T0214583

Lecture Notes in Computer Science 11178

Commenced Publication in 1973
Founding and Former Series Editors:
Gerhard Goos, Juris Hartmanis, and Jan van Leeuwen

Rena Bakhshi · Paolo Ballarini
Benoît Barbot · Hind Castel-Taleb
Anne Remke (Eds.)

Computer Performance Engineering

15th European Workshop, EPEW 2018
Paris, France, October 29–30, 2018
Proceedings

 Springer

Editors
Rena Bakhshi
eScience Center
Amsterdam
The Netherlands

Hind Castel-Taleb
Telecom SudParis
Evry
France

Paolo Ballarini
University Paris-Saclay
Gif-sur-Yvette
France

Anne Remke
Westfälische Wilhelms Universität Münster
Münster
Germany

Benoît Barbot
Université Paris-Est Créteil
Créteil
France

ISSN 0302-9743   ISSN 1611-3349   (electronic)
Lecture Notes in Computer Science
ISBN 978-3-030-02226-6   ISBN 978-3-030-02227-3   (eBook)
https://doi.org/10.1007/978-3-030-02227-3

Library of Congress Control Number: 2018957280

LNCS Sublibrary: SL2 – Programming and Software Engineering

This Springer imprint is published by the registered company Springer Nature Switzerland AG
The registered company address is: Gewerbestrasse 11, 6330 Cham, Switzerland

Preface

This LNCS volume contains the proceedings of the 15th European Performance Engineering Workshop (EPEW), held in Paris, France, during October 29–30, 2018. At its 15th edition the annual EPEW workshop series is a well-established workshop aimed at providing researchers from both academia and industry with a forum for debate/networking over a broad range of topics across the performance engineering realm, including, dependability and security modeling, performance-oriented model verification and testing, hardware and software systems case studies, applications/extensions of queuing theory, and network design. Following the tradition of EPEW, the papers presented at the 2018 edition reflect the diversity of modern performance engineering, where theoretical aspects (involving formalisms such as graphs, trees, queueing networks, stochastic automata as well as mathematical methods such as simulation, product form solutions, game theory, optimization, model checking) are often combined with specific applications (e.g., delay-tolerant networks, mobile cloud computing, smart buildings, fault-tolerant systems, distributed databases).

EPEW 2018 received 27 submissions from nine countries around the world, including Asia, North America, and Europe. Each paper was peer reviewed by an average of three Program Committee (PC) members and assessed on the basis of its relevance to the workshop community, its novelty, and its technical quality. The review outcome led to the selection of 17 high-quality contributions for publication in the proceedings and presentation at the workshop.

We would like to thanks the keynote speakers we were honored to host at EPEW 2018, namely, Dr. Gerardo Rubino, a senior researcher at Inria/IRISA Rennes (France) with a strong background both in quality of services for network applications as well as in quantitative analysis of probabilistic models, and Dr. Benny Van Houdt, a senior lecturer at the computer science department of the University of Antwerp (Belgium) with strong diverse expertise in performance evaluation of computer systems and networks.

We would also like to warmly thank all PC members and external reviewers for their quality work in the review process. Furthermore we would like to thank both the SAMOVAR laboratory of Télécom SudParis, the LACL laboratory of the University of Paris-Est Créteil, and the MICS laboratory of CentraleSupélec for their support in making the organization of EPEW 2018 possible. We are very grateful both to the EasyChair team, for their useful conference system that we used for managing papers submission/reviewing process, and to Springer for their editorial support. Above all, we would like to thank the authors of the papers for their contribution to this volume. We hope these contributions will be as useful and inspiring to the readers as they were to us.

September 2018

Rena Bakhshi
Paolo Ballarini
Benoît Barbot
Hind Castel
Anne Remke

Organization

Program Committee

Elvio Gilberto Amparore	University of Turin, Italy
Urtzi Ayesta	LAAS-CNRS, France
Rena Bakhshi	Netherlands eScience Center, The Netherlands
Paolo Ballarini	CentraleSupelec, France
Simonetta Balsamo	Università Ca' Foscari di Venezia, Italy
Benoit Barbot	Paris-Est Creteil University, France
Marco Beccuti	University of Turin, Italy
Marco Bernardo	University of Urbino, Italy
Marco Biagi	University of Florence, Italy
Olivier Brun	LAAS-CNRS, France
Laura Carnevali	University of Florence, Italy
Hind Castel	Telecom SudParis, France
Tadeusz Czachórski	Institute of Theoretical and Applied Informatics, Polish Academy of Sciences, Poland
Dieter Fiems	Ghent University, Belgium
Jean-Michel Fourneau	DAVID, Université de Versailles St. Quentin, France
Stephen Gilmore	University of Edinburgh, UK
Boudewijn Haverkort	University of Twente, The Netherlands
András Horváth	University of Turin, Italy
Gábor Horváth	Budapest University of Technology and Economics, Hungary
Emmanuel Hyon	Paris Nanterre University, France
Alain Jean-Marie	Inria, France
William Knottenbelt	Imperial College London, UK
Samuel Kounev	University of Würzburg, Germany
Lasse Leskelä	Aalto University, Finland
Andrea Marin	University of Venice, Italy
Marco Paolieri	University of Southern California, USA
Nihal Pekergin N.	Paris-Est Creteil University, France
Agapios Platis	University of the Aegean, Greece
Philipp Reinecke	Cardiff University, UK
Anne Remke	WWU Münster, Germany
Markus Siegle	University of the Bundeswehr Munich, Germany
Miklos Telek	Budapest University of Technology and Economics, Hungary
Nigel Thomas	Newcastle University, UK
Petr Tuma	Charles University, Czech Republic
Enrico Vicario	University of Florence, Italy

Joris Walraevens   Ghent University, Belgium
Qiushi Wang   Nanyang Technological University, Singapore
Katinka Wolter   Freie Universität zu Berlin, Germany
Huaming Wu   Tianjin University, China

Additional Reviewers

Hüls, Jannik
Pilch, Carina
Santoni, Francesco
Walter, Jürgen

Keynotes

Performance Evaluation Targeting Quality of Experience

Gerardo Rubino

Inria, France

When we must evaluate the performance of a computing facility, a communication network, a Web service, we typically build a model and, then, we use it to analyze one or several metrics that we know are important for capturing the performance aspect of interest of the considered system (mean response time, mean backlog of jobs/packets/requests/..., loss probabilities, etc.). Typical tools for analyzing the model are queuing theory results, Markov chain algorithms, discrete event simulation, etc. If we specifically consider the case of applications or services operating on the Internet and focusing on video, or audio, or voice content (IP telephony, video streaming, video-conferences, ...), in most cases the ultimate target is the perception the user has about the delivered service, how satisfied she is with its quality, and this perception concentrates in that of the quality of the content (how good was the reception of the transmitted voice over the IP channel, or of the play of the movie requested to the VoD server, etc.). We call it Perceptual Quality (PQ), and it is the main component of the user-centered Quality of Experience for these fundamental classes of applications. In theory, PQ is the mandatory criteria to take care of the user when designing the system. Needless to say, these classes of apps and/or services are responsible for a very important component of today's and tomorrow's Internet traffic, and they represent a large fraction of total traffic in volume. The PQ is usually evaluated using subjective tests, that is, by means of panels of human observers. In this area many standards exist, depending on the type of media, the type of usage, etc. A subjective testing session provides, at the end, a number measuring the PQ, that is, quantifying this PQ. When quantifying (when measuring), we typically refer to the Mean Opinion Score (MOS) of the video or voice sequence, and a standard range for MOS is the real interval [1, 5], '1' the worst, '5' the best. In this presentation, we will argue that using an appropriate approach to measure this PQ, we can rely on our classic tools in performance evaluation (queuing models, low level stochastic processes, etc.) while focusing our effort in analyzing directly this PQ central aspect of our systems. Instead of saying "if the offered traffic and the system service rate satisfy relation R, then the throughput of the system is high, which is good, but the delay is also a little bit high, which is not very nice,...", we can say "if the offered traffic and the system service rate satisfy relation R, then the PQ is high enough". That is, instead of showing how the throughput, the mean backlog, the mean response time, ... evolve with some param-eters that can be controlled to tune the system's performance, we can work directly with the PQ, the ultimate target, and still use our M/M/* queues, Jackson networks, or whatever model is relevant in our study. This allows obtaining results concerning our final goal, that is, keep the user happy when looking at the video stream, or when using her telephone, at a reasonable cost. Detailed examples will be given using the author own proposal for the automatic measure of PQ, called PSQA (for Pseudo Subjective Quality Assessment) and based on Machine Learning tools., that provides a rational function of several parameters returning the current PQ, parameters that may include those low level metrics.

Mean Field Models for (Large-Scale) Load Balancing Systems

Benny Van Houdt

University of Antwerpen, Belgium

This talk focuses on the behavior of load balancing systems and is composed of three parts.

In the first part we revisit a classic mean field result on load balancing in large distributed systems. More specifically, we focus on the celebrated power-of-two choices paradigm and its mean field limit. We subsequently introduce a theorem for the class of density dependent population processes established in the 1970s by Kurtz and discuss some of the technical issues involved to extend this result to the stationary regime. We end the first part by illustrating the accuracy of the mean field limit using simulation.

In the second part we introduce the refined mean field approximation, which is a technique to compute a $1/N$ correction term to improve the accuracy of classic mean field limits. This technique can be used to more accurately approximate the performance of small systems, e.g., consisting of $N = 10$ servers, and can be applied to any density dependent population processes with limited effort. We focus on the different computational steps involved to compute this correction term and illustrate its accuracy on various numerical examples.

In the final part of the talk we discuss some recent results on load balancing schemes that select servers based on workload information (as opposed to queue length information). Such systems are motivated by load balancing systems that use late binding or redundancy. We present explicit results for the workload and response time distribution when the job sizes follow an exponential distribution and indicate how to compute these distributions for non-exponential jobs sizes.

This talk is based on joint work with Nicolas Gast (Inria) and Tim Hellemans (University of Antwerp).

Contents

On the Degradation of Distributed Graph Databases with Eventual Consistency

Paul Ezhilchelvan[1]([⊠]), Isi Mitrani[1], and Jim Webber[2]

[1] School of Computing, Newcastle University, Newcastle upon Tyne NE4 5TG, UK
{paul.ezhilchelvan,isi.mitrani}@ncl.ac.uk
[2] Neo4j UK, 41-45 Blackfriars Rd, London SE1 8NZ, UK
Jim.Webber@neo4j.com

Abstract. The 'eventual consistency' approach to updates in a distributed graph database leaves open the possibility that edge information may be corrupted. The process by which this occurs is modeled, with the aim of estimating the time that it takes for the database to become corrupted. A fluid approximation is developed and is evaluated for different parameter settings. Comparisons with simulations show that the results are very accurate.

1 Introduction

Managing distributed data typically means adopting either strongly or eventually consistent update policies. In the former approach, replicas of a data item are updated in an identical order at all servers [7]. When update requests are launched concurrently, users will see an identical update sequence, irrespective of the actual physical server they use for accessing the data. However, this single-server abstraction imposes a significant performance penalty, since update requests need to be ordered (and replicated) prior to being acted upon. Further, according to the CAP theorem (see [2,6]), if the network partitions the servers, request ordering and access to data may be interrupted and the availability of services can be reduced.

In view of these disadvantages, large distributed data stores such as Google Docs, Dynamo [5] and Cassandra [4], opt instead for an eventually consistent update policy (see [10]). Update requests are processed as soon as they arrive. This enhances system performance and availability but leaves a time window in which values of a replicated data item at different servers can be mutually inconsistent. These windows may occasionally lead to incorrect data operations. Eventual consistency is a viable model for applications where availability is paramount and where the consequences of any incorrect operations can be dealt with through compensations and state reconciliations.

For example, Bailis and Ghodsi [1] refer to an ATM service where eventual consistency can allow two users to simultaneously withdraw more money than their (joint) bank account holds; such an anomaly, on being detected, is reconciled by invoking exception handlers. Given that an ATM service is expected to be available 24/7, the eventually consistent approach is appropriate.

© Springer Nature Switzerland AG 2018
R. Bakhshi et al. (Eds.): EPEW 2018, LNCS 11178, pp. 1–13, 2018.
https://doi.org/10.1007/978-3-030-02227-3_1

In this paper, we focus on the effects of adopting the eventually consistent policy in systems where occasional incorrect operations are not immediately or readily observed, and can lead to large scale propagation of erroneous states. Reconciliation at a later time can become impossible. The systems of interest here are Graph Databases (see Robinson et al. [9]), which are a rapidly growing database technology at present.

A graph database consists of *nodes* and *edges*, representing entities and relations between them, respectively. For example, node A may represent a person of type Author and B an item of type Book. A and B will have an edge between them if they have a relation, e.g. A is an author of B. The popularity of the graph database technology owes much to this simple structure from which sophisticated models can be easily built and efficiently queried. Examples of operations performed on a graph database are: counting the number of fans following a famous person on Twitter, ranking the most frequently accessed pages in the web, etc.

When nodes are connected by an edge, the database stores some reciprocal information. For example, if there is an edge between A and B, then A would have a field *wrote B* and B would have a field *written by A*; similarly, if there is an edge between a music fan F and a singer S, then they would have the reciprocal fields *following S* and *being followed by F*. Storing this reciprocal information is a critical design decision. In a distributed graph database this is a non-trivial problem since the information at nodes across different servers must remain mutually compatible. Any updates in one connected node at one server must be reflected in the other node(s) at a different server(s).

When a query writes a distributed edge, the eventual consistency policy cannot ensure that the necessary updates are implemented in a timely or consistently-ordered fashion across the servers involved. This can cause major problems. Suppose that two queries operate (nearly) simultaneously on a given distributed edge, each starting from a different server. Then the two updates can be implemented in a different order at the two servers, leading to a mutual incompatibility between two nodes. While such a state exists, there may be a stream of queries reading one node and another stream reading the other. One of the two streams is obviously reading incorrect information (from a global point of view).

A query that reads incorrect information about one edge and updates another edge, introduces incorrect information at both nodes of the second edge. Those two nodes may then be mutually compatible, yet incorrect. Such errors cannot be detected by simple compatibility tests. Moreover, they are propagated throughout the database by subsequent queries that carry out updates based on incorrect information. Eventually, the quality of information held by the database becomes so degraded that the database becomes unusable.

The contribution of this paper is to model the above process of degradation. This has not, to the best of our knowledge, been done before. This work is thus the first in formally assessing the damage that the eventually consistent update policy can inflict on a distributed graph database.

We provide easily implementable, efficient and accurate solutions that allow us to determine the time it takes for the database to lose its utility. These solutions are then used in experiments aimed at examining quantitatively the effect that various parameters have on the degradation process. At the same time, the accuracy of the estimates is evaluated by comparisons with simulations.

The model is described in Sect. 2. Section 3 develops the solutions, based on fluid approximations. The numerical and simulation results are presented in Sect. 4.

2 The Model

A popular implementation of a graph database contains, for each node, a list of adjacency relations describing the incoming and outgoing edges associated with that node. When an edge is updated, the corresponding entries in both the origin and the destination nodes must be updated. If those two nodes are stored on the same server, then the edge is said to be 'local'. A local update is assumed to be instantaneous. An edge connecting two nodes stored on different servers is said to be 'distributed'. A 'write' operation for a distributed edge is carried out first on one of its servers and then, after a small but non-zero delay, on the other.

This implementation of distributed writes makes it possible to introduce faults in edge records. Consider an edge e, spanning two servers, S_1 and S_2. A query Q_1, containing a write operation for e, arrives in S_1 at time t and is performed in S_2 at time $t + \delta$. At some point between t and $t + \delta$, another query, Q_2, also writing e, arrives in S_2 and is performed in S_1 some time later. The result of this occurrence, which will be referred to as a 'conflict', is that the S_1 entry for e is written in the order Q_1, Q_2, while the S_2 entry is written in the order Q_2, Q_1. One of these entries may be considered correct, but an external observer cannot tell which is which. Such edges are called 'half-corrupted'.

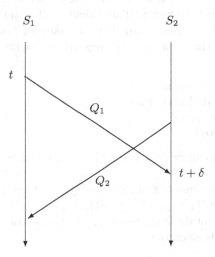

Fig. 1. Conflict between Q_1 and Q_2

The mechanism of conflict is illustrated in Fig. 1, where the time at S_1 and S_2 is shown flowing downwards.

A subsequent query which happens to read the correct entry of a half-corrupted edge, and completes a write operation for it without a conflict, will repair the fault and make the edge record clean again. However, if it reads the incorrect entry and writes any edge, it causes the target to become 'semantically corrupted', or simply 'corrupted'. The correct and incorrect reads are equally likely, so each occurs with probability $1/2$.

Any edge can become corrupted by being written on the basis of reading incorrect information. Corrupted edges cannot be repaired, since there is no post-facto solution to the graph repair problem in the general case.

Queries that update edges arrive in a Poisson stream with rate λ per second. We assume that each query contains a random number of read operations, K, followed by one write operation. This is a conservative assumption, since more than one writes per query would increase the rate of corruption. The variable K can have an arbitrary distribution, $P(K = k) = r_k$. In practice K tends to be at least 2, i.e. $r_0 = r_1 = 0$. The K edges read, and the one written by the query are assumed to be independent of each other (but note below that they are not equally likely).

The edges in the database are divided into T types, numbered $1, 2, \ldots, T$ in reverse order of popularity. The probability that a read or a write operation accesses an edge of type i is p_i, with $p_1 > p_2 > \ldots > p_T$. The number of edges of type i is N_i, and typically $N_1 < N_2 < \ldots < N_T$. The total number of edges is N. In every type, a fraction f of the edges are distributed and the rest are local. The probability of accessing a particular edge of type i, for either reading or writing, is p_i/N_i.

At time 0, all edges are clean (free from corruption). When a certain fraction, γ (e.g., $\gamma = 0.1$), of all edges become corrupted, the database itself is said to be corrupted for practical purposes. The object of the analysis is to provide an accurate estimate of the length of time that it takes for this to happen.

At any moment in time, an edge belongs to one of the following four categories.

Category 0: Local and clean.
Category 1: Distributed and clean.
Category 2: Half-corrupted.
Category 3: Corrupted.

Only distributed edges can be in category 2, but any edge, including local ones, can be in category 3.

Denote by $n_{i,j}(t)$ the number of type i edges that are in category j at time t. The set of vectors $\mathbf{n}_i(t) = [n_{i,0}(t), n_{i,1}(t), n_{i,2}(t), n_{i,3}(t)]$, for $i = 1, 2, \ldots, T$, define the state of the database at time t. At all times, the elements of vector $\mathbf{n}_i$ add up to N_i. Any state such that

$$\sum_{i=1}^{T} n_{i,3}(t) \geq \gamma N, \tag{1}$$

will be referred to as an 'absorbing state'. The absorbing states correspond to a corrupted database.

The value of interest is U, the average first passage time from the initial state where $\mathbf{n}_i(0) = [(1-f)N_i, fN_i, 0, 0]$ (i.e., a clean database), to an absorbing state.

The above assumptions and definitions imply that a read operation performed at time t would return a correct answer with probability α, given by

$$\alpha = \sum_{i=1}^{T} \frac{p_i}{N_i} [n_{i,0}(t) + n_{i,1}(t) + \frac{1}{2} n_{i,2}(t)]. \tag{2}$$

The probability, β, that all the read operations in a query arriving at time t return correct answers, is equal to

$$\beta = \sum_{k=1}^{\infty} r_k \alpha^k. \tag{3}$$

Suppose that the distribution of K is geometric with parameter r, starting at $k = 2$; in other words, $r_k = (1 - r)^{k-2} r$. Then the above expression becomes

$$\beta = \frac{\alpha^2 r}{1 - \alpha(1 - r)}. \tag{4}$$

Consider now the probability, q_i, that a query of type i arriving at time t and taking a time δ to complete a write operation, will be involved in a conflict. That is the probability that another query of type i arrives between t and $t + \delta$ and writes the same edge, but starting at its other end. This can be expressed as

$$q_i = 1 - e^{-\frac{1}{2}\lambda p_i \delta / N_i}; \quad i = 1, 2, \ldots, T. \tag{5}$$

Note that in practice δ is dominated by network delays. The actual processing time associated with a write operation is negligible.

If the time to complete a distributed write is not constant, but is distributed exponentially with mean δ, then the conflict probability would be

$$q_i = \frac{\lambda p_i \delta}{2N_i + \lambda p_i \delta}; \quad i = 1, 2, \ldots, T. \tag{6}$$

When δ is small, there is very little difference between these two expressions.

An incoming query that is involved in a conflict would change the category of a distributed edge from 1 to 2, provided that all read operations of both queries return correct results. Hence, the instantaneous transition rate, $a_{i,1,2}$, from state $[n_{i,0}, n_{i,1}, n_{i,2}, n_{i,3}]$ to state $[n_{i,0}, n_{i,1} - 1, n_{i,2} + 1, n_{i,3}]$, can be written as

$$a_{i,1,2} = \frac{\lambda p_i n_{i,1}}{N_i} q_i \beta^2. \tag{7}$$

Conversely, an incoming query writing a category 2 edge can change it to a category 1 edge, provided that all its read operations return correct results and it is not involved in a conflict. Hence, the instantaneous transition rate, $a_{i,2,1}$, from state $[n_{i,0}, n_{i,1}, n_{i,2}, n_{i,3}]$ to state $[n_{i,0}, n_{i,1} + 1, n_{i,2} - 1, n_{i,3}]$, is given by

$$a_{i,2,1} = \frac{\lambda p_i n_{i,2}}{N_i} (1 - q_i)\beta. \tag{8}$$

The other possible transitions convert an edge of category 0, 1 or 2 into an edge of category 3. This happens when a query writes after receiving an incorrect answer to at least one of its reads. Denoting the corresponding instantaneous transition rates by $a_{i,j,3}$, for $j = 0, 1, 2$, we have

$$a_{i,j,3} = \frac{\lambda p_i n_{i,j}}{N_i} (1 - \beta). \tag{9}$$

Using these transition rates, one can simulate the process of corrupting the database and obtain both point estimates and confidence intervals for the average time to corruption, U. However, the systems of practical interest tend to be large, and such simulations take a long time to run. It is therefore desirable to develop an analytical solution that is both efficient to implement and provides accurate estimates for U. That is our next task.

3   Fluid Approximation

Instead of describing the system state by integer-valued functions specifying numbers of edges of various types and categories, it is convenient to use continuous fluids of those types and categories. So now $n_{i,j}(t)$ is a real-valued function indicating the amount of fluid present at time t in a 'bucket' of type i and category j $(i = 1, 2, \ldots, T; j = 0, 1, 2, 3)$. The total amounts of different types, and the initial states, are the same as before.

Fluids flow out of, and into buckets, at rates consistent with the transition rates described in the previous section. Thus, the bucket labeled $(i, 0)$ (local of type i and clean) has an outflow at the rate given by (9), and no inflow. This can be expressed by writing

$$n'_{i,0}(t) = -\frac{\lambda p_i(1 - \beta)}{N_i} n_{i,0}(t), \tag{10}$$

where β is given by (3) and (2).

The bucket labeled $(i, 1)$ (distributed of type i and clean) has two outflows, at rates given by (7) and (9) respectively, and an inflow at rate given by (8). The corresponding equation is,

$$n'_{i,1}(t) = -\frac{\lambda p_i(\beta^2 q_i + 1 - \beta)}{N_i} n_{i,1}(t) + \frac{\lambda p_i \beta(1 - q_i)}{N_i} n_{i,2}(t). \tag{11}$$

Similarly, bucket $(i, 2)$ (half-corrupted of type i) has two outflows, at rates given by (8) and (9) respectively, and an inflow at rate given by (7). This implies

$$n'_{i,2}(t) = -\frac{\lambda p_i(\beta(1 - q_i) + 1 - \beta)}{N_i} n_{i,2}(t) + \frac{\lambda p_i \beta^2 q_i}{N_i} n_{i,1}(t). \tag{12}$$

Finally, bucket $(i, 3)$ (corrupted of type i) has three inflows, at rates given by (9), and no outflows. Hence,

$$n'_{i,3}(t) = \frac{\lambda p_i(1 - \beta)}{N_i}[n_{i,0}(t) + n_{i,1}(t) + n_{i,2}(t)]. \tag{13}$$

The object is to determine the value U such that

$$\sum_{i=1}^{T} n_{i,3}(U) = \gamma N. \tag{14}$$

Unfortunately, the above differential equations are coupled in a complicated way. Not only do the unknown functions appear in each others equations, but they also depend on β, which in turn depends on α, which depends on the unknown functions. Moreover, that dependency is non-linear. Consequently, an exact solution for this set of equations does not appear to be feasible. We need another level of approximation.

Denote by $\bar{n}_{i,j}$ the average value of the function $n_{i,j}(t)$ over the interval $(0, U)$:

$$\bar{n}_{i,j} = \frac{1}{U} \int_0^U n_{i,j}(t)dt. \tag{15}$$

Replacing, in the right-hand side of (2), all functions by their average values, allows us to treat the probability α as a constant:

$$\alpha = \sum_{i=1}^{T} \frac{p_i}{N_i}[\bar{n}_{i,0} + \bar{n}_{i,1} + \frac{1}{2}\bar{n}_{i,2}]. \tag{16}$$

Then the probability β will also be a constant. Also, where one unknown function appears in the differential equation of another, replace the former by its average value. The resulting equations are linear, with constant coefficients, and are easily solvable. The solution of (10), which involves only $n_{i,0}(t)$, becomes

$$n_{i,0}(t) = (1 - f)N_i e^{-a_{i,0}t}, \tag{17}$$

where $a_{i,0} = \lambda p_i(1 - \beta)/N_i$.

In Eq. (11), $n_{i,2}(t)$ is replaced by $\bar{n}_{i,2}$. The solution is then

$$n_{i,1}(t) = \frac{b_{i,1}\bar{n}_{i,2}}{a_{i,1}}[1 - e^{-a_{i,1}t}] + fN_i e^{-a_{i,1}t}, \tag{18}$$

where $a_{i,1} = \lambda p_i(\beta^2 q_i + 1 - \beta)/N_i$ and $b_{i,1} = \lambda p_i \beta(1 - q_i)/N_i$.

Similarly, in Eq. (12), $n_{i,1}(t)$ is replaced by $\bar{n}_{i,1}$. This yields

$$n_{i,2}(t) = \frac{b_{i,2}\bar{n}_{i,1}}{a_{i,2}}[1 - e^{-a_{i,2}t}], \tag{19}$$

where $a_{i,2} = \lambda p_i[\beta(1 - q_i) + 1 - \beta]/N_i$ and $b_{i,2} = \lambda p_i \beta^2 q_i/N_i$.

Replacing $n_{i,j}(t)$ by $\bar{n}_{i,j}$ in Eq. (13), makes the right-hand side constant and therefore

$$n_{i,3}(t) = t\frac{\lambda p_i(1-\beta)}{N_i}(\bar{n}_{i,0} + \bar{n}_{i,1} + \bar{n}_{i,2}). \tag{20}$$

Hence, according to (14), the time to corruption U can be estimated as

$$U = \gamma N \left[\sum_{i=1}^{T}\frac{\lambda p_i(1-\beta)}{N_i}(\bar{n}_{i,0} + \bar{n}_{i,1} + \bar{n}_{i,2})\right]^{-1}. \tag{21}$$

Integrating (17), (18) and (19) over the interval $(0, U)$ and dividing by U, we obtain the following expressions:

$$\bar{n}_{i,0} = \frac{(1-f)N_i}{a_{i,0}U}[1 - e^{-a_{i,0}U}]; \tag{22}$$

$$\bar{n}_{i,1} = \frac{b_{i,1}\bar{n}_{i,2}}{a_{i,1}} + (fN_i - \frac{b_{i,1}\bar{n}_{i,2}}{a_{i,1}})\frac{1}{a_{i,1}U}[1 - e^{-a_{i,1}U}]; \tag{23}$$

$$\bar{n}_{i,2} = \frac{b_{i,2}\bar{n}_{i,1}}{a_{i,2}}[1 - \frac{1}{a_{i,2}U}(1 - e^{-a_{i,2}U})]. \tag{24}$$

This is a set of non-linear simultaneous equations for the averages $\bar{n}_{i,0}$, $\bar{n}_{i,1}$ and $\bar{n}_{i,2}$. They can be solved by consecutive iterations.

Start with some initial estimates for $\bar{n}_{i,j}$; call them $\bar{n}_{i,j}^{(0)}$. Using (16), get an initial estimate for α and hence for β; call those $\alpha^{(0)}$ and $\beta^{(0)}$. Then (21) provides an initial estimate for U, called $U^{(0)}$.

Substituting the initial estimates into the right-hand sides of (22), (23) and (24), yields new values for the averages $\bar{n}_{i,j}$; call them $\bar{n}_{i,j}^{(1)}$. They in turn provide new values, $\alpha^{(1)}$ and $\beta^{(1)}$, and a new estimate, $U^{(1)}$.

In step m of this procedure, the values $\bar{n}_{i,j}^{(m-1)}$, $\beta^{(m-1)}$ and $U^{(m-1)}$ are used to compute $\alpha^{(m)}, \beta^{(m)}, \bar{n}_{i,j}^{(m)}$ and $U^{(m)}$. The process terminates when the results of two consecutive iterations are sufficiently close to each other.

In effect, the above procedure computes a fixed point for the mapping $\bar{n}_{i,j} \to \bar{n}_{i,j}$ defined by (22), (23) and (24). Such a fixed point exists by Brouwer's theorem [3] because the averages are bounded and the mapping is continuous.

In the next section, the fluid approximation is used to study the behaviour of a reasonably realistic sample database. The accuracy of the approximation is evaluated by comparisons with simulations.

4 Numerical and Simulation Results

The example database contains five types of edges. Their numbers are: $N_1 = 10^4, N_2 = 10^5, N_3 = 10^6, N_4 = 10^7$ and $N_5 = 10^8$. The corresponding probabilities of access are $p_1 = 0.5, p_2 = 0.26, p_3 = 0.13, p_4 = 0.07$ and $p_5 = 0.04$. The number of read operations per query is distributed geometrically, starting at 2:

$r_k = (1 - r)^{k-2}r$, with $r = 0.07$. Thus, on the average, there are just over 15 reads per query.

The time to complete a distributed write operation is assumed constant, equal to 0.005 s.

In all types, a fraction 0.3 of the edges are distributed and the rest are local (for an argument in support of this fraction, see [8]). The database starts clean at time 0 and is considered to be corrupted when a fraction $\gamma = 0.1$ of all edges are corrupted.

In Fig. 2, the average period until corruption is plotted against the arrival rate of queries, λ. The latter is varied in the range $(100, 5000)$ queries per second. The time U is measured in hours.

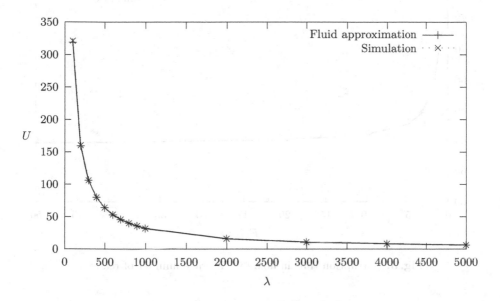

Fig. 2. Corruption time in hours vs. arrival rate/sec.

We observe that U decreases with λ. This was of course to be expected, since a higher arrival rate leads both to higher probability of conflicts, and faster spread of incorrect information. In this database, type 1 forms a relatively small nucleus of edges that are quite likely to be accessed; once they become involved in conflicts, corruption spreads rapidly.

The figure also aims to compare the fluid approximation results with those obtained by simulation. That is, the transition steps governed by the rates (7), (8) and (9) were simulated until an absorption state was reached.

The two plots are practically indistinguishable; the relative differences that exist are smaller than 1%. On the other hand, the fluid approximation plot took a fraction of a second to compute (each point required fewer than 10 fixed-point iterations), whereas the simulated one took more than half an hour.

The next experiment examines the effect of the average number of read operations per query, $E(K)$, on the time to corruption. The arrival rate is fixed at $\lambda = 500$ queries per second. The other parameters are as in Fig. 2.

For the purpose of this evaluation, the requirement that there should be at least two reads per query has been dropped. The random variable K has the normal geometric distribution with parameter r: $r_k = (1 - r)^{k-1}r$, $k = 1, 2, \ldots$. In Fig. 3, r decreases from 0.99 to 0.02, which means that $E(K) = 1/r$ increases from 1.01 to 50. The time to corruption, U, is again measured in hours.

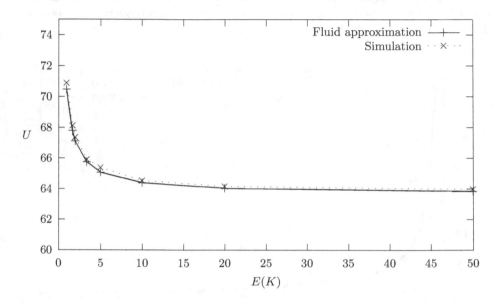

Fig. 3. Corruption time in hours vs. average number of reads

As expected, the more edges are read by queries, the higher the probability of reading a corrupted edge, and hence the shorter the time to a corrupted database. Less obvious, however, is the observation that the resulting decrease in U is highly non-linear. Indeed, increasing $E(K)$ beyond 10 almost ceases to make a difference. We see roughly the same U, whether there are 10 or 50 reads per query.

The accuracy of the fluid approximation is again very good over the entire range of $E(K)$.

It may also be of interest to examine the effect of the fraction of distributed edges, f, on the interval U. In Fig. 4, that fraction is varied between $f = 0.1$ and $f = 1$. The arrival rate is fixed at $\lambda = 100$ (in order to prolong the time to corruption), and the number of reads per query is distributed geometrically starting with 2, with parameter $r = 0.07$ and mean just over 15.

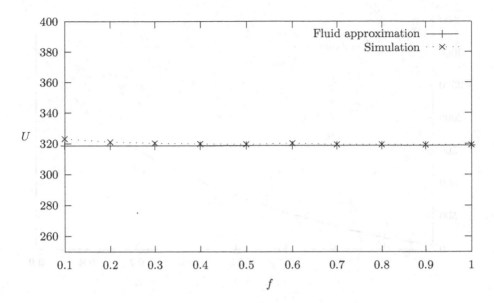

Fig. 4. Varying fraction of distributed edges

The fluid approximation plot is flat. This is not entirely surprising, since the expression for the probability α involves only the sums $\bar{n}_{i,0} + \bar{n}_{i,1}$, and not the individual averages. Moreover, local edges are just as easily corrupted by incorrect reads as distributed ones.

The simulation agrees with the approximation for most of the range, but begins to diverge from it when $f = 0.1$. It seems that when the fraction of distributed edges is very small, the accuracy of the fluid approximation diminishes.

In the final experiment, the parameter that is varied is the fraction, γ, of edges that should become corrupted before the database is considered to be corrupted. The arrival rate is fixed at $\lambda = 500$, and all other parameters are as in Fig. 2.

Figure 5 shows how the time to corruption grows when the definition of corruption becomes more demanding. The plot is a convex curve, which is slightly counter-intuitive. One might guess that the more edges are corrupted, the faster even more edges would be corrupted. That would produce a concave curve. In fact the opposite is observed. The likely explanation is that the fewer the remaining clean edges, the longer it takes for a random access to hit one and corrupt it.

The fluid approximation estimates are almost indistinguishable from the simulation ones, while being several orders of magnitude faster to compute.

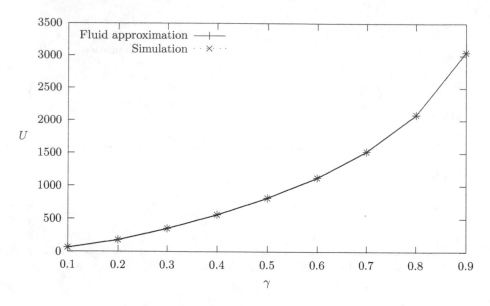

Fig. 5. Varying fraction of corrupted edges

5 Conclusions

The problem that we have addressed—to construct and solve a quantitative model of database deterioration—is of considerable practical importance. The fluid approximation that has been developed is fast and provides accurate estimates of the time to corruption. The only area where there is a suggestion of inaccuracy is when the fraction of distributed edges is very small.

It may be possible to improve the approximation so that it can handle more extreme parameter values. One idea would be to break the interval $(0, U)$ into smaller portions and apply the fixed-point iterations consecutively to each portion. This, and other possible extensions would be a suitable topic for future research.

References

1. Bailis, P., Ghodsi, A.: Eventual consistency today: limitations, extensions, and beyond. Queue **11**(3), 20–32 (2013)
2. Brewer, E.A.: Towards robust distributed systems. In: Proceedings of the 19th Annual ACM Symposium on Principles of Distributed Computing, Portland, 16–19 July 2000
3. Brouwer, L.E.J.: Uber Abbildungen von Mannigfaltigkeiten. Mathematische Annalen **71**, 97–115 (1911)
4. http://cassandra.apache.org/
5. DeCandia, G., et al.: Dynamo: Amazon's highly available key-value store. SIGOPS Oper. Syst. Rev. **41**(6), 205–220 (2007)

6. Gilbert, S., Lynch, N.: Brewers conjecture and the feasibility of consistent, available, partition-tolerant web services. ACM SIGACT News **33**(2), 51–59 (2002)
7. Herlihi, M.P., Wing, J.M.: Linearizability: a correctness condition for concurrent objects. ACM TOPLAS **12**(3), 463–492 (1990)
8. Huang, J., Abadi, D.J.: Leopard: lightweight edge-oriented partitioning and replication for dynamic graphs. Proc. VLDB Endow. **9**(7), 540–551 (2016)
9. Robinson, I., Webber, J., Eifrem, E.: Graph Databases, New Opportunities for Connected Data. O'Reilly Media, Sebastopol (2015). ISBN 978-1491930892
10. Vogels, W.: Eventually consistent. Comm. ACM **52**(1), 40–44 (2009)

To What Extent Does Performance Awareness Support Developers in Fixing Performance Bugs?

Alexandru Danciu[1(✉)] and Helmut Krcmar[2]

[1] fortiss GmbH, Guerickestr. 25, 80805 Munich, Germany
alexandru.danciu@mytum.de
[2] Technische Universität München, Boltzmannstr. 3, 85748 Garching, Germany
krcmar@in.tum.de

Abstract. Current research on performance awareness evaluates approaches primarily for their functional correctness but does not assess to what extent developers are supported in improving software implementations. This article presents the evaluation of an existing approach for supporting developers of Java Enterprise Edition (EE) applications with response time estimations based on a controlled human-oriented experiment. The main goal of the experiment is to quantify the effectiveness of employing the approach while optimizing the response time of an implementation. Subjects' optimizations are quantified by the amount of fixed performance bugs. Having employed the approach, subjects fixed on average over three times more performance bugs. The results further indicate that in the absence of a performance awareness aid, the success of optimizing a previously unknown implementation is far less dependent of the behavior and skill level of the developer.

Keywords: Performance awareness · Response time estimation
Controlled experiment · Palladio Component Model · Java EE

1 Introduction

The concept of performance awareness aims at aiding the development process with observations on the performance of software and the ability to react upon the findings, if necessary [16]. Among other layers, performance awareness addresses the support of developers with insights to complement their optimizations. Many promising performance awareness approaches aim at automating performance evaluations and integrating feedback in development environments. However, existing approaches are primarily validated for their functional correctness [1,5]. The resulting evaluations, therefore, do not assess to what extent performance awareness could support developers. The influence of these approaches on developers and the quality of their implementations remains unknown. Horký et al. [6] report the failed attempt to investigate the influence of their approach

© Springer Nature Switzerland AG 2018
R. Bakhshi et al. (Eds.): EPEW 2018, LNCS 11178, pp. 14–29, 2018.
https://doi.org/10.1007/978-3-030-02227-3_2

(b) Integration of estimations for reused components

(a) Integration of response time estimations within code editor

(c) Tooltip information

Fig. 1. Developer feedback example

on the response time of implementations produced by students. On the basis of a few and in some cases strongly diverging results, no statistically significant improvement could be found by the availability of the approach. As an alternative, the usefulness of the approach was explained using scenarios. The approach presented by Danciu et al. [3] at the 12th European Workshop on Performance Engineering has so far only been evaluated with regard to the prediction accuracy. The aim of this paper is to investigate if this approach can help developers improve the performance of software implementations. The contribution of this paper is the execution of a controlled experiment aimed at quantifying the impact of the approach described by Danciu et al. [3] on developers and answering the following research questions:

– Are developers performing better while employing the approach?
– How do developers spend their time while executing a maintenance task?
– How does the success of developers relate to a methodical investigation of the code?

We first provide an overview of the approach for integrating performance awareness in Java EE development environments in Sect. 2. The design, results, and threats to validity of the experiment are described in Sects. 3, 4, and 5 respectively. In Sect. 6 similar approaches and the scope of their validation are presented. Finally, we state a conclusion and provide an outlook on future work (Sect. 7).

2   Performance Awareness Approach

Depending on the dimension, Tůma [16] distinguishes awareness of performance relevant mechanisms, of performance expectations, of developers and

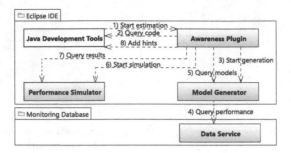

Fig. 2. Architectural Overview

performance-aware applications. The approach presented by Danciu et al. [3] aims at supporting developers of Java EE components with insights on the expected response time for the operations they are currently developing. Response time estimations for component operations under development are derived based on the measured performance of reused components. Developers trigger response time estimations by selecting a specific Java class and executing the corresponding context menu action. Estimation results are presented to the developer within the code editor using symbols, text highlighting, links, and tooltips, as depicted in Fig. 1.

Hints on Method Declaration Level. The exceeding of the warning or error threshold for estimated response times is displayed at the level of the corresponding method declaration (see Fig. 1a). A yellow or red speedometer is used as a symbol opposite the declaration.

Hints on Method Invocation Level. Separate markers indicate which individual method invocations already exceed the configured response time thresholds for the superordinate method declaration (see Fig. 1b). A yellow or red square surrounding the invocation is used as a symbol. Chained methods are also accounted for. Hints are also inserted recursively into the underlying call hierarchy of a method declaration. Thus, the declarations of invoked methods within the same project are also augmented with markers.

Tooltip. Tooltips are used to display the actual predicted or measured response times (see Fig. 1c). If there are several markers within a row, the symbols get superimposed. However, the tooltip displays a list of all hint details.

The performance awareness plugin can be configured based on Eclipse preferences. Developers are able to specify (i) a threshold for displaying warning messages, (ii) a threshold for displaying error messages, (iii) the number of simulated users, and (iv) the think time of simulated users. Developers are also able to refine the model creation using Java annotations. The awareness plugin, however, can use default values for these settings.

The architecture consists of the *Awareness Plugin*, the *Model Generator*, the *Performance Simulator*, and the *Data Service* (see Fig. 2). The *Java Development Tools* (JDT) implement the standard user interfaces for managing and editing Java source code in Eclipse. By selecting a specific class, developers are able to request estimations for the expected response time of the contained method declarations (1). The Awareness Plugin determines the Java class and the surrounding project to be analyzed (2) to configure and trigger the creation of performance models (3). The Model Generator then parses the corresponding source code to an abstract syntax tree (AST) which is then transformed to a Palladio Component Model (PCM) [12]. The Data Service supplies response time measurements for the reused component operations that are used to enhance the PCM model (4). The resulting models are retrieved (5) and supplied as input for the Performance Simulator (6). The outcomes are analyzed (7) and reported back to the developer interface. If the estimated response time of a method declaration or method invocation exceeds a specific threshold, either a performance warning or a performance error is displayed within the code editor of the developer (8). Details of the performance model generation and simulation process can be found in [3].

3   Experimental Design

The impact of employing the presented approach during software development is assessed based on a controlled experiment, which is conducted according to Wohlin et al. [19]. The goal of the experiment is to quantify the effectiveness of employing the approach during a software development task in terms of the resulting response time of an implementation. The time frame and the setting represent important factors for the expected outcomes of the development task. The more time subjects are accorded, the more complex tasks can be conducted. During a longer time frame, however, the effective time spent on the task can vary between subjects. To address this factor, the task is carried out during a shorter time frame under supervision. While relying on volunteers as subjects, a shorter time frame promises more participants. The experiment is, therefore, designed for at most one hour and conducted within a computer lab providing identical workplaces to all subjects.

As a development task, both the implementation of new and the maintenance of existing functionality can be considered. In the context of complex business software, the implementation of new functionality represents a risk to the outcome of the experiment. During a relatively short time frame, only simple requirements can be implemented and the subjects' results might not differ significantly. Horký et al. [6] require the implementation of an XML parser within their experiment and report a small share of acceptable solutions. The implementation of new functionality while relying on complex Java EE frameworks promises even fewer working solutions. Therefore, subjects are required to perform a maintenance task comprising the optimization of an existing implementation in terms of response time.

3.1 Hypotheses, Variables and Treatments

RQ1: Are Developers Performing Better While Employing the Approach? The realized optimization can be quantified by measuring the resulting response times. In the context of complex business software, this represents, however, a huge challenge. To exclude errors and interference, extensive measurements have to be conducted. Response times also heavily depend on the executed workloads and the database content. Therefore, the subjects' optimizations are quantified by the amount of fixed performance bugs. According to Jin et al. [8] performance bugs represent inefficient code sequences resulting in a significant performance degradation and which can be resolved by relatively simple source code modifications. Based on the goals of the experiment, we formulate the following main hypotheses for this paper:

- H_0: The employment of the approach has no impact on the amount of performance bugs fixed during the optimization task.
- H_1: The employment of the approach has a positive impact on the amount of performance bugs fixed during the optimization task.

The amount of fixed performance bugs represents the dependent variable, and the availability of the approach the independent variable. We choose a between-subjects design so that a participant is part of either the experiment group or the control group. The computers of the lab are equipped with the Java EE IDE. The performance awareness plugin is activated only for a subset of these IDEs. Each workstation is identified by a number. Through the workstation assignment, subjects are distributed to either the experiment or the control group. Due to the number of available workstations and the availability of volunteers, the experiment is conducted in multiple iterations resulting in different group sizes.

RQ2: How Do Developers Spend Their Time While Executing a Maintenance Task? Context switches and work fragmentation have a negative impact on the productivity of developers while executing maintenance tasks [14]. After leaving the IDE and then returning back, developers need time to resume their activities [11]. For quantifying the amount of interruptions experienced by subjects during the experiment we measure how often the IDE is left and how much time is spent outside the IDE.

RQ3: How Does the Success of Developers Relate to a Methodical Investigation of the Code? Robillard et al. [13] analyze the impact of applying a methodical approach while investigating code on the effectiveness of developers during a maintenance task. The authors describe a methodical approach as the application of cross-reference and keyword searches. In contrast, an opportunistic approach relies on scrolling and browsing. Based on the definitions of Robillard et al. [13] we quantify the methodical investigation of the code as the number of inspected classes which are relevant for fixing bugs.

The assignment of subjects to treatments is performed randomly. It is assumed that the performance of subjects depends on their experience in software development. To control this factor, blocking is applied. The experience level of subjects is not known in detail upon the experiment. Also, the classification of experience is difficult and comprises different layers, such as software performance, architecture, programming language, frameworks, and IDEs. We, therefore, distinguish between students (Bachelor's and Master's) and practitioners (from research or industry) for blocking. While repeating the experiment with a different amount of subjects, the application of blocking might not be possible within each iteration. For example, during an iteration with two subjects having different experience levels, blocking would not be applicable. Within the affected iterations, a pure randomization is performed. In a subsequent iteration, the equilibrium is restored by assigning the blocks to the opposite treatment without randomization. Overall, treatments are assigned in such a way that a balanced design is achieved and both groups have the same number of subjects.

This experiment design represents, according to Wohlin et al. [19], a standard design type with one factor and two treatments, which can further be conceptualized as completely randomized design or as paired comparison design. An advantage of the paired comparison design lies in the collection of double the amount of samples. However, learning effects can take place during the experiment, thus requiring different objects and tasks for the two stages [9]. Due to the complexity of the optimization task and the limited availability of suitable implementations, a completely randomized design is chosen.

3.2 Experiment Subjects

Students and researchers of the Department of Informatics of the Technische Universität München, researchers of the fortiss An-Institut Technische Universität München and software developers from industry are invited to volunteer as subjects for the experiment. Volunteers are required to possess at least basic programming skills to be accepted as subjects. An informal interview is conducted before the admission to the experiment to assess whether a volunteer has visited at least one course and already gained some practical experience in the area of software engineering. While having to optimize an existing implementation, knowledge in the domains of Eclipse, Java, Java EE, JPA, or software performance management are not supposed. During the experiment, however, subjects must fill out a form eliciting their knowledge in these areas. Students invited to participate study either computer science, information systems, or games engineering. Subjects are invited to participate based on convenience sampling [19].

3.3 Experiment Objects

The open source Java EE project *Cargo Tracker*[1] is used as the implementation for the optimization task due to its intuitive user interface, its code comprehensiveness and its ease of deployment. Cargo Tracker demonstrates how Java EE applications can be developed using approaches such as domain-driven design and implements the business logic of a cargo shipping company. The source code

---

[1] https://github.com/javaee/cargotracker.

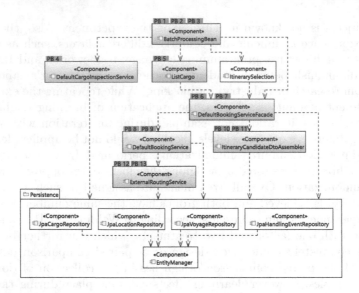

Fig. 3. Relevant Cargo Tracker components and localization of performance bugs (Color figure online)

comprises 83 classes, eleven interfaces and three enums distributed among 27 packages. Due to its lightweight and loosely coupled components, the implementation provides relatively simple methods. Therefore, a new component reusing a great share of existing functionality is created and called *BatchProcessingBean*. This component provides functionality for the identification and rescheduling of late cargos and serves as an entry point for the optimization scenario.

Due to its high quality, the Cargo Tracker source code provides relatively little potential for optimization. Therefore, new performance bugs are inserted systematically into the implementation. The performance antipatterns described by [15] serve as a basis. Wert [18] classifies performance antipatterns in the four abstraction levels architecture, design, implementation, and deployment. During the experiment, subjects are not provided any architectural descriptions, but source code. Therefore, only antipatterns on the implementation level are suitable for the experiment. Due to the focus of the application on reading and writing database records, the following antipatterns are instantiated within the source code as performance bugs (PB) [15]:

- Sisyphus database retrieval: Queries for individual entities are replaced with the retrieval of collections, which afterwards are iterated to identify the relevant entity (PB1, PB4, PB6, PB8, PB9, PB10, PB11, PB12, and PB13).
- Empty semi trucks: The retrieval of a collection of objects from the database is replaced with multiple queries for single entities (PB7).

Furthermore, the Cargo Tracker implementation provides three more opportunities for the instantiation of antipatterns: (i) inserting redundant database queries (PB2), (ii) always calling a service that is only required under certain conditions

(PB3), and (iii) removing existing caching mechanisms (PB5). Other antipatterns, such as the Tower of Babel [15], cannot be implemented without significantly changing the application design. The type and quantity of instantiated antipatterns reflects the application's characteristics, which in turn reflects a typical Java EE implementation. Bugs are implemented only on statement level, e.g., by substituting method calls or changing the control flow. Subjects are also requested to alter only Java code. Figure 3 illustrates the relevant components of the application. Classes enhanced with performance bugs are depicted in color.

The performance awareness plugin does not aim at identifying bugs, instead it integrates measurements in the code editor and makes developers aware of expected method response times. Inefficient code sequences may include, however, method calls reported by the awareness plugin. The complete resolution of a performance bug is rated with one point. Incomplete or syntactically incorrect fixes are awarded half a point. When optimizations are applied to statements that are not affected by any performance bugs, or when minor improvements, such as avoiding unnecessary variable declarations, are performed, no points are awarded at all. The awareness plugin also reports hints for expensive statements which cannot be avoided without destroying functionality.

The experiment objects provided to subjects comprise a Java EE IDE, a local application server, a deployment script and a browser. The IDE is based on the Eclipse[2] platform 4.5.2. The performance awareness plugin is preinstalled in the IDE, however, is only visible for the experiment group. Initially, the plugin has access to response time measurements for the EntitiyManager methods but does not supply any insights. Only after an estimation is triggered by the developer, the corresponding performance models are created and simulated. The Cargo Tracker source is included in the workspace of the IDE as a Java EE project. The deployment script automates the activities of compiling, building and deploying the application to a local Glassfish[3] server. After applying source code changes, subjects have to run the script and are then able to test the new version using a browser. Running and testing the application does not require any prior Java EE knowledge at all.

Instrumentation. Subjects are provided written instructions at the beginning of the experiment. This document describes (i) the experiment procedure in terms of phases and duration, (ii) an imaginary scenario where subjects act as the developer of the BatchProcessingBean of the Cargo Tracker application, (iii) the response time goals set for the application, (iv) the features and the user interface of the application, (v) the development environment, (vi) the task of optimizing the response time of the BatchProcessingBean, and (vii) experiment rules. Subjects of the experiment group are also informed about the usage of the performance awareness plugin. The instructions are printed and written in English. Subjects are allotted ten minutes for reading the instructions and 40 min to perform the optimization task. All relevant actions performed by the subjects are captured automatically by the IDE.

---

[2] https://www.eclipse.org/.
[3] https://javaee.github.io/glassfish/.

Analysis Procedure. Depending on the distribution of samples, this analysis employs either the paired t-test or the Mann-Whitney test. The characteristic of normal distribution is evaluated using the Kolmogorov-Smirnov test and the Shapiro-Wilk test [4]. We use the Pearson correlation coefficient (PCC) to assess the correlation between the behavior of subjects and their effectiveness.

4   Impact of Performance Awareness

The experiment was executed during a period of four weeks and comprised eight iterations. Overall, 26 subjects participated in the experiment without receiving any incentive. Participants included 21 students and 5 practitioners, implying an imbalanced distribution. Figure 4 illustrates the distribution of subjects to groups. Participating students cover the degree programs of computer science, information systems, and games engineering. All participating researchers are active in the field of business information systems engineering and engaged in industry projects. Only one industrial software engineer volunteered. During the seventh iteration, only workstations of the control group were available in the computer lab, leading to the imbalance of one additional practitioner towards the control group and one student towards the experiment group. All subjects completed the experiment.

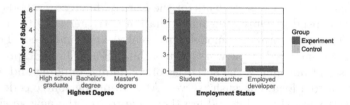

Fig. 4. Classification of subjects

4.1   Descriptive Statistics

Subjects of the experiment group fixed on average over three times more performance bugs than subjects of the control group. Three subjects of the experiment group and nine of the control group could not fix any bugs at all. The highest number of bugs fixed within the experiment group was 5.5 (one bug only fixed partially) and within the control group 3. The dispersion and skewedness of the two samples are illustrated in Fig. 5. While the highest score of three fixed bugs within the control group exceeds the interquartile range, it is displayed here as an outlier [4]. The maximum value of the control group calculated by the box-plot is 1. Subjects of the experiment group executed at least one, an average of 2.231, and at most 5 response time estimations. Subjects having fixed no bugs at all executed one estimation. Most subjects having fixed more than one bug also executed multiple estimations. One subject fixed five bugs while executing

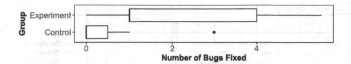

Fig. 5. Dispersion and skewedness of samples

one estimation. During the experiment, each response time estimation run took about five minutes.

Figure 6 illustrates how frequently individual performance bugs were fixed by the two groups. One subject of the experiment and one of the control group fixed PB1 only partially and received half the points. One subject of the control group provided an additional optimization, which is reported separately in Fig. 6. Instead of replacing the Sisyphus database retrieval with a more specific query, the result set was reused within a subsequent loop. The bug types empty semi trucks (PB7) and caching (PB5) were not addressed by the control group at all. Subjects of the experiment group did not destroy any functionality due to hints for expensive statements that cannot be avoided.

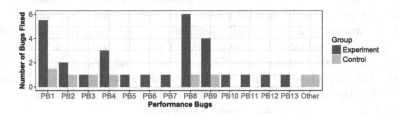

Fig. 6. Histogram of fixed performance bugs by group

Figure 7 illustrates the performance of each group according to the highest degree and the employment status of the subjects. Subjects of the experiment group performed better with an increasing experience level. The impact of the highest degree and the employment status on the number of fixed bugs is lower within the control group.

The number of times the subjects left the IDE is similar within both groups. Overall, subjects left the IDE on average 63.6 times (median of 58). In the case of the availability of the performance awareness plugin, subjects spent an average of 10.6% more time within the IDE. The overall time spent inside the IDE is 82%.

The top-level class was visited by all participants, though it reuses directly and indirectly six other classes relevant for the optimization task. While employing the awareness plugin participants visited on average 4.4 relevant classes (median of 5) compared to a mean of 2.5 (median of 2) achieved by participants of the control group.

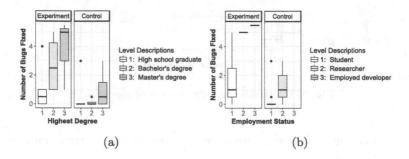

Fig. 7. Dispersion and skewedness by highest degree and employment status

4.2 Hypothesis and Correlation Testing

For the selection of a suitable hypothesis test, we first examine whether the samples of the number of fixed performance bugs are normally distributed. The results of the Kolmogorov-Smirnov and the Shapiro-Wilk tests are listed in Table 1. The null hypothesis of both tests assumes a normal distribution of samples. The p-value of the Kolmogorov-Smirnov test for the experiment group is higher than $\alpha = 0.05$, indicating a normally distributed sample. However, this does not apply to the control group. The Shapiro-Wilk test indicates that none of the two samples are normally distributed. Therefore, the Mann-Whitney test is applied to evaluate H_0. The p-value of the directed test is considerably lower than $\alpha = 0.05$ (p-value $= 0.005723$, U $= 131$) and, therefore, allows us to reject the null hypothesis H_0 and accept the alternative hypothesis. Hence, we conclude that the number of fixed performance bugs is significantly increased by the availability of the performance awareness plugin.

Table 1. Test for normal distribution

Group	Kolmogorov-Smirnov test		Shapiro-Wilk test	
	D	p-value	W	p-value
Experiment	0.327	0.124	0.8092	0.008795
Control	0.3898	0.03845	0.5759	0.00004089

The results of the survey for eliciting the skill level of participants are based on an ordinal scale and, therefore, cannot be used in any mathematical operations. When assuming the same difference between the skill levels (e.g., interval scale) the test for correlation indicates a high correlation between the amount of fixed bugs and the expertise only for the participants using the awareness plugins. The corresponding boxplots displayed in Fig. 7 also indicate that subjects with a higher experience level also achieve better results with the availability of the plugin. In contrast, the experience level has less impact if subjects are not supported with performance awareness. The lack of familiarity with an application prevents subjects from utilizing their expertise. The presence of hints on the response time of methods within the source code supports developers in proceeding more effectively during the optimization task. The performance awareness plugin also enables less experienced subjects to implement optimizations.

Subjects of the experiment group spent statistically significantly more time within the IDE than subjects of the control group. The most successful subjects of the control group also spent more time than the average of the group within the IDE. However, the test for correlation between the number of fixed bugs and the time spent inside the IDE does not indicate any significant correlation.

Subjects of the experiment group visited statistically significantly more relevant classes than subjects of the control group. The test for correlation between the methodical inspection of relevant classes and the effectiveness of developers employing the aid returns a PCC of 0.56 and a p-value of 0.04 indicating a significant linear correlation. As many subjects of the control group didn't fix any bugs at all, the results of the correlation test are not robust. We conclude, that the awareness plugin enables a methodical investigation of code during maintenance tasks and, therefore, increases the effectiveness of developers.

During the experiment, a single response time estimation took about five minutes due to the lab's low performing computers. In contrast, the same operation takes about 90 s on up-to-date hardware. Hence, only eight estimations could be obtained during the allotted time frame. It can be assumed that subjects using the plugin would perform even better when provided with faster workstations.

5   Threats to Validity

Threats to conclusion, internal, construct, and external validity [19] are discussed in this section.

Conclusion Validity. The selection of hypothesis tests for this experiment is performed considering underlying assumptions on the distribution of samples and levels of measurement. The results and the activity of subjects is measured automatically by the IDE. The assessment of optimizations is based on a well-defined scheme accounting for alternative or incomplete solutions.

Internal Validity. The performance of subjects can vary significantly, so that their selection represents a threat to internal validity. Subjects might lack the required skills for performing the optimization task. To participate in the experiment, at least basic programming skills were required. None of the subjects abandoned the experiment. Within each group, at least 30% of the subjects managed to identify or fix a performance bug. Due to the voluntary participation, a relatively high motivation of the subjects can be assumed. Prior knowledge of the Cargo Tracker application among the experiment participants can be excluded based on the analysis of the survey. Participants were also distributed randomly to treatments. By employing blocking, the impact of subjects' experience was controlled. To address learning effects, subjects participate only once and are assigned only one treatment.

Construct Validity. The operationalization of response time behavior as a set of performance bugs represents a simplification of the underlying construct since bugs can differ in their impact. In the context of Java EE applications, the impact of bugs depends on database content and cannot be generally quantified. A simplified representation of the response time behavior is therefore necessary. Using a single application as an object, the concept of Java EE might be under-represented. The application, however, is composed of a variety of components and covers the broad spectrum of Java EE technologies. Only five of the performance antipatterns identified in literature are instantiated as performance bugs. However, only antipatterns on the implementation level can be addressed by the performance awareness approach, and other types do not apply to the application. The application of the treatment aims at improving the response time behavior of components. While optimizing the response time, other aspects such as resource utilization or throughput might be aggravated. Thus, the results of this experiment might not be generalizable to other constructs.

External Validity. Several studies examine the suitability of students as subjects in carrying out experiments in the field of software engineering [7]. According to Kitchenham et al. [10], students are generally suitable for evaluating the use of a technology by software engineers with less experience. The majority of the subjects, however, already had a bachelor's degree and industrial programming experience. About half of the subjects possessed more than a year of industrial experience. The Cargo Tracker implements all relevant Java EE technologies and is in this regard representative for the industry. However, the application is relatively simple. The lack of familiarity with the application and its domain could compensate for the simplicity. It is expected that the benefit of performance awareness will be even higher in the context of a more complex application. Similar optimization tasks can occur in practice. However, the results of the experiment are not necessarily transferable to development tasks. This threat was deliberately accepted in order to allow for a short procedure with the highest possible number of participants and a low drop-out rate. In contrast to the development of simple algorithms, the implementation of Java EE components requires more knowledge.

6 Related Work

Research in the area of performance awareness proposes both measurement-based and model-based approaches supporting developers with insights based on past observations and predictions. Approaches can be further classified by their level of automation, the focused domain, the type of insights provided and their integration in development environments. Automated approaches integrated in the development environment are described in this section.

Measurement-Based Approaches. Existing measurement-based approaches focus on several domains, such as parallel programs, component-based applications, Java programs, or database management systems. The insights provided cover aspects such as resource consumption, anti-patterns, or response times. The Stochastic Performance Language (SPL) presented by Bulej et al. [1] provides a means for specifying expectations of the performance of individual methods. The authors evaluate how well SPL formulas are suitable for specifying ratios between the performance of different methods. Heger et al. [5] describe an approach for the automatic recognition of performance degradation and the identification of the root causes based on unit tests. The authors validate how well the approach can identify a sample of both synthetically injected and real-world performance regressions. Horký et al. [6] present an approach for the support of performance awareness by extending the source code documentation of methods with a description of their response time behavior. As already described in Sect. 1, the authors report that no statistically significant improvement could be found by the availability of the approach due to the few and in some cases strongly diverging results.

Model-Based Approaches. Model-based approaches focus on domains such as event-driven systems, object-relational mapping, storage systems, or software as a service. The insights provided cover aspects such as response time, and suggestions for optimization. Weiss et al. [17] describe an approach for predicting the response time of persistence layer services based on tailor-made benchmarks. The influence of the approach on the implementation of the developers is not evaluated by the authors. An approach for feedback-driven development of cloud applications based on the integration of monitoring data in the IDE is described by Cito et al. [2]. The authors describe an initial implementation of the approach for the SAP HANA Cloud Platform but no evaluation.

7   Conclusion and Future Work

This work presented the evaluation of an approach for supporting developers of Java EE applications with performance awareness within a controlled experiment. Subjects fixed on average over three times more performance bugs while using the approach. Statistical tests indicate that the number of fixed performance bugs is significantly increased by the availability of the performance awareness plugin.

Future research will investigate the impact of the performance awareness approach in new scenarios. The present experiment focused on the availability of the awareness plugin. It would also be desirable to compare the results while employing different tools. Here, other approaches for performance awareness as well as classical tools for performance analysis can be considered. For example, subjects might be required to employ Java profilers to optimize components. In addition, the approach to performance awareness should also be evaluated in the context of a development task.

Subjects had to explicitly request response time predictions during this experiment. Due to the duration of each prediction run, the approach could not provide continuous feedback, e.g. automatically after each code change. The approach will be optimized for this scenario. In the context of further experiments, it could then be investigated whether the influence on developers persists while predictions are displayed unsolicited.

References

1. Bulej, L., Bureš, T., Keznikl, J., Koubková, A., Podzimek, A., Tůma, P.: Capturing performance assumptions using stochastic performance logic. In: 3rd ACM/SPEC International Conference on Performance Engineering, pp. 311–322 (2012)
2. Cito, J., Leitner, P., Gall, H.C., Dadashi, A., Keller, A., Roth, A.: Runtime metric meets developer: building better cloud applications using feedback. In: ACM International Symposium on New Ideas, New Paradigms, and Reflections on Programming and Software, pp. 14–27 (2015)
3. Danciu, A., Chrusciel, A., Brunnert, A., Krcmar, H.: Performance awareness in Java EE development environments. In: Beltrán, M., Knottenbelt, W., Bradley, J. (eds.) EPEW 2015. LNCS, vol. 9272, pp. 146–160. Springer, Cham (2015). https://doi.org/10.1007/978-3-319-23267-6_10
4. Elliott, A.C., Woodward, W.A.: Statistical Analysis Quick Reference Guidebook: With SPSS Examples. Sage, Thousand Oaks (2007)
5. Heger, C., Happe, J., Farahbod, R.: Automated root cause isolation of performance regressions during software development. In: 4th ACM/SPEC International Conference on Performance Engineering, pp. 27–38 (2013)
6. Horký, V., Libic, P., Marek, L., Steinhauser, A., Tůma, P.: Utilizing performance unit tests to increase performance awareness. In: 6th International Conference on Performance Engineering, pp. 289–300 (2015)
7. Höst, M., Regnell, B., Wohlin, C.: Using students as subjects–a comparative study of students and professionals in lead-time impact assessment. Empir. Softw. Eng. 5(3), 201–214 (2000)
8. Jin, G., Song, L., Shi, X., Scherpelz, J., Lu, S.: Understanding and detecting real-world performance bugs. SIGPLAN Not. 47(6), 77–88 (2012)
9. Kitchenham, B., Fry, J., Linkman, S.: The case against cross-over designs in software engineering. In: 11th International Workshop on Software Technology and Engineering Practice, pp. 65–67 (2003)
10. Kitchenham, B.A., et al.: Preliminary guidelines for empirical research in software engineering. IEEE Trans. Softw. Eng. 28(8), 721–734 (2002)
11. Minelli, R., Mocci, A., Lanza, M.: I know what you did last summer - an investigation of how developers spend their time. In: 23rd IEEE International Conference on Program Comprehension, pp. 25–35 (2015)
12. Reussner, R., Becker, S., Happe, J., Koziolek, H., Krogmann, K., Kuperberg, M.: The Palladio Component Model. Universität Karlsruhe (2007)
13. Robillard, M.P., Coelho, W., Murphy, G.C.: How effective developers investigate source code: an exploratory study. IEEE Trans. Softw. Eng. 30(12), 889–903 (2004)
14. Sanchez, H., Robbes, R., Gonzalez, V.M.: An empirical study of work fragmentation in software evolution tasks. In: 22nd IEEE International Conference on Software Analysis, Evolution, and Reengineering, pp. 251–260 (2015)
15. Smith, C.U., Williams, L.G.: More new software performance antipatterns: even more ways to shoot yourself in the foot. In: Computer Measurement Group Conference, pp. 717–725 (2003)
16. Tůma, P.: Performance awareness: keynote abstract. In: 5th ACM/SPEC International Conference on Performance Engineering, pp. 135–136 (2014)

17. Weiss, C., Westermann, D., Heger, C., Moser, M.: Systematic performance evaluation based on tailored benchmark applications. In: 4th ACM/SPEC International Conference on Performance Engineering, pp. 411–420 (2013)
18. Wert, A.: Performance problem diagnostics by systematic experimentation. Ph.D. thesis, KIT-Bibliothek (2015)
19. Wohlin, C., Runeson, P., Hst, M., Ohlsson, M.C., Regnell, B., Wessln, A.: Experimentation in Software Engineering. Springer, Heidelberg (2012). https://doi.org/10.1007/978-3-642-29044-2

Deriving Symbolic Ordinary Differential Equations from Stochastic Symmetric Nets Without Unfolding

Marco Beccuti[1], Lorenzo Capra[2], Massimiliano De Pierro[1],
Giuliana Franceschinis[3(✉)], and Simone Pernice[1]

[1] Dip. di Informatica, Università di Torino, Turin, Italy
[2] Dip. di Informatica, Università di Milano, Milan, Italy
[3] DISIT, Università del Piemonte Orientale, Alessandria, Italy
giuliana.franceschinis@uniupo.it

Abstract. This paper concerns the quantitative evaluation of Stochastic Symmetric Nets (SSN) by means of a fluid approximation technique particularly suited to analyse systems with a huge state space. In particular a new efficient approach is proposed to derive the deterministic process approximating the original stochastic process through a system of Ordinary Differential Equations (ODE). The intrinsic symmetry of SSN models is exploited to significantly reduce the size of the ODE system while a symbolic calculus operating on the SSN arc functions is employed to derive such system efficiently, avoiding the complete unfolding of the SSN model into a Stochastic Petri Net (SPN).

Keywords: Stochastic Symmetric Nets
Ordinary Differential Equations · Symmetries · Symbolic analysis
Symbolic structural techniques

1 Introduction

SSNs [8] are a colored extension of SPNs [11]: both formalisms are widely used for modeling and analysing Discrete Event Dynamic Systems. The underlying stochastic process, a Continuous Time Markov Chain (CTMC), can be automatically generated and studied using numerical and simulative techniques or approximated by an ODE system.

This paper extends the result described in [4] in which: (1) we identified a class of SSNs whose underlying CTMC can be approximated by an ODE system according to Kurtz's theorem [9]; (2) we proposed an algorithm to generate a reduced ODE system exploiting the SSN model symmetries. This algorithm requires an unfolding step before generating the reduced system.

To overcome this limitation we propose a new approach based on a symbolic calculus for SSN arc functions to generate the compact ODE system without prior unfolding. Such calculus was introduced in [5] where a language extending

© Springer Nature Switzerland AG 2018
R. Bakhshi et al. (Eds.): EPEW 2018, LNCS 11178, pp. 30–45, 2018.
https://doi.org/10.1007/978-3-030-02227-3_3

the arc expressions syntax of SSNs and some operators on the language elements were presented and applied to SSN structural properties computation. The calculus was implemented in the SNexpression tool [6]. In [7] a more comprehensive formalization of SSN structural properties and the generalization of all operators (with some limitations on composition) to work on multisets extended the method applicability. In this paper the ability to symbolically manipulate the arc functions of SSNs is exploited to build the reduced set of Symbolic ODEs (SODEs) directly. The three main contributions are: (1) the definition of the formulae for the derivation in symbolic form of the terms to be included in each SODE, (2) the definition of an approach to compute the cardinality of specific language expressions representing groups of similar terms in a single ODE, that can thus be *compressed* in a single term in the SODE, and (3) the definition of a procedure to express the *enabling degree* of transition instances appearing in the SODE in symbolic form. The main steps required to automatically derive the complete set of SODE have been implemented.

This is the first approach in which the syntax of SSNs is exploited to directly generate a compact ODE system (we refer to [13] for a general overview on PNs and fluid approximation). Indeed, even in efficient PN tools (e.g., Snoopy [10]) the compact representation of colored models is exploited in model construction and for some basic analysis, but not for the deterministic simulation. In the context of a fluid framework for PEPA, a result similar to that in [4] was presented in [14], but the aggregation is based on exact fluid lumpability.

The paper is organized as follows: in Sect. 2 the background and the notation needed to understand the new approach are introduced. In Sect. 3 the new approach is illustrated on a case study and the main properties needed to automatically generate the SODE are presented. In Sect. 4 we report a set of experimental results illustrating the method efficiency. Conclusions and directions for future work are discussed in Sect. 5.

2   Background

In this section, after presenting the case study used for illustrating the new approach, the SSN formalism is introduced and a description on how to derive the SODE system from an SSN model is presented, recalling the results in [4].

2.1   Our Case Study in a Nutshell

Our case study is inspired by the model presented in [12]: Botnets are networks of compromised machines under the control of an attacker that uses those compromised machines for a variety of malicious/nefarious purposes.

Typically, initial infection involves a malware, called *Trojan horse*, which installs a malicious code into a vulnerable machine. The injected malicious code begins its bootstrap process and attempts to join the Botnet. A machine connected to the Botnet becomes a *bot* and can send spam (a working bot) or infect new machines (a propagation bot). The bot is inactive most of the time to reduce the probability to be detected and becomes active only for very short periods. An infected machine can be recovered if an anti-malware software discovers the virus or if the computer is physically disconnected from the network. The corresponding SSN model is reported in Fig. 1. In the next subsections its main components are introduced together with the elements of the formalism.

2.2   The SSN Formalism

The SSN formalism [8] adds *colors* to the SPN formalism, so that information can be associated with the tokens in the net. This feature usually leads to a more compact system representation which may be exploited during both the construction and the solution of the model [4,8].

An SSN is a bipartite directed graph with two types of nodes: *places* and *transitions*. Places, graphically represented as circles, coincide with the state variables of the system. For instance the places of the Botnet model in Fig. 1 are *NoConBot*, *ConBot*, *InactiveBot* and *ActiveBot*, corresponding to four possible phases through which a machine under attack can flow. Places contain *tokens*, whose colors are defined by the *color domain* $cd()$, expressed as Cartesian product of *color classes* C_i. Color classes can be partitioned in *static subclasses* $\{C_{i,j}, j = 1, \ldots, k\}$. Colors in a class represent entities of the same nature but only colors within the same static subclass are guaranteed to *behave similarly*. A color class may be *ordered* and in this case a successor function denoted by ! is defined on it, which determines a circular order on its elements. In the model of Fig. 1 there are two color classes: *Mac* and *Loc*. The former is partitioned into four static subclasses of cardinality one (the machine infection states): **N**(ormal), **I**(nfected), **W**(orking Bot), **P**(ropagation Bot). The latter, representing machine locations, is not partitioned into subclasses. The color domains of all the places is $Mac \times Loc$ (representing pairs ⟨machine infection state,location⟩).

Transitions, graphically drawn as boxes, represent the system events: in our example, the flow through attack phases and changes in the infection state of a machine. The instances of a transition t are defined by its *color domain* $cd(t)$ defined as a list of typed variables (with types chosen among the color classes) or as the Cartesian product of its variables types (assuming an implicit order among its variables). The transition variables appear in the functions labeling its arcs. A *transition instance* $\langle t, c \rangle$ binds each variable to a specific color of proper type. A *guard* can be used to restrict the allowed instances of t: it is a logical expression defined on $cd(t)$, and its terms, called *basic predicates* allow one to (1) compare colors assigned to variables of the same type ($x = y, x \neq y$); (2) test whether a color belongs to a given static subclass ($x \in C_{i,j}$); (3) compare the static subclasses of the colors assigned to two variables ($d(x) = d(y)$, $d(x) \neq d(y)$).

For instance *RecInitInf* is a transition in the model of Fig. 1. Its color domain is $Mac \times Mac \times Loc$ (assuming variables' order x, y, l), restricted by the guard $[x \in I \wedge y \in N]$ to the colors that associate variables x and y to the subset of machines in *infected* and *not infected* state respectively.

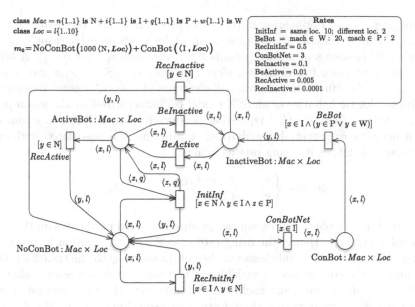

class $Mac = n\{1..1\}$ is $N + i\{1..1\}$ is $I + q\{1..1\}$ is $P + w\{1..1\}$ is W
class $Loc = l\{1..10\}$

$m_0 = \text{NoConBot}\big(1000\,\langle N, Loc\rangle\big) + \text{ConBot}\big(\langle I, Loc\rangle\big)$

Rates

InitInf = same loc. 10; different loc. 2
BeBot = mach $\in$ W : 20, mach $\in$ P : 2
RecInitInf = 0.5
ConBotNet = 3
BeInactive = 0.1
BeActive = 0.01
RecActive = 0.005
RecInactive = 0.0001

Fig. 1. SSN model for the Botnet.

The state of an SSN, called *marking*, is defined by the number of colored tokens in each place. The initial marking of the model in Fig. 1, representing one infected machine and 1000 not infected machines in each location, is

$$NoConBot(1000\langle N, Loc\rangle) + ConBot(\langle I, Loc\rangle). \qquad (1)$$

Places and transitions are connected through arcs decorated with *arc functions* defining both the enabling conditions for the transition instances and the state change caused by their firing. The function on the arc connecting place p and transition t has domain $cd(t)$ and codomain $Bag[cd(p)]$, where $Bag[A]$ is the set of multisets built on set A, and if $b \in Bag[A], a \in A, b[a]$ denotes the multiplicity of a in multiset b. Given a transition instance, the input and output arc functions map the transition color into (multi)sets of colored tokens matching the corresponding place color domain. Input and output arcs are denoted $I, O[p, t] : cd(t) \to Bag[cd(p)]$. A transition instance $\langle t, c\rangle$ is enabled in marking m if $\forall p \in {}^\bullet t, \forall c' \in cd(p)I[p,t](c)[c'] \le m[p][c']$ (${}^\bullet t$ and $t^\bullet$ represent the set of input and output places of t, respectively). An enabled instance may fire causing a state change from m to m' defined as follows: $\forall p, m'[p] = m[p] - I[p,t](c) + O[p,t](c)$.

The *arc functions* are formally expressed as sums of tuples, with each tuple element chosen from a set of predefined *basic functions* whose domain is the transition color domain and whose codomain is $Bag[C_i]$, for a given color class C_i. The tuples may have an associated guard, expressed with the same syntax of transition guards, allowing to include or exclude the tuple from the sum depending on the truth value of the guard for a given transition instance. The basic functions are: *projection*, denoted by a variable in the transition color domain (e.g., x and l appearing in the arc expression $\langle x, l \rangle$); *successor*, denoted $!x$, where x is a variable whose type is an ordered class; a constant function returning all elements in a class (or subclass), denoted S_{C_i} (or $S_{C_{i,j}}$). A linear combination of basic functions is a *class* function, e.g. $S_{C_i} - x$, where x is of type C_i, is a class function returning all elements of class C_i except element x.

The stochastic behavior of an SSN model is characterized by the assumption that the firing of any enabled transition occurs after a random delay sampled from a negative exponential distribution. A function ω is associated with each transition and defines its firing rate as follows:

$$\omega(t, c) = \begin{cases} r_i & if\ cond_i(c),\ i = 1, \ldots, n; \\ r_{n+1}\ otherwise \end{cases}$$

where $cond_i$ is a boolean expression comprising standard predicates on the transition color instance. Hence, the firing rate $r_i \in \mathbb{R}^+$ of a transition instance can depend only on the static subclasses of the colors assigned to the transition variables and on the comparison of variables of the same type. We assume that the conditions $cond_i$ are mutually exclusive. For instance, the rate associated with transition *InitInf* representing the infection propagation event is 10.0 if $q = l$, otherwise 2; also *BeBot*, representing the start of Working or Propagation Bot activity, has rate 20.0 if $(y \in W)$ and 2 if $(y \in P)$. The stochastic process driving the dynamics of an SSN model is a CTMC, where the states are identified with SSN markings and the state changes correspond to the marking changes in the model. In this context we assume that all the transitions of the SSN use an infinite server policy, and we define the intensity of $\langle t, c \rangle$ in marking m as:

$$\varphi(m, t, c) = \omega(t, c) \min_{\langle p_j, c' \rangle : I[p_j, t](c)[c'] \neq 0} \left\lfloor \frac{m[p_j][c']}{I[p_j, t](c)[c']} \right\rfloor$$

where the last factor is $e(m, t, c)$, the enabling degree of $\langle t, c \rangle$ in m.

2.3 From SSN Models to ODE

In [2] a class of SPN was identified whose stochastic behavior can be approximated through a deterministic process in agreement with the Kurtz's results in [9]: considering an SPN model whose places are all covered by P-semiflows and whose transitions use an *infinite server policy*, the underlying CTMC satisfies the *density dependent property* (i.e. the intensities of the transitions can be expressed as a function of the density of the tokens $\frac{m(p)}{N}$ where N is a constant depending on the P-semiflows and the initial marking) and it is possible to derive a set of ODE providing a good deterministic approximation of the average number of tokens in the places when the number of interacting objects (i.e. tokens) is large. In [4] we showed that similar results can be derived for SSN models and we described how to automatically generate the ODE system from an SSN model through the net unfolding: the average number of tokens in each place of the unfolded net is approximated through the following ODE:

$$\frac{dx_i(\nu)}{d\nu} = \sum_{j=1}^{|T|} \varphi(x(\nu), t_j)(O[p_i, t_j] - I[p_i, t_j]) \tag{2}$$

where $x(\nu)$ is a vector of real numbers representing the average number of tokens in the model places at time ν, T is the set of the net transitions, and $\varphi(x(\nu), t_j)$ is a function defining the intensity of transition t_j in the state $x(\nu)$ as follows:

$$\varphi(x(\nu), t_j) = \omega(t_j) \min_{l:I[p_l, t_j] \neq 0} \frac{x_l(\nu)}{I[p_l, t_j]}, \tag{3}$$

where $\omega(t_j)$ is obtained by $\omega(t, c)$ through the unfolding of $\langle t, c \rangle$ into t_j.

In [4], we proposed a translation method which reduces the size of the ODE system by automatically exploiting the model symmetries. This is achieved through the notion of *"symbolic" ODE* (SODE): a compact representation for a set of equivalent ODE, where the actual color identity is abstracted away, but the ability to distinguish different colors and to establish their static subclass is retained. However, this method still required an initial unfolding of the model to generate the ODE system that is automatically reduced in a second step. The goal of this paper is instead to directly derive the SODE from the SSN.

2.4 Symbolic Manipulation of SSN Arc Functions

In this section the definitions and notations required to explain how to derive the set of SODE are introduced: the method is based on symbolic manipulation of expressions of a language $\mathcal{L}$ (that look like SSN arc functions with a few syntactical extensions) through a set of operators (difference, transpose, composition).

The elements of language $\mathcal{L}$ have the following syntax:

$$\sum_j \lambda_j [g'_j] T_j [g_j], \lambda_j \in \mathbb{N}$$

where T_j is a tuple of class functions while $[g_j]$ and $[g'_j]$ are called respectively *guard* and *filter*. These expressions denote functions $D \to Bag[D']$; D and D' are in turn defined as Cartesian products of color classes. The components in a tuple T_j correspond one-to-one to the elements in the Cartesian product D': they are *intersections* ($\cap$) of basic class functions from set[1] $BS = \{v, S - v, S_C, S_{C_k}\}$ denoting functions $D \to Bag[C]$, where C is one of the basic color classes in D', v is a variable of type C, and C_k is a static subclass of C. The functions in BS are a subset of SSN class functions. The intersection is not part of the arc functions syntax, but allows any SSN arc function to be rewritten to a $\mathcal{L}$ expression. For instance (v_i, v_j variables of type C): $\langle S_{C_k} - v_i, v_i \rangle [v_i \in C_k]$ ($\notin \mathcal{L}$) $\equiv \langle S_{C_k} \cap (S - v_i), v_i \rangle [v_i \in C_k]$ ($\in \mathcal{L}$); $\langle S - v_i - v_j, v_i, v_j \rangle [v_i \neq v_j]$ ($\notin \mathcal{L}$) $\equiv \langle (S - v_i) \cap (S - v_j), v_i, v_j \rangle [v_i \neq v_j]$ ($\in \mathcal{L}$). Symbols $[g_j]$, $[g'_j]$ are defined on D and

---

[1] To keep the presentation simple, ordered classes are not considered here, but the presented results extend to models including them.

D', respectively. Symbol $[g]$, where g is a SSN standard predicate defined on D, denotes a function $D \to D$: $[g](d) = d$ if $g(d) = true$, $[g](d) = \emptyset$ if $g(d) = false$. Observe that the SSN arc function syntax may include guards but not filters.

Language $\mathcal{L}$ is closed with respect to a set of operators among which the *transpose* and the *difference*; SNexpression (www.di.unito.it/~depierro/SNex) implements the rules for symbolically treating these operators.

Definition 1 (Transpose). *Let $f : D \to Bag[D']$ be a function, its transpose $f^t : D' \to Bag[D]$ is defined as: $f^t(x)[y] = f(y)[x], \forall x \in D', y \in D$.*

Definition 2 (Difference). *Let $f, g : D \to Bag[D']$ be two functions. The difference $f - g : D \to Bag[D']$ is defined as: $f - g(x) = f(x) - g(x), \forall x \in D$.*

The multiset difference is: $b, b' \in Bag[A], a \in A$, $(b - b')[a] = max(0, b[a] - b'[a])$.

In the sequel the language, its operators and its properties are the key formal tools to define the SODE characterizing an SSN model without unfolding it. In particular the difference and transpose operators allow us to define and express in symbolic form the functions $\mathcal{R}(t, p)$ and $\mathcal{A}(t, p)$, where t is a transition and p is a place connected to t. Function $\mathcal{R}(t, p)$, called *Removed By*, defines which instances $\langle t, c' \rangle$ of t withdraw tokens of color $c \in cd(p)$ from place p. Function $\mathcal{A}(t, p)$, called *Added By*, defines which instances $\langle t, c' \rangle$ add tokens of color $c \in cd(p)$ into place p. $\mathcal{R}(t, p)(c)[c']$ and $\mathcal{A}(t, p)(c)[c']$ denote the number of tokens of color c withdrawn by/ added by instance $\langle t, c' \rangle$ from/to p.

$$\mathcal{R}(t, p) : cd(p) \to Bag[cd(t)]; \quad \mathcal{R}(t, p) = (I[t, p] - O[t, p])^t$$

$$\mathcal{A}(t, p) : cd(p) \to Bag[cd(t)]; \quad \mathcal{A}(t, p) = (O[t, p] - I[t, p])^t$$

For instance, place *ActiveBot* (whose cd is $Mac \times Loc$) is connected to transition *RecActive* with $cd : x \in Mac, y \in Mac, l \in Loc$ and with guard $y \in N$. The expression for $\mathcal{R}(RecActive, ActiveBot) = (\langle x, l \rangle[y \in N])^t$, is $\langle \tilde{x}, S_N, \tilde{l} \rangle$ denoting a function from $cd(ActiveBot)$ to $Bag[cd(RecActive)]$. Here the names $\tilde{y}$ and $\tilde{l}$ indicate respectively the first occurrence of class Mac and of class Loc in $cd(ActiveBot)$, while the color identifying an instance of $RecActive$ is indicated as $\langle x, y, l \rangle$. As expected the instances of $RecActive$ that remove tokens of color $\langle \tilde{x}, \tilde{l} \rangle$ from $ActiveBot$ are those with $x = \tilde{x}, y \in N, l = \tilde{l}$.

3   The Symbolic ODE Generation Method

The approach for deriving the SODE corresponding to a given place p comprises two steps. Let $x[p, c]$ be the number of c-colored tokens in place p at time ν (in order to keep notation simple we will omit time dependency).

Step 1. For each transition t connected to place p: if there is an arc from p to t compute $\mathcal{R}(t, p)$, if there is an arc from t to p compute $\mathcal{A}(t, p)$.
Step 2. The differential equation for place p and color $c \in cd(p)$ is defined as:

$$\frac{dx[p, c]}{d\nu} = \sum_{\langle t, c' \rangle : p \in t^\bullet, c' \in \mathcal{A}(t, p)(c)} \varphi(x(\nu), t, c')(\mathcal{A}(t, p)(c)[c']) - \sum_{\langle t, c' \rangle : p \in {}^\bullet t, c' \in \mathcal{R}(t, p)(c)} \varphi(x(\nu), t, c')(\mathcal{R}(t, p)(c)[c']), \quad (4)$$

Each sum spans over all instances $\langle t, c' \rangle$ that withdraw (negative sum) or add (positive sum) tokens of color c from/to p. The *intensity* of $\langle t, c' \rangle$ is multiplied by $\mathcal{A}(t, p)(c)[c']$ or $\mathcal{R}(t, p)(c)[c']$ (i.e., by the number of tokens of color c added to or withdrawn from p by $\langle t, c' \rangle$) to get the actual flow of tokens in/out p.

Due to the symmetry of SSN arc functions the above procedure can be done for just an *arbitrary* color $c \in cd(p)$. This statement is only partially true, in fact the symmetry is surely preserved only in subsets of $cd(p)$ containing colors that cannot be distinguished through standard predicates operating on $cd(p)$: for this reason a partial unfolding of the places may be needed (e.g. due to the presence of static subclasses). In order to apply the symbolic approach the intensity $\varphi(x(\nu), t, c')$ must also be symmetric: this may require the partial unfolding of transitions. Special care should be taken in case the $cd(t)$ includes variables with same type: in this case one should treat separately instances in which the same color or different colors are assigned to these variables since this may influence both the rate of $\langle t, c' \rangle$ and the number of tokens of color c flowing in or out of p.

Symbolic Representation of ODE. Due to symmetries, each summation over the color domain of a given transition t in Eq. (4) may be computed efficiently by grouping instances with "similar" rate and same number of tokens moved into or out of the place. This may be achieved by expressing Eq. (4) in a compact, *symbolic* way. As anticipated, a preliminary partial unfolding of some nodes of the original SSN may be needed: each place p' in the partially unfolded net, derives from a place p in the original model and an SSN predicate g on $cd(p)$ taking into account the partition of color classes in subclasses, and the possibility that elements of same class in the tuples of $cd(p)$ be equal or different. In the partially unfolded net a filter $[g]$ prefixes the function on any arc connected to p'; notation $p_{[g]}$ shall be used for the place names in the partially unfolded net to put in evidence the original place name and predicate g. If $cd(p)$ contains only one occurrence of C and g is $[c \in C_j]$ we shall use the notation p_{C_j}. For what concerns transitions, each t' in the partially unfolded net must satisfy $\forall c_1, c_2 \in cd(t') : \omega(t', c_1) = \omega(t', c_2) = \omega(t')$, in this case the unfolded transitions t' deriving from transition t in the original model shall be characterized by a guard which is the conjunction of t guard and the condition $cond_i$ associated with value r_i in the definition of $\omega(t)$. This kind of partial net unfolding will be illustrated on the example.

The terms of the SODE corresponding to place p are based on the symbolic expressions $\mathcal{A}(t, p)$ and $\mathcal{R}(t, p)$, formally expressed as weighted sums of *tuples* $\sum_i \lambda_i F_i$, $\lambda_i \in \mathbb{N}$, $F_i = [g_i] T_i [g_i']$, $\forall c \in cd(p), \forall c' \in cd(t)$ $F_i(c)[c'] \leq 1$. Each term of $\mathcal{R}$ and $\mathcal{A}$ can be seen as a *parametric* set of t's instances, each one withdrawing/putting λ_i tokens of color c from/to p. Hence we need to compute the *cardinality* of each parametric set, that may depend on $c \in cd(p)$.

Definition 3 (Constant-size function). *A guarded function* $F[g] : D \to Bag[D']$ *is constant-size if and only if* $\exists k \in \mathbb{N} : \forall c \in D, g(c) \Rightarrow |F(c)| = k$.

The above definition includes the particular case $g \equiv true$. The *cardinality* $|F[g]|$ of a constant-size function is equal to $|F(c)|$, for any c s.t. $g(c)$ is true.

A guarded tuple $T[g] \in \mathcal{L}$ is constant size if and only if, for each T's component (a class function) f, $f[g]$ is constant size. The following property defines a syntactical condition for a (guarded) class function $f[g]$ being constant size:

Property 1. $f[g]$ is *constant-size* if: f either belongs to the basic-set BS of class functions or it takes one of these forms

$$(a) \quad \bigcap_{j \in Q, |Q| < |C|} S - v_j \qquad b) \quad S_{C_k} \bigcap_{j \in J, |J| < |C_k|} S - v_j$$

where in (b) for each v_j: $g \Rightarrow v_j \in C_k$.

The cardinalities of terms of type (a) and (b) are $|C| - |Q|$ and $|C_k| - |J|$, respectively. The cardinalities of functions in BS can be easily inferred. For instance, function $S - v_1 \cap S - v_2[v_1 \neq v_2]$, where v_1, v_2 are two variables of type C, is constant size, with cardinality $|C| - 2$.

When transposing a given expression with the SNexpression tool each term $[g']T[g]$ in the resulting sum is such that $T[g]$ is constant size. We finally state a syntactical condition on a filter $[g']$ ensuring that $[g']T[g] \in \mathcal{L}$ is constant-size.

Property 2. $[g']T[g] \in \mathcal{L}$ is *constant-size* if $T[g]$ is constant size and

1. g' is a conjunctive form composed only of (in)equations $c_i = (\neq)c_j$, $i < j$,
2. for each (in)equation $c_i = (\neq)c_j$ the corresponding class-C functions f_i, f_j in T are such that $f_j \equiv f_i$,

Condition (2) says that tuple components referred to by any (in)equation in the filter must be equal. A constructive proof of Property 2, given in terms of an algorithm computing tuple cardinality, is provided in [3].

Example: the tuple $[c_1 \neq c_2 \wedge c_2 \neq c_3]\langle S_{C1} - c, S_{C1} - c, S_{C1} - c, S, c\rangle[c \in C1]$ has domain C and co-domain $C \times C \times C \times C$ (i.e. C^4); each c_i appearing in the filter represents the $i - th$ element in tuple T, $C = C1 \cup C2$ hence $|C| = |C1| + |C2|$ and $|C1| = 4, |C2| = 2$. Observe that the first three elements in the tuple are equal, and this is coherent with the hypothesis that elements compared in some term of the filter g' must be equal. The tuple can be divided in two independent sub-tuples: the first $[c_1 \neq c_2 \wedge c_2 \neq c_3]\langle S_{C1} - c, S_{C1} - c, S_{C1} - c\rangle[c \in C1]$ and the second $\langle S, c\rangle[c \in C1]$. The guard makes the elements $S_{C1} - c$ constant size: without this guard the size would be $|C1|$ if $c \notin C1$ and $|C1| - 1$ if $c \in C1$.

The filter of the second subtuple is *true*. The filter of the first subtuple doesn't involve any equality while it comprises two inequalities. The cardinality of the tuple elements are: $|S_{C1} - c| = |C1| - 1$, $|S| = |C|$, $|c| = 1$.

The first subtuple has as many elements as the number of possible colorings of a graph G with three nodes, each one associated with one of the three variables c_1, c_2, and c_3, and an edge between pairs of variable-nodes that appear in an inequality of the filter. Since $|S_{C1} - c| = |C1| - 1 = 3$ in this case $P(G, 3) = 12$. The filter of the second subtuple is *true*, hence its cardinality is simply $|S||c| = |C| = 6$. Finally the cardinality of the complete tuple is $12 * 6 = 72$.

Property 3. Any expression $e \in \mathcal{L}$ can be rewritten as a weighted sum of constant-size terms $[g_i']T_i[g_i]$.

The SNexpression tool can be instrumented to produce expressions in the form introduced in Property 3. The expression obtained from the tool does not have a canonical form: depending on the order of application of the rewriting rules the expression terms may be grouped in different ways; it is however guaranteed that the terms $F_i = [g_i]T_i[g_i']$ appearing in $\mathcal{R}$ or $\mathcal{A}$ are pairwise disjoint and *constant-size*. Thus, according with the transpose semantics, a term $[g_i]T_i[g_i']$ of $\mathcal{R}$ or $\mathcal{A}$ represents a set of $n_i = |[g_i]T_i[g_i']|$ t's colour instances each one withdrawing/adding exactly λ_i (the term's coefficient in the weighted sum) tokens from/to place p (these instances satisfy the predicate g_i').

If, in addition, all t colour instances matching $[g_i]T_i[g_i']$ had the *same* enabling-degree and hence consequently the same intensity (denoted by $\varphi(x(\nu), t)$), we could directly express the SODE relating place p:

$$\frac{dx[p,c]}{d\nu} = \sum_{t:p\in t^\bullet, F_i \text{ in } \mathcal{A}(t,p)} \lambda_i n_i \varphi(x(\nu), t) - \sum_{t:p\in {}^\bullet t, F_j \text{ in } \mathcal{R}(t,p)} \lambda_j n_j \varphi(x(\nu), t) \quad (5)$$

Each term in the SODE is a product of four factors: the cardinality of the expression identifying a set of (n_i) homogeneous transition instances, the number (λ_i) of tokens withdrawn/added by any transition instance in the set, the base rate ω of any transition instance in the set, and its enabling degree (the two factors are combined in φ). The last factor depends on the number of colored tokens required by the arc functions labelling the input arcs of any transition instance in the set. Some terms $[g_i]T_i[g_i']$ of $\mathcal{A}$ or $\mathcal{R}$ may have to be split into equivalent sums of tuples representing classes of transition instances with the same enabling degree. The procedure for computing the enabling degree is described later.

The Botnet Example. Let us illustrate the idea on the Botnet example to point out the main problems that have to be solved to automatize the whole process. Only the equation for place $NoConBot_N$, obtained by partially unfolding place $NoConBot$, is developed completely since similar arguments apply to the other places. The method generates one distinct equation for each place in the partially unfolded net: since all places in the BotNet model have $cd(p) = Mac \times Loc$ and only Mac is partitioned in four static subclasses, each place p will be unfolded into four new places p_I, p_N, p_W and p_P, and filters $[c \in X]$, where X stands for a static subclass of Mac, will prefix the functions on the arcs connected to place p_X as shown in Fig. 2. In some cases it is possible to simplify the partially unfolded net taking into account the transition guards: in Fig. 2 for instance some filters are not present because the transition guards make them redundant (e.g. see the arc from $RecActive$ to $NoConnBot_N$), moreover if the combination filter-transition guard results in a surely empty function, then the arc can be deleted (this is the case for the arc from $ActiveBot_W$ and transitions $InitInf_{[g]}$). On the Botnet example only a subset of colors can be found in the model places as explained hereafter: this allows to further simplify the partially unfolded model. The first element (Mac) of tokens in $NoConBot$ can only be in N or in I, those

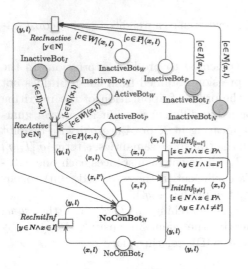

Fig. 2. Partially unfolded (sub)net (note filters $[c \in N/I/P/W]$) including all transitions connected to place $NoConBot_N$.

Table 1. List of rates in the $NoConBot_N$ equation and functions $\mathcal{A}$ and $\mathcal{R}$ needed to derive it, where $g = (c \in N)$.

Rates in SODE for $NoConBot_N$
$\omega_1 = \omega(RecActive, c, c' \in P, l)$
$\omega_2 = \omega(RecActive, c, c' \in W, l)$
$\omega_3 = \omega(RecInactive, c, c' \in P, l)$
$\omega_4 = \omega(RecInactive, c, c' \in W, l)$
$\omega_5 = \omega(InitInf, c, c' \in I, c'' \in P, l, l)$
$\omega_6 = \omega(InitInf, c, c' \in I, c'' \in P, l, l' \neq l)$
$\omega_7 = \omega(RecInitInf, c, c' \in I, l)$

place $(NoConBot_N, c, l); g = c \in N$	
$\mathcal{A}(RecActive, .)$	$\langle S_{Mac}, c, l \rangle [g]$
$\mathcal{A}(RecInactive, .)$	$\langle S_{Mac}, c, l \rangle [g]$
$\mathcal{R}(InitInf_{[l=q]}, .)$	$\langle c, S_I, S_P, l, l \rangle [g]$
$\mathcal{R}(InitInf_{[l \neq q]}, .)$	$\langle c, S_I, S_P, l, S - l \rangle [g]$
$\mathcal{A}(RecInitInf, .)$	$\langle S_I, c_1, l \rangle [g]$

in Active/InactiveBot can only be in W and P (see grey-colored empty instances in Fig. 2), finally those in place ConBot can only be in I.

Table 1 shows the expressions $\mathcal{A}$ and $\mathcal{R}$ for each transition connected to place $NoConBot_N$ from which we can generate a differential equation with several terms, depending on the number of terms in the expressions $\mathcal{A}$ and $\mathcal{R}$. Observe that some term may need to be transformed into an equivalent sum of terms to separate the transition instances with different enabling degree or rate.

In our model we assume that all transitions have uniform base rate except $InitInf$ and $BeBot$: the former has a different rate depending whether the two locations l' (of the machine which is going to be infected) and l (of the bot which is going to propagate the infection) are equal or different. The latter has a different rate for working bot and propagation bot generation. Hence the partial unfolding shall generate two instances of $InitInf$, $InitInf_{[l=l']}$ and $InitInf_{[l \neq l']}$ (see Fig. 2), and two instances of $BeBot$: $BeBot_W$ and $BeBot_P$.

In the following equation we denote with $x[p_X, c, l]$ the mean number of tokens in the place instance $\langle p_X, c, l \rangle$ (where X is one of the static subclasses in Mac). Thus, the differential equation corresponding to $\langle NoConBot_N, c, l \rangle$ is:

$$\frac{dx[NoConBot_N, c, l]}{d\nu} = |P|\omega_1 x[ActiveBot_P, c', l] + |W|\omega_2 x[ActiveBot_W, c', l] +$$
$$+ |P|\omega_3 x[InactiveBot_P, c', l] + |W|\omega_4 x[InactiveBot_W, c', l] + \omega_7 x[NoConBot_I, c', l] +$$
$$- |P||I|\omega_5 \min(x[NoConBot_I, c', l], x[ActiveBot_P, c'', l]) +$$
$$- |P||I|(|Loc| - 1)\omega_6 \min(x[NoConBot_I, c', l], x[ActiveBot_P, c'', l]),$$

where rates ω_i are defined in Table 1. Coefficients $|P|$ and $|W|$ in the first four terms are the cardinality of the tuples $\langle S_P, c_1, l_1 \rangle$ and $\langle S_W, c_1, l_1 \rangle$ respectively: these are obtained by splitting the term $\langle S_{Mac}, c_1, l_1 \rangle[c_1 \in N]$, common to $\mathcal{A}(RecActive, NoConBot_N)$ and $\mathcal{A}(RecInactive, NoConBot_N)$, into $\langle S_P, c_1, l_1 \rangle[g] + \langle S_W, c_1, l_1 \rangle[g]$ (the terms $\langle S_I, c_1, l_1 \rangle[g] + \langle S_N, c_1, l_1 \rangle[g]$) do not appear because they correspond to instances of $RecActive$ and $RecInactive$ that will never be enabled). Coefficients $|P||I|$ and $|P||I|(|Loc| - 1)$ in the last two terms of the SODE are the cardinalities of tuples $\langle c_1, S_I, S_P, l_1, l_1 \rangle$ and $\langle c_1, S_I, S_P, l_1, S_{Loc} - l_1 \rangle$, respectively. We omit the factor 1 preceding the ω_i, derived from the coefficient of the corresponding term in $\mathcal{A}$ or $\mathcal{R}$.

Computation of the Enabling Degree. Let us consider the SODE for place p. The contribution due to a transition t connected to p is expressed by $\mathcal{R}(t, p)$ or $\mathcal{A}(t, p)$, whose weighted terms $\lambda_i[g_i]T_i[g_i']$ represent parametric sets of $n_i = ||[g_i]T_i[g_i']||$ instances of t, that withdraw/add λ_i tokens from/to p. We need a method to derive the enabling degree of such instances, by possibly splitting terms with $n_i > 1$ into subterms denoting instances with same enabling degree.

Let $F_i = [g_i]T_i[g_i']$ be one such term. Due to symmetries, for each place $p' \in {}^{\bullet}t$ we just have to evaluate the arc function $I[p', t]$ on an arbitrary element of the parametric set F_i. This operation corresponds to a *composition* of two elements of $\mathcal{L}$: $I[p', t] \circ Tr_i$, where Tr_i is a cardinality-1 symbolic tuple *representative* of F_i. This particular composition is supported by the SNexpression tool and results in an element of $\mathcal{L}$.

Definition 4 (Composition). *Given l_1 and l_2 in $\mathcal{L}$ where l_2 has constant size equal to 1, the composition $l_1 \circ l_2$ is defined as $l_1 \circ l_2(c) = l_1(l_2(c))$; where l_1 is evaluated on the single element in the (multi)set returned by $l_2(c)$.*

The representative tuple Tr_i has the same co-domain as F_i and domain D_e, which may be equal to D of F_i or be extended. If $n_i = 1$ the representative tuple Tr_i coincides with $[g_i]T_i[g_i']$. Otherwise it is defined as $[g_i]T_i'[g_i'']$, according to Table 2, which maps T_i components to the corresponding T_i' ones; a conjunction of additional predicates may be introduced. The type of class-functions on the first row is the only admitted in constant-size tuples. Symbols c_h are new variables (index h must exceed the number of repetitions of C in D) that occur only once in Tr_i. These symbols cause an extension of the original domain.

Table 2. Syntactical rules to derive a representative tuple

T_i component	$f, |f[g_i']| = 1$	S	S_{Ck}	$\bigcap_{w \in A} S - c_w$	$S_{Ck} \bigcap_{w \in A} S - c_w$
T_i' component	f	c_h	c_h	c_h	c_h
$g_i'' = g_i' \wedge \ldots$	-	-	$c_h \in Ck$	$\bigwedge_{w \in A} c_h \neq c_w$	$c_h \in Ck \bigwedge_{w \in A} c_h \neq c_w$

As an example, consider $\langle S - c_1 \cap S - c_2, c1 \rangle[c_1 \neq c_2]$, with domain C^2. Its representative, with domain C^3, is $\langle c_3, c_1 \rangle[c_1 \neq c_2 \wedge c_1 \neq c_3 \wedge c_2 \neq c_3]$.

The following property formalizes the notion of *representative* tuple:

Property 4. Let $c' \in D_e$, and let $c'_D \in D$ denote the projection on D of c'

$$- \forall c' \in D_e : Tr_i(c') \in [g_i]T_i[g'_i](c'_D);$$
$$- \forall c \in D : [g_i]T_i[g'_i](c) = \bigcup_{c' \in D_e,\, c'_D = c} Tr_i(c').$$

The composition $I[p',t] \circ Tr_i$ results in $\sum_j \lambda_j F_j$, $F_j = [g_j]T_j[g'_j]$. If this summation contains a single term then λ_1 is the coefficient to be used as divisor of $x[p']$, in the formal expression of the enabling degree of t. Otherwise it can be rewritten[2] so that its terms are pairwise disjoint ($F_{j_1} \cap F_{j_2} \equiv \emptyset$), and guards $[g'_j]$ are either equal or mutually exclusive.

We can thus partition the summation into subsums $\sum_{j_1} + \sum_{j_2} \ldots$ of terms characterized by having the same guard, i.e., $(\sum_{j_h} \lambda_{j_h}[g_{j_h}]T_{j_h})[g'_h]$. The guard of each subsum (that, we recall, is a function $cd(t) \rightarrow cd(t)$) identifies a subset of t's instances that require the same number λ_{j_h} tokens of a color c_{j_h} from place p', so that the enabling degree (w.r.t. input place p') can be expressed as: $x[p']/\lambda_h^*$, $\lambda_h^* = max(\{\lambda_{j_h}\})$. These guards are applied as *filters* to split the parametric set F_i of t's instances, into subsets with constant enabling degree (w.r.t. p'): formally $\lambda_i F_i \mapsto \lambda_i(\sum_h [g'_h \wedge g_i]T_i[g'_i])$.

By repeatedly applying the procedure on the obtained subterms on the remaining places of $\bullet t$, we finally get the SODE expression for F_i, that will take the form: $\lambda_i \sum_h n_{i_h} \omega_t e_{i_h}(x)$, where $e_{i_h}(x) = min_{p' \in \bullet t}(x[p']/\lambda_{i_h}^*)$, $\sum_h n_{i_h} = n_i$.

Example. Let us illustrate the procedure on the Botnet model. When building the SODE of place $\langle NoConBot_N, c \in N, l \in Loc \rangle$ all the connected transitions should be considered: they are shown in Fig. 2. Let us consider only one of them: $InitInf_{[l \neq l']}$: in Table 1 we find the expression for $\mathcal{R}((InitInf_{[l \neq l']}, c, c' \in I, c'' \in P, l, l'), (NoConBot_N, c \in N, l \in Loc))$, namely $\langle c, S_I, S_P, l, S - l \rangle[c \in N]$. The last term in the SODE of $NoConBot_N$ originates from this expression which represents $|I||P|(|Loc| - 1)$ transition instances. A representative tuple for it is: $\langle c, c', c'', l, l' \rangle[c \in N, c' \in I, c'' \in P, l \neq l']$; to compute its enabling degree we need to know how many tokens are required in each input place ($ActiveBot_P$ and $NoConBot_N$) to ensure its enabling. We already have the number of tokens (of color $\langle c \in N, l \in Loc \rangle$) required in $NoConBot_N$ since it is the coefficient of the considered term in $\mathcal{R}$ that is 1; the multiset of tokens required in $ActiveBot_P$ by the representative instance of $InitInf_{l \neq l'}$ can be computed by performing the composition $\langle c'', l' \rangle[c'' \in P] \circ \langle c, c', c'', l, l' \rangle[c \in N, c' \in I, c'' \in P, l \neq l']$ resulting in $\langle c'', l' \rangle[c'' \in P]$, so it is only one token, hence the enabling degree is $e(x, InitInf_{[l \neq l']}, c, c' \in I, c'' \in P, l, l') = min(x(NoConBot_I, c, l), x(ActiveBot_P, c'', l'))$. Similar arguments apply to $InitInf_{[l = l']}$. In the other terms of the SODE the *min* function does not appear because the corresponding transitions have only one input place: for each of them the procedure illustrated above indicates that only one colored token is required by the input arc function composed with the representative tuple (so the divisor in the enabling degree formula is simply 1).

---

[2] In the SNexpression implementation there is an option to enforce such rewriting.

4 Experimental Results

In this section we report some experimental results showing the effectiveness of the proposed method. All the experiments are performed using a prototype implementation which combines: (1) GreatSPN [1] to draw the model and to generate R scripts encoding the ODE systems derived by the unfolded net; (2) SNexpression [6], a java tool, to compute and support the user into the creation of the SODE system applying the approach presented in this paper; (3) the R framework to solve the ODE systems (i.e. *deSolve package*).

The experiments consisted in (1) generating and solving the SODE system using the new approach and (2) unfolding the SSN model to evaluate the cost of this operation, which is the dominating cost of the method [4] as $|Loc|$ increases, and compare the results obtained from the ODE system of the unfolded model against those obtained from the SODE system.

The SODE system and the reduced ODE system generated with the method in [4] have the same number of equations, however the equations may not be identical because the new method may group homogeneous transition instances. In the Botnet model the equation associated with $NoConBot_N$ has one term representing $|Loc| - 1$ terms in the corresponding equation from the unfolding. As a consequence the number of terms in the ODE system grows linearly with $|Loc|$ while in the SODE it is constant.

We also compared the results obtained by solving the SODE system with those obtained from the ODE system of the unfolded model when the initial marking is that in Eq. 1: using the R function *lsoda()* for numerically solving the systems, the difference between the computed solutions is smaller than $1.0e^{-11}$.

The SODE system comprises 7 equations (the number of places in the partially unfolded net is 16 but 9 of them are always empty) and the total number of terms is 28. The procedure to derive the seven SODE from the net structure takes slightly less than one second (including the initial partial unfolding) and does not depend on $|Loc|$. In Table 3 the number of terms and equations of the ODE system obtained from the unfolded net and the reduction ratio achieved when the SODE system is adopted are shown. The fourth and fifth column contain the execution time required to solve the ODE and the SODE system on a 2.50 GHz Intel i3-3120M processor with 4 GB of RAM. In Table 4 the time required by the unfolding step is shown as a function of $|Loc|$; it was not possible to generate the unfolded model for $|Loc| = 200$ for insufficient memory. From these results we can conclude that the SODE approach is effective and overcomes the limitations of the methods that require the complete unfolding.

Table 3. ODE vs. SODE system size

$|Loc|$	Num. of terms		Mean solution time (sec.)	
	ODE	ODE/SODE	ODE	SODE
1	42 (11 eq.)	2.511 (1.57)	0.3790	0.0846
10	600 (110 eq.)	21.43 (15.7)	38.8110	0.2381
20	1600 (220 eq.)	57.14 (31.43)	572.1798	0.2920
50	7000 (550 eq.)	250 (78.58)	>4 h	0.2479

Table 4. Unfolding time.

$|Loc|$	Unfolding (sec.)
10	2.484
50	13.219
100	43.949
150	320.979
200	Out of memory

5   Conclusions and Future Work

In this paper we have proposed a new approach for generating a reduced set of ODE approximating the dynamic behavior of a SSN model: this is based on the observation that, due to the model symmetries, groups of *equivalent* equations, generated from the unfolded model could be substituted by a unique representative [4] so that the reduced system could be solved more efficiently.

The novelty of the present paper consists in the ability to automatically derive a Symbolic ODE for each group of *equivalent* ODE without ever computing the (complete) unfolding of the SSN. The new method is based on a recently developed extension of a symbolic calculus for the computation of SSN structural properties and its implementation in the SNexpression tool. In the paper the steps required to generate the system of SODE are defined in details. Some preliminary experimental results are reported to compare the new method with a previous method based on the model unfolding. The results have been obtained through a prototype implementation which combines different tools as GreatSPN, SNexpression and the R framework. The performance improvement observed on a relatively simple example may lead to substantial saving in more complex cases with good symmetric structure (large color classes with a few static subclasses). The complete implementation of the whole automatic procedure for generating the system of SODE of a SSN model is in progress.

The proposed method relies on the specific way of modeling symmetric systems provided by the SSN formalism. It is not straightforward to extend it to other formalisms that allow to express symmetries at the level of the model syntax, in some cases this may be achieved by showing a correspondence between formalism constructs: this is an interesting topic for future work.

Another foreseen evolution is to extend our approach for cases in which the deterministic approximation is not suited. In particular we will investigate how to combine SSN formalism with the diffusion approximation proposed by Kurtz [9] in which the deterministic process is replaced by the Ito's process.

Acknowledgments. This work is original and the contribution of G. Franceschinis was supported by the *Università del Piemonte Orientale*. The work of M. Beccuti was supported by *Fondazione CRT* for the project *Experimentation and study of models for* *the evaluation of the performance and the energy efficiency of the Competence Center for Scientific Computing at the Università di Torino.*

References

1. Baarir, S., Beccuti, M., Cerotti, D., De Pierro, M., Donatelli, S., Franceschinis, G.: The GreatSPN tool: recent enhancements. ACM SIGMETRICS Perf. Eval. Rev. **36**(4), 4–9 (2009). Special Issue on Tools for Performance Evaluation
2. Beccuti, M., Bibbona, E., Horvath, A., Sirovich, R., Angius, A., Balbo, G.: Analysis of Petri net models through stochastic differential equations. In: Ciardo, G., Kindler, E. (eds.) PETRI NETS 2014. LNCS, vol. 8489, pp. 273–293. Springer, Cham (2014). https://doi.org/10.1007/978-3-319-07734-5_15
3. Beccuti, M., Capra, L., De Pierro, M., Franceschinis, G., Pernice, S.: Deriving symbolic ordinary differential equations from Stochastic Symmetric Nets without unfolding. Technical report TR-INF-2018-07-03-UNIPMN, DiSIT, Università del Piemonte Orientale, Alessandria, Italy (2018)
4. Beccuti, M., et al.: From symmetric nets to differential equations exploiting model symmetries. Comput. J. **58**(1), 23–39 (2015)
5. Capra, L., De Pierro, M., Franceschinis, G.: A high level language for structural relations in well-formed nets. In: Ciardo, G., Darondeau, P. (eds.) ICATPN 2005. LNCS, vol. 3536, pp. 168–187. Springer, Heidelberg (2005). https://doi.org/10.1007/11494744_11
6. Capra, L., De Pierro, M., Franceschinis, G.: A tool for symbolic manipulation of arc functions in symmetric net models. In: Proceedings of the 7th International Conference on Performance Evaluation Methodologies and Tools, ValueTools 2013, Torino, Italy, pp. 320–323. ICST, Brussels (2013)
7. Capra, L., De Pierro, M., Franceschinis, G.: Computing structural properties of symmetric nets. In: Campos, J., Haverkort, B.R. (eds.) QEST 2015. LNCS, vol. 9259, pp. 125–140. Springer, Cham (2015). https://doi.org/10.1007/978-3-319-22264-6_9
8. Chiola, G., Dutheillet, C., Franceschinis, G., Haddad, S.: Stochastic well-formed coloured nets for symmetric modelling applications. IEEE Trans. Comput. **42**(11), 1343–1360 (1993)
9. Kurtz, T.G.: Strong approximation theorems for density dependent Markov chains. Stoch. Process. Appl. **6**(3), 223–240 (1978)
10. Liu, F., Heiner, M., Gilbert, D.: Coloured Petri nets for multilevel, multiscale and multidimensional modelling of biological systems. Brief. Bioinf. **11** (2017)
11. Molloy, M.K.: Performance analysis using stochastic Petri nets. IEEE Trans. Comput. **31**(9), 913–917 (1982)
12. E. V. Ruitenbeek and W. H. Sanders. Modeling peer-to-peer botnets. In Proceedings of the 5th International Conference on Quantitative Evaluation of Systems), QEST 08, Washington, DC, USA, pp. 307–316. IEEE CS (2008)
13. Silva, M.: Individuals, populations and fluid approximations: a Petri net based perspective. Nonlinear Anal.: Hybrid Syst. **22**, 72–97 (2016)
14. Tschaikowski, M., Tribastone, M.: Exact fluid lumpability for Markovian process algebra. In: Koutny, M., Ulidowski, I. (eds.) CONCUR 2012. LNCS, vol. 7454, pp. 380–394. Springer, Heidelberg (2012). https://doi.org/10.1007/978-3-642-32940-1_27

Mean Value Analysis of Closed
G-Networks with Signals

Jean-Michel Fourneau[✉]

DAVID, UVSQ, Univ. Paris-Saclay, Versailles, France
Jean-Michel.Fourneau@uvsq.fr

Abstract. We consider a closed network of queues with external signals. These signals trigger customer between queues and they arrive following a rate which depends on the number of active customers in the station. We consider three types of stations: they may have one server, an infinite number of servers or no servers at all. In that case, the customers behave like inert customers and they only react to signal. We prove that, under irreducibility conditions, such a network has a stationary distribution which is multiplicative. As the network is finite, all the states are not reachable and the distribution is known up to a normalization constant. To avoid the computation of this constant, we also prove a mean value analysis algorithm which allows to determine the average queue size and the average waiting time without computing the probabilities. We also present some extensions of the model.

1 Introduction

This paper generalizes in many directions the result obtained by Gelenbe in [12] where G-networks with trigger signals were introduced and were shown to have a product form steady-state distribution. First, we consider a closed network with customers and three types of stations: single server stations, infinite server stations and stations without server. Second, the signals arrive from the outside and are routed with a state dependent probability to a station in a the network. A signal triggers a customer movement from the station where it is received to any other queue in the network. Despite these uncommon features, we prove that such a network has a product form steady-state distribution. We also prove an "arrival see time average" property [ASTA] to relate the state seen by a incoming customer (due to routing or trigger) with the steady-state distribution for a network with a customer less. This property allows to develop a MVA like algorithm to compute the average queue length and the expected sojourn time.

G-networks of queues with signals have received a considerable attention since the seminal paper by Gelenbe [11] in 1991 where he introduced networks with positive and negative customers. A negative customer deletes a positive customer if there is any in the queue at its arrival. Then it disappears. If the queue is empty, it also disappears immediately. A negative customer is never kept in the queue. It is now seen as a signal which deletes a customer. Such a network

© Springer Nature Switzerland AG 2018
R. Bakhshi et al. (Eds.): EPEW 2018, LNCS 11178, pp. 46–61, 2018.
https://doi.org/10.1007/978-3-030-02227-3_4

with positive and negative customers are associated with models of Random Neural networks [13] and are therefore suitable to model control algorithms. Since then, many papers on networks of queues with signals have been published (see for instance a annotated bibliography [5]). It is worthy to remark that most of the results are obtained for open networks of queues (see [6] for one notable exception). Indeed, most of the signals studied so far implies the destruction of customers. In a closed network, such a behavior leads to an empty network after some time. Some numerical algorithms have been designed to solve explicitly the flow equations which are more general than the ones we get for Jackson or Gordon networks of queues [9]. For closed networks of queues, one must also compute the normalization constant. To avoid this computation, we develop an exact Mean Value Analysis approach. We prove for the first time, to the best of our knowledge, an ASTA property for a network with signals. It is well-known that in a closed Gordon Newell network, an arriving customer sees the steady-state distribution of the network with one customer less. Such a question was not considered so far for closed network of generalized queues with restart or trigger signals. The answer we provide here allows to compute the average queue size without computing the steady-state distribution: this is an extension of the well-known MVA algorithm [23].

Recently G-network with triggers have been proposed to model data processing and energy consumption [10,14–16,18]. In this model, denoted as Energy Packet Networks (EPN in the following), we can represent the flow of intermittent sources of energy like batteries and solar or wind based generators and their interactions with IT devices consuming energy like sensors, cpu, storage systems and networking elements. The main idea of EPNs is to represent energy in terms of discrete units called Energy Packets (or EP). Each EP represents a certain number of Joules. EP are produced by intermittent source of energy (solar, wind). Thus, the flows of EP is associated with random processes. EPs can be stored in a battery from which they can leak after a random delay. They also interact with devices which need energy to perform some works. Again this interaction is associated with some random processes. Note that a EPN is not only a theoretical concept. A more practical approach where power packets are really implemented as a pulse of current characterized by an intensity, a voltage and a time duration had been presented in the electrical engineering literature (see for instance [24]. These packets are associated with a protocol, control information and some hardware for switching and routing.

In the original Energy Packet Network model presented for instance in [17], we model the energy as EPs and the workload ad Data Packets (DPs). To transmit a DP between two nodes, one must use one EP. In a G-network, this is modeled with two types of queues: a battery queue and a workload queue (see Fig. 1). EP are stored in a battery queue while DP are queued before service in the workload queue. Each node in the network is associated with a queue to store the DP and a battery (the EP queue) to keep the energy. The EPs are sent to the DP queue and triggers the customer movement between workload queues in the network. When an EP arrives at a DP queue which is not backlogged, the energy is lost.

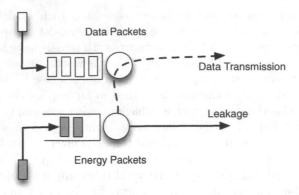

Fig. 1. The classical EP network model: 2 types dedicated respectively to EP and DP, the migration of a DP is provoked by the movement of an EP.

We hope that the theoretical results we provide in this paper will be useful for that research direction. This paper is merely theoretical as we prove that the queueing network has a product form steady-state distribution if the associated Markov chain is ergodic. The proof of the product form result is based on the resolution of the global balance equation. One may use other theoretical approaches to establish the result. But it not clear that the CAT and RCAT theorems proved by Harrison [1,19,21] are easier here. G-networks have also been modeled as networks of synchronized automata [4,7] and a proof based on properties of tensors has been proposed associated with this representation. We think that the proof we present here are easier. To simplify the presentation the proof is postponed in an appendix.

The technical part of the paper is organized as follows. In the next section we present the model and we state that the network of queues has a product form steady state distribution. Many details of the proof are postponed into an appendix for the sake of readability. As the network is closed and the number of customers is constant, not all the states are reachable and the distribution is known up to a normalization constant. To avoid the computation of this constant, we develop in Sect. 3 a mean value analysis algorithm to obtain the mean queue length and the average waiting time. This algorithm requires that we relate the state seen by an arriving customer or a signal and the steady-state distribution. In Sect. 4, we present some possible extensions of these results and an example of a closed network with energy packets and data packets.

2   Description of the Model

We investigate generalized networks with an arbitrary number N of queues, one class of customers and one type of signals (i.e. triggers as introduced by Gelenbe in [12]. We consider that the networks contains three types of station: stations with one server (in set $\mathcal{F}$), stations with an infinite number of servers (in set $\mathcal{I}$) and stations without server (in set $\mathcal{Z}$). In a station without any server, the customers do not receive service but they react to the signal. The stations received customers which are waiting for service, are served before migration to another queue, but they can also react to a signal as usual with G-networks of queues with signals. We consider here a trigger signal defined by Gelenbe in [12]. At its arrival to a non empty queue (say i) a trigger moves a customer to queue j according to routing matrix $\mathbf{T}$ and it disappears immediately. If queue i is empty, the trigger signal vanishes instantaneously. Triggers are never queued. Triggers arrive to the system following to a Poisson process with rate λ^t and they are routed to station i with a state dependent probability which will be detailed in the following paragraphs. Note that matrix $\mathbf{T}$ is stochastic but we do not require it is irreducible.

In most of the papers in the literature, G-networks with signals have an open topology because many signals imply the deletion of customers. Here we assume that the signals are external and only implies customer movement. Thus, we have a balance for the customers in the queues. If the queue is empty, it remains empty after reception of a trigger. If there is a backlog, we still have the same total number of customers after the reception of a signal. Therefore it is possible to consider a closed network where the total number of customers is constant. Let K be this number of customers in the network.

Let us turn back to the routing of triggers to queues. Let $\boldsymbol{x} = (x_1, \ldots, x_N)$ be the state of the system where x_i is the number of customers in station i. Thus $K = ||\boldsymbol{x}||_1$. We consider the following quantity:

$$S(\boldsymbol{x}) = \sum_{i \in \mathcal{F}} 1_{x_i > 0} + \sum_{i \in \mathcal{I}} x_i + \sum_{i \in \mathcal{Z}} x_i$$

The probability that a trigger entering the network of queues is routed to queue i is:

- $\frac{1_{x_i \geq 0}}{K}$ if i is station with one server,
- $\frac{x_i}{K}$ if i is an infinite server station,
- $\frac{x_i}{K}$ if i is station without server,

and it vanishes before joining a station with probability $\frac{K - S(\boldsymbol{x})}{K}$. Indeed we have $S(\boldsymbol{x}) \leq K$ and these probabilities are all well-defined. The remaining of the model is more classical. Service times are exponentially distributed with rate μ_i for a server at station i (for i in $\mathcal{F}$ and $\mathcal{I}$). At the completion of their service, the customers move between queues according to routing matrix $\mathbf{R}$. Note that this matrix is initially defined as a rectangular matrix because it models the routing between a queue in $\mathcal{F} \cup \mathcal{I}$ to a queue in $\mathcal{F} \cup \mathcal{I} \cup \mathcal{Z}$. We complete this matrix to obtain a square matrix with null rows corresponding to nodes in $\mathcal{Z}$. Note that $\mathbf{R}$ is not stochastic as it contains some null rows.

Assumption 1. *We assume in the following that:*

- $\lambda^t > 0$.
- $\mu_j > 0$ *for all j in $\mathcal{I} \cup \mathcal{F}$.*

– *Consider the directed graph built as follows: the set of nodes is the set of stations and there exists an arc from node i to node j if either $\mathbf{R}[i,j] > 0$ or $\mathbf{T}[i,j] > 0$. Let DG be this directed graph. We assume that DG is strongly connected,*

Clearly $(\boldsymbol{x})_t$ is a continuous time Markov chain. It has a finite number of states. As we assume that the directed graph of the customer movement (due to signals or routing of customers after their service) is strongly connected, it is also irreducible. Therefore it is ergodic and the steady-state distribution exists. The following result characterizes this distribution.

Theorem 1. *Let K be the number of customers in the network. Under Assumptions 1, the Markov chain $(\boldsymbol{x})_t$ has the following steady-state distribution:*

$$\pi(K, \boldsymbol{x}) = \frac{1}{G(K)} 1_{(\sum_i x_i = K)} \prod_{i \in \mathcal{F}} \rho_i^{x_i} \prod_{i \in \mathcal{I}} \frac{\rho_i^{x_i}}{x_i!} \prod_{i \in \mathcal{Z}} \frac{\gamma_i^{x_i}}{x_i!}, \tag{1}$$

where ρ_i and γ_i are defined by the flow equations: for all queue i in $\mathcal{F}$ and in $\mathcal{I}$:

$$\rho_i = \frac{\sum_{j \in \mathcal{F} \cup \mathcal{I}} \mu_j \rho_j \mathbf{R}[j,i] + \sum_{j \in \mathcal{F} \cup \mathcal{I}} \frac{\lambda^t}{K} \rho_j \mathbf{T}[j,i] + \sum_{j \in \mathcal{Z}} \frac{\lambda^t}{K} \gamma_j \mathbf{T}[j,i]}{\mu_i + \frac{\lambda^t}{K}}, \tag{2}$$

and finally for all queue i in $\mathcal{Z}$

$$\gamma_i = \frac{\sum_{j \in \mathcal{F} \cup \mathcal{I}} K \mu_j \rho_j \mathbf{R}[j,i] + \sum_{j \in \mathcal{F} \cup \mathcal{I}} \lambda^t \rho_j \mathbf{T}[j,i] + \sum_{j \in \mathcal{Z}} \lambda^t \gamma_j \mathbf{T}[j,i]}{\lambda^t}. \tag{3}$$

Proof: The proof of product form is based on the analysis of the Chapman Kolmogorov equation for steady-state. For the sake of readability we now give the equation and some explanations for several terms in the equation. The analysis is then postponed in an appendix.

Let us first give the global balance equation. In the following e_j will be a vector the components of which are all equal to 0 except component j which is equal to 1.

$$\pi(K, \boldsymbol{x}) \left[\sum_{i \in \mathcal{F}} \mu_i 1_{x_i > 0} + \sum_{i \in \mathcal{I}} \mu_i x_i + \lambda^t \left(\sum_{i \in \mathcal{F}} \frac{1_{x_i > 0}}{K} + \sum_{i \in \mathcal{I} \cup \mathcal{Z}} \frac{x_i}{K} \right) \right]$$

$$= \sum_{i \in \mathcal{F}} \sum_{j \in \mathcal{F} \cup \mathcal{I} \cup \mathcal{Z}} \mu_i \pi(K, \boldsymbol{x} + e_i - e_j) \mathbf{R}[i,j] 1_{x_j > 0} \qquad [1]$$

$$+ \sum_{i \in \mathcal{I}} \sum_{j \in \mathcal{F} \cup \mathcal{I} \cup \mathcal{Z}} x_i \mu_i \pi(K, \boldsymbol{x} + e_i - e_j) \mathbf{R}[i,j] 1_{x_j > 0} \qquad [2]$$

$$+ \sum_{i \in \mathcal{F}} \sum_{j \in \mathcal{F} \cup \mathcal{I} \cup \mathcal{Z}} \pi(K, \boldsymbol{x} + e_i - e_j) \mathbf{T}[i,j] 1_{x_j > 0} \lambda^t \frac{1_{x_i + 1 > 0}}{K} \qquad [3]$$

$$+ \sum_{i \in \mathcal{I}} \sum_{j \in \mathcal{F} \cup \mathcal{I} \cup \mathcal{Z}} \pi(K, \boldsymbol{x} + e_i - e_j) \mathbf{T}[i,j] 1_{x_j > 0} \lambda^t \frac{x_i + 1}{K} \qquad [4]$$

$$+ \sum_{i \in \mathcal{Z}} \sum_{j \in \mathcal{F} \cup \mathcal{I} \cup \mathcal{Z}} \pi(K, \boldsymbol{x} + e_i - e_j) \mathbf{T}[i,j] 1_{x_j > 0} \lambda^t \frac{x_i + 1}{K}. \qquad [5]$$

$$\tag{4}$$

The first two terms of the right hand side describe the services in stations in $\mathcal{F}$ and $\mathcal{I}$. Remember that in stations of $\mathcal{Z}$ the services do not occur. The last three terms describe the effect of trigger signals arriving at queue i with a state dependent probability and moving a customer to another queue somewhere else in the network (say j). The left hand side of the equation contains the description of service with state dependent service rate for stations in $\mathcal{I}$ and in $\mathcal{F}$. The last two terms of the l.h.s. describe the arrival of a trigger signal. Note that we avoid to take into account null transitions on both sides of the balance equation. Remember that some triggers may vanish without any effect.   □

Once the theorem has been established, we still have to prove is the existence of the rates ρ_i (for i in $\mathcal{F}$ and $\mathcal{I}$) and γ_j (for j in $\mathcal{Z}$). We begin with a technical lemma.

Lemma 1 (Stochastic). *For all queue j in $\mathcal{F} \cup \mathcal{I} \cup \mathcal{Z}$, matrix $\mathbf{M}$ defined in Eq. 5 is stochastic.*

$$\mathbf{M[j,i]} = \frac{\mu_j \mathbf{1}_{j \in \mathcal{I} \cup \mathcal{F}}}{\mu_j \mathbf{1}_{j \in \mathcal{I} \cup \mathcal{F}} + \lambda^t/\mathbf{K}} \mathbf{R[j,i]} + \frac{\lambda^t/\mathbf{K}}{\mu_j \mathbf{1}_{j \in \mathcal{I} \cup \mathcal{F}} + \lambda^t/\mathbf{K}} \mathbf{T[j,i]}. \tag{5}$$

Furthermore matrix $\mathbf{M}$ is irreducible.

Proof: Consider an arbitrary index j in $\mathcal{I} \cup \mathcal{F}$.

$$\mathbf{M[j,i]} = \frac{\mu_j}{\mu_j + \lambda^t/\mathbf{K}} \mathbf{R[j,i]} + \frac{\lambda^t/\mathbf{K}}{\mu_j + \lambda^t/\mathbf{K}} \mathbf{T[j,i]}.$$

And rows j of matrix $\mathbf{R}$ and $\mathbf{T}$ are distributions of probability. Therefore as a convex sum of distributions of probability the i-th row of $\mathbf{M}$ is a distribution of probability.

Now assume that j is in $\mathcal{Z}$. We have:

$$\mathbf{M[j,i]} = \mathbf{T[j,i]}.$$

As matrix $\mathbf{T}$ is stochastic by assumption, the i-th row of $\mathbf{M}$ is also a distribution of probability. Finally, all rows of $\mathbf{M}$ are distributions of probability and therefore matrix $\mathbf{M}$ is stochastic.

Now remember that DG is strongly connected. The adjacency matrix $\mathbf{A}$ of directed graph DG is defined by

$$\mathbf{A[i,j]} = \mathbf{1}_{\mathbf{R[i,j]}>0} \text{ OR } \mathbf{1}_{\mathbf{T[i,j]}>0}$$

As λ^t and μ_j (for all j in $\mathcal{I} \cup \mathcal{F}$) are positive, we also have:

$$\mathbf{A[i,j]} = \mathbf{1}_{\mathbf{M[i,j]}>0}$$

Matrix $\mathbf{M}$ is irreducible because it is associated with adjacency matrix $\mathbf{A}$ which is strongly connected by the third part of Assumptions 1.

Property 1 (Existence). *Under Assumptions 1, the system of fixed point equations (Eqs. 2 and 3) has a solution.*

Proof: let us denote by v the vector defined by

$$\begin{bmatrix} \mathbf{v(i)} = \rho_i(\mu_i + \lambda^t/K) & i \in \mathcal{F} \cup \mathcal{I}, \\ \mathbf{v(i)} = \gamma_i \lambda^t/K & i \in \mathcal{Z}. \end{bmatrix}$$

After substitution in Eq. 2, we have for all i in $\mathcal{I} \cup \mathcal{F}$:

$$\mathbf{v}[i] = \sum_{j \in \mathcal{F} \cup \mathcal{I}} \mathbf{v}[j]\mathbf{M}[j,i] + \sum_{j \in \mathcal{Z}} \mathbf{v}[j]\mathbf{T}[j,i]. \tag{6}$$

Similarly for Eq. 3 we get for all i in $\mathcal{Z}$:

$$\mathbf{v[i]} = \sum_{j \in \mathcal{F} \cup \mathcal{I}} \mathbf{v[j]M[j,i]} + \sum_{j \in \mathcal{Z}} \mathbf{v[j]T[j,i]}. \tag{7}$$

Thus, combining both equations in vector form, taking into account that $\mathbf{M}[j,i] = \mathbf{T}[j,i]$ for all j in $\mathcal{Z}$:

$$\mathbf{v} = \mathbf{vM}. \tag{8}$$

The previous lemma states that matrix $\mathbf{M}$ is stochastic and irreducible. Thus there exists an eigenvector associated with eigenvalue 1 and $\mathbf{v}$ is an arbitrary positive multiple of this eigenvector. Remember that for a closed queuing network, we can consider any multiple of the eigenvector as the unique solution for the probability distribution is obtained after normalization.   □

As usual it remains to compute G. A natural idea consists in a generalization of the convolution algorithm proposed by Buzen [2], to networks of queues with signals. In the following we develop another idea which allows to compute the expected queue length and average waiting time without computing the normalization constraint.

3   Mean Value Analysis

We have to prove an arrival theorem to relate the probability seen by an arriving customer to the steady-state probability (the so-called ASTA property). We follow the approach presented by Harrison and Patel in [20]. Let us introduce some additional notation. Let $\pi_{Ai}(K, \boldsymbol{x})$ be the probability that an arriving customer at queue i sees state $\boldsymbol{x}$. This is due to a transition from state $\boldsymbol{x} + \boldsymbol{e}_j$ to state $\boldsymbol{x} + \boldsymbol{e}_i$. In state $\boldsymbol{x}$ the total number of customers is $K - 1$. We begin with some technical properties.

Property 2. *Due to the product form solution for the steady-state distribution, we have, for all state $\boldsymbol{x}$:*

$$G(K)\pi(K, \boldsymbol{x} + \boldsymbol{e}_j) = G(K-1)\pi(K-1, \boldsymbol{x})a_j,$$

where:

$$\begin{bmatrix} a_j = \rho_j, & \text{if } j \in \mathcal{F} \\ a_j = \frac{\rho_j}{x_j+1}, & \text{if } j \in \mathcal{I} \\ a_j = \frac{\gamma_j}{x_j+1}, & \text{if } j \in \mathcal{Z} \end{bmatrix}$$

Proof: Assume first that $j \in \mathcal{F}$. Then

$$G(K)\pi(K, \boldsymbol{x} + \boldsymbol{e}_j) = 1_{(1+\sum_i x_i = K)}\rho_j^{x_j+1} \prod_{i \in \mathcal{F}, i \neq j} \rho_i^{x_i} \prod_{i \in \mathcal{I}} \frac{\rho_i^{x_i}}{x_i!} \prod_{i \in \mathcal{Z}} \frac{\gamma_i^{x_i}}{x_i!}$$

Thus:

$$G(K)\pi(K, \boldsymbol{x} + \boldsymbol{e}_j) = 1_{(\sum_i x_i = K-1)}\rho_j \prod_{i \in \mathcal{F}} \rho_i^{x_i} \prod_{i \in \mathcal{I}} \frac{\rho_i^{x_i}}{x_i!} \prod_{i \in \mathcal{Z}} \frac{\gamma_i^{x_i}}{x_i!} = \rho_j G(K-1)\pi(K-1, \boldsymbol{x})$$

The proof is similar for $j \in \mathcal{I}$ and $j \in \mathcal{Z}$. It is omitted for the sake of conciseness.
□

Theorem 2 (Arrivals See Time Average). *An arriving customer at queue i sees the steady-state distribution in a network with one customer less:*

$$\pi_{Ai}(K, \boldsymbol{x}) = \pi(K-1, \boldsymbol{x})$$

Proof: The process is stationary. Therefore, $\pi_{Ai}(K, \boldsymbol{x})$ can be expressed as the ratio of the expected number of transitions giving an arrival to node i at state $\boldsymbol{x}$ (i.e. $A_i(\boldsymbol{x})$) and the expected number at any internal state $\boldsymbol{y}$, i.e. $\sum_y A_i(\boldsymbol{y})$:

$$\pi_{Ai}(K, \boldsymbol{x}) = \frac{A_i(\boldsymbol{x})}{\sum_y A_i(\boldsymbol{y})}. \tag{9}$$

A customer arriving at queue i sees state $\boldsymbol{x}$ during a transition from state $\boldsymbol{x} + \boldsymbol{e}_j$ to state $\boldsymbol{x} + \boldsymbol{e}_i$. This transition occurs after a service completion or after the reception of a trigger signal at station j. Remember that the service rates or the trigger routing probability may be state dependent. Thus:

$$\begin{aligned}
Ai(\boldsymbol{x}) = &\sum_{j \in \mathcal{F}} \pi(K, \boldsymbol{x} + \boldsymbol{e}_j)\mu_j \mathbf{R}[\mathbf{j}, \mathbf{i}] \\
&+ \sum_{j \in \mathcal{I}} \pi(K, \boldsymbol{x} + \boldsymbol{e}_j)\mu_j(x_j + 1)\mathbf{R}[\mathbf{j}, \mathbf{i}] \\
&+ \sum_{j \in \mathcal{F}} \pi(K, \boldsymbol{x} + \boldsymbol{e}_j)\frac{\lambda^t}{K}\mathbf{T}[\mathbf{j}, \mathbf{i}] \\
&+ \sum_{j \in \mathcal{I} \cup \mathcal{Z}} \pi(K, \boldsymbol{x} + \boldsymbol{e}_j)\frac{\lambda^t(x_j + 1)}{K}\mathbf{T}[\mathbf{j}, \mathbf{i}].
\end{aligned}$$

Reordering the summations, we get:

$$\begin{aligned}
Ai(\boldsymbol{x}) = &\sum_{j \in \mathcal{F}} \pi(K, \boldsymbol{x} + \boldsymbol{e}_j)\left[\mu_j \mathbf{R}[\mathbf{j}, \mathbf{i}] + \frac{\lambda^t}{K}\mathbf{T}[\mathbf{j}, \mathbf{i}]\right] \\
&+ \sum_{j \in \mathcal{I}} \pi(K, \boldsymbol{x} + \boldsymbol{e}_j)(x_j + 1)\left[\mu_j \mathbf{R}[\mathbf{j}, \mathbf{i}] + \frac{\lambda^t}{K}\mathbf{T}[\mathbf{j}, \mathbf{i}]\right] \\
&+ \sum_{j \in \mathcal{Z}} \pi(K, \boldsymbol{x} + \boldsymbol{e}_j)\frac{\lambda^t(x_j + 1)}{K}\mathbf{T}[\mathbf{j}, \mathbf{i}].
\end{aligned}$$

Using the definition for matrix $\mathbf{M}$ we obtain after substitution:

$$Ai(\boldsymbol{x}) = \sum_{j \in \mathcal{F}} \pi(K, \boldsymbol{x} + e_j) \left[\mu_j + \frac{\lambda^t}{K} \right] \mathbf{M}[\mathbf{j}, \mathbf{i}]$$

$$+ \sum_{j \in \mathcal{I}} \pi(K, \boldsymbol{x} + e_j)(x_j + 1) \left[\mu_j + \frac{\lambda^t}{K} \right] \mathbf{M}[\mathbf{j}, \mathbf{i}] \tag{10}$$

$$+ \sum_{j \in \mathcal{Z}} \pi(K, \boldsymbol{x} + e_j) \frac{\lambda^t(x_j + 1)}{K} \mathbf{M}[\mathbf{j}, \mathbf{i}].$$

Let us now turn back to Property 2 from which we easily obtain:

$$\pi(K, \boldsymbol{x} + e_j) = \pi(K - 1, \boldsymbol{x}) a_j \frac{G(K - 1)}{G(K)},$$

which is substituted into Eq. 10 to get:

$$Ai(\boldsymbol{x}) = \frac{G(K - 1)}{G(K)} \sum_{j \in \mathcal{F}} \pi(K - 1, \boldsymbol{x}) a_j \left[\mu_j + \frac{\lambda^t}{K} \right] \mathbf{M}[j, i]$$

$$+ \frac{G(K - 1)}{G(K)} \sum_{j \in \mathcal{I}} \pi(K - 1, \boldsymbol{x})(x_j + 1) a_j \left[\mu_j + \frac{\lambda^t}{K} \right] \mathbf{M}[j, i]$$

$$+ \frac{G(K - 1)}{G(K)} \sum_{j \in \mathcal{Z}} \pi(K - 1, \boldsymbol{x}) a_j \frac{\lambda^t(x_j + 1)}{K} \mathbf{M}[j, i].$$

Taking into account the definition of a_j for the various queues and the definition of $\mathbf{v}[i]$, we get after substitution:

$$Ai(\boldsymbol{x}) = \frac{G(K - 1)}{G(K)} \sum_{j \in \mathcal{F}} \pi(K - 1, \boldsymbol{x}) \mathbf{v}[j] \mathbf{M}[j, i]$$

$$+ \frac{G(K - 1)}{G(K)} \sum_{j \in \mathcal{I}} \pi(K - 1, \boldsymbol{x})(x_j + 1) \mathbf{v}[j] \mathbf{M}[j, i]$$

$$+ \frac{G(K - 1)}{G(K)} \sum_{j \in \mathcal{Z}} \pi(K - 1, \boldsymbol{x}) \mathbf{v}[j] \mathbf{M}[j, i]$$

Thus,

$$Ai(\boldsymbol{x}) = \frac{G(K - 1)}{G(K)} \pi(K - 1, \boldsymbol{x}) \sum_{j \in \mathcal{F} \cup \mathcal{I} \cup \mathcal{Z}} \mathbf{v}[j] \mathbf{M}[j, i].$$

Remember that $\mathbf{v}$ is the eigenvector of matrix $\mathbf{M}$. Thus,

$$Ai(\boldsymbol{x}) = \frac{G(K - 1)}{G(K)} \pi(K - 1, \boldsymbol{x}) \mathbf{v}[i]. \tag{11}$$

Combining this last equation and Eq. 9, we finally get

$$\pi_{Ai}(K, \boldsymbol{x}) = \pi(K - 1, \boldsymbol{x}).$$

and the proof is complete. □

We now present the algorithm to compute de average queue size and the expected sojourn time in each queue. It is similar to a classical MVA algorithm for a single class closed queueing network as detailed in [2, 20]. Let us first introduce some notation:

- $T_i(K)$ is the sojourn time at queue i when the number of customers in the network is K,
- $N_i(K)$ is the average queue size at queue i when the number of customers in the network is K,
- $\Lambda_i(K)$ is the arrival rate at queue i when the number of customers in the network is K.

The first step is to define an equivalent service time. Remember that some stations (i.e. in $\mathcal{Z}$) do not have a server and in some stations the signals trigger customers movement. Let S_i be the average equivalent service time.

$$S_i = \frac{1}{\mu_i 1_{i \in \mathcal{I} \cup \mathcal{F}} + \frac{\lambda^t}{K}}$$

Little equation give two sets of equations as in the classical MVA approach:

$$N_i(K) = \Lambda_i(K) T_i(K)$$

And:

$$K = \Lambda_i(K) (\sum_j T_j(K) \frac{\mathbf{v}[j]}{\mathbf{v}[i]})$$

Finally, the theorem on the state seen by an arriving customer allows to relate the sojourn time to the average queue size:

$$T_i(K) = (1 + N_i(K - 1)) S_i$$

These three sets of equations allow a computation for $T_i(K)$, $N_i(K)$ and $\Lambda_i(K)$ for all values of K beginning with $K = 1$. When $K = 1$, the quantities are initialized with:

$$T_i(1) = S_i, \ \Lambda_i(1) = \frac{1}{\sum_j S_j \frac{\mathbf{v}[j]}{\mathbf{v}[i]}}, \ N_i(1) = \frac{S_i}{\sum_j S_j \frac{\mathbf{v}[j]}{\mathbf{v}[i]}}.$$

□

4   An Example and Some Possible Extensions

Let us first present a simple example (depicted in Fig. 2) to illustrate some features of the model. The network is decomposed into two sub-networks which are connected by the movement of customers provoked by signals. The first sub-network is a ring containing queues labeled 1, 2 and 3. The second sub-network is a tandem with two queues labeled 4, and 5. The signals arriving in the first sub-network move a customer to queue 4 while they provoke a migration to queue 1 when they arrive in the second sub-network.

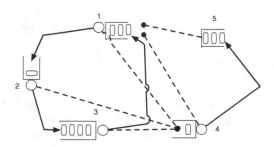

Fig. 2. An example with a two sub-networks topology. The migrations of customers provoked by signals are represented by a hatched lines with a dot to indicate the destination.

Station 5 does not have any server. Therefore the customers accumulate until the station receives a signal to move to station 1. Such a model was proposed for the optimization of the Energy Packets arrival. Indeed, a very simple idea is to provide energy to stations where packets are waiting. The trigger signal (as mentioned in the introduction) represents EP which are needed to move the customers to another part of the network (between the two sub-networks in the example). The ordinary movements of customers based on matrix **R** are not supposed to need energy (or at least the energy is insignificant).

We now propose some extensions of the model. First, one may replace the external source of triggers by a sub-network of queues with positive and negative customers as in Fig. 3. This is the original model we first consider and the following property explains how to decompose the model into two parts, the second one being solved by Theorem 1.

Property 3. *As proved in [3], an open network of positive and negative customers is quasi-reversible and the flows of signals (whatever they are) leaving the network follow Poisson processes. Therefore we may add in the model of Theorem 1 an open subnetwork sending trigger signal to the closed sub-network instead of assuming an external Poisson arrival of signals.*

One may also consider stations with multiple servers. Here we only consider stations with 0, 1 or an infinite number of servers. We have to find the associate routing probability which provides a product form. We also have to extend the MVA algorithm to deal with these stations. Concerning the routing probabilities of signals for stations without server, we have obtained preliminary results showing that it is possible to have much more general routing functions for these stations. We hope to provide more general results in the near future.

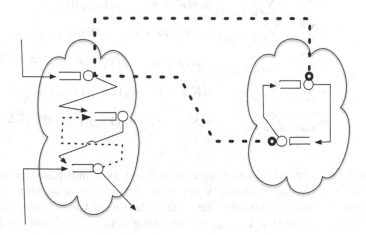

Fig. 3. Mixed topology. The signals are generated by the first sub-network (on the left) and sent to the closed subnetwork (on the right). The first sub-network is open and it contains positive and negative customers. Positive customers (resp. negative customers) movements are represented by solid lines (resp. doted lines). The emission of trigger signals is represented by hatched lines.

Finally, we have considered here the single class version of the problem. G-networks with multiple classes of customers and signals have already been studied in the literature (for instance [8] for Processor Sharing queues). We think that it is possible to extend both the proof of product form and arrival theorem for network with multiple classes of customers and signals, at least for Processor Sharing queues and Infinite Server queues.

5   Concluding Remarks

We obtained one of the first closed form expression for closed networks of queues with signals. It is also to the best of our knowledge the first time that an arrival theorem for a closed network with signals is proved. This allows to generalize the MVA approach for networks with more complex movement of customers. The result rises many interesting theoretical questions for closed networks with triggers, signals, or more general synchronizations of queues (for instance, the closed version of networks with load balancing presented in [22]). We want to address some of these problems in the near future.

Appendix: Proof of Theorem 1

Consider again the global balance equation at steady-state.

$$\pi(K,\boldsymbol{x})[\sum_{i\in\mathcal{F}}\mu_i 1_{x_i>0} + \sum_{i\in\mathcal{I}}\mu_i x_i + \lambda^t(\sum_{i\in\mathcal{F}}\frac{1_{x_i>0}}{K} + \sum_{i\in\mathcal{I}\cup\mathcal{Z}}\frac{x_i}{K})]$$

$$= \sum_{i\in\mathcal{F}}\sum_{j\in\mathcal{F}\cup\mathcal{I}\cup\mathcal{Z}}\mu_i\pi(K,\boldsymbol{x}+\boldsymbol{e}_i-\boldsymbol{e}_j)\mathbf{R}[i,j]1_{x_j>0} \qquad [1]$$

$$+ \sum_{i\in\mathcal{I}}\sum_{j\in\mathcal{F}\cup\mathcal{I}\cup\mathcal{Z}}x_i\mu_i\pi(K,\boldsymbol{x}+\boldsymbol{e}_i-\boldsymbol{e}_j)\mathbf{R}[i,j]1_{x_j>0} \qquad [2]$$

$$+ \sum_{i\in\mathcal{F}}\sum_{j\in\mathcal{F}\cup\mathcal{I}\cup\mathcal{Z}}\pi(K,\boldsymbol{x}+\boldsymbol{e}_i-\boldsymbol{e}_j)\mathbf{T}[i,j]1_{x_j>0}\lambda^t\frac{1_{x_i+1>0}}{K} \qquad [3]$$

$$+ \sum_{i\in\mathcal{I}}\sum_{j\in\mathcal{F}\cup\mathcal{I}\cup\mathcal{Z}}\pi(K,\boldsymbol{x}+\boldsymbol{e}_i-\boldsymbol{e}_j)\mathbf{T}[i,j]1_{x_j>0}\lambda^t\frac{x_i+1}{K} \qquad [4]$$

$$+ \sum_{i\in\mathcal{Z}}\sum_{j\in\mathcal{F}\cup\mathcal{I}\cup\mathcal{Z}}\pi(K,\boldsymbol{x}+\boldsymbol{e}_i-\boldsymbol{e}_j)\mathbf{T}[i,j]1_{x_j>0}\lambda^t\frac{x_i+1}{K} \qquad [5]$$

Divide both sides by $\pi(\boldsymbol{x})$ and take into account the multiplicative solution proposed in Eq. 1. As the probability depends on the type of station, we have to decompose the summation into three parts, based on the set of stations we consider. We also notice that $1_{x_i+1>0} = 1$ and that $x_i 1_{x_i>0} = x_i$ and we simplify some terms.

$$\sum_{i\in\mathcal{F}}\mu_i 1_{x_i>0} + \sum_{i\in\mathcal{I}}\mu_i x_i + \lambda^t(\sum_{i\in\mathcal{F}}\frac{1_{x_i>0}}{K} + \sum_{i\in\mathcal{I}\cup\mathcal{Z}}\frac{x_i}{K})$$

$$= \sum_{i\in\mathcal{F}}\sum_{j\in\mathcal{F}}\mu_i\rho_i/\rho_j\mathbf{R}[i,j]1_{x_j>0} \qquad [1]$$

$$+ \sum_{i\in\mathcal{F}}\sum_{j\in\mathcal{I}}\mu_i\rho_i/\rho_j x_j\mathbf{R}[i,j] \qquad [2]$$

$$+ \sum_{i\in\mathcal{F}}\sum_{j\in\mathcal{Z}}\mu_i\rho_i/\gamma_j x_j\mathbf{R}[i,j] \qquad [3]$$

$$+ \sum_{i\in\mathcal{I}}\sum_{j\in\mathcal{F}}\mu_i\rho_i/\rho_j\mathbf{R}[i,j]1_{x_j>0} \qquad [4]$$

$$+ \sum_{i\in\mathcal{I}}\sum_{j\in\mathcal{I}}\mu_i\rho_i/\rho_j x_j\mathbf{R}[i,j] \qquad [5]$$

$$+ \sum_{i\in\mathcal{I}}\sum_{j\in\mathcal{Z}}\mu_i\rho_i/\gamma_j x_j\mathbf{R}[i,j] \qquad [6]$$

$$+ \sum_{i\in\mathcal{F}}\sum_{j\in\mathcal{F}}\rho_i/\rho_j\mathbf{T}[i,j]1_{x_j>0}\lambda^t\frac{1}{K} \qquad [7]$$

$$+ \sum_{i\in\mathcal{F}}\sum_{j\in\mathcal{I}}\rho_i/\rho_j x_j\mathbf{T}[i,j]\lambda^t\frac{1}{K} \qquad [8]$$

$$+ \sum_{i\in\mathcal{F}}\sum_{j\in\mathcal{Z}}\rho_i/\gamma_j x_j\mathbf{T}[i,j]\lambda^t\frac{1}{K} \qquad [9]$$

$$+ \sum_{i\in\mathcal{I}}\sum_{j\in\mathcal{F}}\rho_i/\rho_j\mathbf{T(i,j)}\mathbf{T}[i,j]\lambda^t\frac{1}{\mathbf{K}} \qquad [10]$$

$$+\sum_{i\in\mathcal{I}}\sum_{j\in\mathcal{I}}\rho_i/\rho_j x_j \mathbf{T}[i,j]\lambda^t\frac{1}{K} \qquad [11]$$

$$+\sum_{i\in\mathcal{I}}\sum_{j\in\mathcal{Z}}\rho_i/\gamma_j x_j \mathbf{T}[i,j]\lambda^t\frac{1}{K} \qquad [12]$$

$$+\sum_{i\in\mathcal{Z}}\sum_{j\in\mathcal{F}}\gamma_i/\rho_j \mathbf{T}[i,j]1_{x_j>0}\lambda^t\frac{1}{K} \qquad [13]$$

$$+\sum_{i\in\mathcal{Z}}\sum_{j\in\mathcal{I}}\gamma_i/\rho_j x_j \mathbf{T}[i,j]\lambda^t\frac{1}{K} \qquad [14]$$

$$+\sum_{i\in\mathcal{Z}}\sum_{j\in\mathcal{Z}}\gamma_i/\gamma_j x_j \mathbf{T}[i,j]\lambda^t\frac{1}{K} \qquad [15]$$

We exchange the role of indices i and j in all the terms of the r.h.s. and we factorize the terms $(1+4+7+10+13)$, $(2+5+8+11+14)$, $(3+6+9+12+15)$:

$$\sum_{i\in\mathcal{F}}\mu_i 1_{x_i>0} + \sum_{i\in\mathcal{I}}\mu_i x_i + \lambda^t\Big(\sum_{i\in\mathcal{F}}\frac{1_{x_i>0}}{K} + \sum_{i\in\mathcal{I}\cup\mathcal{Z}}\frac{x_i}{K}\Big)$$

$$=\sum_{i\in\mathcal{F}}1_{x_i>0}1/\rho_i\Big[\sum_{j\in\mathcal{F}\cup\mathcal{I}}\mu_j\rho_j\mathbf{R}[j,i] \ + \ \sum_{j\in\mathcal{F}}\rho_j\mathbf{T}[j,i]\frac{\lambda^t}{K}$$

$$+\sum_{j\in\mathcal{I}}\rho_j\mathbf{T}[j,i]\frac{\lambda^t}{K} \ + \ \sum_{j\in\mathcal{Z}}\gamma_j\mathbf{T}[j,i]\frac{\lambda^t}{K}\Big]$$

$$+\sum_{i\in\mathcal{I}}x_i/\rho_i\Big[\sum_{j\in\mathcal{F}\cup\mathcal{I}}\mu_j\rho_j\mathbf{R}[j,i] \ + \ \sum_{j\in\mathcal{F}}\rho_j\mathbf{T}[j,i]\frac{\lambda^t}{K}$$

$$+\sum_{j\in\mathcal{I}}\rho_j\mathbf{T}[j,i]\frac{\lambda^t}{K} \ + \ \sum_{j\in\mathcal{Z}}\gamma_j\mathbf{T}[j,i]\frac{\lambda^t}{K}\Big]$$

$$+\sum_{i\in\mathcal{Z}}x_i/\gamma_i\Big[\sum_{j\in\mathcal{F}\cup\mathcal{I}}\mu_j\rho_j\mathbf{R}[j,i] \ + \ \sum_{j\in\mathcal{F}}\rho_j\mathbf{T}[j,i]\frac{\lambda^t}{K}$$

$$\sum_{j\in\mathcal{I}}\rho_j\mathbf{T}[j,i]\frac{\lambda^t}{K} \ + \ \sum_{j\in\mathcal{Z}}\gamma_j\mathbf{T}[j,i]\frac{\lambda^t}{K}\Big].$$

The first and second term of the l.h.s. cancel with the first and second term of the r.h.s. due to the first flow equation (i.e. Eq. 2). It remains:

$$\lambda^t \sum_{i \in \mathcal{Z}} \frac{x_i}{K} = \sum_{i \in \mathcal{Z}} x_i / \gamma_i \left[\sum_{j \in \mathcal{F} \cup \mathcal{I}} \mu_j \rho_j \mathbf{R}[j,i] + \sum_{j \in \mathcal{F}} \rho_j \mathbf{T}[j,i] \frac{\lambda^t}{K} \right.$$

$$\left. \sum_{j \in \mathcal{I}} \rho_j \mathbf{T}[j,i] \frac{\lambda^t}{K} + \sum_{j \in \mathcal{Z}} \gamma_j \mathbf{T}[j,i] \frac{\lambda^t}{K} \right].$$

And this last equation is equivalent to the second flow equation for station in $\mathcal{Z}$ (i.e. Eq. 3). And the proof is complete.   □

References

1. Balsamo, S., Harrison, P.G., Marin, A.: A unifying approach to product-forms in networks with finite capacity constraints. In: Misra, V., Barford, P., Squillante, M.S. (eds.) SIGMETRICS 2010, Proceedings of the 2010 ACM SIGMETRICS International Conference on Measurement and Modeling of Computer Systems, pp. 25–36. ACM, New York (2010)
2. Bolch, G., Greiner, S., De Meer, H., Trivedi, K.: Queueing Networks and Markov Chains. Wiley, Hoboken (1998)
3. Chao, X., Miyazawa, M., Pinedo, M.: Queueing Networks: Customers, Signals and Product Form Solutions. Wiley, Hoboken (1999)
4. Dao Thi, T.H., Fourneau, J.M.: Stochastic automata networks with master/slave synchronization: product form and tensor. In: Al-Begain, K., Fiems, D., Horváth, G. (eds.) ASMTA 2009. LNCS, vol. 5513, pp. 279–293. Springer, Heidelberg (2009). https://doi.org/10.1007/978-3-642-02205-0_20
5. Do, T.V.: An initiative for a classified bibliography on G-networks. Perform. Eval. **68**(4), 385–394 (2011)
6. Fourneau, J.M.: Closed G-networks with resets: product form solution. In: Fourth International Conference on the Quantitative Evaluation of Systems (QEST 2007), Edinburgh, UK, pp. 287–296. IEEE Computer Society (2007)
7. Fourneau, J.-M.: Product form steady-state distribution for stochastic automata networks with domino synchronizations. In: Thomas, N., Juiz, C. (eds.) EPEW 2008. LNCS, vol. 5261, pp. 110–124. Springer, Heidelberg (2008). https://doi.org/10.1007/978-3-540-87412-6_9
8. Fourneau, J.M., Kloul, L., Quessette, F.: Multiple class G-networks with iterated deletions. Perform. Eval. **42**(1), 1–20 (2000)
9. Fourneau, J.M., Quessette, F.: Computing the steady-state distribution of G-networks with synchronized partial flushing. In: Levi, A., Savaş, E., Yenigün, H., Balcısoy, S., Saygın, Y. (eds.) ISCIS 2006. LNCS, vol. 4263, pp. 887–896. Springer, Heidelberg (2006). https://doi.org/10.1007/11902140_92
10. Fourneau, J.M., Marin, A., Balsamo, S.: Modeling energy packets networks in the presence of failures. In: 24th IEEE International Symposium on Modeling, Analysis and Simulation of Computer and Telecommunication Systems, MASCOTS, London, United Kingdom, pp. 144–153. IEEE Computer Society (2016)
11. Gelenbe, E.: Product-form queuing networks with negative and positive customers. J. Appl. Prob. **28**, 656–663 (1991)

12. Gelenbe, E.: G-networks with instantaneous customer movement. J. Appl. Prob. **30**(3), 742–748 (1993)
13. Gelenbe, E.: G-networks: an unifying model for queuing networks and neural networks. Ann. Oper. Res. **48**(1–4), 433–461 (1994)
14. Gelenbe, E.: Energy packet networks: ICT based energy allocation and storage. In: Rodrigues, J.J.P.C., Zhou, L., Chen, M., Kailas, A. (eds.) GreeNets 2011. LNICST, vol. 51, pp. 186–195. Springer, Heidelberg (2012). https://doi.org/10.1007/978-3-642-33368-2_16
15. Gelenbe, E.: A sensor node with energy harvesting. SIGMETRICS Perform. Eval. Rev. **42**(2), 37–39 (2014)
16. Gelenbe, E., Ceran, E.T.: Energy packet networks with energy harvesting. IEEE Access **4**, 1321–1331 (2016)
17. Gelenbe, E., Ceran, E.T.: Central or distributed energy storage for processors with energy harvesting. In: 2015 Sustainable Internet and ICT for Sustainability, SustainIT, pp. 1–3. IEEE (2015)
18. Gelenbe, E., Marin, A.: Interconnected wireless sensors with energy harvesting. In: Gribaudo, M., Manini, D., Remke, A. (eds.) ASMTA 2015. LNCS, vol. 9081, pp. 87–99. Springer, Cham (2015). https://doi.org/10.1007/978-3-319-18579-8_7
19. Harrison, P.G.: Compositional reversed Markov processes, with applications to G-networks. Perform. Eval. **57**(3), 379–408 (2004)
20. Harrison, P.G., Patel, N.M.: Performance Modelling of Communication Networks and Computer Architectures. Addison-Wesley, Boston (1993)
21. Harrison, P.: Turning back time in Markovian process algebra. Theor. Comput. Sci. **290**(3), 1947–1986 (2003)
22. Marin, A., Balsamo, S., Fourneau, J.: LB-networks: a model for dynamic load balancing in queueing networks. Perform. Eval. **115**, 38–53 (2017)
23. Reiser, M., Lavenberg, S.S.: Mean-value analysis of closed multichain queuing networks. J. ACM **27**(2), 313–322 (1980)
24. Takahashi, R., Takuno, T., Hikihara, T.: Estimation of power packet transfer properties on indoor power line channel. Energies **5**(7), 2141 (2012)

Extending the Steady State Analysis of Hierarchical Semi-Markov Processes with Parallel Regions

Marco Biagi[1]([⊠]), Enrico Vicario[1], and Reinhard German[2]

[1] Department of Information Engineering, University of Florence, Florence, Italy
{marco.biagi,enrico.vicario}@unifi.it
[2] Department of Computer Science 7, University Erlangen-Nuremberg, Erlangen, Germany
reinhard.german@fau.de

Abstract. Analysis of hierarchical semi-Markov processes with parallel regions is a technique that evaluates steady-state probabilities of models with multiple concurrent non-Markovian timers in a compositional way without the need of full state space generation. In this paper we extend the technique by removing some of its limitations and increasing its modelling power. By applying the time advancement mechanism known from stochastic state classes, exits in parallel regions with different time origins can be taken into account. Furthermore, exits can be put on state borders such that the model evolution depends on the exited region and a concept for history states is also presented. This significantly increases modeling power, such that the gap between semi-Markov processes with restricted modeling power and non-Markovian models without modeling restrictions but also with less efficient analysis is filled. Experimentations in order to validate the approach and to compare it with another technique were performed in order to better characterise the advantages of the compositional approach.

1 Introduction

Realistic stochastic models often involve multiple concurrent timers with general distributions (*non-Markovian timers*). A large number of formalisms has been defined for the modeling of such systems, each one having different characteristics, such as Stochastic Time Petri Nets [8], Stochastic timed automatas [2] and Input/Output stochastic automatas [4], but often such formalisms are not widespread outside the research context. Other approaches [7,10] are based instead on derivations of more common formalisms like state charts [6] and UML state machines [1]. Furthermore numerous techniques have been proposed for the evaluation of quantitative measures of non-Markovian models, but each technique has limitations that restrict their adoption. Steady-state probabilities can be evaluated for models where the enabling restriction is satisfied, namely when no more than one non-Markovian timer is enabled in each state [5,12], a

© Springer Nature Switzerland AG 2018
R. Bakhshi et al. (Eds.): EPEW 2018, LNCS 11178, pp. 62–77, 2018.
https://doi.org/10.1007/978-3-030-02227-3_5

restriction not often satisfied in realistic models. Regenerative steady-state analysis with stochastic state classes [13] can evaluate the steady-state probabilities beyond the enabling restriction, but only if each cycle in the state space passes through at least one regeneration. In many models this condition is not verified and building the state space often leads to the problem of state space explosion. The approach of [7] exploits the hierarchical structure of the formalism in order to develop a compositional approach for the evaluation of steady state probabilities of the model, notably without the requirement to build the whole state space. The limitation of such work is mainly related to the restricted number of features adopted from the UML state machine formalism. Specifically the derived formalism defines a state machine, where each state can be simple or composite. Simple states have a sojourn time distribution describing how long the system remains in a particular state, while composite states are described by a set of parallel regions, where each region is in turn described by another state machine. Additionally, regions can have final states or exit states describing the condition that needs to be met in order to leave the composite state. One major limitation of the approach is that it doesn't allow to have different successors of a state based on how concurrency is resolved. Additionally the technique imposes restrictions on how exit states can be included in the model. In this paper, we extend such formalism in order to increase its expressiveness. Specifically we remove the limitation to have exit states only at the lower level of the hierarchy of a composite state, allowing to define more complex concurrency patterns. This is achieved by applying the concept of time advancement mechanism known from state classes [8]. It is also combined with a computation of probabilities to reach nested states, which is needed for the final computation of steady-state probabilities. We also add the possibility to have exit states on the border, making possible to have different successor states based on which region finishes first, substantially increasing the expressivity of the formalism. Finally we introduce the possibility to have history states, enabling the definition of more condensed models. The new technique has also been implemented in order to experimentally validate it and to better characterize the advantages of having such a compositional approach.

The paper is organized as follows: in Sect. 2 we present the extended formalism and give a formalization of it; in Sect. 3 we describe the analysis technique; in Sect. 4 we report an application example and study technique performances; finally conclusions are drawn in Sect. 5.

2   Hierarchical Semi-Markov Process with Parallel Regions

Adopted formalism is derived from UML state machines [1], allowing only the usage of a subset of its features but also adding some extensions to model quantitative aspects as done in, e.g., [10]. A previous version of the formalism was presented in [7], but here it is enriched with the concept of history states which allows for a more concise representation, and for exit states on the border, which allow to have distinct successor states based on which region concludes first.

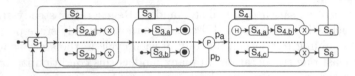

Fig. 1. Example model defined with the formalism

2.1   Description and Graphical Representation

The model describes a state machine, thus a system that can be in exactly one state at any given time. The time elapsed in a particular state is stochastically distributed, and when such time expires the system changes its state. Each state can be *simple* or *composite*. Time spent in a simple state is described by a stochastic distribution and there are no additional details regarding the internal representation of the state. Instead the internal state of a composite state is described by a set of one or more parallel regions, each one described again as a state machine. When a composite state is entered, each region has its own internal state and only when a specific condition between regions is met the composite state is left. Recursively applying this concept allows to define hierarchical models, since in the same composite state it is possible to have sub-states that in turn are composite, thus having more levels of details in the same composite state. The highest of such levels will be called hereafter *top level*.

An example model is shown in Fig. 1. At any given time at top level, the system can be in states S_1, S_2, S_3, S_4, S_5 or S_6, where S_1 is the initial state identified by an arrow with a black circle on its origin. States S_1, S_5 and S_6 are simple states, while states S_2, S_3 and S_4 are composite states where their internal representation is described through regions and sub-models. Additionally, the successor of state S_3 is a *P-pseudonode*, introduced in [9], that is used to handle discrete probabilistic branching. Specifically, after state S_3 with probability p_a next state is S_4 and with probability p_b next state will be S_1. In this example, composite states are all defined by a set of two regions, each one describing a nested state machine. When state S_2 is entered, both regions have their own current state, $S_{2,a}$ and $S_{2,b}$, respectively. In this case the end condition is defined by exit pseudostates, which denote that the composite state is left when one of the exit pseudostate is reached first. Exit pseudostates are graphically represented as a circle with a cross. Composite state S_3 is modeled with a different kind of end condition, by using final pseudostates, which denote that the state is left when both final states are reached. Final states are graphically represented as a circle with an inscribed black circle. Finally, state S_4 uses again exit pesudostates, but they are placed on the border of the composite state, meaning that the state reached when state S_4 is left depends on which region completes at first its execution. If the upper region ends first, next state will be S_5, otherwise, if the lower region ends first, S_6 will be the next state. Moreover, the upper region of state S_4 has an initial state depending on its history. A history state allows a region to keep track of the state it was in when it was last exited. When the system enters again in such a region, the region returns to this same state. The first time the state is entered a *default history state* is specified, in this case it is $S_{4,a}$. This is represented as described by the UML specification [1]. Note also that if the absorbing state was reached in the previous execution, next time the region is entered the default history state will be selected. According to this history states have a meaning only in regions where exit pesudostates are present. As a restriction, we require that all regions on a level directly below a composite state must have the same type of end pseudostate.

2.2 Formal Definition

First we recall the definition of semi-Markov processes (SMP) [11]. Consider a stochastic process $\{X(t), t \geq 0\}$ with a countable number of states. It starts in an initial state X_0 at time $t = 0$, stays for a sojourn time T_1 and then changes its state to a new value X_1. In general it stays in a state X_n for a duration T_{n+1} and then jumps to a state X_{n+1}.

Definition 1. *A stochastic process $X(t), t \geq 0$ is called SMP if it has a countable number of states and the sequence $\{X_0, (X_n, T_n), n \geq 1\}$ satisfies $P(X_{n+1} = j, T_{n+1} \leq t | X_n = i, T_n, X_{n-1}, T_{n-1}, \ldots, X_1, T_1, X_0) = P(X_1 = j, T_1 \leq t | X_0 = i) = G_{i,j}(y)$.*

The matrix $\mathbf{G}(y) = [G_{i,j}(y)]$ is called global kernel of the SMP process.

Definition 2. *A hierarchical SMP with parallel regions (HSMP) is a tuple $\theta = \langle R, \rho, S, P, F, \phi, \eta \rangle$, where R is the set of regions; $\rho : R \to S$ is a function that identifies the initial state of a region; $S = S_s \cup S_c \cup S_a$ is the set of states where S_s are simple states, S_c are composite states, $S_a = S_a^E \cup S_a^F$ are absorbing states, S_a^E are absorbing states of type exit, S_a^F are absorbing state of type final; $P : S \times S \to \mathbb{R}$ is the matrix that describes the discrete probability that the successor of a state will be specific state; $F : S_s \to CDF$ associates each simple state to a cumulative distribution function; $\phi : S_c \to \theta$ associates the composite state with another HSMP that describes its internal representation.*

The definition is recursive since each composite state is described through a nested HSMP. It is worth noting that for convenience this definition defines branching with a matrix P and not as a pseudostate. It would also be easy to associate state transitions with timing. If we consider the model of a particular region, without considering sub-states of composite states, the underlying process constitutes a semi-Markov process. The reason is that the state space of the process is composed by the states of the region, where the sojourn time depends only on the current state and not on the history as required by Definition 1. In particular if the current state is a simple state $s \in S_s$, the distribution of time to reach next state is simply given by $F(s)$, if instead the current state is a composite state it can be evaluated as will be shown in Sect. 3 and the distribution does also not depend on the history.

Finally it should be noted that exits on borders and history states are not directly formalized in the above definition, because as we will see in Sect. 3 they need special handling to be considered.

3 Analysis Technique

The steady-state analysis of an *HSMP* presented in [7] is extended here notably to increase its applicability. Specifically it can now be applied to analyze models with history states, with exits on borders and with a complex structure of exit states, not handled by the previous version of the technique.

The analysis technique allows to evaluate steady-state probabilities for top level states and for states nested inside composite states of the *HSMP*. As in the steady-state analysis of an *SMP* [11], the idea behind the analysis is to build the *embedded DTMC* of the top level *SMP*, evaluate its steady-state probabilities and then evaluate steady-state probabilities of the top level *SMP* using mean sojourn times of states. Subsequently, the steady state probability of nested states can be evaluated by evaluating the ratio of time spent in each nested state.

The analysis is organized in the following 6 steps: (1) **Sojourn time distributions** are evaluated for each composite state, without considering possible exits in parallel regions (Sect. 3.1); (2) **Exit distributions** are computed, defined as the probability to leave a region at time t due to an exit in a parallel region (Sect. 3.2); (3) **Reaching probabilities of sub-states** are computed, considering also possible exits in parallel regions (Sect. 3.3); (4) If exits on the border are present, **probabilities to exit from a specific exit** are computed (Sect. 3.4); (5) **Mean sojourn times** are evaluated, considering also possible exits in parallel regions (Sect. 3.5); (6) **Steady-state probabilities** of the *HSMP* are evaluated (Sect. 3.6).

In the following each step will be explained in detail, first without considering history states, then describing required extensions for analyzing models with history states in Sect. 3.7

3.1 Evaluation of the Sojourn Time Distributions

The first step of the analysis is to evaluate the sojourn time distributions of composite states, without considering possible exits that may occur in parallel regions on the same level or at higher hierarchy levels. This is done with a bottom-up approach starting from the deepest level where only simple states are present and then going up through the hierarchy exploiting sojourn times of composite states evaluated in previous steps. Following this approach, when evaluating the sojourn time distribution of a state $s_k \in S_c^i$ of an *HSMP* $\theta^i = \langle R^i, \rho, S^i, P^i, F^i, \phi^i, \eta^i \rangle$, we first evaluate the distribution of time to reach the end state of each region and then compose them. In particular, being $\phi^i(s_k) = \theta^j = \langle R^j, \rho^j, S^j, P^j, F^j, \phi^j, \eta^j \rangle$ the *HSMP* describing the internal representation of the composite state s_k, we need to evaluate it for each region $r_q \in R^j$. Let ψ_{r_q} be the distribution of time to reach the end state of the region r_q, it can be derived from the transient probabilities of the underlying *SMP*. Transient probabilities of an *SMP* can be evaluated according to Eq. 1 [11].

$$\mathbf{V}_{r_q}(t) = \mathbf{E}_{r_q}(t) + \int_0^t d\mathbf{G}_{r_q}(u)\mathbf{V}_{r_q}(t - u) \tag{1}$$

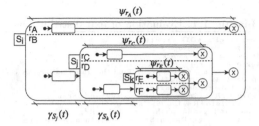

Fig. 2. Evaluation of the exit distribution of a region

Where $\mathbf{V}_{r_q}(t)$ is the matrix of transient probabilities to be in a state of the SMP at time t given an initial state, $\mathbf{E}_{r_q}(t) = I - diag(H_1(t), \ldots, H_{|T_{r_q}|}(t))$ is the local kernel of the process, T_{r_q} is the set of states of the process and $H_i(t)$ is sojourn time distribution of the state $s_i \in T_{r_q}$. Let $\bar{e}$ be the vector with 1 in the position of absorbing states of the SMP and 0 otherwise and $\bar{l}$ the vector having 1 in the position of the initial state of the SMP given by $\rho(r_q)$ and 0 otherwise, the sojourn time distribution of the region is given by $\psi_{r_q}(t) = 1 - \bar{l} * \mathbf{V}_{r_q}(t) * \bar{e}$. After evaluating $\psi_{r_q}(t)$ for each region of the composite state s_k, its sojourn time distribution can be derived. If end states are final states, the distribution of the sojourn time of s_k is the maximum over the sojourn time of its regions, evaluated as $\Omega_{s_k}(t) = \prod_{q=1}^{|R^j|} \psi_{r_q}(t)$, otherwise if all end states are exit states its distribution of sojourn time is given by the minimum over the sojourn times of its region evaluated as $\Omega_{s_k}(t) = 1 - \prod_{q=1}^{|R^j|}(1 - \psi_{r_q}(t))$.

3.2   Evaluation of Exit Distributions

The evaluation of the mean sojourn time of a state needs to take into account its distribution of sojourn time, but also the possibility that an exit occurs during its sojourn in some parallel region. According to this we evaluate the distribution of probability $F_{r_i}^{exit}(t)$ that sojourn in a region r_i is interrupted at time t due to an exit occurring in a parallel region of the same composite state or in a higher level parallel region. Consider Fig. 2 where $F_{r_F}^{exit}(t)$ needs to be evaluated. An early exit in such region can occur if an exit occurs in region r_E, r_C or r_A. $F_{r_i}^{exit}(t)$ can be evaluated with a top-down approach exploiting the fact that the behavior in each region is independent from other regions except that when an exit occurs. Additionally we assume that the evaluated distribution needs to have as time origin the time at which r_i is entered. Since higher level parallel regions were entered before the entrance in region r_i, we need to condition the probability that such regions will cause an exit to the fact that time has already passed when region r_i is entered.

First is useful to recall that the conditioning of a distribution to the passage of time can be done using *time advancement* operation introduced in [8]:

Definition 3. *Let τ_A and τ_B be two random variables of the sojourn time in two concurrent states A and B distributed according to the probability density*

Listing 1.1. Evaluation of exit distributions

```
1     procedure  evaluateExitDistribution(r_i, ψ̄)
2         //Bottom-up reasearch of parents
3         parentStates = []; //Stack
4         parentRegions = [r_i]; //Stack
5         parent = getParentState(r_i);  //Find the state that directly contains r_i
6         while( parent is not null)
7             parentStates.push(parent);
8             containingRegion = getParentRegion(parent);
9             if( containingRegion is not null)
10                parentRegions.push(containingRegion);
11                parent = getParentState(containingRegion);
12            else
13                parent = null;
14        //Top-down evaluation of the distribution
15        F_{r_i}^{exit}(t) = U(t - ∞);
16        currentState = parentStates.pop();
17        while( currentState is not null)
18            currentRegion = parentRegions.pop();
19            regions = getRegions(currentState);//Get regions of the composite state
20            regions = regions.removeElement(currentRegion);
21
22            if( currentRegion has exit pseudostate)
23                for( r in regions)
24                    F_{r_i}^{exit}(t) = min(F_{r_i}^{exit}(t), ψ_r(t));
25
26            nextState = parentStates.pop();
27            if( nextState is not null)
28                smp = buildSMP(currentRegion);  //Build the model of the region
29                γ(t) = smp.evaluateTransientTo(nextState);  //Evaluate time to be
                     absorbed
30                F_{r_i}^{exit}(t) = timeAdvancement(F_{r_i}^{exit}(t), γ(t));  //Apply the time advancement
31
32            currentState = nextState;
33        return F_{r_i}^{exit}(t);
```

functions $f_{\tau_A}(t)$ and $f_{\tau_B}(t)$, respectively. Let's assume that $\tau_A < \tau_B$. When A is exited, the remaining sojourn time τ'_B in B is reduced by τ_A, $\tau'_B = \tau_B - \tau_A$ and is distributed as $f_{\tau'_B}(t) = \int_{Min(\tau_A)}^{Max(\tau_A)} f_{\tau_B}(t+x) f_{\tau_A}(x) dx$. This operation is called time advancement or time shift.

Let $\overline{\psi}$ be the set of sojourn time distributions of each region of the model evaluated in Sect. 3.1. The top-down algorithm for the evaluation of exit distributions for region r_i is reported in Listing 1.1.

In order to better understand the algorithm we apply it to the model of Fig. 2. We want to evaluate the exit distribution for region r_F, so procedure parameters are r_F and $\overline{\psi}$. From line 3 to 13, the model is visited with a bottom-up approach creating two stacks of parent states of the considered region and regions containing such parent states. At the end of this first step $parentStates = [S_k, S_j, S_i]$ and $parentRegions = [r_F, r_D, r_B]$. Note that the two stacks are equipped with the classic $push()$ and $pop()$ operations. Then the procedure from line 15 to 32 effectively evaluates the exit distribution by iterating with a top-down approach until the target region is reached. The exit distribution is initialized at line 15, with a unit step function in ∞. Then the top-down approach iterates from S_i over S_j to S_k. At lines 19 and 20 all parallel regions of the current region are found. Then from line 22 to line 24, if the current region has a final pseudostate, it has no exit and so also its parallel regions do not contribute to the exit distribution. Otherwise the total exit distribution is given by the minimum between the previous regions exit distributions and the sojourn time distribution of these regions. Finally if another level in the hierarchy is present, we need to apply a time advancement to the evaluated distribution, equal to the time required to

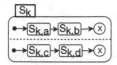

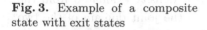

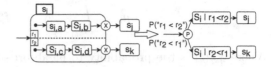

Fig. 3. Example of a composite state with exit states

Fig. 4. Example of a composite state with exits on the border reaching distinct successor

be absorbed in the state containing the target region, so that at the next step all considered distributions will continue to have the same time origin. To help understand, Fig. 2 highlights the distributions used in the evaluation of $F_{r_i}^{exit}(t)$. At first step $F_{r_i}^{exit}(t) = \psi_{r_A}(t)$ since r_A is the only parallel region to r_B and the minimum between the step function in ∞ and $\psi_{r_A}(t)$ is the sojourn time distribution of r_A. The algorithm goes down to the next level, and first the distribution $\gamma_{S_j}(t)$ that represents time to be absorbed in S_j is evaluated, then a time advancement operation is applied to $F_{r_i}^{exit}(t)$ by subtracting $\gamma_{S_j}(t)$. At next step the minimum between previous $F_{r_i}^{exit}(t)$ and $\psi_{r_C}(t)$ is evaluated and then a time advancement of $\gamma_{S_k}(t)$ is applied. Finally the minimum between previously evaluated $F_{r_i}^{exit}(t)$ and $\psi_{r_E}(t)$ gives the final result of the evaluation.

This algorithm evaluates the $F_{r_i}^{exit}(t)$ distribution for each region of the model. The approach has a limitation: it can't be applied if a lower level region contains cycles which includes a composite state. The reason is that if cycles with a composite states are present, when evaluating the exit distribution we need to evaluate the time to be absorbed by the target state in order to apply the time advancement conditioning. But if cycles are present, it is possible to enter in a sub-region, exit and then enter again and according to this the evaluation of the absorbing time is no longer compositional, but requires to analyze the model as a whole instead that through a succession of isolated evaluations. Note that this restriction applies only to the case of regions with exit states, if only final states are present there is no need to evaluate the absorbing probabilities.

Finally it is important to highlight that the early version of the technique presented in [7] didn't use this algorithm and thus it was limited to the case in which exit states were possible only at bottom levels of composite states.

3.3 Evaluation of the Reaching Probabilities of Nested States

Consider the composite state of Fig. 3. When we evaluate the steady-state probabilities of sub-states $S_{k,b}$ or $S_{k,d}$ we need to consider both the ratio between the sojourn time spent in the parent state and in the nested state and also the probability that the nested state will be visited. The reason is that in both regions of the composite state it is possible that an exit occurs in the other parallel region before the nested state will be reached. More generally, the probability μ_{s_i} to visit a sub-state s_i given that the parent state is visited is $\mu_{s_i} \leq 1$ if it is not the initial state of the region and there are parallel regions or higher level regions with exit states, thus in that cases it needs to be evaluated. The value μ_{s_i} of a state s_i in a region r_j can be evaluated from Eq. 2.

$$\mu_{s_i} = \int_{D_{\tau_1 < \tau_2}} \gamma_{s_i}(\tau_1) f^{exit}_{r_j}(\tau_2) d\overline{\tau} \tag{2}$$

Where $\gamma_{s_i}(t)$ is the probability to be absorbed in state s_i at time t given that the region r_j is entered a time $t = 0$, $f^{exit}_{r_j}$ is exit density evaluated from the distribution $F^{exit}_{r_j}(t)$, $\overline{\tau} = <\tau_1, \tau_2>$ and $D_{\tau_1 < \tau_2}$ is the joint domain of the two functions restricted to $\tau_1 < \tau_2$, thus where the absorption occurs before any exit.

3.4   Evaluation of Probabilities to Exit from Border Points

Exit states on the border allow us to define different successors of a composite state, based on which region completes first. Consider the composite state s_i shown in the left part of Fig. 4. If region r_1 exits first, the successor state will be s_j, and if region r_2 exits first, the successor state will be s_k.

Evaluation of sojourn time distribution of a composite state with exits on the border is not different compared to exits not on the border. Its sojourn time continues to be the minimum between the sojourn times of its regions and this will be later used to evaluate the mean sojourn time of the state. The presence of exits on the border will instead affect evaluation of the distribution and probabilities in the parent region that contains such a composite state. From the parent region point of view, the composite state can be represented as an equivalent model as the one shown in the right part of Fig. 4. In particular the probability of reaching a specific successor can be evaluated as the probability that one region is faster than the other. Moreover if a specific successor is reached, it means that time spent in state s_i is conditioned on the fact that a particular region was faster. Thus depending on the successor, time spent in s_i is different, and this is represented as two distinct states in which the sojourn time is conditioned to one region being faster than the other. According to this the evaluation of models including composite states with exits on borders requires to evaluate the probability that a region will be faster than all other parallel regions, evaluate the conditioned sojourn time distributions and replace such a composite state with the proposed equivalent model.

Consider a composite state s_i with exits on the border and R^i the set of its regions. Let $\alpha^{s_i}_{r_j}$ be the probability that region r_i is faster than all other $|R^i| - 1$ parallel regions, it can be evaluated according to Eq. 3,

$$\alpha^{s_i}_{r_j} = \int_{D_{\tau_j first}} \frac{d\psi_{r_j}(\tau_j)}{d\tau_j} * \prod_{r \in R^i, i \neq j} \frac{d\psi_r(\tau_i)}{d\tau_i} d\overline{\tau} \tag{3}$$

where $D_{\tau_j first}$ is the joint domain of the $|R^i|$ densities restricted to the sub-region where $\tau_j < \tau_i \ \forall i$. Note that Eq. 3 can be efficiently implemented replacing the right factor with the minimum and solving a two dimensions integral instead that a multi dimensions one. Finally, the sojourn time distribution for the state conditioned on having a region r_j faster is given by $\psi_{r_j}(t)$.

3.5   Evaluation of the Mean Sojourn Times

Now the mean sojourn times of each state can be evaluated through a bottom-up approach, taking into account exits in parallel regions. Specifically, the mean sojourn time for any top level state can be evaluated as the mean of its sojourn time distribution $\sigma_{s_i} = \int_0^\infty \Omega_{s_i}(t)dt$. Also if all parallel regions on the same and on higher level has only final pseudostate, we can use the same formula. In all other cases, the possibility that an exit occurs in a parallel region must be considered. In the latter case, the mean sojourn time σ_{s_i} for a composite state s_i contained in a region r_j, can be evaluated as $\sigma_{s_i} = \int_0^\infty v_{r_j}^{s_i}(t) * F_{r_j}^{exit}(t)dt$, where $v_{r_j}^{s_i}(t)$ is the transient probability to be in state s_i, given that region r_j is entered at time $t = 0$ without considering exits in parallel regions, while $F_{r_j}^{exit}(t)$ takes into account possible exits in parallel regions.

3.6   Embedded DTMC and Evaluation of Steady State Probabilities

Consider the top level *HSMP* θ and its transition matrix P. The embedded DTMC of such *HSMP* can be built considering only time point in which the top level state changes. Then the steady-state probabilities $\overline{u}$ of the embedded DTMC of the top state can be evaluated by the system of linear equations $\overline{u} = \overline{u}P$ with the additional constraint $|\overline{u}| = 1$. Finally steady-state probabilities can be evaluated using a top-down approach, considering the steady-state probabilities $\overline{u}$ of the embedded DTMC and weighting them by the mean sojourn times. The top-down approach starts evaluating steady-state probabilities for top level states as $\pi_{s_i} = \frac{u_{s_i} * \sigma_{s_i}}{\sum_{s_j \in S} u_{s_j} * \sigma_{s_j}}$ [11]. Then steady-state probabilities of a sub-state s_i contained in one of the regions of the parent state s_j can be evaluated as $\pi_{s_i} = \pi_{s_j} * \mu_{s_i} * \frac{\sigma_{s_i}}{\sigma_{s_j}}$.

It can be noted that in the early version of the technique presented in [7], μ_{s_i} was not considered and according to this, the technique didn't support the analysis of models where a parallel exit could prevent a sub-state to be reached.

3.7   Analysis with History States

The concept of history states was introduced in [6], as a convenience mechanism to keep track of a state configuration when a region was exited due to some parallel region. In the original formulation a history state could be of two types: *shallow*, that keep track only of the top most level configuration or *deep* that keep track of all sub-levels. In a non-Markovian system, the system state is not only given by the current location but also by the time elapsed in that state. According to this, we can define an additional subdivision of history states types: *Preemptive Repeat Different* (PRD), keeping memory of the location but not of time, and *Preemptive Resume* (PRS) keeping track also of time, thus when the configuration is restored also remaining time is restored. In this work we consider only PRD history states, while PRS history states will be studied in future work. For the sake of simplicity, in the following we also refer only to *shallow* history states, but similar concepts can be applied to *deep* history states.

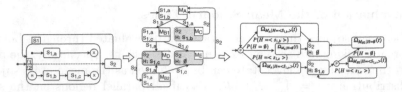

Fig. 5. Example of model with history states and encoding of history in the state space

If a history state is present like in state s_4 of Fig. 1 when the state is entered, the last configuration when it was exited is resumed. In order too keep memory of the last configuration when last exited, we propose to encode this information into the state space. In practice, states of the system need to be differentiated based on the history so as to keep track of it, thus allowing to diversify the future behavior based on such encoded information and start in the correct configuration when the state is visited again. An example is shown in Fig. 5, where on the left a model with one history state and in the center the corresponding state space are shown. If s_1 is exited due to region r_2, we don't need to keep track of history since its exit state was reached. If instead s_1 is exited due to region r_1, we need to keep track of which was the last configuration of r_2, $s_{1,b}$ or $s_{1,c}$. According to this when s_2 is reached we need to keep track of this information. In the state space diagram in the center of Fig. 5 nodes represent current overall configurations of the model considering both higher and lower level states, arcs represent the transition from one state to another and their label report the state whose sojourn time ending causes the change of configuration. In the upper right corner of nodes, a unique name node name is assigned in order to simplify the explanation and in states that need to keep track of history, history information is represented in bold font. The initial node is M_A, where the system is in s_1 and in particular in state $s_{1,a}$ in region r_1 and in state $s_{1,b}$ in region r_2. If the first state to complete its sojourn is $s_{1,a}$, s_1 is exited reaching M_C where we need to keep memory of the state of r_2 that was $s_{1,b}$. Instead if $s_{1,b}$ completes first, M_{B1} is reached. From M_{B1} the system will in any case go to s_2 but with different history depending on which completes first. If $s_{1,c}$ completes first, node M_E is reached and next time r_2 will start from its default history state since it has reached its end state. If instead $s_{1,a}$ completes first, next time r_2 will start again from $s_{1,c}$ and this is encoded in the history. When this happens the initial configuration of s_2 is different from the one represented by node M_{B1}, because in M_{B1} the remaining sojourn time of state $s_{1,a}$ was conditioned on the fact that $s_{1,b}$ completes first. This is why node M_{B2} is different from M_{B1} even though the configurations represent same locations, because in the latter the remaining time of $s_{1,a}$ has a different distribution.

In summary, when dealing with history states we need to enrich the state space with additional information about history and in it must be observed that probabilities to go from M_{B1} to M_D or to M_E require to be evaluated as well as probabilities from M_A to M_C and from M_{B2} to M_D or M_E. Then the SMP of the top level of this model can be built, as shown in the right side of the Fig. 5 based on the above analysis. It worth noting that sojourn time in state s_1 is different if we are in M_{B2} or M_A and also depends on which state we exit. This is similar to what was seen in Sect. 3.4 for exits on the border, since depending on the successor, the sojourn time changes and thus can be handled following a similar approach. When entering in M_A, a pre-selection is needed like the one shown on the right of Fig. 4 and then the sojourn time is different. In particular it decides which is the probability to have a particular history when the state will be exited, then the elapsed sojourn time will be conditioned on the exit having such a particular history. The probability to have a specific configuration when exiting a composite state with history states need to be evaluated. More generally, suppose to have n regions $r_1, \ldots, r_n$ all having history states and suppose that r_j exits, since the evolutions of regions are independent by construction, the probability can be evaluated according to Eq. 4.

$$P\{``H = <h_1, \ldots, h_{j-1}, h_{j+1}, h_n>"\} = \int_0^\infty f_{exit}^{r_j}(t) \prod_{q=1\ldots n, q \neq j} v_{h_q}^{r_q}(t)dt, \quad (4)$$

where h_q is the location of region r_q when the composite state was exited and thus this allows to evaluate the probability to have a particular history $\overline{h} = <h_1, \ldots, h_{j-1}, h_{j+1}, h_n>$ when the state was exited. Note that if a region has not a history state, we can simply remove it from the equation and consider instead the probability that the region was not exited before region r_j. Finally the sojourn time elapsed in the composite states with history state need to be evaluated conditioned on the specific successor. Let s_k be the composite state with n regions $r_1, \ldots, r_n$ all having history states. Given that the configuration when exit occurs in r_q was $\overline{h}$ and thus the successor will encode that history, the sojourn time distribution can be according to Eq. 5.

$$\Omega_{s_k|H=<h_1,\ldots,h_{j-1},h_{j+1},h_n>}(t) = \int_0^t \frac{f_{exit}^{r_j}(\tau) * \prod_{q=1\ldots n, q \neq j} v_{h_q}^{r_q}(\tau)}{P\{``H = <h_1, \ldots, h_{j-1}, h_{j+1}, h_n>"\}} d\tau$$

$$(5)$$

It should be noted that analyzing models with history states substantially increases the complexity of the analysis, in particular if the number of composite states with history states are more then one since it is required to encode the cartesian product of all possible histories causing an increase of the number of states and requiring to evaluate probabilities to have a particular history for all such states. However, on the positive side, the concept of history states requires an extension of the state space just on the level of states with a history state inside. If history states appear on different levels, the extension can also be considered separately. History state analysis can be combined with all other modeling elements of *HSMPs* presented in this paper.

4 Experiments

4.1 Unavailability Analysis of a Fault Tree

A Java numerical implementation of the approach has been developed so as to experimentally validate its correctness. The techniques can be implemented also as an analytical approach, but this requires a restriction of its applicability [7]. The code is available at https://github.com/biagimarco/hierarchicalSMP.

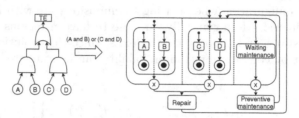

Fig. 6. A fault tree and the equivalent *HSMP* model with repair and maintenance

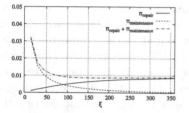

Fig. 7. Steady-state probabilities that the fault tree is unavailable due to a failure, due to preventive maintenance, or both

Table 1. Evaluation times varying N_r and N_s. Upper rows with *HSMP* analysis, lower rows with regenerative analysis

N_r	N_s					
	1	2	3	4	5	6
1	<1 s	<1 s	<1 s	<1 s	<1 s	<1 s
	<1 s	<1 s	<1 s	<1 s	<1 s	<1 s
2	<1 s	<1 s	<1 s	<1 s	<1 s	<1 s
	<1 s	<1 s	<1 s	<1 s	≃1 s	≃3 s
3	<1 s	<1 s	<1 s	<1	<1 s	<1 s
	<1 s	<1 s	≃ 5s	N.D.	N.D.	N.D.
4	<1 s	<1 s	<1 s	<1 s	<1 s	<1 s
	<1 s	≃10 s	N.D.	N.D.	N.D.	N.D.

As an example, we show how the analysis can be applied for the evaluation of steady-state probabilities of a repairable static fault tree with preventive maintenance [14]. Consider the static fault tree shown on the left side of Fig. 6. The fault tree represents a system composed by four components A, B, C and D. If components A and B or components C and D fail at the same time, the whole system fails and becomes unavailable. In that case, a repair operation is performed in order to restore the initial state of the system. Since the unplanned repair operation is slow and more expensive, a preventive maintenance procedure has been adopted in order to periodically maintain the system and thus reduce unplanned repair operations. As shown in the right side of Fig. 6, this system can be represented with an *HSMP* model. Specifically the fault tree is converted in parallel regions where *AND* gates are represented by final states and the *OR* gate is represented by exit states. It is worth noting that static fault trees with only *AND* and *OR* gates can always be modeled as an *HSMP*. A third parallel region models the maintenance period. Exits on the border are used in order to differentiate between unavailability due to a failure of the system and unavailability due to preventive maintenance. Distributions of the system are $F("A") = Exp(1/180)$, $F("B") = Exp(1/240)$, $F("C") = Exp(1/180)$, $F("D") = Exp(1/360)$, $F("Waiting maintenance") = Det(\xi)$, $F("Repair") = Unif(1,3)$, $F("Preventive maintenance") = Unif(0,1)$, where $Exp(\lambda)$ is the exponential distribution of rate λ, $Unif(a,b)$ is the uniform distribution with support $[a,b]$, $Det(\xi)$ is a deterministic time ξ. We want to measure the probability to find the system unavailable and the probability that the system is unavailable due to a preventive maintenance or due to a failure. Figure 7 shows these three measures, varying the value ξ of the time between two subsequent maintenance procedures. If the maintenance occurs too often, the probability to find the system unavailable is higher. Increasing ξ, that means decreasing the frequency of preventive maintenance, reduces the total probability to find the system unavailable but also increases the probability that the system is unavailable due to a failure and not due to a preventive maintenance.

In order to experimentally validate the approach, the same system has also been modeled as a Petri net and analyzed using *Oris tool API* [3]. Evaluated results match for all possible values of ξ.

4.2   Computational Experience with Composability

The strong point of this technique is compositionality, allowing to analyze a model without the need to build its whole state space. In the following a comparison with a technique that instead build the whole state space is performed. The technique that we chose to compare is the regenerative steady-state analysis based on stochastic state classes [13], since currently it is the only technique allowing the evaluation of steady-state probabilities of models with multiple concurrent non-Markovian timers and without the enabling restriction.

The experiment has been performed on a model having a top level composed by a single composite state with a self loop. The composite state consists of N_r parallel regions, each one composed by a sequence of N_s states leading to a final state. Thus the lower level model is composed by $N_r * (N_s + 1)$ states. Sojourn times are all uniform distributions with support $[0,1]$.

The times required to analyze the model with varying N_r and N_s are reported in Table 1. Experiments were performed on a single core of a 2.20 GHz Intel i5-5200U with 8 GB RAM, and each single run was performed with a timeout of 2 min. Increasing the number of regions N_r increases the concurrency degree of the model and thus the regenerative analysis needs to evaluate the state space considering all possible orders in which the transitions can be executed. As one can see, with $N_r = 3$ and $N_r = 4$, 2 min are no more sufficient to analyze the model with the regenerative analysis while with the hierarchical approach requires less then 1 s. The experiment gives an impression of the advantage of this technique when applied to model with high concurrency.

5   Conclusion

Many techniques exist for the analysis of systems with multiple concurrent non-Markovian timers, each one having different limitations and using different formalisms to represent the model. The *HSMP* formalism is inspired by UML state machines [1], a widely diffused formalism and thus easier to be understood. *HSMP* uses state machines in which states can be simple or composite, where simple states have a stochastic sojourn time allowing us to model quantitative aspects while the concept of composite states allows us to define hierarchical models. Leveraging this hierarchical structure a compositional analysis can be defined, enabling the development of an approach that doesn't need to build the whole state space. In this work we better formalize and extend the *HSMP* formalism, and improve the analysis technique by removing some of its limitations and extending it so as to boost its modeling power in the direction to be more similar to that of UML state machines. Specifically, composite states now have no limitation related to exit states, also the possibility to have exit states on the border has been introduced, allowing to define different successors of composite state based on which region finishes first. Additionally, the concept of history states has been added, enabling the definition of more condensed models.

The extended technique was implemented and experimentally validated analyzing a static fault tree under preventive maintenance and comparing results with those of another technique. A comparison with another technique was also performed so as to better highlight the advantage of being compositional.

A future development will be to further extend the technique so as to reduce the gap between the modeling power of UML state machines, for example allowing to have composite states mixing regions with final states and exit states, or to have final and exit states in the same region. Another direction would be to study how to analyze models with *PRS* history states introduced in this work.

References

1. Unified modeling language specification version 2.5.1, December 2017
2. Bertrand, N., et al.: Stochastic timed automata. arXiv (2014)
3. Carnevali, L., Ridi, L., Vicario, E.: A framework for simulation and symbolic state space analysis of non-Markovian models. In: Flammini, F., Bologna, S., Vittorini, V. (eds.) SAFECOMP 2011. LNCS, vol. 6894, pp. 409–422. Springer, Heidelberg (2011). https://doi.org/10.1007/978-3-642-24270-0_30
4. D'Argenio, P.R., Lee, M.D., Monti, R.E.: Input/output stochastic automata. In: Fränzle, M., Markey, N. (eds.) FORMATS 2016. LNCS, vol. 9884, pp. 53–68. Springer, Cham (2016). https://doi.org/10.1007/978-3-319-44878-7_4

5. German, R., Logothetis, D., Trivedi, K.S.: Transient analysis of Markov regenerative stochastic petri nets: a comparison of approaches. In: Petri Nets and Performance Models, pp. 103–112. IEEE (1995)
6. Harel, D.: Statecharts: a visual formalism for complex systems. Sci. Comput. Program. **8**(3), 231–274 (1987)
7. Homm, D., German, R.: Analysis of hierarchical semi-Markov processes with parallel regions. In: Remke, A., Haverkort, B.R. (eds.) MMB&DFT 2016. LNCS, vol. 9629, pp. 92–106. Springer, Cham (2016). https://doi.org/10.1007/978-3-319-31559-1_9
8. Horváth, A., Paolieri, M., Ridi, L., Vicario, E.: Transient analysis of non-Markovian models using stochastic state classes. Perform. Eval. **69**(7–8), 315–335 (2012)
9. Jansen, D.N., Hermanns, H., Katoen, J.-P.: A probabilistic extension of UML statecharts. In: Damm, W., Olderog, E.-R. (eds.) FTRTFT 2002. LNCS, vol. 2469, pp. 355–374. Springer, Heidelberg (2002). https://doi.org/10.1007/3-540-45739-9_21
10. Jansen, D.N., Hermanns, H., Katoen, J.-P.: A QoS-oriented extension of UML statecharts. In: Stevens, P., Whittle, J., Booch, G. (eds.) UML 2003. LNCS, vol. 2863, pp. 76–91. Springer, Heidelberg (2003). https://doi.org/10.1007/978-3-540-45221-8_7
11. Kulkarni, V.G.: Modeling and Analysis of Stochastic Systems. CRC Press, London (2016)
12. Logothetis, D., Trivedi, K.S., Puliafito, A.: Markov regenerative models. In: Computer Performance and Dependability Symposium. IEEE (1995)
13. Martina, S., Paolieri, M., Papini, T., Vicario, E.: Performance evaluation of Fischer's protocol through steady-state analysis of Markov regenerative processes. In: MASCOTS, pp. 355–360. IEEE (2016)
14. Ruijters, E., Stoelinga, M.: Fault tree analysis: a survey of the state-of-the-art in modeling, analysis and tools. Comput. Sci. Rev. **15–16**, 29–62 (2015)

Formal Parameter Synthesis for Energy-Utility-Optimal Fault Tolerance

Linda Herrmann[✉], Christel Baier[✉], Christof Fetzer[✉],
Sascha Klüppelholz[✉], and Markus Napierkowski[✉]

Technische Universität Dresden, Dresden, Germany
{linda.herrmann1,christel.baier,christof.fetzer,sascha.klueppelholz,
markus.napierkowski}@tu-dresden.de

Abstract. Fault-tolerance techniques are widely used to improve the resiliency of hardware/software systems. An important step for the deployment of such techniques in a concrete setting is to find reasonable configurations balancing the tradeoff between resiliency and energy. The paper reports on a case study where we employ probabilistic model checking to synthesize values for tunable system parameters of a redo-based fault-tolerance mechanism. We consider discrete parameters of a finite range (as the number of redos) as well as continuous parameters to encode the error detection rates of the underlying control- and data-flow checkers. To tackle the state-explosion problem, we exploit structural properties of redo-based protocols. The parameter synthesis approach combines probabilistic model checking for Markov chains with parametric transition probabilities and reward values and computer-algebra techniques to determine parameter valuations that minimize the expected overhead given constraints on the utility, depending on a given error probability.

1 Introduction

The paper reports on a case study that addresses the synthesis problem for redo-based fault-tolerance mechanisms. We assume environmental parameters that are part of the input (e.g., error probabilities and energy costs) and configurable parameters (e.g., detection probabilities and the number of redos). The latter are controllable and hence part of the output. The goal is to search for configurations (i.e., values for the tunable parameters) that allow balancing the tradeoff between resiliency, energy and performance.

The authors are supported by the DFG through the Collaborative Research Center SFB 912 – HAEC, the Excellence Initiative by the German Federal and State Governments (cluster of excellence cfAED and Institutional Strategy), the Research Training Groups QuantLA (GRK 1763) and RoSI (GRK 1907), the DFG-project BA-1679/11-1, and the DFG-project BA-1679/12-1.

R. Bakhshi et al. (Eds.): EPEW 2018, LNCS 11178, pp. 78–93, 2018.
https://doi.org/10.1007/978-3-030-02227-3_6

The considered fault-tolerance mechanism is inspired by the hardware-assisted fault-tolerance protocol HAFT [1]. HAFT enables error[1] detection and correction for a finite sequence of instructions (in the further named application), that is affected by bit-flips. The operating principle of HAFT at the relevant abstraction level is as follows: The fault-tolerance technique partitions the application into transactions, and performs error detection and correction transaction-wise. Error detection is enabled by replicating instructions, and comparing for differences. Replicated instructions can also be affected by errors, and thus might cause error correction to be invoked although the application would have been correct when not using error detection. An erroneous transaction is corrected by redoing the transaction. Also during a redo errors can occur and further redos might be necessary. If after a pre-defined number of redos still an error is detected, the application is aborted. Error detection and correction cause overhead costs. As a measure, we take the number of instructions executed for error handling. This measure correlates with the energy consumption for error detection and correction, since the additional energy consumption only comes from additional instruction execution. In this paper we build on Markov chains with parameters for transition probabilities and rewards as underlying semantic model. The discrete protocol parameters, e.g., the number of redos and transaction length, induce a family of parametric Markov chains that yield the basis for finding reasonable configurations. Finding optimal solutions in uncountably infinite parameter sets is in general undecidable [3,4]. We restrict ourselves to families with finitely many members, as the set of reasonable transaction lengths as well as the number of redos can safely be assumed to be finite as well.

Our primary configuration objective is resilience: the probability of terminating without an undetected error shall be very high. Aborting the application is preferred to terminating with a wrong result, thus, the conditional probability of aborting in case of not terminating correctly shall be high. As a subordinate objective, the energy consumption has to be low. This opens the following synthesis problems: (1) What is a good transaction length? Long transactions increase the probability of a transaction to be erroneous and increase the overhead in redos, while short transactions cause error detection to be performed very often and thus increase the overall costs for error detection. (2) What is an optimal number of maximal redos? Redos enable error correction and thus application recovering, but during a redo there is an additional chance of having undetected errors and causing the application to terminate with a wrong result. (3) How many instructions shall be replicated? Increasing this amount increases the chance of detecting an error, but also increases the overhead and the chance of some replica being affected by an error.

Challenges. To address this synthesis problem, we apply variants of probabilistic model checking [5,6] that take as input parametric Markov chains as described

---

[1] Following the taxonomy of [2], we use the term "fault" to describe bit-flips. Errors are caused by faults that affected the applications run. Failures in our sense are caused by errors that could not be detected by the fault-tolerance mechanism and thus lead to a wrong computation of the application.

above. These variants yield rational functions for probabilities of reaching some goal state and expected accumulated rewards. We will refer to this variants as parametric probabilistic model checking (PPMC). PPMC yields rational functions, describing system characteristics, instead of single values. The rational functions can then be analyzed for optimality. This comes with several challenges. (1) An application typically consists of billions of instructions, realistic transaction lengths range from several hundred instructions to the extremal case of handling the whole application as one transaction. We need to include both, the details of a transaction, and the execution of millions of transactions, in the model. This results in very large models, which is in contrast to PPMC requiring models to be small. (2) Only the detection probabilities but not the maximal number of redos and the transaction length can be handled as parameters. For the latter, PPMC needs to be invoked once for each considered configuration, which is especially problematic due to the large model sizes. (3) The error probability crucially depends on the hardware and the application scenario. Moreover, tiny error probabilities[2] can lead to numerical instability when treated in a nonparametric fashion. Thus, environmental and tunable parameters are part of the model, but PPMC hardly scales for larger models with multiple parameters [5].

Contribution. In this paper, we report on a case study for the synthesis problem for fault-tolerance mechanisms and show how to overcome the mentioned challenges. The main idea is to exploit the regularity of our model with repeating transaction blocks. Hence, we apply PPMC to families of very small sub-models, modeling only one transaction, but detailed and still parametric in the full set of probability and reward parameters. With this we obtain rational functions for probabilities of successful error detection and aborting as well as energy overhead for each transaction. We present a new, suited factorization approach that allows to combine the transaction-level results and obtain rational functions for the whole application. Our approach allows handling the transaction length as a parameter and PPMC has to be invoked only once for each considered number of maximal redos. Finally, we exemplarily utilize the rational functions to find sweet spots in the tradeoff between resiliency and energy. Here, a surprising result is, that for reasonable error probabilities, increasing the maximal number of redos to more than just one, degrades the resiliency while only introducing additional overhead costs.

2   Related Work

Parameter synthesis for probabilistic systems using formal methods has been done widely before. In, e.g., [10] parametric model checking is applied to synthesize optimal values for transition probabilities in Markov models, as we do

---

[2] [7] gives an error rate of 0.066 FIT (failures in time, the expected number of failures in 10^9 h) per Mbit. This corresponds to having an error in a single instruction within an hour with probability about $4 \cdot 10^{-15}$. Other error rate estimates from [8] and [9] give error probabilities of $3.7 \cdot 10^{-15}$ and $2.7 \cdot 10^{-15}$.

for the amount of instructions to be replicated. Rate parameters are synthesized in [11] in a CTMC modelling stochastic biochemical networks, and in [12] for a real-time storage system that is affected by randomly occurring bit-flips. In [13], a parameter synthesis approach is presented and applied to repair systems by tuning transition probabilities. Some instances of adaptive systems with configurable transition probabilities are configured in [14], using stochastic methods like Monte Carlo Sampling and particle swarm optimization. None of these works addresses the parameter synthesis problem for redo-based fault-tolerance mechanisms and exploits the regularity of the model structure to address the imposed scalability challenges. Furthermore, our approach also spans parameters that affect the structure of the Markov model and thus cannot be handled easily with standard parametric model-checking techniques.

3 Preliminaries

We will provide a brief summary of the relevant concepts for Markov chains. For more details, we refer to, e.g., [15]. A *discrete-time Markov chain* (DTMC) is a tuple $\mathcal{M} = (S, P)$ with a finite set of states S and transition probabilities $P : S \times S \to [0,1] \cap \mathbb{Q}$ such that for all $s \in S : \sum_{t \in S} P(s,t) \in \{0,1\}$. A *path* in $\mathcal{M}$ is a finite or infinite sequence of states $\pi = s_0 s_1 \ldots$ such that $P(s_i, s_{i+1}) > 0$ for all $i \geq 0$. We denote the set of all paths in $\mathcal{M}$ by $Paths_{\mathcal{M}}$. For a finite path $\pi = s_0 s_1 \ldots s_n$ we write $P(\pi) = \prod_{i=0}^{n-1} P(s_i, s_{i+1})$. A path π is maximal if it is infinite or π is finite and $\sum_{t \in S} P(s_n, t) = 0$.

Let $G \subseteq S$ and $s_0 \in S$. The probability of eventually reaching some state in G from s_0, denoted by $\mathrm{Pr}_{s_0}(\Diamond G)$, is derived using the standard definition of the induced probability distribution on the set of measurable sets of maximal paths. The event $\Diamond G$ is called a *reachability property*.

A *reward function* $rew : S \to \mathbb{Q}^{\geq 0}$, assigns each state a non-negative value (e.g., energy consumed in that state). The accumulated reward induced by rew is a random variable $AccRew : Paths_{\mathcal{M}} \to \mathbb{R}$ assigning each path in $\mathcal{M}$ the sum of its state rewards, i.e. $AccRew(s_0 s_1 \ldots s_n) = \sum_{i=0}^{n} rew(s_i)$. Let $G \subseteq S$ be a set of states such that $\mathrm{Pr}_{s_0}(\Diamond G) = 1$. The *expected accumulated reward* until reaching G from s_0, denoted by $\mathbb{E}_{s_0}(\Diamond G)$, is the expectation value of $AccRew$ in $\mathcal{M}$ restricted to the set of paths ending in G, i.e., $\mathbb{E}_{s_0}(\Diamond G) = \sum_{\pi \in \Pi} P(\pi) \cdot AccRew(\pi)$, where $\Pi = \{s_0 \ldots s_n \in Paths_{\mathcal{M}} \mid s_n \in G, s_i \notin G \text{ for } 0 \leq i < n\}$.

For $G \subseteq S$ and $\mathrm{Pr}_{s_0}(\Diamond G) > 0$ the *conditional expected accumulated reward* until reaching G from s_0 under the condition of reaching G is, with Π as above:

$$\mathbb{E}_{s_0}(\Diamond G \mid \Diamond G) = \sum_{\pi \in \Pi} \frac{P(\pi) \cdot AccRew(\pi)}{\mathrm{Pr}_{s_0}(\Diamond G)}.$$

4 Redo-Based Fault-Tolerance Model

In this section, we introduce the fault-tolerance model. A detailed description can be found in the extended version of this paper [16]. The model contains adjustable *attributes* for, e.g., the error probability. It consists of components for the underlying hardware, the application, and the fault-tolerance protocol. The latter contains a control-flow checker (CFC), a data-flow checker (DFC), and a transaction redo manager (TRM) implementing the redo/abort-schema.

Application. An application performs a fixed number of instructions $inst\_num$, each instruction is prone to errors (see paragraph "Errors and Failures" below). The instruction flow is partitioned into transactions, each consisting of ta_len instructions. The number of transactions to be performed is $ta\_num = inst\_num/ta\_len$. We assume three types of instructions: *control-flow instructions*, where errors affect only the control-flow (e.g., jump), *data-flow instructions*, where errors affect the data-flow (e.g. add), and *transaction management instructions*, implementing the transaction mechanism (e.g., begin-of-transaction and end-of-transaction instructions). Errors in the latter do only affect the control flow. Errors in the data-flow also affect and thus falsify the control-flow. The ratio of control-flow and data-flow instructions can be set via the attribute cf_df_ratio. The amount of transaction management instructions is controlled by the attribute tmi_num. The application starts in a location "start transaction", performs a transaction and then reaches a "wait" location. Eventually, it either receives an ABORT or a COMMIT from the TRM. An ABORT indicates that an error could not be corrected. Then, the application switches to location "abort". Receiving COMMIT causes the application to complete the transaction. If all instructions are executed, it terminates, reaching location "done". Otherwise, it increases a counter $ta\_counter$ and starts a new transaction.

Error Detection. The TRM initially waits for the application to complete a transaction. Then, it invokes both, CFC and DFC in parallel, and waits for the results. The DFC checks all data-flow instructions for errors. The CFC checks all instructions for errors, since all instructions affect the control flow. For each data-flow-corrupted transaction there is a chance p_detn_DFC of the DFC to detect this error. For each transaction with correct data-flow, there is a chance of p_fp_DFC to detect an error anyway, i.e., to have a false positive. Analogous attributes p_detn_CFC and p_fp_CFC are defined for the CFC.

Error Correction. After checking, the checkers report their results to the TRM, which switches to location "answers received". If one of the checkers detected an error, a redo is invoked by the TRM, i.e., the transaction is re-executed and a redo-counter $redo\_counter$ is increased. The re-executed transaction can again be corrupted, thus, error detection is invoked and might result in a further redo. This is repeated until the preset attribute max_redos is reached by the redo counter. Then, the TRM sends an ABORT signal to the application. If in the original transaction or in one of its re-executions no error is detected, the TRM sends a COMMIT-signal to the application.

Errors and Failures. The hardware model tracks the state of the applications internal memory. When starting the application, the hardware location is "correct". Each instruction can be corrupted with probability p_e, which causes the location to switch to "error". When being erroneous, and a redo is invoked by the TRM, the location switches back to "correct". When being erroneous and no redo is invoked, the location is changed to "failure". A failure increases the chance of a subsequent error in an instruction to p_e_incr. Once the application has a failure in its internal memory, it will persist until the application either terminates (with this failure) or is aborted due to another error.

Transaction Outcomes. After performing, checking, correcting, and committing or aborting a transaction, there are four possible outcomes. (1) The hardware state is "correct" and the application received a commit, i.e., is in a location "transaction completed" (short: cc). This outcome is reached if either no error occurred and also no error was detected, or if an error occurred, was detected and could be corrected. (2) The hardware is "correct" but the application was aborted (short: ca), arising, if no error occurred in the original transaction, but a false positive triggered redos, and redos failed. (3) If an error occurred in the original application but could not be detected, the hardware model ends up in location "failure" and the application receives a commit, completing the transaction (short: fc). (4) If the hardware after some transaction ends in the previous mentioned outcome fc and in some transaction afterwards an abort signal is sent, then the hardware model is in location "failure" and the application is in location abort (short: fa).

5   State-Space Reduction and Factorization

Semantics and Structure of the Model. The fault-tolerance model is a Markov decision process (MDP) (see, e.g., [17]), i.e., a discrete-time Markov chain (DTMC) enhanced with nondeterminism. In an MDP there can be several distributions per state. The non-determinism is resolved by a *strategy*. Each strategy $\mathfrak{S}$ induces a DTMC and thus, together with a starting state $s_0 \in S$, a probability distribution $\mathrm{Pr}_{s_0}^{\mathfrak{S}}$ on the set of measurable sets of paths in the induced DTMC. The MDP $\mathcal{M}$ for our model serves as operational model whose states are tuples consisting of the local states of all components. The initial state s_0 is the state where the hardware is "correct", the application's location is "start" and all other modules wait for being invoked. All counters (i.e., *redo_counter*, *ta_counter*) are set to 0 and variables indicating redos to false. For each state, the outgoing transitions arise from all possible synchronous and asynchronous transitions enabled in the components.

Reduction to Markov Chain. The nondeterminism in $\mathcal{M}$ solely arises from interleaving execution of the CFC and DFC. None of the individual components of the model contains nondeterministic choices. Since no variables or locations outside CFC and DFC change during execution of CFC and DFC and no transitions in the CFC and DFC make use of the internal state of the respective other checker component, the state of the MDP after error detection does not depend on the chosen interleaving. Furthermore, none of our configuration criteria in Sect. 6 distinguishes between states in the non-deterministic part of the MDP, i.e., states that model the error detection process. Thus, we can rely on results that have been established in the context of partial-order reduction for MDPs [18–20]: for the chosen configuration criteria it is irrelevant which interleaving is chosen and we can replace $\mathcal{M}$ with, e.g., the DTMC in which first the CFC performs error detection and then the DFC checks the data-flow.

Factorization. The model size increases significantly when increasing ta_num (i.e., by decreasing the transaction length). Furthermore, even for small models, PPMC performs badly on our model. When choosing $max\_redos = 1$ and $ta\_num = 5$, the model consists of only 876 states, but computation times of simple probabilistic properties are unfeasible large[3]. Realistic applications consist of many more transactions, e.g., in Sect. 6 we will analyze a model with $ta\_num = 10^{10}$.

We will use the structure of the model to simplify the model checking process. For technical reasons, we slightly modify the model: instead of terminating in abort states, we stepwise increase the transaction counter up to its maximum value (without changing other variable values). This gives us a DTMC with a regular structure with repeating phases (Fig. 1). One phase represents one transaction and after each phase there are four possible outcomes cc, ca, fc, and fa (cf. Sect. 4). Internal details of each phase such as program execution, error detection and correction are omitted here.

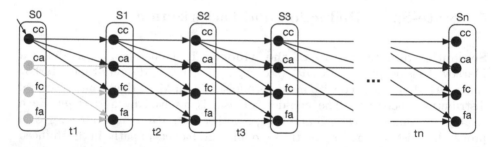

Fig. 1. The structure of the DTMC on transaction level. Each arrow indicates the execution of one transaction, including error detection and correction. The outcome of each transaction is one of the states in {(correct,commit)(cc), (correct,abort)(ca), (failure,commit)(fc), (failure,abort)(fa)}. Light-grey states in S_0 mark states that are not reachable.

For the rest of this section we fix $ta\_num = n$. We denote the set of outcome states after the i-th transaction by $S_i = \{(cc, i), (ca, i), (fc, i), (fa, i)\}$ (cf. Fig. 1), and identify the initial state with $s_0 = (cc, 0) \in S_0$, since the hardware is "correct", the application is not aborted and no transaction is performed yet. Note that for all $0 \leq i < n$ the probabilities of reaching state $t \in S_{i+1}$ from $s \in S_i$ do not depend on the counter value i. Thus, we can choose an arbitrary $0 \leq i < n$

---

[3] Computing the probability of correct termination single threaded on a 2.5 Ghz Intel Core Processor did not finish within 2 h, for $ta\_num = 5$. The model was parametrized in the detection probabilities and the error probabilities.

and define a probability matrix $P = (\text{Pr}_s(\Diamond t))_{s \in S_i, t \in S_{i+1}}$. P is a 4×4-matrix that describes the probabilistic effects of a single transaction. Note that the matrix elements are rational functions. The probability of reaching outcome goal $\in S_n$ (thus, after the n-th transaction) can be computed by $\text{Pr}_{s_0}(\Diamond goal) = (P^n)_{s_0, goal}$.

Lemma 1. *Let rew be a reward structure with $rew(s_n) = 0$ for all $s_n \in S_n$, $E = (\mathbb{E}_s(\phi t | \Diamond t))_{s \in S_i, t \in S_{i+1}}$ for some arbitrary $0 \le i < n$, and let pe be a 1×4 vector with $pe = \left(\sum_{t \in S_{i+1}} P_{s,t} \cdot E_{s,t} \right)_{s \in S_i}$. Then we have*

$$\mathbb{E}_{s_0}(\phi S_n) = \left(\sum_{k=1}^{n} P^{k-1} \cdot pe \right)_{s_0}.$$

The proof relies on Bayesian decomposition for expectation values and can be found in the extended version of this paper [16]. The matrices P and E and the vector pe can be computed with existing PPMC implementations on very small models (modeling only one transaction). Thus, we can compute rational functions for both, reachability properties and expected accumulated rewards by combining PPMC (on very small models) and a computer algebra system. Furthermore, the structures of the small models do not depend on ta_num and ta_len, thus ta_len can be treated as a parameter.

6 Configuration

In this section, we exemplarily configure an instance of our fault-tolerance model with respect to the configuration parameters p_detn_CFC, p_detn_DFC, ta_len and max_redos. During model checking we handle p_detn_CFC, p_detn_DFC and ta_len as parameters, and, using the factorization approach from Sect. 5, compute rational functions for each $max\_redos \in \{0, 1, 2, 3\}$. We also handle the error probability p_e as parameter, and exemplarily configure the fault-tolerance model for all $p\_e \in \{10^{-8}, 10^{-10}, 10^{-15}\}$. The models, rational functions, and additional files can be downloaded[4].

Fault-Tolerance Setting. The model instance is mainly inspired by HAFT [1], i.e., instructions in our model correspond to instructions on CPU level, and error detection is enabled by duplicating instructions. The amount of duplicated instructions is configurable and represents the detection probability, e.g., replicating 80% of all data-flow instructions means $p\_detn\_DFC = 0.8$. Replicating all instructions gives error detection probabilities of 1, i.e., we neglect the probability of the same error occurring in both, an original instruction and its replication, which would cause the error to be undetectable. Furthermore we assume that transaction management instructions are not replicated.

Model Attributes. We fix the following model attributes: The application runs for exactly 10^{12} ($inst\_num$) instructions, 10% (cf_df_ratio) being control-flow

---

[4] https://wwwtcs.inf.tu-dresden.de/ALGI/PUB/EPEW18.

instructions, and two (*tmi_num*) transaction management instructions ("begin of transaction" and "end of transaction") are inserted per transaction. The increased error probability is defined as $p\_e\_incr = (p\_e)^{\frac{8}{10}}$. False positives are errors that occur in replicated instructions or in transaction management instructions, i.e., with $cf\_df\_ratio = 0.1$ we have:

$$p\_fp\_CFC = 1 - \left((1 - p\_e)^{ta\_len \cdot 0.1 \cdot p\_detn\_CFC} \cdot (1 - p\_e)^{ta\_len \cdot 0.9 \cdot p\_detn\_DFC}\right.$$

$$\left. \cdot (1 - p\_e)^{tmi\_num}\right) \qquad \text{and}$$

$$p\_fp\_DFC = 1 - \left((1 - p\_e)^{ta\_len \cdot 0.9 \cdot p\_detn\_DFC}\right).$$

Reward Structures. In the analysis we focus on the expected energy-overhead for error detection and correction. For this we introduce a reward structure that assigns one energy unit each time an instruction is executed for error detection or correction. Formally, we define a reward structure assigning states where the TRM is in location "answers received" the following reward for the energy overhead, depending on whether a transaction or one of its redos was executed:

if *redo_counter* = 0 : $ta\_len \cdot p\_detn\_CFC + ta\_len \cdot 0.9 \cdot p\_detn\_DFC + tmi\_num$,

if *redo_counter* > 0 : $ta\_len \cdot p\_detn\_CFC + ta\_len \cdot 0.9 \cdot p\_detn\_DFC + tmi\_num + ta\_len$.

Configuration Criteria. The goal of this section is to exemplarily find good parameter values that optimize the chosen protocol instance with respect to the following criteria: (1) the probability of terminating correctly should be at least 0.9995, (2) the conditional probability of aborting, in case of not terminating correctly, should be greater than 0.15, and (3) from all configurations meeting the conditions above, one with least energy overhead should be chosen.

Finding Optimal Configuration. Using probabilistic model checking, we compute parametric matrices P and E (as defined in Sect. 5). For this we use the parametric model checker Storm [21]. The matrices are parameterized over the error probability, detection probabilities, and the transaction length. As P and E depend on the number of redos, this causes separate runs of Storm for $max\_redos \in \{0, 1, 2, 3\}$. To systematically explore the design space, we first fix the error probabilities and replace the parameters with constants within P and E, as these values can be assumed to be given. We will consider three scenarios with $p\_e \in \{10^{-10}, 10^{-12}, 10^{-15}\}$. For each $max\_redos \in \{0, 1, 2, 3\}$ we then consider a discrete number of combinations for the detection probabilities $(p\_detn\_DFC, p\_detn\_DFC \in \{0, 0.001, 0.1, 0.5, 0.75, 0.9, 0.95, 0.99, 0.999\})$ and transaction length $(ta\_len \in \{100, 200, 500, 1000, 2000, 5000, 10^4, 10^6, 10^{10}, 10^{12}\})$ to fill decision tables (or plot the respective rational function). For this step we applied the Python-based computer algebra system SymPy [22][5].

---

[5] Computing the matrices took 50 s for $max\_redos = 0$, 173 s for $max\_redos = 1$, 140 min for $max\_redos = 2$, and about one day and 3 h for $max\_redos = 3$. Evaluating the rational functions to set up decision tables using SymPy [22] took less then a second per evaluation point for $max\_redos = 0$ and about 3 s per point for $max\_redos = 3$.

The Maximal Number of Redos. We start with analyzing the effect of the maximal number of redos. Without any fault-tolerance mechanism[6], the probability of terminating correctly is $3 \cdot 10^{-83}$ for $p\_e = 10^{-10}$, 0.15 for $p\_e = 10^{-12}$, and for $p\_e = 10^{-15}$ it is 0.998. Figure 2 shows the probability of terminating correctly, when varying max_redos. For all chosen error probabilities and detection probabilities, performing a single redo pays off drastically. For example, when the transaction length is 1000 and the detection probabilities both are set to 0.9, allowing a single redo increases the probability of terminating correctly from 0.027 to 0.827, when $p\_e = 10^{-12}$. When performing error detection without redo-based correction, increasing detection probabilities cause the probability of terminating correctly to shrink, since more instructions are replicated and thus more replicas can be affected by errors. Allowing redos neglect this effect. Also for all transaction lengths, except for the extremal case where the whole application is a single transaction, allowing redos increases the probability of terminating correctly significantly. Allowing more than one redo does only marginally increase the probability of terminating correctly, except for transaction lengths above 10^{10}. Figure 3 shows that each redo decreases the chance of aborting in case of not terminating correctly (Criteria 2). For two redos, this chance is almost zero for all configurations except for extremely large transaction lengths and small error probabilities. The correlation of the energy overhead and

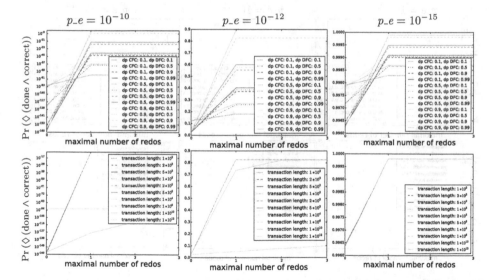

Fig. 2. Probability of terminating correctly in dependence on the maximal number of redos. First row: ranging detection probabilities, $ta\_len = 1000$. Second row: ranging transaction length, $p\_detn\_CFC = p\_detn\_DFC = 0.9$. From left to right: error probability $10^{-10}, 10^{-12}, 10^{-15}$. Note that y-scales in the left column are in log scale.

---

[6] Due to the nature of PPMC, these values need to be computed in a separate run. Applying the factorization approach of Sect. 5, this took less than three seconds.

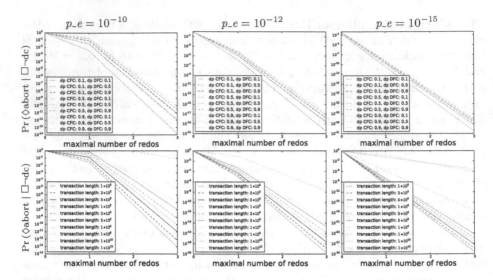

Fig. 3. Conditional probability of aborting in case of not terminating correctly in dependence of the maximal number of redos (dc is short for done ∧ correct.) First row: ranging detection probabilities. Second row: ranging transaction lengths. From left to right: error probability $10^{-10}, 10^{-12}, 10^{-15}$. Note that y-scales are in log scale.

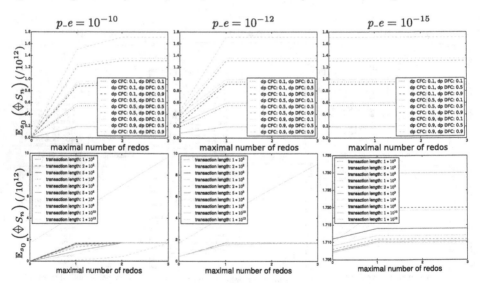

Fig. 4. Expected overhead in dependence of the maximal number of redos. First row: ranging detection probabilities. Second row: ranging transaction length. From left to right: error probability $10^{-10}, 10^{-12}, 10^{-15}$.

the maximal number of redos is depicted in Fig. 4. For low error probabilities, the overhead is only marginally affected by the maximal number of redos, since, when errors are unlikely and thus error correction is invoked only seldom, the overhead is mainly defined by the number of replicated instructions executed for error detection. For higher error probabilities, expectably more errors occur and thus more error correction needs to be performed. So the overhead increases, when allowing more redos. Thus, choosing to perform at most one redo increases the probability of correct termination. Allowing another redo does not further increase this probability significantly, but decreases the probability of aborting in case of not terminating correctly without decrease in the overhead. Hence, from now on we fix $max\_redos = 1$.

Optimal Transaction Lengths. Figure 5 shows from top to bottom results for the three configuration criteria. For $p\_e = 10^{-10}$ the probability of terminating correctly is hardly affected by varying transaction lengths below 10^6. Choosing longer transaction length decreases the probability substantially. Large transaction lengths do increase the probability again, when p_detn_DFC is small, but short transaction lengths are in general to be preferred. For lower error probabilities, the turning point moves to the right. For error probability 10^{-15} it is beyond the maximal possible transaction length. The conditional probability of

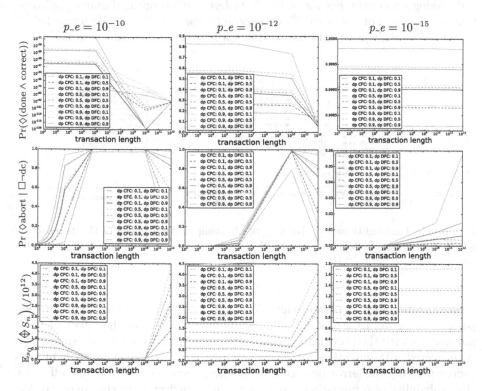

Fig. 5. In dependence of the transaction length for ranging detection probabilities, $max\_redos = 1$: First row: probability of terminating correctly. Second row: conditional probability of aborting in case of not terminating correctly (dc is short for done $\wedge$ correct). Third row: expected energy overhead. From left to right: error probability $10^{-10}, 10^{-12}, 10^{-15}$.

aborting when not terminating correctly (Fig. 5, second row) first increases with increasing transaction lengths, then stays on a level near one for middle-large transaction lengths and finally drops again, in the same point as the probability of terminating correctly rises for some detection probabilities. Again, the turning points move to the right when decreasing error probabilities. Regarding the overhead, small transaction lengths cause less transactions to be erroneous and thus less error correction to be performed. Nevertheless, very small transaction lengths cause error detection to take place very often and thus lead to a higher overhead. This is visible in the third row of Fig. 5. For error probabilities 10^{-10} and 10^{-12}, increasing the transaction length up to 10^{10} decreases the overhead, but after this point, the overhead increases significantly. For error probability 10^{-15} the effect is barely visible. The decrease of energy overhead also arises because the probability of aborting increases with higher transaction length (cf. Fig. 6): The higher this probability, the sooner the application is likely to be aborted. After an abort no more overhead is produced. Thus the overhead drops with increasing abort rates, and rises, when very large transaction lengths cause a shrinking abort rate. For $p\_e = 10^{-10}$, $ta\_len = 10^6$ is optimal under the investigated lengths. For $p\_e = 10^{-10}$, we choose $ta\_len = 10^{10}$, and for $p\_e = 10^{-15}$, errors are unlikely enough to handle the application as one transaction.

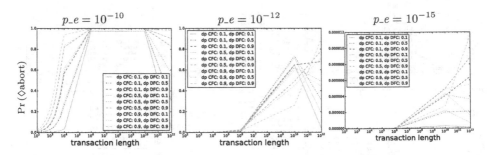

Fig. 6. The (unconditional) probability of aborting in dependence of the transaction length for ranging detection probabilities, $max\_redos = 1$: From left to right: error probability $10^{-10}, 10^{-12}, 10^{-15}$.

Error Detection Probabilities. We now fix the remaining configuration parameters, p_detn_CFC and p_detn_DFC. Figure 7 shows the effect of these parameters with the previously chosen configurations for max_redos and ta_len. As expected, all three values increase when increasing the detection probabilities. Increasing only one error detection probability certainly has a visible effect on the probability of terminating correctly, yet it is ineffective to choose one detection probability to be very low and the other one to be very high. To configure the remaining parameters of the fault-tolerance technique, we use a decision table, exemplarily for $p\_e = 10^{-15}$. Figure 8 shows results for $max\_redos = 1$ and $ta\_len = 10^{12}$. All depicted lines satisfy the first two configuration criteria. The energy overhead does not differ much, but the conditional probability

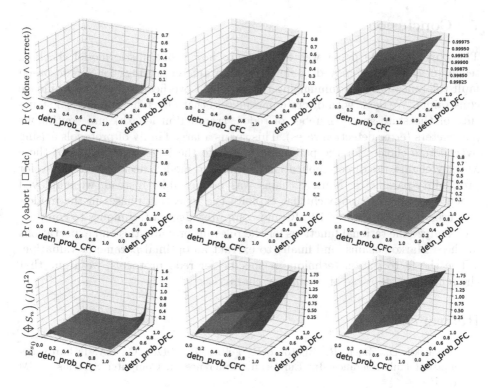

Fig. 7. In dependence of the detection probabilities, for $max\_redos = 1$: First row: probability of terminating correctly. Second row: conditional probability of aborting in case of not terminating correctly (dc is short for done $\wedge$ correct). Third row: expected overhead. From left to right: $p\_e = 10^{-10}$ and $ta\_len = 10^{6}$, $p\_e = 10^{-12}$ and $ta\_len = 10^{10}$, $p\_e = 10^{-15}$ and $ta\_len = 10^{12}$.

p_detn_CFC	p_detn_DFC	Criteria 1	Criteria 2	Criteria 3
0.95	0.99	0.99992	0.19	$1.851 \cdot 10^{12}$
0.95	0.999	0.99994	0.21	$1.86 \cdot 10^{12}$
0.99	0.95	0.99993	0.19	$1.855 \cdot 10^{12}$
0.99	0.99	0.99997	0.43	$1.892 \cdot 10^{12}$
0.99	0.999	0.99997	0.57	$1.9 \cdot 10^{12}$
0.999	0.95	0.99994	0.23	$1.864 \cdot 10^{12}$
0.999	0.99	0.99998	0.59	$1.901 \cdot 10^{12}$
0.999	0.999	0.99998	0.88	$1.909 \cdot 10^{12}$

Fig. 8. Decision table for $p\_e = 10^{-15}$, $ta\_len = 10^{12}$ and $max\_redos = 1$.

of aborting when not terminating correctly can be increased significantly when accepting a little more overhead. Thus, it would be worth choosing a configuration that replicates some more instructions, accepting a little more overhead, e.g., $p\_detn\_CFC = p\_detn\_DFC = 0.999$.

7   Conclusion

The purpose of the paper was to illustrate how probabilistic model checking techniques can be employed to determine parameter settings for a redo-based fault-tolerance protocol minimizing the expected overhead subject to resilience constraints. We dealt with discrete parameters that affect the topological structure of the state space (number of redos, transaction length) and continuous parameters (error detection rates). This spans a large family of protocols arising by concrete choices for the parameters. Due to the huge state spaces of these Markov chains, the direct application of standard model checking techniques for probability-parametric Markov chains was not feasible. Instead, we employed a new factorization approach that exploits the repeating phases in the models and used a combination of PPMC and computer-algebra techniques to compute and analyze the rational functions for the relevant probabilities and expectations in these Markov chains, and finally to extract an optimal parameter valuation. While the factorization technique is specific for redo protocols, we argue that the remaining steps are of exemplary character.

References

1. Kuvaiskii, D., Faqeh, R., Bhatotia, P., Felber, P., Fetzer, C.: HAFT: hardware-assisted fault tolerance. In: European Conference on Computer Systems. ACM (2016)
2. Saha, G.K.: Approaches to software based fault tolerance. Comput. Sci. J. Mold. **13**(2), 193–231 (2005)
3. Apt, K.R., Kozen, D.: Limits for automatic verification of finite-state concurrent systems. Inf. Process. Lett. **22**(6), 307–309 (1986)
4. Lanotte, R., Maggiolo-Schettini, A., Troina, A.: Parametric probabilistic transition systems for system design and analysis. Form. Asp. Comput. **19**(1), 93–109 (2007)
5. Hahn, E.M., Hermanns, H., Zhang, L.: Probabilistic reachability for parametric Markov models. Softw. Tools Technol. Transf. **13**(1), 3–19 (2011)
6. Quatmann, T., Dehnert, C., Jansen, N., Junges, S., Katoen, J.P.: Parameter synthesis for Markov models: faster than ever. In: Artho, C., Legay, A., Peled, D. (eds.) ATVA 2016. LNCS, vol. 9938, pp. 50–67. Springer, Cham (2016). https://doi.org/10.1007/978-3-319-46520-3_4
7. Sridharan, V., Liberty, D.: A study of dram failures in the field. In: High Performance Computing, Networking, Storage and Analysis, pp. 1–11, November 2012
8. Li, X., Huang, M.C., Shen, K., Chu, L.: A realistic evaluation of memory hardware errors and software system susceptibility. In: USENIX Annual Technical Conference, p. 6 (2010)
9. Sridharan, V., Stearley, J., DeBardeleben, N., Blanchard, S., Gurumurthi, S.: Feng Shui of supercomputer memory positional effects in DRAM and SRAM faults. In: 2013 SC - International Conference for High Performance Computing, Networking, Storage and Analysis (SC), pp. 1–11, November 2013
10. Cubuktepe, M., et al.: Sequential convex programming for the efficient verification of parametric MDPs. In: Legay, A., Margaria, T. (eds.) TACAS 2017. LNCS, vol. 10206, pp. 133–150. Springer, Heidelberg (2017). https://doi.org/10.1007/978-3-662-54580-5_8

11. Češka, M., Dannenberg, F., Paoletti, N., Kwiatkowska, M., Brim, L.: Precise parameter synthesis for stochastic biochemical systems. Acta Informatica **54**(6), 589–623 (2017)
12. Han, T., Katoen, J., Mereacre, A.: Approximate parameter synthesis for probabilistic time-bounded reachability. In: Proceedings of the 29th IEEE Real-Time Systems Symposium, pp. 173–182 (2008)
13. Bartocci, E., Grosu, R., Katsaros, P., Ramakrishnan, C.R., Smolka, S.A.: Model repair for probabilistic systems. In: Abdulla, P.A., Leino, K.R.M. (eds.) TACAS 2011. LNCS, vol. 6605, pp. 326–340. Springer, Heidelberg (2011). https://doi.org/10.1007/978-3-642-19835-9_30
14. Chen, T., Han, T., Kwiatkowska, M., Qu, H.: Efficient probabilistic parameter synthesis for adaptive systems. DCS, Technical report RR-13-04, p. 13 (2013)
15. Baier, C., Katoen, J.-P.: Principles of Model Checking. MIT Press, Cambridge (2008)
16. Herrmann, L., Baier, C., Fetzer, C., Klüppelholz, S., Napierkowski, M.: Formal parameter synthesis for energy-utility-optimal fault tolerance (extended version) (2018). https://wwwtcs.inf.tu-dresden.de/ALGI/PUB/EPEW18
17. Puterman, M.L.: Markov Decision Processes: Discrete Stochastic Dynamic Programming. Wiley, Hoboken (1994)
18. Baier, C., Größer, M., Ciesinski, F.: Partial order reduction for probabilistic systems. In: Quantitative Evaluation of Systems, pp. 230–239. IEEE (2004)
19. D'Argenio, P.R., Niebert, P.: Partial order reduction on concurrent probabilistic programs. In: Quantitative Evaluation of Systems, pp. 240–249. IEEE (2004)
20. Groesser, M., Baier, C.: Partial order reduction for Markov decision processes: a survey. In: de Boer, F.S., Bonsangue, M.M., Graf, S., de Roever, W.P. (eds.) FMCO 2005. LNCS, vol. 4111, pp. 408–427. Springer, Heidelberg (2006). https://doi.org/10.1007/11804192_19
21. Dehnert, C., Junges, S., Katoen, J.P., Volk, M.: A storm is coming: a modern probabilistic model checker. In: Majumdar, R., Kunčak, V. (eds.) CAV 2017. LNCS, vol. 10427, pp. 592–600. Springer, Cham (2017). https://doi.org/10.1007/978-3-319-63390-9_31
22. Meurer, A., et al.: SymPy: symbolic computing in Python. PeerJ Comput. Sci. **3**, e103 (2017)

Performance Model of Apache Cassandra Under Heterogeneous Workload Using the Quantitative Verification Approach

Al Amjad Tawfiq Isstaif[(✉)] and Nizar Alhafez

Higher Institute for Applied Sciences and Technology, Damascus, Syria
{alamjadtawfiq.isstaif,nizar.alhafez}@hiast.edu.sy

Abstract. We report our experience using PRISM, a leading quantitative verification engine, to formulate a performance model of Apache Cassandra, a popular NoSQL database, under a simple form of hybrid operational/analytical workload, since such heterogeneous workloads have shown to have significant implications for the deployment and elastic strategies of these databases. Some current literature suggest that, compared to classical performance modelling tools, quantitative verification provides a more rigorous analysis framework. We aim to explore the effectiveness and applicability of this approach in practice which we identify as relevant to our use case. We present a partial model of a single Cassandra node that predicts its maximum throughput under various system and workload parameters and validate this model experimentally. Furthermore, we show the limitations of extending this model using PRISM to address other interesting properties, identifying the need for scalable analytical modelling approaches for realistic highly concurrent systems under heterogeneous workloads.

Keywords: Probabilistic model checking · Quantitative verification
PRISM · NoSQL · Apache Cassandra · Performance analysis
Heterogeneous workload

1 Introduction

Due to their benefits in horizontal scalability, NoSQL databases are having an increasingly important role as backends of Big Data applications. With the increasing adoption of Big Data analytics applications, such databases are being extensively used for diverse transactional, analytical and hybrid workloads.

In practice, mixing analytical and transactional workloads is known to create undesired consequences on the performance of NoSQL databases [12]. In Cassandra, this has led to new deployment models that sort out hybrid workloads into isolated homogeneous workloads. Each workload is then applied to a separate replica of the database cluster, which is tuned independently in order to achieve the desired performance properties of its applied workload, avoiding any interference that may be caused by other workloads. Furthermore, there

© Springer Nature Switzerland AG 2018
R. Bakhshi et al. (Eds.): EPEW 2018, LNCS 11178, pp. 94–109, 2018.
https://doi.org/10.1007/978-3-030-02227-3_7

has been extensive research works to develop workload-aware elastic strategies for NoSQL data stores, particularly the works of [1–3]. These works show how the data access pattern and the heterogeneity of the workload have significant implications for the optimal deployment configurations of such systems in the cloud. Developing performance models that take such workload characteristics into account can lead to more effective capacity planning and autonomous management of these NoSQL databases. Our work represents an initial step in this direction with Apache Cassandra as an example.

As for the modelling approach, we consider the cloud elasticity as instance of the general class of self-adaptive systems (as presented in several works such as [7] and [8]). Among other model-based performance analysis approaches for self-adaptive systems surveyed in [4], the work in [7] utilizes the quantitative verification approach using the probabilistic model checker (PRISM). This provides a rigorous analysis approach, which has the important benefit of establishing the correctness of performance requirements of dynamic and self-adaptive systems under possible autonomous reconfiguration or environment changes. In particular, the work in [7] presents performance and reliability models developed using PRISM for a hypothetical service-based software system, where the QoS requirements of this system are specified using ProProST, a formal specification system based on probabilistic logics, that are verified against these models. The PRISM engine is then integrated into the closed monitor-analyse-plan-execute (MAPE) control loop to proactively detect any possible QoS violations and ensure adaptation plans do not result in QoS violations as well.

Nevertheless, while all the surveyed performance modelling approaches in [4] have provided proof-of-concept implementations of their target self-adaptive systems, none of these works have conducted case studies on realistic systems. To this end, our aim is to explore the usage of PRISM to develop a performance model of a realistic system that has the potential to improve elasticity decisions. A well known issue that constitutes the main limitation of this approach is the state-space explosion and large solution times [5]. Our goal is to explore to which extent it is feasible to develop analytical performance models for realistic systems using PRISM with fast solution times.

Our initial aim is to develop a full model of a single Cassandra node that detects any resource bottlenecks under a simple form of hybrid operational/analytical workload. However, representing both disk and network resources with realistic capacities leads to prohibitively large models and long solution times. Building on insights related to the system internals of Cassandra, and within restrictive assumptions, we are able to develop a continuous-time Markov chain (CTMC) partial model of a single Cassandra node, addressing how concurrent read queries of multiple types are handled by Cassandra multithreading architecture. We show by experimental validation how this model can be used to predict the performance in terms of maximum throughput of a single node under a mixed workload with various proportions of read and scan operations. While we show this model can be extended to a reasonable number of request types that could still be solved effectively by PRISM, a serious limitation prohibits its extensibility to capture more interesting behaviour of our target system. Furthermore, our experience shows that we resort to a rather simple model where the benefits of PRISM are questionable. We thus identify the need for scalable analytical modelling approaches for the QoS requirements of highly concurrent distributed systems under heterogeneous workloads.

The rest of the paper is organised as follows. Section 2 summarises related work. Section 3 describes the internals of Apache Cassandra involved in the study. Section 4 introduces the proposed model, which is subsequently validated in Sect. 5. Section 6 presents the limitations of PRISM. Finally, we present our conclusions as well as proposed future work in Sect. 7.

2   Related Work

In this section we present previous work related to (1) benchmarks of mixed workloads performed on NoSQL databases, (2) previous performance models of Apache Cassandra and finally (3) relevant work on using PRISM for performance analysis.

2.1   Benchmarks of Mixed Workloads on NoSQL

We derived our initial insights related to the behaviour of Cassandra under mixed workloads from the experiments presented in [10] and [12]. As for [10], a comprehensive performance evaluation and benchmark study has been conducted over six database systems (including Cassandra) using workloads found in Big Data analytics applications. For databases that support scan operations, analytical workloads were modeled using the Yahoo! Cloud Serving Benchmark (YCSB) [11] to construct a mixed workload consisting of read, write and scan operations. These database systems were also benchmarked against the same workloads, excluding scan operations, so that their performance would be comparable to the performance of databases that do not support scans. Comparing the maximum throughput measured with and without scans, the study shows that the maximum throughput of these systems decreases significantly. This insight remains true irrespective of the cluster size, as the benchmarks were performed on various number of nodes, and the linear scalability has been confirmed for Cassandra in most of the tests.

The negative effect of mixing scan operations has also been confirmed in a public benchmark of NoSQL databases [12], where several YCSB workloads were applied to various cluster sizes of Cassandra. These workloads included standard YCSB workloads alongside a customized workload representing mixed operational/analytical workload (60% read, 25% update, 10% insert, and 5% scan). In this study, the Cassandra throughput decreased from over 300,000 operations per second under balanced read and write workload, to less than 130,000 operations per second under this mixed workload. Again, these insights remain true irrespective of the cluster size. We think this is due to the fact that clusters in both [10] and [12] have been configured with no replication factor. Furthermore, nodes under all cluster sizes were filled so that they will have the same amount of data.

2.2 Performance Models of Apache Cassandra

To the best of our knowledge, the research work which has been conducted on performance modelling of NoSQL databases is limited, and the available models specific to Cassandra are all based on the simulative approach applied under normal transactional workloads [13–15]. Our work is different from all the previous works in focusing on considering a simple heterogeneous workload that includes the scan operation, which generally represents the analytical component of a workload, alongside normal read operations on a single node database. Furthemore, it takes into account the effect of the variation in the proportion of scan operations on the maximum throughput that could be served by the node. However, because of the limitations of developing workable solutions using PRISM (reported later in Sect. 6), we are not able to extend our approach to predict end-to-end latencies of the requests as in these works.

The work presented in this paper is also different at the abstraction level. Previous models of Cassandra focus on modelling the latencies of the requests as they travel through the computing resources of CPU, network and disk. In this work, however, we leverage the insights related to the internals of Cassandra multithreading architecture based on the Staged Event-Driven Architecture (SEDA). In this architecture, the request life-cycle is broken into several stages, and the read and write operations have different system paths. This enables us to develop a partial model of the single stage of reading data from disks, considering how scan and read operations compete for the same resource excluding the effect of write operations.

Furthermore, we focus only on modelling a single node Cassandra system. The general behaviour of read and scan operations in the cluster is directly related to the replication factor and consistency levels which have been thoroughly modelled and studied in [13]. We think that the study of scan queries found in analytical workloads applied on a cluster should be the subject of a future work that builds on our present work and on [13].

2.3 Performance Analysis Using PRISM

The work in [5] explains the usage of PRISM in performance and reliability analysis, where PRISM can be used to represent continuous-time Markov chains (CTMCs) and Markov reward models. Furthermore, the works in [6] and [9] have shown the applicability of probabilistic model checking to formulate queuing network based models with several layers of existing models in the literature and the advantage of this approach compared to classical performance modelling tools. Our work could be considered as a further contribution to define the limitations of using PRISM to model the performance of realistic case studies. In particular, we consider the effect of incorporating multiple request types and realistic queue sizes. Another relevant case study is [8], where PRISM is used to model dependable and cost-aware horizontal scaling decision making for NoSQL databases applied to Cassandra. The focus of [8] is on transient-analysis of performance during the scale-up and scale-down events of the NoSQL cluster using a Markov Decision Process (MDP) in order to provide performance guarantees regarding latency violations for various elastic policies. In contrast, this work focuses on steady-state analysis of the node under different sets of workload and system parameters using a CTMC-based model.

3   Cassandra Internals

In this section, we present a brief overview of system internals of a single Cassandra node related to our use case. Firstly, we outline how local read and write requests follow different paths in the system, showing how write operations resort to extremely fast sequential disk writes that do not directly interfere with generally disk-bound read operations. We then illustrate Cassandraś internal multithreading architecture based on SEDA. We show, in particular, how this architecture handles requests and background operations as a collection of explicitly defined stages, each with a separate thread pool, which helps to avoid congestion in a particular resource.

3.1   Read and Write Paths

Among other NoSQL databases, Cassandra is known to be capable of handling write-heavy workloads thanks to its in-memory writes where their durability is ensured by a persistent write-ahead commit log. Writes are initially handled by an in-memory structure called **Memtable** which is periodically flushed into disk in the form of a persistant structure called **SSTable**. An SSTable (Sorted Strings Table) is an immutable structure, so new data elements are added as new SSTables that are periodically merged and compacted in order to reduce read access time. To ensure that writes do not directly affect the performance of reads, separate disks are used for storing both SSTables and the commit log. Data written to the commit log remain there until the Memtable is flushed into disk. These background operations of flushing data from memory to disk and compacting SSTables might affect the performance of read operations in write-heavy workloads. In such cases, the compaction operations could be throttled so their effect would only consume a limited proportion of available disk bandwidth. However, this has no effect on the performance of write operations. This is due to the fact that clients of write requests do not need to wait the data to be fully written in data directory as writes can be acknowledged once written to the commit log. As a result, write operations resort to extremely fast sequential disk writes and thus are considered to be CPU-bound.

On the contrary, read operations include random access disk reads hitting several SSTables until finding the appropriate records, so they are considered disk-bound operations. Various forms of in-memory caching are used to accelerate read operations. Furthermore, the virtual file system cache is used to store chunks of these SSTables. If the size of data stored on the node fits in the RAM, all read operations can be served from memory. Only in such a case, both read and write operations would be considered to be CPU-bound.

3.2 Internal Multithreading Architecture

Operations of Cassandra are handled by several thread pools organized based on a Staged Event-Driven Architecture (SEDA). In this architecture, the lifecycle of request is broken down into various stages. A dedicated thread pool exists for each stage, making one thread responsible for only a single stage of the request lifecycle. By the end of each stage, a thread submits its work to available threads in the next stage. If all threads are busy, the job is submitted to a message queue instead. Once a thread is available, it fetches any waiting jobs from its message queue. If there is no room at the message queue, the requester is blocked until a room exists.

In Cassandra, there are three types of stages: `request`, `transport` and `internal`. Stages under the `request` type are dedicated to directly handle incoming requests, most notably are the `ReadStage` and `MutationStage` for local read and write operations respectively. Stages of the `internal` type include background operations such as SSTable compaction and flushing Memtables to disk. The `transport` type includes the single `Native-Transport-Requests` stage, which is used to handle network requests and responses for native clients sending Cassandra Query Language (CQL) queries. Two threads are used for each request: one for sending and another for receiving.

Both inserts and updates are handled by the `MutationStage`. Similarly, both read and scan operations are performed during the `ReadStage`. However, scan operations are constructed as range queries which are handled differently than normal ones. Thus, unlike reads, scans take considerably longer times in order to collect all the matching number of records. The maximum thread pool sizes of both `ReadStage` and `MutationStage` default to 32 concurrent threads. However, this defaults to 128 threads in the case of the `Native-Transport-Requests` stage.

4 Cassandra Model

In this section, we firstly summarize the assumptions behind our model. Secondly, we present a two-dimensional birth-death CTMC model both in mathematical formulation and in using PRISM. Then, we illustrate our methodology to parameterize our model. Finally, we report how we use the PRISM experiments feature to predict the maximum throughput of a single node under various proportions of read and scan operations.

4.1 Model Assumptions

We focus in our work on modelling the `ReadStage` thread pool under a mix of read and scan operations in a single Cassandra node system. Scans are considered to be a special type of read operations because they are handled by the same `ReadStage` thread pool. While multiple threads would be running concurrently, we assume this can be modeled as a finite-capacity queuing station with a single server and a capacity size corresponding to a thread pool size of 32 concurrent threads. We assume that scan operations need longer time to be serviced by the server, and so a decreased throughput is observed under mixed workloads. Furthermore, we assume independent Poisson for request arrivals, and exponential distribution for all service times.

We exclude the effect of write operations handled by the `MutationStage` thread pool which we will argue that is safe in most cases. We assume read-mostly workloads where background operations triggered by write operations have insignificant effect on read operations. We have shown in Sect. 3 that write operations can affect the performance of read operations only in two main cases: firstly under write-heavy workloads where flushing and compaction operations start to significantly consume disk bandwidth, and secondly when read workloads start to become CPU-bound where data can fit entirely in memory.

Before and after retrieving data from disk, network transfers are handled by the `Native-Transport-Requests` thread pool which has a default size of the maximum of 128 concurrent threads. This would be naturally modeled as another finite-capacity queuing station that submits and retrieves jobs from the queuing station corresponding to the `ReadStage`. However, due to the limitations we will report in Sect. 6, we are unable to include these two queuing stations in the same model as this combination would generate a prohibitively large model.

Excluding network transfer time makes it impossible to compute the end-to-end latencies of requests. However, assuming a large network bandwidth, it becomes safe to assume read and scan workloads are disk rather than network bound. Thus, assuming we have the general case of disk-bound workloads, this makes the `ReadStage` model useful to estimate the number of system active jobs under various target throughputs. Furthermore, it allows us to estimate the queuing station refusal ratio which, as we show, can be used to predict the maximum throughput under a certain proportion of read and scan operations.

4.2 Mathematical Formulation

In this section, we present the mathematical formulation of the limited-capacity queuing station model, corresponding to the `ReadStage` thread pool. As we explained in detail in the previous section, read requests would correspond to threads submitted to this queue with jobs waiting to be served in a first-come-first-served (FCFS) fashion. Both read and scan requests would be submitted to the same queue. These two request types would have different service rates related to the average time needed to fetch data from disk for each request type.

Our mathematical formulation is built upon the birth-death Markov process, which is a well-known analytical equivalent of a queuing station. In this formulation, a single state variable represents the number of waiting jobs in the queue and a continuous-time Markov chain (CTMC) is used to model how often the value of this variable changes as jobs arrive and leave the system. We extend this formulation by suggesting a two-dimensional birth-death process to model the state of two variables representing the number of current requests of each of the two types currently held by the queue (illustrated in Fig. 1). The sum of these two variables at any time should represent the total number of requests which should not exceed the maximum allowed number of threads in the thread pool stage. In this extended model we would have to consider two types of rates describing (1) arrival rates of both read and scan operations and (2) service rates of both read and scan operations. The first group of parameters represents the properties of the workload while the other represents the behaviour of the system under a specific configuration as we will elaborate in Sect. 4.4.

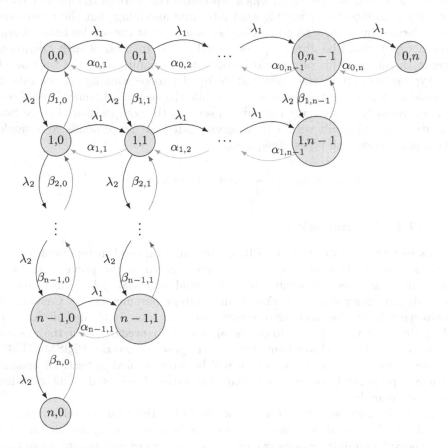

Fig. 1. The two-dimensional CTMC-based mathematical formulation of the ReadStage thread pool holding active read and scan jobs concurrently.

Each type of request has its own arrival rate, λ_1 and λ_2. Assuming that inter-arrivals follow an exponential distribution, the total arrival rate of requests, λ, would correspond to the sum of these two rates $\lambda = \lambda_1 + \lambda_2$. Furthermore, assuming p_{read} and p_{scan} are the proportions of each of the read and scan operations in the workload respectively, the arrival rates of each request type can be derived from λ as follows: $\lambda_1 = p_{read} * \lambda$ and $\lambda_2 = p_{scan} * \lambda$.

For each of the read and scan operations, we would have two service rates: $\alpha_{i,j}$ and $\beta_{i,j}$ respectively. Unlike arrival rates, these would vary according to the current state of the queue and thus are parameterized by indexes accordingly. In the two extreme cases of read-only or scan-only workloads, the values of these rates would not depend on the current state of the queue featuring the constant values of μ_1 and μ_2 which correspond to the maximum service rate of each request type under the condition of being served alone. Thus, $\alpha_{0,j} = \mu_1$ and $\beta_{i,0} = \mu_2$. In the general case of a state (i, j), which represents the state of the queue having i waiting scan jobs and j waiting read jobs, and assuming that these requests are performed by a single server, we further assume that the service time (of any request type) would be directly proportional to the fraction of each operation type in the queue. This rate would be obtained by multiplying the fraction of this type of request at the current state by the corresponding service rate if it would be served alone on this server. While the backward transitions of $\alpha_{i,j}$ and $\beta_{i,j}$ would typically represent parallel service, the composition of these two transitions would result with a total service rate that corresponds to a single server processing both types of requests:

$$\alpha_{i,j} = \mu_1 * \frac{j}{i+j} \quad \text{and} \quad \beta_{i,j} = \mu_2 * \frac{i}{i+j} \tag{1}$$

4.3   PRISM Formulation

In this section, we introduce the PRISM formulation used in representing the previous mathematical structure. As we have shown in the previous section, our main interest is the number of active read and scan jobs, which are to be predicted under certain workload and system parameters. As Cassandras´ architecture limits the number of concurrent read jobs (explained in Sect. 3), calculating this value in the long run allows us to predict when the system reaches its maximum throughput. For this purpose we use the PRISM CTMC module to represent our model, which will be later verified in Sect. 4.5 against a PRISM property in order to calculate the ratio of accepted requests using steady-state analysis.

The PRISM model is composed of two modules: the `jobs` module for generating the workload and the `read_stage` module for representing the queuing station. The `jobs` module includes two events: `accept_read` and `accept_scan` that are triggered unconditionally according to the overall arrival rate of requests. Each request type is generated according to a rate directly proportional to its share in the workload. The module is illustrated in Listing 1.1.

```
module jobs
  [accept_read] true -> lambda * read_proportion: true ;
  [accept_scan] true -> lambda * scan_proportion: true ;
endmodule
```

Listing 1.1. jobs module

In Listing 1.2, we show the **read_stage** module which holds the variables **active_read** and **active_scan**, representing the active number of read and scan jobs currently waiting in the queue respectively.

```
formula read_stage_active = active_read +    active_scan ;
module read_stage
   active_read: [0..capacity] init 0;
   active_scan: [0..capacity] init 0;
   [accept_read] read_stage < capacity -> active_read' =
       active_read+1;
   [accept_scan] read_stage < capacity -> active_scan' =
       active_scan+1;
   [process_read] active_read > 0 ->   read_rate *
       (active_read/read_stage): (active_read' =
       active_read-1);
   [process_scan] active_scan > 0 ->   scan_rate *
       (active_scan/read_stage): (active_scan' =
       active_scan-1);
endmodule
```

Listing 1.2. read_stage module

The Listing 1.2 shows the various events handled by the **read_stage** module. The first two events are triggered in synchronization with the corresponding **accept_scan** and **accept_read** events of the **jobs** module, representing the action of accepting the incoming requests as long as the maximum capacity (configured to be a constant value, 32) has not been reached. The current capacity is represented by the **read_stage_active** formula which returns the sum of active jobs in the system of both types at any time. Processing these active jobs is represented by the collection of **processed_read** and **processed_scan** events. These events are triggered as long as there are active jobs in the system waiting to be processed, according to the rates in Eqs. (1) and (2) illustrated in the previous section.

4.4 Model Parameterization

In this section we present our methodology to obtain the group of parameters related to system configuration and state: the service rates of read and scan operations which correspond to the **read_rate** and **scan_rate** variables in the PRISM formulation and μ_1 and μ_2 in the mathematical formulation.

These two rates represent the hard disk service rates of both read and scan operations under a specific system configuration. This configuration can be either normal configuration or an optimized configuration for a specific workload type. In our experiments, we examine the service rates of read and scan operations under normal system configuration, taking into account the following two factors: (1) the scan length and (2) the total number of records currently held at the node. The scan length factor corresponds to the number of records that need to be obtained to match the scan operation. We examine the two constant scan

Table 1. A summary of measured disk service rates (operations per second)

Number of records	Reads	Normal scans	Aggressive scans
1 million record	23294	2172	225
8 million record	312	92	30
16 million record	235	110	40

lengths, 100 records (normal scans) and 1000 records (aggressive scans). The total number of records factor corresponds to the total size of records currently held by the database. We examine three different data sizes: firstly, the case when the entire data can fit into memory (1 million records), and secondly when data is served mostly from disk (8 and 16 million records). Table 1 illustrates the measured service rates (as operations per second) under the described scenarios.

In order to measure these rates, a single node would be stressed by workload of a single request type under the target system state, and the maximum reported throughput would be considered as the service rate of this request type. To ensure these rates represent truly the disk service rates, we need to ensure that the applied workloads are not network bound. We achieve this by monitoring network bandwidth (using standard Linux monitoring tools) during the period of the tests, ensuring it does not reach the maximum network bandwidth between the client and the server which could be measured using `iperf` tool.

Using the YCSB benchmark with the default parameters used in the standard Workload E (a YCSB workload where ranges of records are queried), we generate these workloads by modifying the proportion of operations so that scan or read operations would be %100. Before each stress test, the node is loaded with the required number of records. The default size for each record is 1KB. We also set value of the `maxscanlength` property to specify the number of records to be scanned by a single scan operation, according to a constant distribution (specified by the `scanlengthdistribution`). We then record the average throughput values as recorded by YCSB at the end of each stress test. Each experiment is run on the real system for a period of 30 min to ensure the recorded values represent stable system behaviour.

4.5   PRISM Experiments to Predict Maximum Throughput

In this section, we use a PRISM property to represent the ratio of accepted requests of the `read_stage` queuing station in order to predict the maximum throughput of a single node in the long run under certain workload parameters and system configuration and state. This ratio can be calculated using the following PRISM property, which corresponds to the steady-state probability of the `read_stage` having at least one free room for an incoming request:

S=? [(read_stage < capacity)]

Furthermore, this property can also be used to specify the requirement for having no dropped requests by providing a threshold value for the acceptance ratio. The verification of this property would return true if the expected value of this property in the steady state is over 0.99. As we will show experimentally in the next section, we consider the 0.99 ratio as a good approximation of the behaviour of the system, since requests, that could not be handled by thread pools of Cassandra, are not actually dropped but are instead saved in the message queue of the thread pool waiting for the system to handle them:

S>0.99 [(read_stage < capacity)]

To predict the maximum throughput, we perform PRISM experiments verifying our model against the previous property over a range of arrival rates, lambda, using appropriate step sizes, until we reach the arrival rate value where the property does not hold. We calculate the maximum throughputs considering major changes in read and scan proportions in the workload, increasing the read proportion with %25 steps (and decreasing the scan proportion accordingly). Thus we examine the workloads with the following read proportions: %25 (scan-mostly), %50 (balanced), %75 (read-mostly). These workloads are examined alongside the considered factors of scan length and data size, described earlier in Sect. 4.4. Figure 2 shows the results of these experiments plotted alongside real measurements obtained from the experimental setup, which we will describe in Sect. 5.

5   Experimental Evaluation

To validate the results of our model, we setup a single node Cassandra on a bare metal server and install the YCSB workload generator on another bare metal server. Both servers have 2 CPU cores and 8 GBs of memory. Cassandra server has a 1TB SSD hard disk which is used solely for the storage of data while the commit log is configured on another disk, which is considered the best practice to avoid any interference between normal workloads and recent data written on the commit log. The operating system is Ubuntu 16.04 with Sun Java 1.8 and Cassandra version 3.1.

To validate the maximum throughput of the workloads and system parameters described in the previous section, the YCSB workload generator is used to load the database with the corresponding data size. Then the node is stressed repeatedly, each time by a new workload; with the two types of scan operations (normal and aggressive) and with the %25 variation in scan proportion described in the previous section. In order to stress the node, the workload is run with different increasing number of target throughputs (using the -target option) until no further increase is possible. The results of these experiments are recorded in Fig. 2 and plotted alongside the values obtained from the corresponding PRISM models. Except for the 16 million record under aggressive scans where we have very low maximum throughput values, comparing the results obtained from the real system and from our PRISM model, we notice that our model is sensitive to

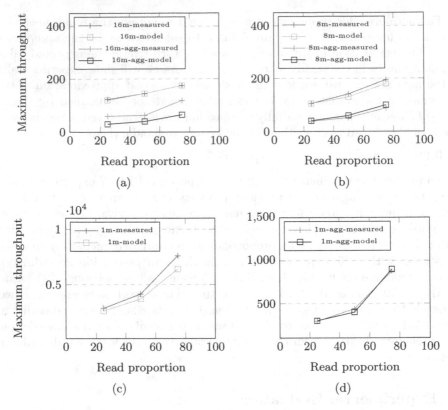

Fig. 2. A set of four plots describing the maximum throughputs of a single Cassandra node both as measured experimentally and as obtained from the PRISM model, under various proportions of read operations. (a) and (b) describes the maximum throughputs under 16 and 8 million records both under normal and aggressive scans; while (c) and (d) describe the maximum throughputs under 1 million record separating normal and aggressive scans in two plots.

all major changes in the ratio of scan operations under all experimented system states. Average relative errors range from 6% to 12%.

6   PRISM Limitations

In this section, we point out the limitations we have encountered during our attempts to develop useful performance models that can be solved by PRISM effectively. As mentioned in Sect. 4.1, extending our model with an additional queuing station to consider network transfer results in a model that could not be solved by PRISM. The limitation is mainly due to the relatively large size of the queue representing the `Native-Transport-Requests` thread pool (128 threads). Referring to the details presented in Sect. 4.3, the two variables `active_read` and `active_scan` have a defined integer range, namely 0 to 32, corresponding to the maximum size for this thread pool which directly affects the number of states in the model. Following a similar approach to represent the `Native-Transport-Requests` thread pool, this yields four additional variables which represent both read and scan network requests as well as network responses: `active_read_req`, `active_scan_req`, `active_read_res` and `active_scan_res`. These variables are necessary to represent receiving network requests and submitting them to the `ReadStage` before being submitted back to the network stage as network responses. As shown in Table 2, adding all these variables to a single model results in a prohibitively large state space which could not be solved under any of PRISM solution engines. Providing a much lower and unrealistic size of maximum threads for the `Native-Transport-Requests`, namely 32, the state space persists to be too large to have a fast solution time. Excluding variables related to network requests (assuming that request size is negligible), the model size is reduced considerably. However, this still results with an impractical solution time of several minutes. Limiting the model to the `ReadStage`, we are able to extend the it to include up to 4 request types with reasonable solution time.

Table 2. Comparison of model sizes (number of states) and fastest solution times (seconds) for various extensions of our PRISM model. Solution times were obtained using the JOR (Jacobi with over-relaxation) numerical method.

Model	Used variables with ranges	State space size	Solution time
ReadStage only	active_read (32), active_scan (32)	561	0.02
ReadStage with network transfer (realistic queue sizes)	active_read (32), active_scan (32), active_read_req (128), active_scan_req (128), active_read_res (128), active_scan_res (128)	6,778,438,128	n/a
ReadStage with network transfer (unrealistic queue sizes)	active_read (32), active_scan (32), active_read_req (32), active_scan_req (32), active_read_res (32), active_scan_res (32)	33,044,616	416.249
ReadStage with network responses only	active_read (32), active_scan (32), active_read_res (128), active_scan_res (128)	4,703,985	328.457
ReadStage only (4 request types)	active_read (32), active_scan[1,3] (32)	58,905	0.924
ReadStage only (6 request types)	active_read (32), active_scan[1,5] (32)	2,760,681	19.732

7   Conclusions and Future Work

In this paper, we have investigated the limitations of the PRISM model checker in the performance analysis of a realistic system. While PRISM formalism has shown to be very useful to rigorously define an accurate analytical performance model for our use case, our experience shows that having multiple request types alongside multiple layers of queuing stations with realistic queue sizes produces models with prohibitively large state space and long solutions times. We showed how we had addressed this problem by identifying and modelling a sub-component of the target systems that is still useful to capture high-level system behaviour. However, our work shows the limitations of using PRISM to solve analytical models of realistic highly concurrent distributed systems under heterogeneous workloads. We aim, in future work, to further analyze the performance of realistic big data workloads over cluster configuration of Cassandra, and to identify appropriate modelling approaches to provide performance guarantees for workload-aware auto-scaling strategies of NoSQL databases.

References

1. Cruz, F., et al.: MeT: workload aware elasticity for NoSQL. In: Proceedings of the 8th European Conference on Computer Systems - EuroSys, pp. 183–196 (2013)
2. Kassela, E., Boumpouka, C., Konstantinou, I., Koziris, N.: Automated workload-aware elasticity of NoSQL clusters in the cloud. In: 2014 IEEE International Conference on Big Data (Big Data) (2014). https://doi.org/10.1109/bigdata.2014.7004232
3. Anwar, A., Cheng, Y., Gupta, A., Butt, A.R.: MOS: workload-aware elasticity for cloud object stores. In: Proceedings of the 25th ACM International Symposium on High-Performance Parallel and Distributed Computing, pp. 177–188 (2016)
4. Becker, M., Luckey, M., Becker, S.: Model-driven performance engineering of self-adaptive systems: a survey. In: Proceedings of the 8th international ACM SIGSOFT Conference on Quality of Software Architectures, QoSA 2012, pp. 117–122 (2012)
5. Kwiatkowska, M., Norman, G., Parker, D.: PRISM: probabilistic model checking for performance and reliability analysis. ACM SIGMETRICS Perform. Eval. Rev. **36**, 40–45 (2009)
6. Berczes, T., Guta, G., Kusper, G., Schreiner, W., Sztrik, J.: Comparing the performance modeling environment MOSEL and the probabilistic model checker PRISM for modeling and analyzing retrial queueing systems. Technical report no 07–17 in RISC Report Series, Research Institute for Symbolic Computation (RISC), Johannes Kepler University Linz, Austria (2007)
7. Calinescu, R., Grunske, L., Kwiatkowska, M., Mirandola, R., Tamburrelli, G.: Dynamic QoS management and optimization in service-based systems. IEEE Trans. Softw. Eng. **37**, 387–409 (2011)
8. Naskos, A., Gounaris, A., Katsaros, P.: Cost-aware horizontal scaling of NoSQL databases using probabilistic model checking. Cluster Comput. **20**, 2687–2701 (2017)
9. Bérczes T., Guta, G., Kusper, G., Schreiner, W., Sztrik, J.: Analyzing a proxy cache server performance model with the probabilistic model checker PRISM. In: Automated Specification and Verification of Web Systems (2009)
10. Rabl, T., Gómez-Villamor, S., Sadoghi, M., Muntés-Mulero, V., Jacobsen, H.-A., Mankovskii, S.: Solving big data challenges for enterprise application performance management. Proc. VLDB Endow. **5**, 1724–1735 (2012)

11. Cooper, B.F., Silberstein, A., Tam, E., Ramakrishnan, R., Sears, R.: Benchmarking cloud serving systems with YCSB. In: Proceedings of the 1st ACM Symposium on Cloud Computing - SoCC 2010 (2010). https://doi.org/10.1145/1807128.1807152
12. Benchmarking Top NoSQL Databases: Apache Cassandra, Couchbase, HBase, and MongoDB [Internet]. End Point Corporation, 2015 April. https://www.datastax.com/wp-content/themes/datastax-2014-08/files/NoSQL_Benchmarks_EndPoint.pdf
13. Dipietro, S., Casale, G., Serazzi, G.: A queueing network model for performance prediction of Apache Cassandra. In: Proceedings of the 10th EAI International Conference on Performance Evaluation Methodologies and Tools (2017). https://doi.org/10.4108/eai.25-10-2016.2266606
14. Gandini, A., Gribaudo, M., Knottenbelt, W.J., Osman, R., Piazzolla, P.: Performance evaluation of NoSQL databases. In: Horváth, A., Wolter, K. (eds.) EPEW 2014. LNCS, vol. 8721, pp. 16–29. Springer, Cham (2014). https://doi.org/10.1007/978-3-319-10885-8_2
15. Huang, X., Wang, J., Qiao, J., Zheng, L., Zhang, J., Wong, R.K.: Performance and replica consistency simulation for quorum-based NoSQL system Cassandra. In: van der Aalst, W., Best, E. (eds.) PETRI NETS 2017. LNCS, vol. 10258, pp. 78–98. Springer, Cham (2017). https://doi.org/10.1007/978-3-319-57861-3_6

Modelling Smart Buildings Using Fault Maintenance Trees

Alessandro Abate[2], Carlos E. Budde[1(✉)], Nathalie Cauchi[2],
Arnaud van Harmelen[1], Khaza Anuarul Hoque[4], and Mariëlle Stoelinga[1,3]

[1] Formal Methods and Tools Group, University of Twente,
Enschede, The Netherlands
{c.e.budde,a.vanharmelen,m.i.a.stoelinga}@utwente.nl
[2] Department of Computer Science, University of Oxford, Oxford, UK
{alessandro.abate,nathalie.cauchi}@cs.ox.ac.uk
[3] Department of Software Science, Radboud University, Nijmegen, The Netherlands
[4] Department of Electrical Engineering and Computer Science,
University of Missouri, Columbia, USA
hoquek@missouri.edu

Abstract. Increasingly many industrial spheres are enforced by law
to satisfy strict RAMS requirements—reliability, availability, maintain-
ability, and safety. Applied to Fault Maintenance Trees (FMTs), formal methods offer flexible and trustworthy techniques to quantify the
resilience of (abstract models of) systems. However, the estimated metrics are relevant only as far as the model reflects the actual system:
Refining an abstract model to reduce the gap with reality is crucial for
the usefulness of the results. In this work, we take a practical approach
at the challenge by studying a Heating, Ventilation and Air-Conditioning
unit (HVAC), ubiquitous in smart buildings. Using probabilistic and statistical model checking, we assess RAMS metrics of a basic fault maintenance tree HVAC model. We then implement four modifications aug-
menting the expressivity of the FMT model, and show that reliability,
availability, expected number of failures, and costs, can vary by orders
of magnitude depending on involved modelling details.

Keywords: Fault maintenance trees · Reliability · Availability
Maintenance · Model checking · PMC · SMC · Smart buildings · HVAC

1 Introduction

The current rapid momentum in the number of available sensing devices and
the advances in communication technologies has resulted in a growing interest
towards making things "smart." This shift has not escaped the building sector,
where engineers and researchers are working towards a new type of building
termed *smart buildings*. These are equipped with sensors to deliver services that
are cost effective, compliant with RAMS—reliability, availability, maintainabil-
ity, and safety—requirements, ubiquitous, and ensuring occupant comfort and

© Springer Nature Switzerland AG 2018
R. Bakhshi et al. (Eds.): EPEW 2018, LNCS 11178, pp. 110–125, 2018.
https://doi.org/10.1007/978-3-030-02227-3_8

productivity, e.g. proper temperature and high air quality. A key element is the correct application of timely and cost-effective maintenance: Comfort and correct building operation, i.e. reliable and dependable, can be maintained only as long as the components are available and operating with sufficient performance.

In this work we focus on the Heating, Ventilation and Air-Conditioning unit (HVAC) of a smart building, whose optimised operation is essential for the correct running of the premises. Early fault detection and maintenance can improve the lifespan and reliability of an HVAC. In the literature, maintenance can be optimised following different methods—see e.g. [17]. *Fault maintenance trees* (FMT, [19]) are a novel technique to model and analyse systems, which allow planning maintenance strategies to balance costs and system (failure) resilience. FMTs extend dynamic fault trees (DFT, [11]) encompassing degradation and maintenance concepts. Degradation modelling represents component health decay via elemental modules known as Extended Basic Events. Maintenance modelling incorporates different maintenance concepts like inspections, repairs, and replacements. Typically, FMT analysis is performed via statistical model checking (SMC, [19]). Analysing (smart buildings using) FMTs via probabilistic model checking (PMC) was introduced in [5]. In that work, component degradation of an HVAC is discretised in time using phases, with a stepwise degradation behaviour approximated via Erlang distributions, and using inspection and repair modules to regulate maintenance actions.

Standing on the FMT model framework introduced in [5], in the following sections we present a sequence of modelling setups which extend the central case study of that work. We enhance the modelling and analysis of the HVAC FMT by adding realistic flavours, to attune the maintenance policies towards their application in the real world. To that aim, we first perform an encoding of the FMT in terms of continuous-time Markov chains and priced time automata, which we then respectively analyse using PMC and SMC. For each technique we highlight the trade-offs and limitations encountered. From that basis, we extend the FMT model in four stages: First, we individualise maintenance actions and make a clear distinction between *cleans* and *repairs*. Second, we drop the Erlang approximation of time periods in lieu of *truly deterministic intervals*. Third, we model component redundancy by introducing *spare gates* for some elements of the HVAC. Fourth and last, we refine the degradation of some extended basic events to follow a *continuous stochastic (generalised) behaviour*.

We use both PMC and SMC to analyse the first two modelling setups, i.e. the basic setting and the first extension; for all other extensions we use only SMC. PMC explores all states of the model (relevant for the current property query) and does not need statistical bounds to decide convergence. In contrast, SMC uses statistical theory to infer conclusions with arbitrary levels of confidence and precision. On each stage we demonstrate the implications and the resulting modifications needed for analysing system reliability, availability, expected number of failures, and the total costs. We also delineate the impact on these key performance indicators w.r.t. the previous models.

This article has the following structure: Sect. 2 presents the fundamental theoretical basis; Sect. 3 introduces the central case study, an HVAC unit, where the root HVAC model inspired in [5] is presented in Sect. 3.1; The four modelling extensions are introduced and analysed in Sects. 3.2, 3.3, 3.4 and 3.5; Sect. 4 concludes this work and outlines possible tracks of future research.

2   Preliminaries

Fault Maintenance Trees. *Fault trees* are directed acyclic graphs describing combinations of failures in system components, that can lead to a system failure or *Top Level Event* (TLE) at the root of the tree [21]. The leaves in fault trees are *basic events* which denote atomic component failures, typically following the exponential distribution. The internal nodes or *gates* describe how failures in basic events and lower level gates interact, as they propagate towards the TLE. The internal events are labelled as *intermediate events* (IE). Each gate models a different interaction: to propagate a failure, AND gates require all children to fail, OR gates require any child to fail, etc. [20]. In standard fault trees a closed-form solution exists for many RAMS metrics, provided the exact distributions of the basic events are known. *Dynamic fault trees* introduce gates with time- or order-dependent behaviour for which this is no longer true [22]. For instance, the children in priority-AND gates are ordered, and the gate fails if all children fail from left to right. Other than FMTs, there seems to be relatively scarce literature on DFTs that support component health decay combined with preventive maintenance, e.g. acting *before component failure* [20]. In [13] a tool is presented to compute RAMS metrics from DFTs in the presence of a maintenance policy. FMTs offer a formalism for this: They are a superset of DFTs which can model and assess various maintenance concepts [19]. Extensions over DFTs include:

- *Extended Basic Events* (EBEs): basic events whose failures follow an Erlang distribution. Its stepwise degradation allows identifying light decay, allowing restorations before an actual failure (that may trigger a TLE) occurs;
- *Repair Modules* (RM): perform periodic checks that can trigger maintenance actions. This encompasses with the phased degradation of EBEs, allowing early detection of degradation and potentially cheaper maintenance, as opposed to repair boxes that can repair a component only after it has failed.

Metrics. To measure compliance with RAMS requirements, it is common to set a time horizon $T > 0$ and quantify failures in the time window $[0, T]$. Maintenance is also a cost-driven concept, hence the operational and maintenance costs incurred within the time window provide further insight on how well the system is performing. The following *Key Performance Indicators* (KPIs) are commonly used to assess system resilience in the presence of maintenance actions:

– *Reliability* at time T is the probability of not observing a system failure, i.e. a TLE, in the time window $[0, T]$;
– *Availability* at time T is the proportion of time that the system is not failed in the time window $[0, T]$;
– *Expected number of failures* (ENF) at time T is the expected number of times a TLE is observed in the time window $[0, T]$;
– *Expected cost* at time T is the total expected cost incurred in the time window, including operational and maintenance costs (such as costs associated with system inspections and repair of components).

Modelling and Analysis of FMTs. FMTs can be given semantics via Bayesian networks, generalised stochastic Petri nets, etc. [14]. We use continuous-time Markov chains (CTMC) and priced time automata (PTA): two widely extended modelling formalisms with rich tool support, whose expressiveness meets our modelling requirements. For these semantics, the KPIs of interest can be quantified via *quantitative model checking* [7], a well-established formal verification technique used to verify the correctness of finite-state automata. Model checking algorithms take as input (i) a formal model of the system, usually some type of labelled automaton, and (ii) the property queries to verify, usually expressed in terms of a temporal logic. To check whether the model satisfies a property, the algorithms explore exhaustively and automatically all (reachable) states. Quantitative model checking is a broad field that comes in different flavours [8]. In particular we use two (complementary) techniques to analyse our models:

– *Probabilistic model checking* (PMC, [15]) performs a state space analysis in probabilistic (finite) state automata. These are usually state transition models like CTMC, with probability as transitions rates and labels on the transitions and the states. A *probabilistic model checker* computes the probabilities of reaching certain states, or the expected reward over a time horizon.
– *Statistical model checking* (SMC, [24]) samples finitely many runs of "model behaviour," typically execution traces, and uses statistical analysis to estimate an answer to the query from such (random) sample, where the probability of converging to an incorrect answer can be arbitrarily bounded.

Thus, using PMC/SMC one can analyse e.g. CTMC/PTA models of an FMT, computing (approximate) values for the relevant KPIs, which serve to assess the resilience and RAMS compliance of the modelled system.

3 Fault Maintenance Tree Model of an HVAC System

This work is centred around a Heating, Ventilation and Air-Conditioning unit (HVAC) that regulates the internal environment in smart buildings. HVACs offer a decomposition in subsystems fitting nicely the FMT approach. The concrete model studied is taken from [5]: Fig. 1 shows a visual description of the setup.

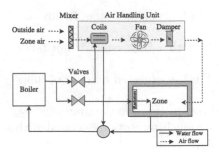

Fig. 1. HVAC system schematic [5].

The HVAC is divided in two circuits, one for air and the other for water flow. Two valves in the water circuit, one for the supply air heating coil and one for the radiators, control the water flow rate. A boiler heats up the supply water, which is then transferred into the heating coil and the radiators. The radiators transfer the water heat directly into the room (or *zone*). The return water goes through the collector back towards the boiler. In the air circuit, the mixer blends outside air with zone air. This goes to the heating coil to warm it up to the desired temperature. The air is then sent back into the zone via the supply fan, at a rate controlled by the Air Handling Unit dampers (AHU).

In smart buildings, comfort and running costs depend heavily on the proper functioning of the HVAC unit. Moreover, these are complex machines that can fail in various ways, and repairs can be quite costly. The trade-off between system performance and maintenance costs offers a rich scenario to model with FMTs, and to analyse with model checking in order to estimate relevant KPI metrics.

The degree of confidence in, and utility of, the computed metrics is a function of the realism of the underlying model. With that motivation, the next sections present five (incremental) versions of the HVAC, using FMT models to measure KPIs. We start from the basic case in Sect. 3.1, which mainly corresponds to the model presented in [5]. In Sect. 3.2 we enhance the model by refining the maintenance actions. In those two setups deterministic time delays are emulated via Erlang distributions: In Sect. 3.3 we use true deterministic delays instead. Finally, in Sect. 3.4 we introduce component redundancy by means of spare gates, and in Sect. 3.5 we model EBE degradation using continuous stochastic functions.

3.1 HVAC-0: The Basic Setting

In [5], HVAC failures can derive from malfunctions in the heating coil, the supply fan, or the radiators. Similarly, here we decompose the HVAC FMT into the failures affecting its subsystems; see Fig. 2a for a graphical description. The leaves of the tree are EBEs whose degradation behaviour is detailed in Fig. 2b. Values for N and MTTF, which are the number of degradation phases and mean time to failure respectively, are obtained from [2,12] and are based on a real dataset of measurements on an HVAC system. For instance, EBE 1 models the failure of the AHU via a random variable with distribution Erlang$(4, {}^4/20)$.

We label the degradation phases (states) of EBEs to allow differentiated maintenance actions. With **new** we label the initial phase of an EBE, corresponding to perfect condition. With **failed** we label the last phase, e.g. phase 4 for EBE 1, corresponding to a failure that may propagate in the tree. With **thresh** we label all other phases to indicate a degraded—but still functional—condition.

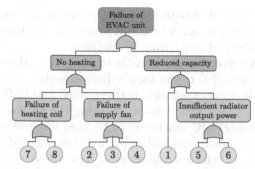

EBE ID	Failure mode	N	MTTF (years)
1	AHU damper broken	4	20
2	Fan motor failure	3	35
3	Supply fan obstructed	4	31
4	Fan bearing failure	6	17
5	Radiator failure	4	25
6	Radiator stuck valve	2	10
7	Heater stuck valve	2	10
8	Heat pump failure	4	20

(a) FMT leaves are EBEs, IEs reflect the subsystem affected by failures in the children.

(b) Detailed EBEs; degradation values from [2, 12].

Fig. 2. FMT of HVAC-0

The maintenance policies modelled in [5] distinguish between *inspections*, *repair checks*, and *overhauls*, which in our setting take place every half, two, and fifteen years respectively. Deterministic time delays, e.g. for performing these periodic maintenance checks, are emulated via Erlang distributions. Overhauls trigger a *replace* action that renews the whole HVAC, sending all EBEs back to their states representing the new phase. Replace actions take one week to complete. Instead, inspections and repair checks can trigger a *clean* action, that reverts one degradation phase in all the EBEs. Clean actions take one day to complete. When an inspection takes place, a clean is triggered if any EBE is in a thresh state. Similarly, a clean is triggered if any EBE is in a thresh or failed state during a repair check. Maintenance actions act on all EBEs: A clean sends all EBEs back one degradation phase—except those in a new state. Notice these semantics are a modelling choice and *not* a general characteristic of FMTs.

The total costs incurred are divided into operational and maintenance costs. Operational costs accrue €1 per day of system uptime and €4 per day of system downtime. Maintenance costs are €5000 per replace action triggered, €100 per clean action triggered, and €5 per periodic inspection. Repair checks and overhauls incur no additional costs when they take place. These values are based on previous research and expert-knowledge applied to an industrial case study [6].

In [5], the HVAC FMT is modelled using a CTMC with rewards, and the KPIs are computed with PMC via the PRISM model checker [16]. A state-space reduction technique is devised to build "an equivalent abstract CTMC," allowing PRISM to analyse the whole model and estimate (an approximation of) the metrics. We reproduce that approach for HVAC-0, and extend the analysis repertoire with SMC via the UPPAAL tool [9]. SMC estimates confidence intervals rather than point values like PMC does. Once a confidence level and termination epsilon have been set for SMC and PMC respectively, the results yielded by these techniques coincide if the SMC interval contains the PMC value.

UPPAAL operates with PTAs, a proper superset of CTMC that can encode (general) stochastic and non-linear dynamic behaviour. To substantiate the semantic coincidence of the models encoded in both tools, we first study subsystems of HVAC-0 for which the non-reduced (*exact*) PRISM model (i.e. without the state-space reduction technique devised in [5]) can be analysed.

In Fig. 3a we show the metrics for five time horizons in the largest of these subsystems, where only EBEs 2, 3, and 4 (i.e. the supply fan subsystem) are missing from the model of Fig. 2a. The metrics coincide between SMC and PMC exact, and differ slightly (as expected) for PMC *reduced*, i.e. using the abstract CTMC. When studying the full system, PMC exact cannot be used due to the state space explosion and the physical memory constraints [5,15]. Thus only SMC and PMC reduced can be compared, for which a difference as that observed in Fig. 3a is expected. This is corroborated in the full system analysis of HVAC-0, as it can be observed in Fig. 3b. The metrics for the total costs are not shown due to space constrains but they exhibit the same trends.

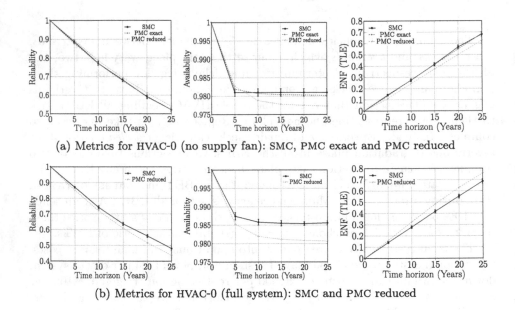

(a) Metrics for HVAC-0 (no supply fan): SMC, PMC exact and PMC reduced

(b) Metrics for HVAC-0 (full system): SMC and PMC reduced

Fig. 3. Comparative model checking for FMT of HVAC-0

In Fig. 3a, reliability and ENF values for SMC are lower than for PMC reduced, whereas in Fig. 3b they are higher. This is due to an interplay between the cleaning actions and the state-space reduction, which (for each time horizon) substitutes OR gates by EBEs with 4 phases and the MTTF of the replaced subsystem. Only EBE 4 has more than 4 phases—see Fig. 2b. Thus in PMC reduced *the number of phases* of all replaced subtrees is greater or equal for the system of Fig. 3a, but *lower* for the full HVAC-0 of Fig. 3b, viz. for the supply fan subtree. Therefore, only for PMC reduced of the full system, cleaning actions have less opportunities to act, which derives in more failures and explains Fig. 3.

3.2   HVAC-1: Refinement of Maintenance Actions

In the basic setting of Sect. 3.1, inspections and repair checks overlap considerably: Both can trigger the same maintenance action, namely a clean, and both will do so in the same system configurations. The only situations when a clean would be triggered by a repair check and not by an inspection, is when there is at least one failed—but no degraded—component. The likelihood of these scenarios decreases with the amount of EBEs and their number of degradation phases.

A more problematic modelling effect is that, when triggered by an inspection, a clean can "repair" a failed EBE and make it operational again. If e.g. EBE 1 is failed and EBE 2 is degraded, an inspection will trigger a clean because EBE 2 is in a `thresh` state; since cleaning actions are system-wide this also affects EBE 1, which then moves from its `failed` to a `thresh` state, becoming operational.

We argue this is not a realistic behaviour: Thus as first improvement over HVAC-0 we propose a more clear distinction between inspections and repairs. The former will remain as is, but repair checks will effectively trigger a *repair* maintenance action iff some EBE is in its `failed` state. As opposed to a clean triggered by an inspection, a repair *will only affect failed components, sending them back $N - 2$ degradation phases*. In particular, EBEs in a `thresh` or `new` state are not affected by repair actions. Repairs thus restore the health of failed components significantly albeit not entirely—only replacements triggered by overhauls leave components "as good as new." Repairs are necessarily more complex than cleans: They take longer (2 days) and cost more (€800).

The intuition behind this modification, code name HVAC-1, is that a technician fixes periodically all broken components, which has been named age repair or *age replacement* and is also related to *block replacement* [1,4].

Hence, to become operational again, a failed system must now wait for the next repair check, which takes four times longer than an inspection. This should increase system downtime and reduce availability. It is less clear how system reliability, ENF, and costs would be affected: The degradation mechanisms remain unchanged and the likelihood of failures may not be altered. In turn, total costs might increase due to the higher cost of repairs w.r.t. cleans.

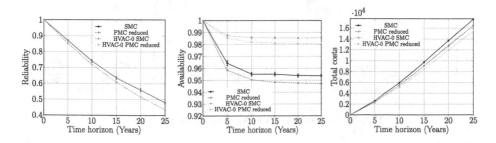

Fig. 4. Metrics for HVAC-1 (full system): SMC and PMC reduced

Figure 4 shows that system un-availability in HVAC-1 is 2 to 3 times higher than in HVAC-0; other metrics are much less affected. Due to space constraints, ENF values are not shown. However, they correlate to those obtained in HVAC-0. Since *PMC exact* creates a state-space explosion, here we opt for PMC reduced; the results obtained validate those achieved via SMC and highlight the trade-off between state-space reduction and deviation from SMC metrics.

3.3   HVAC-2: Deterministic Time Periods

In the previous section we give a first glimpse of how significantly a model refinement can impact a KPI. Here, building on top of HVAC-1, we focus on the modelling of events in time. In the FMTs from Sects. 3.1 and 3.2 and following [5], periodic events like inspections and overhauls are emulated using 3-phase Erlang distributions. Originally, this was needed because the model had semantics exclusively in terms of CTMCs. For the HVAC-2 model presented in this section we employ (more realistic) *deterministic* time periods instead [1,4].

This refinement has a twofold motivation: First, on the modelling side, events occurring at specific time points are a common maintenance policy—e.g. inspections are scheduled *exactly* every six months. Accurately modelling this is relevant for cost analyses, specially for (high) one-time investments like overhauls. Second, on the analysis side, Erlang approximations as phase-type distributions tend to the desired behaviour as the number of phases increases [10]. Thus, to achieve more deterministic-like delays, the state space of PMC models must grow, since e.g. Erlang phases are integral variables in the CTMCs of PRISM. To reach the desired level of realism, all variables encoding periodic time delays (inspections, cleans, etc.) require $\geqslant 10$ values. This would result in $\gg 10^8$ states, meaning PMC via PRISM cannot be performed [15]. Therefore, from this section onwards, we use exclusively PTA models of the HVAC FMT, which can naturally encode (true) deterministic time intervals with no impact on the state space. The KPIs can thus be measured using SMC alone[1].

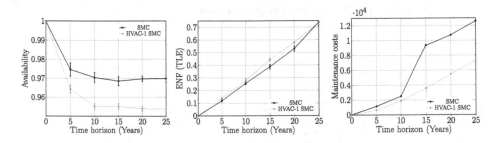

Fig. 5. Metrics for HVAC-2 (full system): SMC

We present the KPIs for HVAC-2 in Fig. 5: The most prominent modification w.r.t. HVAC-1 are in the maintenance costs. The costs incurred by the overhaul

---

[1] Support for reward analysis on PTA with PRISM is ongoing research, see Sect. 4.

at 15 years can be clearly appreciated for HVAC-2, whereas they are spread-out and less noticeable for HVAC-1. Detailed information like this can be crucial e.g. when assessing investment portfolios. The difference in the reliability and ENF values estimated for HVAC-2 are insignificant when compared to HVAC-1. However, availability is higher for the former. Looking at the individual maintenance actions triggered in the simulations of UPPAAL, after 5 years HVAC-1 performs 7 inspections on average, whereas HVAC-2 performs 10; after 25 years we get 37 vs. 48 respectively, etc. This reveals that, on average, the 3-phase Erlang approximation of the deterministic time delays in HVAC-1 is over-approximating. Repair checks are thus performed more frequently in HVAC-2, where the maintenance protocol is *better emulated* than in previous models. This is corroborated by the number of repairs, which is about ten times higher in HVAC-2 than in HVAC-1, accounting also for the generally higher maintenance costs in HVAC-2. Consequently, since the probability and number of failures are not altered, system downtime is lower in HVAC-2 than in HVAC-1. This explains the availability values from Fig. 5. Computation times for these SMC analyses increases considerably w.r.t. HVAC-0 and HVAC-1: While UPPAAL converged to the desired values in a matter of minutes for those models, it took several hours to compute some of the metrics for HVAC-2. This is discussed in Sect. 4.

3.4 HVAC-3: Spares for Affordable Components

In Sects. 3.1, 3.2 and 3.3 we increasingly refined our model to improve realism. Following the same goal, in this section we extend the HVAC to include spares in some subsystems. Redundancy is a common practice in high-resilience or safety-critical systems: RAID data storage uses extra disks to keep system availability high, cars come with a spare wheel, all modern air-conditioned buildings have spare air filters [3], etc. In HVAC-3 we use spare gates (SPARE) to implement *cold spare components* (whose degradation starts only after a fault occurs, [20]) for the valves in the water circuit, i.e. EBEs 6 and 7.

Two reasons motivated the choice of these components: On the one side, valves are relatively affordable parts (compare them to the boiler or the radiators) for which redundancy should require minor investments. On the other side, in Fig. 2b indicates these EBEs fail the most often. The impact observed in resilience should thus be greatest when providing spares for such components.

We add a SPARE with one spare component for EBE 6, and another (independent) SPARE with two spare components for EBE 7[2]. Spare components are assumed identical to main components, and as soon as the main component fails, the corresponding SPARE will switch to a spare without incurring system downtime[3]. When the main component and all spares have failed, the SPARE fails and propagates a signal to the rest of the FMT. We set at €1000 the cost of using a spare component. This way spares are more expensive than repairing the valve (€800), but cheaper than a full system overhaul (€5000). For all previous cases, the cost of

---

[2] Higher redundancies lead to *rare failures* that hinder SMC analyses, see Sect. 4.

[3] Notice that a valve can be replaced in hours, whereas all time horizons are in years.

a triggered maintenance action (e.g. a clean) is independent of the number of EBEs affected by it. For HVAC-3, the cost of using n spares during system operation is $n \times €1000$.

Spares are replenished during repair checks. Costs of using a spare are not incurred immediately, but rather in the next repair check occurring after the use of the spare. The intuition behind this is that the technician that periodically visits the company to perform repairs, is also in charge of replenishing the spares. The company pays him then for all pieces that have been used since his last visit.

Unlike in the previous sections, this extension affects only a subsystem of the HVAC, and in particular does not involve the "Supply fan failure" subtree from Fig. 2a. To highlight the effect of these modifications, we measure the KPIs exclusively for the affected part of the model, i.e. an FMT without EBEs 2–4. Accordingly, when referencing models from previous sections, we allude to the KPIs measured for the corresponding FMTs that also disregard fan failures.

The results of our SMC analyses on HVAC-3 are presented in Fig. 6. To exercise the capabilities of spares we also study a scenario where maintenance occurs half as frequently. Thus with "half maintenance," as opposed to "stnd. maintenance," inspections occur every year, repair checks every four years, and overhauls every thirty years. Notice that here we measure the KPIs for seven time horizons, i.e. for $T \in \{5, 10, 15, \ldots, 35\}$ years of system operation.

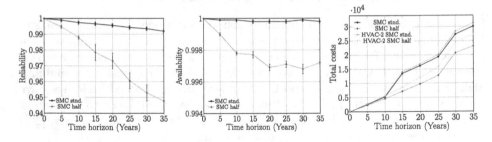

Fig. 6. Metrics for HVAC-3 (no supply fan): SMC

Except for costs, direct comparison of the KPIs from HVAC-3 and its predecessors is omitted, because HVAC-3 is so fault tolerant that its metrics would appear as flat lines on top of the charts. For HVAC-2 with stnd. maintenance, system availability without fan failures converges to 0.97, similarly to the full-system metrics from Fig. 5. For HVAC-3 availability was always above 0.9998, see "SMC stnd." in the availability plot of Fig. 6. With half maintenance, availability for HVAC-2 converged around 0.89 and for HVAC-3 around 0.997. Comparing thus HVAC-3 with half maintenance against HVAC-2 with stnd. maintenance, viz. 0.997 vs. 0.97, we get that using 1 & 2 spares for EBE 6 & 7, *and reducing maintenance checks to a half*, system downtime is reduced by more than 10×.

Reliability exhibits a similar trend: With stnd. maintenance it decreases in a seemingly linear fashion, reaching the value 0.4078 at the 35 years time horizon for HVAC-2, and 0.9919 for HVAC-3. With half maintenance the reliability values of HVAC-2 and HVAC-3 at 35 years are respectively 0.2053 and 0.9477. The values computed for ENF resemble this ratio: 0.9589 vs. 0.0069 for stnd. maintenance and 1.6407 vs. 0.0565 for half maintenance.

This tremendous increment in system resilience is explained by the Erlang degradation modelling in the EBEs. With one component we get N exponential jumps of rate $\frac{N}{\text{MTTF}}$ each. Adding $m - 1$ spares identical to the main component multiplies the number of jumps by $m - 1$, yet keeps the rate constant. Therefore, having $m - 1$ spares is equivalent to having an Erlang(mN, N/MTTF), whose expected value is m MTTF. In the setting of HVAC-3 this means that the MTTF of EBEs 6 and 7 changed to 20 and 30 years respectively, with the corresponding decrease in the probability of failure for a given fixed time window.

Nonetheless, although resilience improved drastically, total costs are actually *lower* for HVAC-3 than for HVAC-2 under both maintenance schemes, see Fig. 6. This is a consequence of the 4-to-1 cost ratio of system downtime/uptime. In spite of the extra maintenance costs incurred to keep stocks of spares, operational costs are much lower due to the very low proportion of system downtime.

It is straightforward to conclude that redundancy (spares) are a must in high-resilience systems. As final comment we mention that SMC analyses took significantly longer than all previous studies. For instance, computing the unreliability at 35 years under stnd. maintenance (0.0081) took 78 h of wall-clock computer time. This issue, discussed in Sect. 4, is due to (i) the addition of two longer time horizons, and (ii) the rarity of observing an event in the time window considered. In comparison, PMC should be less affected by these causes.

3.5   HVAC-4: Randomised Continuous Degradation of EBEs

In all previous sections the EBEs were regarded as atomic elements of the FMT, and modelling did not differ from the basic setting of HVAC-0. Here we refine the degradation semantics of EBEs: Instead of using discrete phases we model degradation continuously. We focus on the "Supply fan failure" subsystem, making the degradation of the fan bearings (EBE 4) resemble a continuous stochastic process known as *Geometric Brownian Motion* (GBM).

We use GBM for two reasons: First, recent studies show GBM can appropriately model bearing degradation [23]. Second, when using N discrete phases of rate λ, time increments between consecutive degradation stages are sampled from N independent and identically distributed (iid) random variables $\sim$ Exponential(λ). Failure times thus follow an N-phase Erlang distribution with expectation MTTF $= N/\lambda$. In contrast, our GBM simulation uses *constant* time increments, and for ever smaller time increments the degradation process is continuous (with probability 1). So degradation is a non-iid non-linear—thus not linearly phased—process, and changes in degradation between consecutive instants are partially stochastic. Consequently, the degradation *speed* of a component is a function of time, and since the expectation of GBM is an exponential function of time, the *failure time follows a log-normal distribution*.

Technically, GBM is the analytical solution to the stochastic differential equation $S(t) = S(0) \exp\left(\left(\mu - \frac{1}{2}\sigma^2\right) t + \sigma W_t\right)$. Next we review its main concepts as used in this section, and refer the interested reader to the abundant literature for a deeper insight into GBM. Let $S(t)$ denote the (continuous) degradation of a system component at time t, with $S(0) = 1$ and Δt the time increment. Then the GBM degradation can be expressed and simulated as

$$S(t + \Delta t) = S(t) \exp\left(\left(\mu - \frac{1}{2}\sigma^2\right) \Delta t + \sigma W_{\Delta t}\right). \tag{1}$$

In Eq. (1) $W_{\Delta t}$ is a Wiener process or "Brownian motion," meaning $W_{\Delta t}$ is normally distributed with zero mean and variance Δt, and has independent Gaussian increments. Parameters μ and σ in Eq. (1) are respectively the *drift* and *diffusion* coefficients. The expected value and variance of $S(t)$ are given by $\mathbb{E}[S(t)] = S(0) \exp(\mu t)$ and $\text{Var}[S(t)] = S(0)^2 \exp(2\mu t)(\exp(\sigma^2 t) - 1)$.

In previous sections, each EBE is characterised by its mean time to failure (MTTF) and number of degradation phases (N). As we now only change the degradation function, we can express the expected degradation value at the MTTF as: $S_{fail} = \mathbb{E}[S(\text{MTTF})] = S(0) \exp(\mu \text{MTTF})$. Hence, assuming $\text{Var}[S(\text{MTTF})] = 1$ and setting $S(0) = 1$ and $S_{fail} = N + 1$, this yields

$$\mu = \frac{\ln(S_{fail}) - \ln(S(0))}{\text{MTTF}} = \frac{\ln(N + 1)}{\text{MTTF}} \tag{2a}$$

$$\sigma = \sqrt{\frac{\ln\left(1 + \frac{\text{Var}[S(\text{MTTF})]}{S(0)^2 \exp(2\mu\text{MTTF})}\right)}{\text{MTTF}}} = \sqrt{\frac{\ln\left(1 + \frac{1}{(N+1)^2}\right)}{\text{MTTF}}}. \tag{2b}$$

Thus, using Eq. (1) with the drift and diffusion from Eq. (2) as degradation function for EBE 4, and keeping EBEs 2 and 3 unmodified w.r.t. HVAC-2, we analyse the FMT for the supply fan subsystem. Since the MTTF values of EBEs 2–4 are among the highest of the model, failures will be rare in the time windows considered. In that sense, this scenario is similar to the one from the previous section, and we thus follow a similar approach: We study a scenario with half maintenance for time horizons $T \in \{5, 10, \ldots, 35\}$.

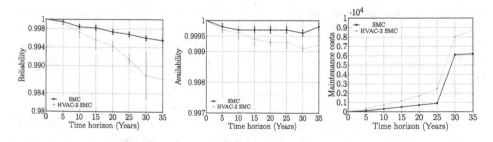

Fig. 7. Metrics for HVAC-4 (supply fan): SMC

The results of experimentation are shown in Fig. 7. Comparing the KPIs against HVAC-2, we observe that HVAC-4 models a more resilient system. This is a direct consequence of using GBM for the degradation of EBE 4, even though it has the lowest MTTF in the subsystem considered. More in detail, the expected degradation of this component in HVAC-4 is continuous and exponentially increasing. The expected time it takes for the GBM to reach a certain degradation value is thus *logarithmic* w.r.t. the degradation value. In contrast, degradation is linearly phased in HVAC-2 for all EBEs, and thus the corresponding expected time is *linear* w.r.t. the degradation state. Because of identical MTTF and failure threshold, the degradation speed in the initial stages of EBE 4 is lower in HVAC-4 than in HVAC-2. Therefore, inspections in HVAC-4 have a higher chance of restoring EBE 4 to its initial value, while in HVAC-2 it is easier to have the component degrade by two phases before the inspection can trigger a clean. As a consequence, given a fixed maintenance scheme and time period, the chances of EBE 4 failing are lower in HVAC-4 than in HVAC-2. This explains the reliability and availability values observed in Fig. 7.

The costs are also an interesting point of comparison. Operational costs are identical for both models, and thus omitted from Fig. 7. Maintenance costs however present a major distinction: HVAC-4 has nearly no costs incurred by repairs, whereas repairs in HVAC-2 increase linearly from €123 after 5 years, to €1984 after 35 years. This is precisely the expected behaviour as per the argument presented above: since most degradation is "early caught" by inspections in HVAC-4, maintenance costs are concentrated in cleans, rather than repairs. This shows, once again, that refining the FMT model can noticeably impact both the resilience KPIs, as well as the costs of system operation and maintenance, in ways and quantities that may concern the interested parties.

4   Concluding Remarks and Future Work

In this work, we demonstrate the importance of the semantic details of an FMT system model, by quantifying the effect of modifications to the model on typical RAMS metrics estimated via PMC and SMC. We propose four (incremental) modelling improvements for a basic HVAC-0 FMT model. We note that (i) the localisation of clean actions to only degraded components increases the unavailability by a factor of $\approx 2.5\times$ (HVAC-1, see Fig. 4), (ii) modelling periodic events with deterministic time delays increases the resilience KPIs and greatly impacts costs (HVAC-2, see Fig. 5), (iii) the use of spares reduces the frequency of maintenance actions while achieving $>100\times$ higher availability and slightly lower costs (HVAC-3, see Fig. 6), and (iv) using GBM to model component degradation increases resilience metrics (in particular reliability) and reduces costs, but makes analyses more involved and, arguably, more realistic (HVAC-4, see Fig. 7). It is thus evident that much can be gained by revisiting an otherwise finished model, and refining any particularly relevant component.

Future Work. There are several areas open for further development. First, from HVAC-2 onwards only SMC could be used because CTMCs cannot emulate deterministic time delays. Current endeavours by the PRISM community to measure reward properties on PTA models [15] are opening the gate to PMC studies of the cases presented in Sects. 3.3, 3.4 and 3.5. Moreover, when the time window is large w.r.t. the event-time-unit simulated (or when the event of interest rarely happens), SMC suffers from longer computation times due to the duration of the (resp. required amount of) simulations, see e.g. Sects. 3.4 and 3.5. If PMC could be used to analyse HVAC-3 and HVAC-4, the time required to converge to an estimate should be faster [15]. Rare event simulation offers an alternative, to apply SMC when the event of interest occurs with very low probability [18]. Parallelly, the next natural step to the EBE refinement from Sect. 3.5 is data validation, i.e. comparing the KPI metrics against measurements from real systems. However, such measurements are scarce due to the long time horizons involved. It would also be interesting to experiment with different degradation functions for distinct EBEs, specialised for the behaviour of each component type concerned. Further relevant extensions include measuring the effect of "on-demand" maintenance in addition to fixed periodic maintenance, and experimenting with different cost schemes to test the robustness of the final conclusions.

Acknowledgements. This work is partially supported by the Alan Turing Institute, UK; Malta's ENDEAVOUR Scholarships Scheme; and the NWO SEQUOIA project.

References

1. Aven, T., Jensen, U. (eds.): Maintenance optimization. Stochastic Models in Reliability, pp. 169–211. Springer, New York (1999). https://doi.org/10.1007/978-0-387-22593-7_5
2. ASHRAE: HVAC systems and equipment. American Society of Heating, Refrigerating, and Air Conditioning Engineers, Atlanta, GA (1996)
3. Au-Yong, C.P., Ali, A.S., Ahmad, F.: Enhancing building maintenance cost performance with proper management of spare parts. JQME **22**(1), 51–61 (2016)
4. Barlow, R.E., Proschan, F.: Mathematical theory of reliability. Science **148**(3674), 1208–1209 (1965)
5. Cauchi, N., Hoque, K.A., Abate, A., Stoelinga, M.: Efficient probabilistic model checking of smart building maintenance using fault maintenance trees. In: BuildSys (2017)
6. Cauchi, N., Macek, K., Abate, A.: Model-based predictive maintenance inbuilding automation systems with user discomfort. Energy **138**(Suppl. C), 306–315 (2017)
7. Clarke, E., Emerson, E., Sistla, A.: Automatic verification of finite-state concurrent systems using temporal logic specifications. ACM Trans. Program. Lang. Syst. **8**, 244–263 (1986)
8. Clarke, E., Grumberg, O., Peled, D.: Model Checking. MIT Press, Cambridge (1999)
9. David, A., Larsen, K., Legay, A., Mikučionis, M., Poulsen, D.: Uppaal SMC tutorial. Intl. J. Softw. Tools Technol. Transf. **17**(4), 397–415 (2015)

10. David, A., Larry, S.: The least variable phase type distribution is Erlang. Communications in statistics. Stoch. Models **3**(3), 467–473 (1987)
11. Dugan, J.B., Bavuso, S.J., Boyd, M.A.: Fault trees and sequence dependencies. In: RAMS, pp. 286–293 (1990)
12. Faisal, I., Mahmoud, M.: Risk-based maintenance (RBM): a quantitative approach for maintenance/inspection scheduling and planning. J. Loss Prev. Process Ind. **16**(6), 561–573 (2003)
13. Guck, D., Spel, J., Stoelinga, M.: DFTCalc: reliability centered maintenance via fault tree analysis (tool paper). In: Butler, M., Conchon, S., Zaïdi, F. (eds.) ICFEM 2015. LNCS, vol. 9407, pp. 304–311. Springer, Cham (2015). https://doi.org/10.1007/978-3-319-25423-4_19
14. Junges, S., Guck, D., Katoen, J.P., Stoelinga, M.: Uncovering dynamic fault trees. In: DSN, pp. 299–310. IEEE, June 2016
15. Kwiatkowska, M., Norman, G., Parker, D.: Probabilistic model checking: advances and applications. In: Drechsler, R. (ed.) Formal System Verification, pp. 73–121. Springer, Cham (2018). https://doi.org/10.1007/978-3-319-57685-5_3
16. Kwiatkowska, M., Norman, G., Parker, D.: PRISM 4.0: verification of probabilistic real-time systems. In: Gopalakrishnan, G., Qadeer, S. (eds.) CAV 2011. LNCS, vol. 6806, pp. 585–591. Springer, Heidelberg (2011). https://doi.org/10.1007/978-3-642-22110-1_47
17. Nicolai, R.P., Dekker, R.: Optimal maintenance of multi-component systems: a review. In: Kobbacy, K.A.H., Murthy, D.N.P. (eds.) Complex System Maintenance Handbook, pp. 263–286. Springer, Heidelberg (2008). https://doi.org/10.1007/978-1-84800-011-7_11
18. Rubino, G., Tuffin, B. (eds.): Rare Event Simulation Using Monte Carlo Methods. Wiley, Hoboken (2009)
19. Ruijters, E., Guck, D., Drolenga, P., Peters, M., Stoelinga, M.: Maintenance analysis and optimization via statistical model checking. In: Agha, G., Van Houdt, B. (eds.) QEST 2016. LNCS, vol. 9826, pp. 331–347. Springer, Cham (2016). https://doi.org/10.1007/978-3-319-43425-4_22
20. Ruijters, E., Stoelinga, M.: Fault tree analysis: a survey of the state-of-the-art in modeling, analysis and tools. Comput. Sci. Rev. **15**, 29–62 (2015)
21. Vesely, W.E., Goldberg, F.F., Roberts, N.H., Haasl, D.F.: Fault tree handbook. Technical report, U.S. Nuclear Regulatory Commission, Washington DC (1981)
22. Volk, M., Junges, S., Katoen, J.P.: Fast dynamic fault tree analysis by model checking techniques. IEEE Trans. Ind. Inform. **14**(1), 370–379 (2018)
23. Wang, D., Tsui, K.L.: Statistical modeling of bearing degradation signals. IEEE Trans. Reliab. **66**(4), 1331–1344 (2017)
24. Younes, H.L.S., Simmons, R.G.: Probabilistic verification of discrete event systems using acceptance sampling. In: Brinksma, E., Larsen, K.G. (eds.) CAV 2002. LNCS, vol. 2404, pp. 223–235. Springer, Heidelberg (2002). https://doi.org/10.1007/3-540-45657-0_17

Performance Impact of Misbehaving Voters

Mohammed Alotaibi[✉] and Nigel Thomas[✉]

Newcastle University, Newcastle upon Tyne, UK
{m.alotaibi1,nigel.thomas}@newcastle.ac.uk

Abstract. In this paper we present three formal performance models, using PEPA, for three types of misbehaving voters when using the DRE-i e-voting system. We use the constructed performance models to study the impact of the intervention of misbehaving voters on the throughput of four main actions of the DRE-i e-voting system. Our performance analysis reveals that the three types of misbehaving voters have a negative impact on the throughput of the DRE-i server actions.

Keywords: Performance models · PEPA · e-Voting

1 Introduction

E-voting systems face a wide range of potential misbehaving components or agents beyond what we used to have in traditional elections. These misbehaviours include misconfigured e-voting components [15,23], errors made by voters, and malicious behaviours made by attackers [16]. Some known attacks on e-voting systems include the replay attack [6], man in the middle attacks, and Cross-Site Scripting (XSS) and Cross-Site Request Forging (CSRF) attacks [7,19]. Investigating the impact of these misbehaviours on e-voting systems performance is an intriguing research topic. One way of studying this impact is through constructing the misbehaving voters' formal performance models and evaluating how their interventions with e-voting system may affect the performance of the e-voting system.

PEPA (Performance Evaluation Process Algebra) [13] is a well-known formalism in constructing performance models for concurrent systems and communication protocols [9,22]. In [2], a formal performance model for the casting-verifying stage of the DRE-i e-voting scheme [11] was constructed using PEPA. In this study, we will model three types of misbehaving voters and their interactions with the DRE-i system using the same formalism. The constructed performance models will be analysed using performance evaluation techniques built in PEPA Eclipse Plug-in [21] to have an insight on the effect of misbehaving voters on the performance of the DRE-i server.

Next, we will provide a brief background about e-voting systems and PEPA. In the third section, we will describe our approach in modelling the misbehaving

R. Bakhshi et al. (Eds.): EPEW 2018, LNCS 11178, pp. 126–141, 2018.
https://doi.org/10.1007/978-3-030-02227-3_9

voters and analysing their impact on the DRE-i e-voting system. Performance models will be shown in section four, and in section five we will present the result and discussion. Finally, conclusion and future work will be presented in Sect. 6.

2 Background

In this section, we will provide a brief background about PEPA (For more details about PEPA, please refer to [13]) and e-Voting schemes (Refer to [10,12] for more details). Also, we will briefly present some known misbehaviours that could affect e-voting systems. At the end of this section, we will present the work related to modelling and analysing e-voting schemes using formal performance models such as PEPA.

2.1 e-Voting

An election enables a participant to choose his candidate for holding a position in a public or private organisation by the voting process. To increase the turnout of voters in elections, researchers suggested electronic voting systems that meet strict accuracy and security requirements. Well-known examples of e-voting systems include DRE-i [11], Helios [1], and iVote [5]. Many countries, states, and organizations have used the e-voting systems in elections such as Estonia [17], Brazil, India, the Australian state of New South Wales (NSW) [5], and the International Association of Cryptologic Research (IACR) [3]. Electronic voting security literature identifies many security requirements for e-voting protocols such as completeness, privacy, soundness and robustness, receipt-freeness, verifiability, fairness, eligibility, and unreusability. To achieve these security features, the electronic voting schemes use different cryptographic building blocks which include blind signatures, mix-nets, encryption algorithms, and interactive and non-interactive proofs.

2.2 e-Voting Misbehaviours

Security of e-voting systems is very influential in the democratic process so many researchers have studied the possible attacks against e-voting systems [12,16]. One of the attacks is the replay attack where a malicious voter retransmits a valid vote or message. The vote replay attack was discovered in different e-voting schemes such as Helios 2.0 [6] and the e-voting schemes by Sako & Kilian and Schoenmakers [18]. Another attack is based on compromising the web-interface of the e-voting client using for example XSS (Cross-Site Scripting) or CSRF (Cross-Site Request Forgery) attacks. In [7] the malicious voter can install a malicious browser extension on the voter's machine to compromise Helios 2.0 e-voting system. Using the CSRF approaches [19], the malicious voter may exploit a weakness in the e-voting web interface and establish an authenticated session with the e-voting server to exchange voting messages with the server.

2.3   Introduction to PEPA

PEPA (Performance Evaluation Process Algebra) is a stochastic modelling formalism for constructing performance models for concurrent systems [13]. It was successfully used in modelling and analysing the performance aspects of systems and protocols. Performance models constructed by PEPA can help systems designers to evaluate the performance characteristics of the system to be deployed. The performance attributes (such as throughput, queue-length, and response time) of models constructed by PEPA can by analysed using Continuous-Time Markov Chain (CTMC) and Ordinary Differential Equations (ODEs) approaches. When using CTMC, the construction and evaluation of PEPA models will be restricted by the size and complexity of modelled systems. PEPA model will encounter the state-space explosion problem when the model comprises a large number of components. To overcome the state-space problem, a fluid approximation approach has been suggested [14] to represent the PEPA model's underlying CTMC as a set of ordinary differential equations (ODEs). PEPA is an abstract compositional description formalism which is used for constructing performance models as a number of interacting components that process activities with rates. In a PEPA model, activity rate is an exponentially distributed random number that shows the rate at which the activity (action) happens during the execution of the model. To evaluate the performance of the PEPA model, the PEPA Eclipse Plug-in tool [21] is used to edit and test the model. It is also used to derive the model's underlying CTMC and the ODE approximation of the model's CTMC. The derived CTMC and ODEs can be solved by the tool to extract the model's performance measures such as expected response time, throughput and utilisation.

The syntax of PEPA language is composed of combinators that express the behaviours and interactions of the model's components. The following is the set of PEPA language's combinators:

Prefix. The prefix combinator "." designates the first behaviour undertaken by the component. The action type a and rate r for component P is encoded in PEPA as $(a, r).P$ which means the action will be carried out and then behaves as component P.

Constant. The constant combinator $\stackrel{def}{=}$ assigns names to behaviours (components). For example, $Q \stackrel{def}{=} (a, r).P$ represents the assignment of the behaviour of $(a, r).P$ to the component Q.

Cooperation. The combinator "$\bowtie_L$" represents the interactions between components. The $(P\bowtie_L Q)$ indicates the cooperation between components P and Q over action types in the cooperation set L. The two components P and Q will proceed independently and concurrently when their cooperation set L is empty. In this case, the parallel composition of P and Q will be expressed as $P||Q$.

Choice. The choice combinator "$+$" denotes the competition between behaviours. $P+Q$ represents a system that may behave as P or Q.

Hiding. The hiding combinator "/" hides the activities in the set L and considers them as an internal delay inside the component. The P/L makes the activities in set L as the unknown type τ where the external observer can witness the delay caused by the hidden activity τ. However, the external observer can not access the hidden activity.

2.4 Related Work

PEPA performance models for the voting scheme of Fujioka, Okamoto, and Ohta [8] was constructed and evaluated in [4,20]. In [20], a set of PEPA models were constructed and analysed for reliable and unreliable voters. In [4], a stochastic simulation technique was used to convert a PEPA model of an e-voting scheme to a set of rate equations. Each rate equation represented an individual action of a component inside the PEPA model and by using these rate equations a simulation description file was constructed that fitted the Dizzy simulation tool. Therefore, the PEPA model of the e-voting scheme was simulated and analysed for a large number of voters. Moreover, the DRE-i e-voting scheme was modelled by PEPA in [2]. The constructed model was evaluated using CTMC and ODEs approaches for a varying number of voters to evaluate the voters' response time when they get involved in the cast-verify stage during the election day.

3 Our Approach

During the election day, legitimate voters who prefer using e-voting systems will use their electronic devices to join the election and cast their votes. This usually will lead to an increase in the throughput of the main activities in the e-voting system. With the intervention of misbehaving voters with the e-voting system, the throughput that is dedicated for legitimate voters will be challenged. We are interested in evaluating the impact of the rate and depth of the intervention of misbehaving voters with the e-voting system. Theretofore, in this section we will present the PEPA models for the DRE-i e-voting server and client, and the three types of misbehaving voters. Also, we will present the rates for the models' actions, and finally we will explain how to evaluate the impact of the misbehaving voters on the DRE-i e-voting system.

3.1 DRE-i Behaviour Description

The Direct Recording Electronic with integrity e-voting scheme (DRE-i) was presented by Hao *et al.* [11]. The scheme is an end-to-end verifiable and self-enforcing cryptographic voting scheme and based on the Direct Recording Electronic voting system technique. This scheme replaces the tallying authority with a cryptographic homomorphic tallying algorithm. The DRE-i scheme can be used in controlled or uncontrolled voting environments for large-scale country-wide political elections or small-size elections like university students' union elections. In this e-voting scheme, a tamper-resistant security module of the e-voting server will generate for each eligible voter n ballots. Each ballot will have two encrypted values known as cryptograms. During election stage, the voter needs to prove his or her eligibility for voting and identity to the voting server. If the voter is eligible for voting, the voter will receive a ballot and will choose one of the two cryptograms. The voter will submit his or her selected vote to the server. Next, the server will sign the received ballot and send it to the voter so the voter can either accept it and cast it as the voter's vote or reveal the content of the signed ballot to verify that the voter's selection reflects his or her intention.

We are interested in modelling and evaluating the casting stage of the DRE-i e-voting system which has four main activities: getting the vote cryptograms, signing the selected cryptogram, casting or verifying the selected vote. From the server side, these actions are *voteCryptogramsReply*, *signTransReply*, *voteCastAck*, and *voteVerifyAck*. Figure 1 demonstrates the interactions between the voting client and voting server to carry out vote casting process.

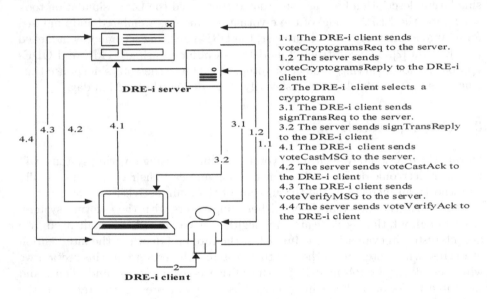

1.1 The DRE-i client sends voteCryptogramsReq to the server.
1.2 The server sends voteCryptogramsReply to the DRE-i client
2 The DRE-i client selects a cryptogram
3.1 The DRE-i client sends signTransReq to the server.
3.2 The server sends signTransReply to the DRE-i client
4.1 The DRE-i client sends voteCastMSG to the server.
4.2 The server sends voteCastAck to the DRE-i client
4.3 The DRE-i client sends voteVerifyMSG to the server.
4.4 The server sends voteVerifyAck to the DRE-i client

Fig. 1. Main collaboration between the *DRE-i* client and server

The legitimate voter will send the following requests: voteCryptogramsReq, signTransReq, voteCastMSG, and voteVerifyMSG to the server. Respectively, the server will reply with the following actions: voteCryptogramsReply, signTransReply, voteCastAck, and voteVerifyAck. In the following two paragraphs we will explain the server and client actions.

3.2 Misbehaving Voters

We have also investigated three misbehaviours that may happen to the DRE-i e-voting system. The first misbehaviour is represented by a rogue client that just replays voteCryptogramsReq messages to get valid ballots from the DRE-i server. We call this type of rogue clients as RCA (Rogue Client of type A) voting client and the steps 1.1 and 1.2 in Fig. 1 show the interactions between the RCA voting client and voting server. This behaviour represents an unsuccessful replay attack where the misbehaving voter tries to request a ballot that has been requested by a legitimate voter but the voting server replies with error message.

The second misbehaviour is represented by a rogue client that sends requests voteCryptogramsReq and signTransReq to the DRE-i server. We call this type of rogue clients as RCB (Rogue Client of type B) voting client and the steps 1.1, 1.2, 2, 3.1, and 3.2 in Fig. 1 show the interactions between the RCB voting client and voting server. In this type of voter misbehaviours, the voter successfully replays a ballot request and gets back the vote cryptograms from the server and then selects a candidate and sends a sign transcript request to the server but the server replies with an error message.

The third misbehaviour is represented by a rogue client that successfully sends requests voteCryptogramsReq, signTransReq, voteCastMSG, and voteV-erifyMSG to the DRE-i server and gets back valid replies. We call this type of rogue clients as RCC (Rogue Client of type C) voting client and the steps 1.1, 1.2, 2, 3.1, 3.2, 4.1, 4.2, 4.3 and 4.4 in Fig. 1 show the interactions between the RCC voting client and the voting server. In this type of misbehaving voters, the malicious voter can successfully cast or verify a vote. This type of misbehaviour can be represented by cross-site scripting (XSS) or Cross-Site Request Forgery (CSRF) attacks.

3.3 Actions Rates

We consider the rogue clients' actions to have rates similar to the rates of the legitimate clients. We assumed that the rogue clients need to wait for one second (1000 ms) to restart the next intervention. The rogue clients will have different rates to complete one intervention with the DRE-i system. To have a good estimate for the rates of the server actions in our performance models, we used the same live experiment in [2] to derive some of the PEPA model rates. Moreover, we assumed that the rates of client actions to be 0.002 for actions that will be done by the client software and 0.0002 for actions to be done by the voter (Tables 1 and 2).

3.4 Throughput Analysis of Server Actions

The throughput of an action is defined as the average number of actions completed by the system during a unit of time (ms) [13]. In PEPA, we can calculate the average number of jobs waiting to be served by an action in the model. This number is called the population(mean queue length). Therefore, we can calculate the average number of valid voters and rogue voters waiting for each server's action. The throughput and population of model actions can be derived by PEPA Eclipse Plug-in immediately after solving the CTMC underlying the model or

Table 1. Action rates for *DRE-i* client.

Action	Rate
voteCryptogramsReq	0.00114
signTransReq	0.00082
voteCastMSG, voteVerifyMSG	0.00087
selectVote, castReply, verifyReply, reselect	0.0002
voteCastingComplete, voteVerificationComplete	0.002
reselectOrEndVotingRate	0.002
wait	0.0000519585

Table 2. Action rates for *DRE-i* server.

Action	Rate
voteCryptogramsReply	0.00114
signTransReply	0.00082
voteCastAck, voteVerifyAck	0.00087

the ODE approximation of the CTMC. Because we are interested in investigating the impact of rogue clients' intervention in the DRE-i system, we need to evaluate the goodput and badput of each server action. Goodput of a server action expresses the throughput dedicated for the average number of legitimate clients waiting to be served by the server action(See formula (1)). The badput of a server action expresses the throughput dedicated for the average number of rogue clients waiting to be served by the server action(See formula (2)).

$$\textbf{Goodput} = \text{action throughput} \times \left(\frac{\text{number of valid voters}}{\text{total number of voters}} \right) \qquad (1)$$

$$\textbf{Badput} = \text{action throughput} \times \left(\frac{\text{number of rogue voters}}{\text{total number of voters}} \right) \qquad (2)$$

4   PEPA Models

We will construct the formal performance models for the typical behaviour of the DRE-i voting scheme using PEPA formalism similar to the PEPA model in [2]. However, in this model we will not model the voter behaviour because we will abstract the voter behaviour inside the voting client. Therefore, in this model we will have the voting client and the voting server components.

Based on Fig. 1 we define the formal performance model for the DRE-i voting scheme using PEPA language as follows:

4.1 DRE-i Server and Client

The system is composed of 30 *DRE-i* legitimate clients and one server. The system starts by receiving the request *voteCryptogramsReq* form the *DRE-i* client and subsequently the *DRE-i* server replies with the action *voteCryptogramsReply*. The client and server continue the interactions as shown in the PEPA description of client and server collaboration below.

Voting client:

$\text{DRE\_Client}_0 \overset{def}{=} (\text{voteCryptogramsReq}, r_{\text{voteCryptogramsReq}}).\text{DRE\_Client}_1$

$\text{DRE\_Client}_1 \overset{def}{=} (\text{voteCryptogramsReply}, r_{\text{voteCryptogramsReply}}).\text{DRE\_Client}_2$

$\text{DRE\_Client}_2 \overset{def}{=} (\text{selectVote}, r_{\text{selectVote}}).\text{DRE\_Client}_3$

$\text{DRE\_Client}_3 \overset{def}{=} (\text{signTranscriptReq}, r_{\text{signTranscriptReq}}).\text{DRE\_Client}_4$

$\text{DRE\_Client}_4 \overset{def}{=} (\text{signTranscriptReply}, r_{\text{signTranscriptReply}}).\text{DRE\_Client}_5$

$\text{DRE\_Client}_5 \overset{def}{=} (\text{castReply}, r_{\text{castReply}}).\text{DRE\_Client}_6 + (\text{verifyReply}, r_{\text{verifyReply}}).\text{DRE\_Client}_7$

$\text{DRE\_Client}_6 \overset{def}{=} (\text{castedVoteMSG}, r_{\text{castedVoteMSG}}).\text{DRE\_Client}_8$

$\text{DRE\_Client}_8 \overset{def}{=} (\text{castedVoteAck}, r_{\text{castedVoteAck}}).$
$\qquad (\text{voteCastingComplete}, r_{\text{voteCastingComplete}}).(\text{wait}, r_{\text{wait}}).\text{DRE\_Client}_0$

$\text{DRE\_Client}_7 \overset{def}{=} (\text{verifiedVoteMSG}, r_{\text{verifiedVoteMSG}}).\text{DRE\_Client}_9$

$\text{DRE\_Client}_9 \overset{def}{=} (\text{verifiedVoteAck}, r_{\text{verifiedVoteAck}}).$
$\qquad (\text{voteVerificationComplete}, r_{\text{voteVerificationComplete}}).\text{DRE\_Client}_{10}$

$\text{DRE\_Client}_{10} \overset{def}{=} (\text{reselectOrEndVoting}, r_{\text{reselectOrEndVoting}}).\text{DRE\_Client}_{11}$

$\text{DRE\_Client}_{11} \overset{def}{=} (\text{reselect}, r_{\text{reselect}}).\text{DRE\_Client}_0 +$
$\qquad (\text{endVoting}, r_{\text{endVoting}}).(\text{wait}, r_{\text{wait}}).\text{DRE\_Client}_0$

Voting server:

$\text{DRE\_SRV}_0 \overset{def}{=} (\text{voteCryptogramsReply}, r_{\text{voteCryptogramsReply}}).\text{DRE\_SRV}_0 +$
$(\text{signTranscriptReply}, r_{\text{signTranscriptReply}}).\text{DRE\_SRV}_0 +$
$(\text{castedVoteAck}, r_{\text{castedVoteAck}}).\text{DRE\_SRV}_0 + (\text{verifiedVoteAck}, r_{\text{verifiedVoteAck}}).\text{DRE\_SRV}_0$

System equation:

$((\text{DRE\_Client}_0[i] \underset{\mathcal{L}_1}{\bowtie} \text{DRE\_SRV}_0[j]))$

where i is the number of voters in the system, j is the number of e-voting servers, and

$\mathcal{L}_1 = \{\text{voteCryptogramsReply}, \text{signTranscriptReply}, \text{castedVoteAck}, \text{verifiedVoteAck}\}$

4.2 RCA DRE-i Clients

The *DRE-i* rogue client of type RCA starts interacting with the system by sending the request *voteCryptogramsReq* to the *DRE-i* server. The server replies with the action *voteCryptogramsReply* to end the collaboration and the *RCA DRE-i* rogue client goes back to the initial state $RCA\_DRE\_Client_0$.

RCA Voting client:

$\text{\textbf{RCA\_DRE\_Client}}_0 \overset{def}{=} (\text{voteCryptogramsReq}, r_{\text{voteCryptogramsReq}}).\text{RCA\_DRE\_Client}_1$

$\text{\textbf{RCA\_DRE\_Client}}_1 \overset{def}{=} (\text{voteCryptogramsReply}, r_{\text{voteCryptogramsReply}}).\text{RCA\_DRE\_Client}_2$

$\text{\textbf{RCA\_DRE\_Client}}_2 \overset{def}{=} (\text{rc\_wait}, r_{\text{rc\_wait}}).\text{RCA\_DRE\_Client}_0$

System equation:

$$((\text{\textbf{DRE\_Client}}_0[i] \bowtie \text{\textbf{RCA\_DRE\_Client}}_0[k]) \underset{\mathcal{L}_1}{\bowtie} \text{\textbf{DRE\_SRV}}_0[j])$$

where i is the number of voters in the system, j is the number of e-voting servers, k is the number of RCA clients, and

$\mathcal{L}_1 = \{\text{voteCryptogramsReply, signTranscriptReply, castedVoteAck, verifiedVoteAck}\}$

4.3   RCB DRE-i Clients

The *DRE-i* rogue client of type RCB starts interacting with the system by sending the request *voteCryptogramsReq* to the *DRE-i* server and successfully receiving the action *voteCryptogramsReply* from the server. In the next step, the RCB client select the candidate. Subsequently, the RCB client sends the request *signTranscriptReq* to the server and the server replies with the action *signTranscriptReply* to end the collaboration and the *RCB DRE-i* rogue client goes back to the initial state $RCB\_DRE\_Client_0$.

RCB Voting client:

$\text{\textbf{RCB\_DRE\_Client}}_0 \overset{def}{=} (\text{voteCryptogramsReq}, r_{\text{voteCryptogramsReq}}).\text{RCB\_DRE\_Client}_1$

$\text{\textbf{RCB\_DRE\_Client}}_1 \overset{def}{=} (\text{voteCryptogramsReply}, r_{\text{voteCryptogramsReply}}).\text{RCB\_DRE\_Client}_2$

$\text{\textbf{RCB\_DRE\_Client}}_2 \overset{def}{=} (\text{selectVoteReq}, r_{\text{selectVoteReq}}).\text{RCB\_DRE\_Client}_3$

$\text{\textbf{RCB\_DRE\_Client}}_3 \overset{def}{=} (\text{signTranscriptReq}, r_{\text{signTranscriptReq}}).\text{RCB\_DRE\_Client}_4$

$\text{\textbf{DRE\_Client}}_4 \overset{def}{=} (\text{signTranscriptReply}, r_{\text{signTranscriptReply}}).\text{DRE\_Client}_5$

$\text{\textbf{RCB\_DRE\_Client}}_5 \overset{def}{=} (\text{rc\_wait}, r_{\text{rc\_wait}}).\text{RCB\_DRE\_Client}_0$

System equation:

$$((\text{\textbf{DRE\_Client}}_0[i] \bowtie \text{\textbf{RCB\_DRE\_Client}}_0[k]) \underset{\mathcal{L}_1}{\bowtie} \text{\textbf{DRE\_SRV}}_0[j])$$

where i is the number of voters in the system, j is the number of e-voting servers, k is the number of RCB clients, and

$\mathcal{L}_1 = \{\text{voteCryptogramsReply, signTranscriptReply, castedVoteAck, verifiedVoteAck}\}$

4.4   RCC DRE-i Clients

In this type of rogue clients, the RCC *DRE-i* rogue client successfully collaborate with the server through sending the client actions *voteCryptogramsReq, signTranssReq, voteCastMSG,* and *voteVerifyMSG* and receiving the server actions *voteCryptogramsReply, signTranscriptReply, castedVoteAck,* and *verifiedVoteAck*.

RCC Voting client:

$\text{RCC\_DRE\_Client}_0 \stackrel{def}{=} (\text{voteCryptogramsReq}, r_{\text{voteCryptogramsReq}}).\text{RCC\_DRE\_Client}_1$

$\text{RCC\_DRE\_Client}_1 \stackrel{def}{=} (\text{voteCryptogramsReply}, r_{\text{voteCryptogramsReply}}).\text{RCC\_DRE\_Client}_2$

$\text{RCC\_DRE\_Client}_2 \stackrel{def}{=} (\text{selectVoteReq}, r_{\text{selectVoteReq}}).\text{RCC\_DRE\_Client}_3$

$\text{RCC\_DRE\_Client}_3 \stackrel{def}{=} (\text{signTranscriptReq}, r_{\text{signTranscriptReq}}).\text{RCC\_DRE\_Client}_4$

$\text{RCC\_DRE\_Client}_4 \stackrel{def}{=} (\text{signTranscriptReply}, r_{\text{signTranscriptReply}}).\text{RCC\_DRE\_Client}_5$

$\text{RCC\_DRE\_Client}_5 \stackrel{def}{=} (\text{castReply}, r_{\text{castReply}}).\text{RCC\_DRE\_Client}_6 +$
$\qquad\qquad\qquad (\text{verifyReply}, r_{\text{verifyReply}}).\text{RCC\_DRE\_Client}_7$

$\text{RCC\_DRE\_Client}_6 \stackrel{def}{=} (\text{castedVoteMSG}, r_{\text{castedVoteMSG}}).\text{RCC\_DRE\_Client}_8$

$\text{RCC\_DRE\_Client}_8 \stackrel{def}{=} (\text{castedVoteAck}, r_{\text{castedVoteAck}}).\text{RCC\_DRE\_Client}_9$

$\text{RCC\_DRE\_Client}_9 \stackrel{def}{=} (\text{voteCastingComplete}, r_{\text{voteCastingComplete}}).$
$\qquad\qquad\qquad (\text{rc\_wait}, r_{\text{rc\_wait}}).\text{RCC\_DRE\_Client}_0$

$\text{RCC\_DRE\_Client}_7 \stackrel{def}{=} (\text{verifiedVoteMSG}, r_{\text{verifiedVoteMSG}}).\text{RCC\_DRE\_Client}_{10}$

$\text{RCC\_DRE\_Client}_{10} \stackrel{def}{=} (\text{verifiedVoteAck}, r_{\text{verifiedVoteAck}}).\text{RCC\_DRE\_Client}_{11}$

$\text{RCC\_DRE\_Client}_{11} \stackrel{def}{=} (\text{voteVerificationComplete}, r_{\text{voteVerificationComplete}}).$
$\qquad\qquad\qquad (\text{rc\_wait}, r_{\text{rc\_wait}}).\text{RCC\_DRE\_Client}_0$

System equation:

$((\text{DRE\_Client}_0[i] \bowtie \text{RCC\_DRE\_Client}_0[k]) \bowtie_{\mathcal{L}_1} \text{DRE\_SRV}_0[j])$

where i is the number of voters in the system, j is the number of e-voting servers, k is the number of RCC clients, and

$\mathcal{L}_1 = \{\text{voteCryptogramsReply}, \text{signTranscriptReply}, \text{castedVoteAck}, \text{verifiedVoteAck}\}$

5   Results and Discussion

After constructing and testing the performance models using the PEPA Eclipse Plug-in tool, we used the ordinary differential equations technique [14] of the

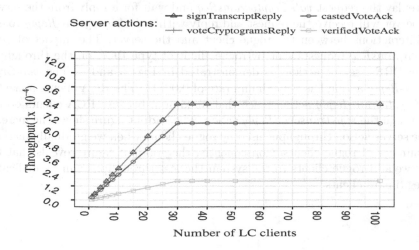

Fig. 2. Throughput for server actions.

tool to evaluate the effect of the intervention of rogue clients on the DRE-i e-voting system. We evaluated the goodput and badput of the server actions for the three types of rogue clients.

First, we investigated the impact of the misbehaving voters on the DRE-i system that had one DRE-i server, thirty legitimate clients, and a varying number of rogue clients. The goodput and badput were analysed. Later, we fixed the number of rogue clients to be 100, the legitimate clients (LC) to be 30, and varied the number of DRE-i servers from one to eight. Before starting the evaluation of the impact of the misbehaving voters' intervention on the performance of the system, we evaluated the throughput of the system. The system had one server, a varying number of legitimate clients, and no rogue clients. We found out that the server action *signTranscriptReply* had reached its maximum rate of 0.000820 when there were 30 legitimate clients in the system. As a result, the *castedVoteAck* and *verifiedVoteAck* reached a maximum throughput of 0.000656 and 0.000164, and *voteCryptogramsReply* reached a maximum throughput of 0.000820 (See Fig. 2). Therefore, we used this configuration, the one server and 30 legitimate clients, to evaluate the impact of the intervention of the three types of the misbehaving voters on the good throughput of the DRE-i system.

5.1   Goodput of Server Actions

In this section, we will show the effect of the three types of interventions of the misbehaving voters when they interact with one DRE-i server. Each intervention type has a different rate to complete one intervention with the DRE-i server. RCA will have the highest rate to complete one intervention, RCB will have a lower rate, and RCC will have the lowest rate.

Impact of RCA Intervention. In the PEPA model of RCA, the rogue client will replay the request *voteCryptogramsReq* and wait for a reply from the server. The server will receive the request and reply with *voteCryptogramsReply* to end the interactions between the rogue client and the server. The impact of *voteCryptogramsReq* requests sent by rogue client of type RCA on the throughput of the DRE-i server actions is demonstrated in Figs. 3 and 4. The *voteCryptogramsReply* action has a maximum rate of 0.00114. The RCA clients make the *voteCryptogramsReply* action reach that maximum because RCA clients do not go through the *signTranscriptReply* action. The badput figure shows the increase of the server action throughput used by rogue clients when we gradually increase the number of rogue clients. Consequently, the goodput figure reveals that the more we add rogue clients to the system the less throughput will be dedicated for legitimate clients.

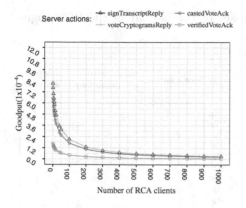

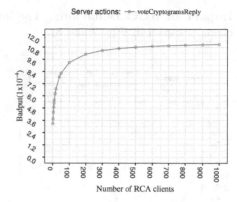

Fig. 3. Goodput for server actions.   **Fig. 4.** Badput for server actions.

Impact of RCB Behaviour. The impact of *voteCryptogramsReq* and *sign-TranscriptReq* requests sent by rogue client of type RCB on the throughput of the DRE-i server actions is demonstrated in Figs. 5 and 6. In this intervention type, the rogue client needs to go through the server action *signTranscriptReply* which has the minimum rate among the rates of the server's actions. The rate of the server's action *signTranscriptReply* will slow down the intervention rate of RCB compared to the intervention rate of RCA. This explains why the *voteCryptogramsReply* action will not exceed the rate of 0.00082.

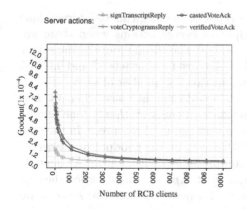

Fig. 5. Goodput for server actions.   **Fig. 6.** Badput for server actions.

The badput and goodput in Figs. 5 and 6 show that the increase in the number of rogue clients in the system increases the badput of the server's actions. Consequently, this will make goodput of the server's actions decrease.

Impact of RCC Behaviour. The impact of the badput of the RCC rogue client is shown in Figs. 7 and 8.

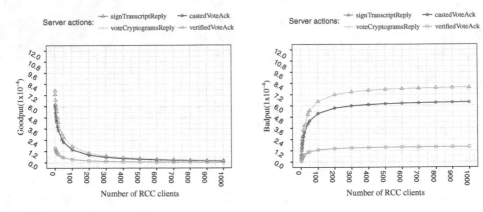

Fig. 7. Goodput for server actions.   **Fig. 8.** Badput for server actions.

The badput and goodput of server actions' *voteCryptogramsReply* and *signTranscriptReply* in this type of intervention are similar to those in the RCB intervention because both RCB and RCC rogue clients need to go through the server action *signTranscriptReply*.

5.2   Scalability of Server's Goodput

After investigating the impact of the three types of the illegitimate interventions on one server, we have studied the goodput of server actions when there are more than one server. As shown in Figs. 9 and 10, the throughputs of the server actions *voteCryptogramReply* and *castedVoteAck* are fixed at 0.0082 and 0.00065 when the system has 30 legitimate clients and varying number of servers.

The throughput for the two server's actions do not increase when we add more servers. The rate of 0.0082 for the action *signTranscriptReply* (one server) is enough to provide the 30 legitimate clients with required resources. In the case when there are one or two servers in the DRE-i system, the goodput of the server action *voteCryptogramReply* when the system interacts with 100 RCA clients is better than the goodput of the server action *voteCryptogramReply* when the system interacts with 100 RCC clients. However, when there are five servers, we notice the contrary. This is because the RCA rogue client has a higher intensity of actions with the DRE-i server than the RCB or RCC rogue client has. The RCB and RCC rogue clients face a bottleneck at the server's action *signTranscriptReply* when they interact with the system. However, when we increase the number of servers, we alleviate the bottleneck in the action *signTranscriptReply*. Therefore, the rogue clients RCB and RCC, and the 30 legitimate clients get more throughput from the server's action *signTranscriptReply*. So, the DRE-i

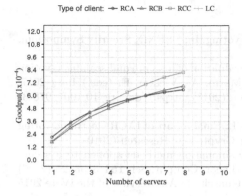

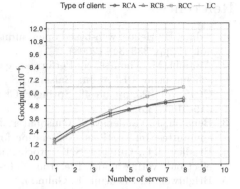

Fig. 9. Goodput for voteCryptogramsReply. $LC = 30$, $RCA = 100$, $RCB = 100$, and $RCC = 100$.

Fig. 10. Goodput for castedVoteAck. $LC = 30$, $RCA = 100$, $RCB = 100$, and $RCC = 100$.

system starts having a better goodput when it has interventions from RCB or RCC rogue clients compared to the goodput it will have when it has interventions from RCA. Moreover, the evaluation of the performance models of the DRE-i system with misbehaving voters shows that adding more servers (up to seven servers) do not make the goodput of the servers' actions reaches the throughput of the DRE-i servers when the system has no misbehaving voters.

6 Conclusion

In this paper, by using PEPA, we presented the performance models of three misbehaving voters when using the large scale and secure DRE-i e-voting system. The constructed performance models captured the high-level interactions between the DRE-i e-voting system, the valid voters, and the misbehaving voters. The evaluation of throughput of the main DRE-i server's actions clearly shows the impact of the interaction of misbehaving voters with the e-voting system. The goodput of server actions went down when added more rogue clients to the system.

The evaluation of the effect of misbehaving voters on the DRE-i e-voting system can be extended to include the analysis of the response time that will be observed by legitimate voters when they cast their votes. Furthermore, the countermeasures to reduce the effect of misbehaving voters on the performance of the DRE-i voting system is an interesting area to be investigated using the formal performance formalism like PEPA.

References

1. Adida, B.: Helios: web-based open-audit voting. In: USENIX Security Symposium, vol. 17, pp. 335–348 (2008)
2. Alotaibi, M., Thomas, N.: Performance evaluation of a secure and scalable e-voting scheme using PEPA. In: Balsamo, S., Marin, A., Vicario, E. (eds.) InfQ 2017. CCIS, vol. 825, pp. 35–48. Springer, Cham (2018). https://doi.org/10.1007/978-3-319-91632-3_3
3. Benaloh, J., Vaudenay, S., Quisquater, J.J.: Final report of IACR electronic voting committee. International Association for Cryptologic Research (2010)
4. Bradley, J.T., Gilmore, S.T.: Stochastic simulation methods applied to a secure electronic voting model. Electron. Notes Theor. Comput. Sci. **151**(3), 5–25 (2006)
5. Brightwell, I., Cucurull, J., Galindo, D., Guasch, S.: An overview of the iVote 2015 voting system (2015)
6. Cortier, V., Smyth, B.: Attacking and fixing helios: an analysis of ballot secrecy. J. Comput. Secur. **21**(1), 89–148 (2013)
7. Estehghari, S., Desmedt, Y.: Exploiting the client vulnerabilities in Internet e-voting systems: Hacking Helios 2.0 as an example. In: EVT/WOTE 2010, pp. 1–9 (2010)
8. Fujioka, A., Okamoto, T., Ohta, K.: A practical secret voting scheme for large scale elections. In: Seberry, J., Zheng, Y. (eds.) AUSCRYPT 1992. LNCS, vol. 718, pp. 244–251. Springer, Heidelberg (1993). https://doi.org/10.1007/3-540-57220-1_66
9. Gilmore, S., Tribastone, M.: Evaluating the scalability of a web service-based distributed e-learning and course management system. In: Bravetti, M., Núñez, M., Zavattaro, G. (eds.) WS-FM 2006. LNCS, vol. 4184, pp. 214–226. Springer, Heidelberg (2006). https://doi.org/10.1007/11841197_14
10. Gritzalis, D.A.: Principles and requirements for a secure e-voting system. Comput. Secur. **21**(6), 539–556 (2002)
11. Hao, F., Kreeger, M., Randell, B., Clarke, D., Shahandashti, S., Lee, P.J.: Every vote counts: ensuring integrity in large-scale electronic voting. In: 2014 Electronic Voting Technology Workshop/Workshop on Trustworthy Elections, EVT/WOTE 2014, vol. 2, pp. 1–25 (2014)
12. Hao, F., Ryan, P.Y.: Real-World Electronic Voting: Design, Analysis and Deployment. CRC Press, Boca Raton (2016)
13. Hillston, J.J.: A compositional approach to performance modelling. Distinguished dissertations in Computer Science, Cambridge University Press, Cambridge (1996)
14. Hillston, J.: Fluid flow approximation of PEPA models. In: Second International Conference on the Quantitative Evaluation of Systems, QEST 2005. IEEE (2005)
15. Kohno, T., Stubblefield, A., Rubin, A.D., Wallach, D.S.: Analysis of an electronic voting system. In: Proceedings of 2004 IEEE Symposium on Security and Privacy, pp. 27–40. IEEE (2004)
16. Lee, P.H.J., Shahandashti, S.F.: Theoretical attacks on E2E voting systems. Real-World Electronic Voting: Design, Analysis and Deployment, p. 219 (2016)
17. Madise, Ü., Martens, T.: E-voting in Estonia 2005. The first practice of country-wide binding Internet voting in the world. Electron. Voting **86** (2006)
18. Smyth, B., Cortier, V.: A note on replay attacks that violate privacy in electronic voting schemes. Ph.D. thesis, INRIA (2011)
19. Sudhodanan, A., Carbone, R., Compagna, L., Dolgin, N., Armando, A., Morelli, U.: Large-scale analysis & detection of authentication cross-site request forgeries. In: 2017 IEEE European Symposium on Security and Privacy (EuroS&P), pp. 350–365. IEEE (2017)

20. Thomas, N.: Performability of a secure electronic voting algorithm. Electron. Notes Theor. Comput. Sci. **128**, 45–58 (2005)
21. Tribastone, M., Duguid, A., Gilmore, S.: The PEPA eclipse plugin. ACM SIGMETRICS Perform. Eval. Rev. **36**(4), 28–33 (2009)
22. Wang, H., Laurenson, D.I., Hillston, J.: Evaluation of RSVP and mobility-aware RSVP using performance evaluation process algebra. In: 2008 IEEE International Conference on Communications, ICC 2008, pp. 192–197. IEEE (2008)
23. Yasinac, A., et al.: Software review and security analysis of the ES&S iVotronic 8.0. 1.2 voting machine firmware. Technical report, Security and Assurance in Information Technology Laboratory, Florida State University (2007)

Information Flow Security for Stochastic Processes

Jane Hillston[1], Andrea Marin[2], Carla Piazza[3(✉)], and Sabina Rossi[2]

[1] University of Edinburgh, Edinburgh, UK
Jane.Hillston@ed.ac.uk
[2] Università Ca' Foscari Venezia, Venice, Italy
{marin,sabina.rossi}@unive.it
[3] Università di Udine, Udine, Italy
carla.piazza@uniud.it

Abstract. In this paper we study an information flow security property for systems specified as terms of a quantitative process algebra, namely Performance Evaluation Process Algebra (PEPA). Intuitively, we propose a quantitative extension of the Non-Interference property used to secure systems from the functional point view by assuming that the observers are able to measure also the timing properties of the system, e.g., the response time or the throughput.

We introduce the notion of *Persistent Stochastic Non-Interference (PSNI)* and provide two characterizations of it: one based on a bisimulation-like equivalence relation inducing a lumping on the underlying Markov chain, and another one based on unwinding conditions which demand properties of individual actions. These two different characterizations naturally lead to efficient methods for the verification and construction of secure systems. A decision algorithm for *PSNI* is presented and an application of *PSNI* to a queueing system is discussed.

1 Introduction

In the last decades, security of information systems has become a crucial topic of research. Finding a formal characterisation of the various properties defined in the context of security, (e.g., confidentiality, anonymity, integrity, etc.) has been an active field of research. Beside numerous definitions of security have been proposed, very few results take into account the time behaviour of the analysed system. However, it is well-known that from the observation of the response times of a system, malicious observers can infer some characteristics that may help an attack to succeed (see, e.g., [2,3,5]). In this paper, we propose a first set of results to cover this gap. We consider systems specified as terms of a quantitative process algebra, namely Performance Evaluation Process Algebra (PEPA). In contrast with most the process algebras used in previous well-known results (e.g., the CCS used for the Non-Interference property [6]), PEPA allows us to specify random delays to model the quantitative properties of the system. Besides, the results that we present can be applied to any Markovian formalism

© Springer Nature Switzerland AG 2018
R. Bakhshi et al. (Eds.): EPEW 2018, LNCS 11178, pp. 142–156, 2018.
https://doi.org/10.1007/978-3-030-02227-3_10

with a synchronisation operator in the style of PEPA cooperation, e.g., the Kronecker's product for Stochastic Automata Networks (see [12,13] and the references therein).

Intuitively, the idea that we propose is a quantitative extension of the Non-Interference property that has been widely used to secure systems from the functional point view [4,6–8,14–18]. Let us consider a system that performs some actions that are intended to be confidential and some others that are observable by an external, possibly malicious, user. Roughly speaking, in the standard, functional, definition of Non-Interference a system S is secure if any external observer is not able to distinguish the behaviour of S performing confidential, secret, activities from the behaviour of the same system but prevented from performing any secret action. In our setting, the definition does not change, however we assume that the observer is able to measure also the timing properties of that system, e.g., the response time or the throughput. In this paper we consider the strictest situation in terms of security requirements, i.e., the observer can see any observable execution path with its delays, i.e., he/she can see the transient behaviour of the system and study correlation properties, averages, etc. The request that for any execution path of the model that performs unobservable, private, actions there exists a corresponding execution path in the model that does not perform private actions (and vice versa) clearly implies that the two models are also indistinguishable when observed in steady-state. However, as shown in the example of Sect. 5, the opposite is in general not true.

We introduce a notion of *stochastic Non-Interference* which is *persistent* in the sense that if a system is secure then all its reachable states are secure too. We show that such property, named *Persistent Stochastic Non-Interference (PSNI)* can be charaterized in terms of a bisimulation-like equivalence relation, between the whole system and the system prevented from performing confidential activities. The property that we propose is strictly related to the lumping of Markov chains since the observation equivalence at the base of our definition relies on the notion of lumpability [10]. Moreover, we provide a characterization of *PSNI* in terms of unwinding conditions which demand properties of individual actions. These two different characterizations naturally lead to efficient methods for the verification and construction of secure systems. We prove that *PSNI* can be verified in polynomial time with respect to the number of states of a system.

We describe an application of *PSNI* to a simple queueing system in which at random instants some private internal operations are performed. Although the functionality of the system is not altered by these operations (and hence the standard Non-Interference is satisfied), the response time is worsen and hence private information can be leaked. We show a simple workaround that makes the system secure and discuss its implications in terms of overall performance.

Structure of the Paper. The paper is organized as follows. In Sect. 2 we introduce the process algebra PEPA, its semantics, and the observation equivalence named *lumpable bisimilarity*. The notion of *Persistent Stochastic Non-Interference (PSNI)* and its characterizations are presented in Sect. 3. In Sect. 4 we describe an algorithm to decide whether a PEPA component is *PSNI*.

Section 5 presents a simple example of a queueing system in which some private operations are preformed. Finally, Sect. 6 concludes the paper.

Table 1. Operational semantics for PEPA components

$$
\frac{}{(\alpha,r).P \xrightarrow{(\alpha,r)} P} \qquad \frac{P \xrightarrow{(\alpha,r)} P'}{P+Q \xrightarrow{(\alpha,r)} P'} \qquad \frac{Q \xrightarrow{(\alpha,r)} Q'}{P+Q \xrightarrow{(\alpha,r)} Q'}
$$

$$
\frac{P \xrightarrow{(\alpha,r)} P'}{P/L \xrightarrow{(\alpha,r)} P'/L}\ (\alpha \notin L) \qquad \frac{P \xrightarrow{(\alpha,r)} P'}{P/L \xrightarrow{(\tau,r)} P'/L}\ (\alpha \in L) \qquad \frac{P \xrightarrow{(\alpha,r)} P'}{A \xrightarrow{(\alpha,r)} P'}\ (A \stackrel{def}{=} P)
$$

$$
\frac{P \xrightarrow{(\alpha,r)} P'}{P \bowtie_L Q \xrightarrow{(\alpha,r)} P' \bowtie_L Q}\ (\alpha \notin L) \qquad \frac{Q \xrightarrow{(\alpha,r)} Q'}{P \bowtie_L Q \xrightarrow{(\alpha,r)} P \bowtie_L Q'}\ (\alpha \notin L)
$$

$$
\frac{P \xrightarrow{(\alpha,r_1)} P'\ \ Q \xrightarrow{(\alpha,r_2)} Q'}{P \bowtie_L Q \xrightarrow{(\alpha,R)} P' \bowtie_L Q'} \qquad R = \frac{r_1}{r_\alpha(P)} \frac{r_2}{r_\alpha(Q)} \min(r_\alpha(P), r_\alpha(Q))\ \ (\alpha \in L)
$$

2   The Calculus

PEPA (Performance Evaluation Process Algebra) is a popular Markovian process algebra introduced in [9] that allows one to model and study the quantitative properties of systems. It consists of two basic elements: the *components* and the *activities.* Activities are pairs (α, r) where α is a label or *action type* belonging to a countable set $\mathcal{A}$, and $r \in \mathbb{R}^+ \cup \{\top\}$ is its *rate* The duration of an activity is a negative exponential distribution with mean r^{-1}. Action type $\tau \in \mathcal{A}$ is the *unknown* type. Activity rates may be $\top$ which should be read as *unspecified.* The syntax for PEPA terms follows the grammar:

$$
P :: = P \bowtie_L P \mid P/L \mid S
$$
$$
S :: = (\alpha, r).S \mid S + S \mid A
$$

where S denotes a *sequential component* and P denotes a *model component* which runs in parallel. Finally, A is a countable set of *constants* and $\mathcal{C}$ denotes the set of all possible components.

Operational Semantics. Table 1 shows the operational semantics of PEPA. The component $(\alpha, r).P$ carries out the activity (α, r) of type α at rate r and subsequently behaves as P. When $a = (\alpha, r)$, the component $(\alpha, r).P$ may be written as $a.P$. $P + Q$ specifies a system which may behave either as P or as Q and where all the current activities of both P and Q are enabled. The first activity to complete distinguishes one of the components, P or Q. The other component of the choice is discarded. The component P/L behaves as P except that any activity of type within the set L are *hidden*, i.e., they are relabelled with the unknown type τ. The meaning of a constant A is given by a defining equation such as $A \overset{def}{=} P$ which gives the constant A the behaviour of the component P. The cooperation combinator $\underset{L}{\bowtie}$ is in fact an indexed family of combinators, one for each possible set of action types, $L \subseteq \mathcal{A} \setminus \{\tau\}$. The *cooperation set* L defines the action types on which the components must synchronise or *cooperate* (the unknown action type, τ, may not appear in any cooperation set). It is assumed that each component proceeds independently with the activities whose types do not occur in the cooperation set L (*individual activities*). However, activities with action types in L require the simultaneous involvement of both components. The shared activity will have the same action type as the two contributing activities and its rate is that of the slower component. If in a component an activity has rate $\top$, then we say that it is passive with respect to that action type. In this case the rate of the shared activity will be that of the other component. For a given P and action type α, the *apparent rate* of α in P, denoted by $r_\alpha(P)$, is the sum of the rates of the α activities enabled in P.

The semantics of each term in PEPA is given via a labelled *multi-transition system* where the multiplicities of arcs are significant. In the transition system, a state or *derivative* corresponds to each syntactic term of the language and an arc represents the activity which causes one derivative to evolve into another. The set of reachable states of a model P is termed the *derivative set* of P ($ds(P)$) and constitutes the set of nodes of the *derivation graph* of P ($\mathcal{D}(P)$) obtained by applying the semantic rules exhaustively. We denote by $\mathcal{A}(P)$ the set of all the *current action types* of P, i.e., the set of action types which the component P may next engage in. We denote by $Act(P)$ the multiset of all the *current activities* of P. Finally we denote by $\mathcal{A}(P)$ the union of all $\mathcal{A}(P')$ with $P' \in ds(P)$, i.e., the set of all action types syntactically occurring in P. For any component P, the *exit rate* from P will be the sum of the activity rates of all the activities enabled in P, i.e., $q(P) = \sum_{a \in Act(P)} r_a$, with r_a being the rate of activity a. If P enables more than one activity, $|Act(P)| > 1$, then the dynamic behaviour of the model is determined by a race condition. As a consqeuence, the nondeterministic branching of the pure process algebra is replaced by a probabilistic branching. Thanks to the exponential assumption, the probability that a particular activity completes is the ratio between its rate and the exit rate from P.

Underlying Markov Chain. Let $P \overset{def}{=} P_0$ with $ds(P) = \{P_0, \ldots, P_n\}$ be a finite PEPA model. Then, the stochastic process $X(t)$ on the space $ds(P)$ is a continuous time Markov chain [9].

The *transition rate* between two states P_i and P_j is denoted by $q(P_i, P_j)$ and corresponds to rate at which the system changes from behaving as component P_i to behaving as P_j, i.e., it is the sum of the activity rates labelling arcs which connect the node corresponding to P_i to the node corresponding to P_j in the derivation graph. Formally:

$$q(P_i, P_j) = \sum_{a \in Act(P_i|P_j)} r_a$$

with $P_i \neq P_j$ and $Act(P_i|P_j) = \{a \in Act(P_i)| P_i \xrightarrow{a} P_j\}$. When P_j is not a one-step derivative of P_i we set $q(P_i, P_j) = 0$. In the following, when possible, we will write q_{ij} instead of $q(P_i, P_j)$. In the definition of the infinitesimal generator $\mathbf{Q}$ of $X(t)$, q_{ij}, $i \neq j$, are the off-diagonal elements of the matrix whereas the diagonal elements are, as usual, the negative sum of the row non-diagonal elements, i.e., $q_{ii} = -q(P_i)$. For any finite and irreducible PEPA model P, the steady-state distribution $\Pi(\cdot)$ exists and it may be found by solving the probability normalising equation and the linear system of global balance equations: $\sum_{P_i \in ds(P)} \Pi(P_i) = 1$ and $\Pi\mathbf{Q} = \mathbf{0}$. Another notion that will be used in the paper is that of *conditional transition rate* from P_i to P_j via an action type α, denoted by $q(P_i, P_j, \alpha)$. This is the sum of the activity rates labelling arcs connecting the corresponding nodes in the derivation graph which are also labelled by the action type α. It is the rate at which a system behaving as component P_i evolves to behaving as component P_j as the result of completing a type α activity. The *total conditional transition rate* from P to $S \subseteq ds(P)$, denoted $q[P, S, \alpha]$, is defined as

$$q[P, S, \alpha] = \sum_{P' \in S} q(P, P', \alpha)$$

where $q(P, P', \alpha) = \sum_{P \xrightarrow{(\alpha, r_\alpha)} P'} r_\alpha$.

Observation Equivalence. When we study a system by means of a process algebraic model, actions, rather than states, are used to capture its observable behaviour. Therefore, we introduce an equivalence notion in which components are regarded as equal if an external observer sees them performing exactly the same actions. In this section we recall a bisimulation-like relation, named *lumpable bisimulation*, for PEPA models that we previously introduced in [10].

Two PEPA components are *lumpably bisimilar* if there exists an equivalence relation between them such that, for any action type α different from τ, the total conditional transition rates from those components to any equivalence class, via activities of this type, are the same.

Definition 1 (Lumpable bisimulation). *An equivalence relation over PEPA components, $\mathcal{R} \subseteq \mathcal{C} \times \mathcal{C}$, is a lumpable bisimulation if whenever $(P, Q) \in \mathcal{R}$ then for all $\alpha \in \mathcal{A}$ and for all $S \in \mathcal{C}/\mathcal{R}$ such that*

- *either $\alpha \neq \tau$,*
- *or $\alpha = \tau$ and $P, Q \notin S$,*

it holds

$$q[P, S, \alpha] = q[Q, S, \alpha].$$

Notice that, in contrast with the notion of strong equivalence [9], lumpable bisimulation allows arbitrary activities with type τ among components belonging to the same equivalence class, and therefore it is less strict.

We are interested in the relation which is the largest lumpable bisimulation, formed by the union of all lumpable bisimulations.

Definition 2 (Lumpable bisimilarity). *Two PEPA components P and Q are lumpably bisimilar, written $P \approx_l Q$, if $(P, Q) \in \mathcal{R}$ for some lumpable bisimulation $\mathcal{R}$, i.e.,*

$$\approx_l = \bigcup \{\mathcal{R} \mid \mathcal{R} \text{ is a lumpable bisimulation}\}.$$

$\approx_l$ is called lumpable bisimilarity *and it is the largest symmetric lumpable bisimulation over PEPA components.*

In [10] we proved that lumpable bisimilarity is a congruence for the so-called evaluation contexts, i.e., if $P_1 \approx_l P_2$ then

- $a.P_1 \approx_l a.P_2$;
- $P_1/L \approx_l P_2/L$;
- $P_1 \bowtie_L Q \approx_l P_2 \bowtie_L Q$ for all $L \subseteq \mathcal{A}$.

3   Persistent Stochastic Non-interference

The security propery named *Persistent Stochastic Non-Interference (PSNI)* tries to capture every possible information flow from a *classified (high)* level of confidentiality to an *untrusted (low)* one. A strong requirement of this definition is that no information flow should be possible even in the presence of malicious processes that run at the classified level.

The definition of *PSNI* is based on the basic idea of Non-Interference [8]: "No information flow is possible from high to low if what is done at the high level *cannot interfere* in any way with the low level".

More precisely, the notion of *PSNI* consists of checking all the states reachable by the system against all high level potential interactions.

In order to formally define our security property, we partition the set $\mathcal{A} \setminus \{\tau\}$ of visible action types, into two sets, $\mathcal{H}$ and $\mathcal{L}$ of high and low level action types. A high level PEPA component H is a PEPA term such that for all $H' \in ds(H)$, $\mathcal{A}(H') \subseteq \mathcal{H}$, i.e., every derivative of H may next engage in only high level actions. We denote by $\mathcal{C}_H$ the set of all high level PEPA components.

A system P satisfies *PSNI* if for every state P' reachable from P and for every high level process H a low level user cannot distinguish P' from $P' \bowtie_{\mathcal{H}} H$. In other words, a system P satisfies *PSNI* if what a low level user sees of the system is not modified when it cooperates with any high level process H.

In order to formally define the *PSNI* property, we denote by $P \setminus \mathcal{H}$ the PEPA component $(P \bowtie_{\mathcal{H}} \bar{H})$ where $\bar{H}$ is any high level process that does not cooperate with P, i.e., for all $P' \in ds(P)$, $\mathcal{A}(P') \cap \mathcal{A}(\bar{H}) = \emptyset$. Intuitively $P \setminus \mathcal{H}$ denotes the component P prevented from performing high level actions.

First we prove that $P \setminus \mathcal{H}$ is well defined, i.e., it does not depend on $\bar{H}$. The proof follows by structural induction on P.

Lemma 1. *Let P be a PEPA component and $\bar{H}$ be a high level process that does not cooperate with P. $P \underset{\mathcal{H}}{\bowtie} \bar{H} \xrightarrow{(\alpha,r)} Q$ if and only if Q is of the form $P' \underset{\mathcal{H}}{\bowtie} \bar{H}$ and $P \xrightarrow{(\alpha,r)} P'$ with $\alpha \in \mathcal{L} \cup \{\tau\}$.*

Notice that the above lemma applies also to P' and more in general to all the processes in $ds(P)$, since they do not cooperate with $\bar{H}$.

Lemma 2. *Let P be a PEPA component. Let $\bar{H}_1$ and $\bar{H}_2$ be two high level processes that do not cooperate with P, i.e., for all $P' \in ds(P)$, $\mathcal{A}(P') \cap \mathcal{A}(\bar{H}_i) = \emptyset$ for $i = 1, 2$. The derivation graphs $\mathcal{D}(P \underset{\mathcal{H}}{\bowtie} \bar{H}_1)$ and $\mathcal{D}(P \underset{\mathcal{H}}{\bowtie} \bar{H}_2)$ are isomorphic as graphs with labels on the edges.*

The formal definition of *PSNI* is as follows.

Definition 3. *Let P be a PEPA component.*

$$P \in PSNI \text{ iff } \forall P' \in ds(P), \forall H \in \mathcal{C}_H,$$

$$P' \setminus \mathcal{H} \approx_l (P' \underset{\mathcal{H}}{\bowtie} H)/\mathcal{H}.$$

We introduce a novel bisimulation-based equivalence relation over PEPA components, named $\approx_l^{hc}$, that allows us to give a first characterization of *PSNI* with no quantification over all the high level components H. In particular, we show that $P \in PSNI$ if and only if $P \setminus \mathcal{H}$ and P are not distinguishable with respect to $\approx_l^{hc}$. Intuitively, two processes are $\approx_l^{hc}$-equivalent if they can simulate each other in any possible high context, i.e., in every context $C[\_]$ of the form $(\_ \underset{\mathcal{H}}{\bowtie} H)/\mathcal{H}$ where $H \in \mathcal{C}_H$. Observe that for any high context $C[\_]$ and PEPA model P, all the states reachable from $C[P]$ have the form $C'[P']$ with $C'[\_]$ being a high context too and $P' \in ds(P)$.

We now introduce the concept of *lumpable bisimulation on high contexts*: the idea is that, given two PEPA models P and Q, when a high level context $C[\_]$ filled with P executes a cetain activity moving P to P' then the same context filled with Q is able to simulate this step moving Q to Q' so that P' and Q' are again lumpable bismilar on high contexts, and vice-versa. This must be true for every possible high context $C[\_]$. It is important to note that the quantification over all possible high contexts is re-itereted for P' and Q'.

We use the following notation. For a PEPA model P, $\alpha \in \mathcal{A}$, $S \subseteq ds(P)$ and a high context $C[\_]$ we define:

$$q_C(P, P', \alpha) = \sum_{C[P] \xrightarrow{(\alpha, r_\alpha)} C'[P']} r_\alpha$$

and

$$q_C[P, S, \alpha] = \sum_{P' \in S} q_C(P, P', \alpha).$$

The notion of *lumpable bisimulation on high contexts* is defined as follows:

Definition 4 (Lumpable bisimilarity on high contexts). *An equivalence rela-tion over PEPA components, $\mathcal{R} \subseteq \mathcal{C} \times \mathcal{C}$, is a* lumpable bisimulation on high contexts *if whenever $(P, Q) \in \mathcal{R}$ then for all high context $C[\_]$, for all $\alpha \in \mathcal{A}$ and for all $S \in \mathcal{C}/\mathcal{R}$ such that*

- *either $\alpha \neq \tau$,*
- *or $\alpha = \tau$ and $P, Q \notin S$,*

it holds
$$q_C[P, S, \alpha] = q_C[Q, S, \alpha].$$

Two PEPA components P and Q are lumpably bisimilar on high contexts, *writ-ten $P \approx_l^{hc} Q$, if $(P, Q) \in \mathcal{R}$ for some lumpable bisimulation on high contexts $\mathcal{R}$, i.e.,*

$$\approx_l^{hc} = \bigcup \{\mathcal{R} \mid \mathcal{R} \text{ is a lumpable bisimulation on high contexts}\}.$$

$\approx_l^{hc}$ *is called* lumpable bisimilarity on high contexts *and it is the largest sym-metric lumpable bisimulation on high contexts over PEPA components.*

The next theorem provides a characterization of *PSNI* in terms of $\approx_l^{hc}$.

Theorem 1. *Let P be a PEPA component. Then*

$$P \in PSNI \text{ iff } P \setminus \mathcal{H} \approx_l^{hc} P.$$

We now show how it is possible to give a characterization of *PSNI* avoiding both the universal quantification over all the possible high level components and the universal quantification over all the possible reachable states.

Before we have shown how the idea of "being secure in every state" can be directly moved inside the lumpable bisimulation on high contexts notion ($\approx_l^{hc}$). However this bisimulation notion implicitly contains a quantification over all possible high contexts. We prove that $\approx_l^{hc}$ can be expressed in a rather simpler way by exploiting local information only. This can be done by defining a novel equivalence relation which focuses only on observable actions that do not belong to $\mathcal{H}$. More in detail, we define an observation equivalence where actions from $\mathcal{H}$ may be ignored. We introduce the notion of *lumpable bisimilarity up to $\mathcal{H}$.*

Definition 5 (Lumpable bisimilarity up to $\mathcal{H}$). *An equivalence relation over PEPA components, $\mathcal{R} \subseteq \mathcal{C} \times \mathcal{C}$, is a* lumpable bisimulation up to $\mathcal{H}$ *if whenever $(P, Q) \in \mathcal{R}$ then for all $\alpha \in \mathcal{A}$ and for all $S \in \mathcal{C}/\mathcal{R}$*

- *if $\alpha \notin \mathcal{H} \cup \{\tau\}$ then*
$$q[P, S, \alpha] = q[Q, S, \alpha],$$
- *if $\alpha \in \mathcal{H} \cup \{\tau\}$ and $P, Q \notin S$, then*

$$q[P, S, \alpha] = q[Q, S, \alpha].$$

Two PEPA components P and Q are lumpably bisimilar up to $\mathcal{H}$, written $P \approx_l^{\mathcal{H}} Q$, if $(P, Q) \in \mathcal{R}$ for some lumpable bisimulation up to $\mathcal{H}$, i.e.,

$$\approx_l^{\mathcal{H}} = \bigcup \{\mathcal{R} \mid \mathcal{R} \text{ is a lumpable bisimulation up to } \mathcal{H}\}.$$

$\approx_l^{\mathcal{H}}$ is called lumpable bisimilarity up to $\mathcal{H}$ and it is the largest symmetric lumpable bisimulation up to $\mathcal{H}$ over PEPA components.

The next theorem shows that the binary relations $\approx_l^{hc}$ and $\approx_l^{\mathcal{H}}$ are equivalent.

Theorem 2. *Let P and Q be two PEPA components. Then*

$$P \approx_l^{hc} Q \text{ if and only if } P \approx_l^{\mathcal{H}} Q.$$

Theorem 2 allows us to identify a local property of processes (with no quantification on the states and on the high contexts) which is a necessary and sufficient condition for *PSNI*. This is stated by the following corollary:

Corollary 1. *Let P be a PEPA component. Then*

$$P \in PSNI \text{ iff } P \setminus \mathcal{H} \approx_l^{\mathcal{H}} P.$$

Finally we provide a characterization of *PSNI* in terms of *unwinding conditions* which demand properties of individual activities. In practice, whenever a state P' of a *PSNI* PEPA model P may execute a high level activity leading it to a state P'', then P' and P'' are indistinguishable for a low level observer.

Theorem 3. *Let P be a PEPA component.*

$$P \in PSNI \text{ iff } \forall P' \in ds(P),$$

$$P' \xrightarrow{(h,r)} P'' \text{ implies } P' \setminus \mathcal{H} \approx_l P'' \setminus \mathcal{H}.$$

Using the equivalence relation $\approx_l^{\mathcal{H}}$ this can be reformulated as follows.

Theorem 4. *Let P be a PEPA component.*

$$P \in PSNI \text{ iff } \forall P' \in ds(P),$$

$$P' \xrightarrow{(h,r)} P'' \text{ implies } P' \approx_l^{\mathcal{H}} P''.$$

Theorems 2, 3 and 4 provide different characterizations of *PSNI* which naturally lead to efficient methods for the verification and construction of secure systems. We also prove some compositionality results that allow us to check the security of a system by only verifying the security of its subcomponents. In particular we prove that *PSNI* is compositional with respect to the low prefix, hiding, and cooperation over a set of low actions.

Proposition 1. *Let P and Q be two PEPA components. If $P, Q \in PSNI$, then*

- $(\alpha, r).P \in PSNI$ *for all $\alpha \in \mathcal{L} \cup \{\tau\}$;*
- $P/L \in PSNI$ *for all $L \subseteq \mathcal{A}$;*
- $P \bowtie_L Q \in PSNI$ *for all $L \subseteq \mathcal{L}$.*

We also prove that if $P \in PSNI$ then the equivalence class $[P]$ with respect to lumpable bisimilarity $\approx_l$ is closed under *PSNI*.

Proposition 2. *Let P and Q be two PEPA components. If $P \in PSNI$ and $P \approx_l Q$ then also $Q \in PSNI$.*

4   A Decision Algorithm for *PSNI*

In this section we briefly describe an algorithm to decide whether a PEPA component is *PSNI*. We first exploit the characterization of *PSNI* given in Corollary 1, i.e., we provide an algorithm that given in input two PEPA components P and Q having finite derivative graphs allows one to decide whether $P \approx_l^{\mathcal{H}} Q$. In virtue of Corollary 1 this will allow us to decide whether a process is *PSNI*. As observed in [10] even if the set $\mathcal{C}$ of PEPA components is infinite, since we are interested in $P \approx_l^{\mathcal{H}} Q$ we can safely focus on the graph $\mathcal{D}(P) \cup \mathcal{D}(Q)$. We intend to exploit the algorithm introduced in [1] for solving the label-compatibility problem. To this aim we need to introduce the notion of directed labeled weighted graphs, the label-compatibility problem, and to show how our problem can be mapped into a label-compatibility one.

Definition 6 (Directed labeled weighted graph). *A directed labeled weighted graph is a tuple $G = (V, Lab, E, w)$ where:*

- *V is a finite set of vertices;*
- *Lab is a finite set of labels;*
- *$E \subseteq V \times V \times Lab$ is a finite set of labeled edges;*
- *$w : E \to \mathbb{R}$ is a weighting function that associates a value to each edge.*

Given $V' \subseteq V$, we denote by $w(v, V', a)$ the sum of the weights of the edges from v to V' having label a.

The following definition of compatibility introduced in [1] extends that of [19] to directed labeled weighted graphs.

Definition 7 (Label-Compatibility Problem). *Let $G = (V, Lab, E, w)$ be a directed labeled weighted graph and $\mathcal{R} \subseteq V \times V$ be an equivalence relation over V. $\mathcal{R}$ is said to be* label-compatible *with G if for each $a \in Lab$, for each $C, C' \in V/\mathcal{R}$, and for each $v, v' \in C$ it holds that $w(v, C', a) = w(v', C', a)$.*

Let $G = (V, Lab, E, w)$ be a directed labeled weighted graph the labeled weighted compatibility problem *over G requires to compute the largest equivalence relation label-compatible with G.*

In [1] it has been proved that the label-compatibility problem always has a unique solution. We now introduce the graph that allows us to map our problem of deciding $P \approx_l^{\mathcal{H}} Q$ into a label compatibility problem.

Definition 8 (Up to $\mathcal{H}$ Lumping Graph). *Let P and Q be PEPA components. The up to $\mathcal{H}$ lumping graph of $P \cup Q$ is the directed labelled weighted graph $\mathcal{LH}_{P \cup Q} = (V_{P \cup Q}, \mathcal{A}, E_{P \cup Q}, w_{P \cup Q})$, where:*

- $V_{P \cup Q}$ *is $ds(P) \cup ds(Q)$*
- $E_{P \cup Q}$ *is the set of labeled edges*

$$E_{P \cup Q} = \{(R, R', \alpha) \mid R \xrightarrow{(\alpha, r)} R'\} \cup \{(R, R, \alpha) \mid \text{ and } \alpha \in \mathcal{H} \cup \{\tau\}\}$$

with R and R' in $V_{P \cup Q}$
- $w_{P \cup Q}$ *is the function which associates to each edge in $E_{P \cup Q}$ the value*

$$w_{P \cup Q}(R, R', \alpha) = \begin{cases} q(R, R', \alpha) & \text{if } \alpha \notin \mathcal{H} \cup \{\tau\} \vee R \neq R' \\ -q[R, V_{P \cup Q} \setminus \{R\}, \alpha] & \text{otherwise} \end{cases}$$

When P and Q coincide we use $\mathcal{LH}_P$ to denote $\mathcal{LH}_{P \cup P}$.

Theorem 5. *Let P and Q be two PEPA components. It holds that $P \approx_l^{\mathcal{H}} Q$ if and only if in the largest equivalence relation label-compatible with $\mathcal{LH}_{P \cup Q}$ the vertices P and Q are equivalent.*

As an immediate consequence of the above theorem we get that we can directly exploit the algorithm presented in [1] with initial relation the total relation over $V_{P \cup Q}$ to decide $\approx_l^{\mathcal{H}}$ in polynomial time with respect to the size of the graph $\mathcal{D}(P) \cup \mathcal{D}(Q)$. We refer to such algorithm as $LCW(\_)$[1].

Corollary 2. *Let P and Q be two PEPA components. Let $\mathcal{LH}_{P \cup Q}$ be the up to $\mathcal{H}$ lumping graph of $P \cup Q$ and $LCW(\_)$ be the algorithm reported in the Appendix. $LCW(\mathcal{LH}_{P \cup Q})$ decides $P \approx_l^{\mathcal{H}} Q$ in time $O(|V_{P \cup Q}| + |E_{P \cup Q}| \log |V_{P \cup Q}|)$.*

Notice that we are interested in deciding whether P is *PSNI*, i.e., whether $P \setminus \mathcal{H} \approx_l^{\mathcal{H}} P$. Exploiting the above result together with Corollary 1 this can be done by computing both $\mathcal{D}(P \setminus \mathcal{H})$ and $\mathcal{D}(P)$. From these two $\mathcal{LH}_{(P \setminus \mathcal{H}) \cup P}$ can be determined in linear time and then $LCW(\_)$ can be exploited. However, from Theorem 5 together with Theorem 4 we can decide whether P is *PSNI* by simply working on $\mathcal{D}(P)$ as stated in the following theorem.

Theorem 6. *Let P be a PEPA component. Let $Comp_P$ be the largest equivalence relation label-compatible with $\mathcal{LH}_P$. P is PSNI if and only if whenever $P' \xrightarrow{(h, r)} P''$ with $P' \in ds(P)$ and $h \in \mathcal{H}$ it holds that $(P', P'') \in Comp_P$.*

This last result lowers the multiplicative constants hidden in the complexity result of Theorem 5, since it avoids the computation and also the management of $\mathcal{D}(P \setminus \mathcal{H})$. Moreover, it substantially reduces the effective complexity of the computation for many non-*PSNI* processes. As a matter of fact during the computation of $Comp_P$ as soon as a split separates two vertices that are connected through a high level transition we can stop the computation and return $P \notin PSNI$. This also suggests strategies for correcting insecure processes.

---

[1] Given a graph $G = (V, Lab, E, w)$ the use of $LCW(G)$ in this paper corresponds to a call to $LCW(G, V \times V)$ in [1].

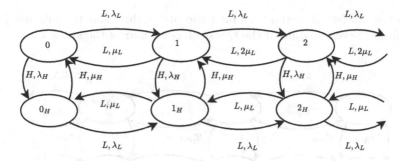

Fig. 1. LTS of the the model that does not satisfy *PSNI*.

5   Example

We consider a distributed system with $n \geq 2$ servers where ordinary jobs arrive according to a homogeneous Poisson process with intensity λ_L. Arrival and departures of ordinary jobs can be observed by a malicious user. The system has an internal job that alternates a phase of sleeping, whose duration is exponential with mean λ_H^{-1}, and a phase of working where it uses one of the n servers for an exponentially distributed time with mean μ_H^{-1}. Each of the ordinary customers requires a service time which is exponentially distributed with mean μ_L^{-1}. If the internal job becomes active and none of the servers is free, then one random ordinary job is preempted and the internal job is executed immediately. Given the exponential distribution of the service time, it is not necessary to discuss the resume policy for the preempted jobs. The waiting room has infinite capacity. The goal is that of hiding the state of the system when the internal process is being executed to the external, possibly malicious, observers. These know how the system works (including the value of μ_L) and the number of available servers.

Notice that in this setting the stability condition is given by:

$$\lambda_L < (n-1)\mu_L + \mu_L \frac{\mu_H}{\mu_L + \mu_H}$$

where the last factor is the probability that the internal process is not active. Figure 1 shows the labelled transition system (LTS) of the PEPA specification of our model as it has been described so far for $n = 2$. States n and n_H denote the system when it contains n ordinary jobs and the internal process is not active (state n) and active (state n_H), respectively. It is interesting to observe that if the malicious user can only estimate the throughput of the ordinary jobs, then the system could be considered safe since this must be λ_L if the stability condition is met. Nevertheless, a smart observer could pay attention to the transient behaviour of the system, and hence could reasonably estimate the number of ordinary jobs in the system. For instance if $n = 2$, and in a time interval we have k arrivals and h departures, such that $k - h \geq 2$, then the next departure of an ordinary job should occur in an expected time of $(2\mu_L)^{-1}$ if the internal job is not active and μ_L^{-1}, otherwise. In other words, the observer can apply some statistical methods to infer the probability that the internal job is active from the observation of the transient behaviour of the system.

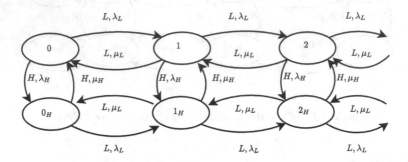

Fig. 2. LTS of the model that satisfies *PSNI*.

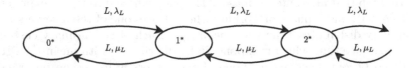

Fig. 3. LTS of the model as seen by an external observer.

Formally, we can say that the model of Fig. 1 does not satisfy the conditions of *PSNI*. In fact, the rate outgoing from state i_H to $(i-1)_H$ is different from from that going from i to $i-1$, where $i > 1$. One simple, but expensive, way to obtain a secure system according to *PSNI* is that of devoting one server to the execution of the internal process. The system of Fig. 1 can be modified to obtain that shown in Fig. 2. With these modification, the observer cannot distinguish the model of Fig. 2 from that of Fig. 3. However, in the general case of n servers, the stability condition becomes $\lambda_L < (n-1)\mu_L$, and the expected response time is higher than that of the original model. Finally, we notice that due to the independence between the internal process behaviour and the ordinary job service, in stability, the stationary probability π is:

$$\pi(i) = \begin{cases} (1 - \lambda_L/\mu_L)\mu_H/(\lambda_L + \mu_H)(\lambda_L/\mu_L)^i & \textit{if } i = 0, 1, \dots \\ (1 - \lambda_L/\mu_L)\lambda_H/(\lambda_L + \mu_H)(\lambda_L/\mu_L)^i & \textit{if } i = 0_H, 1_H, \dots. \end{cases}$$

Clearly, the stationary probability of the model of Fig. 3 is that of a M/M/1 queue, i.e., $\pi^*(i^*) = (1 - \lambda_L/\mu_L)(\lambda_L/\mu_L)^i$ and we can observe that $\pi^*(i^*) = \pi(i) + \pi(i_H)$, as expected by lumping theory [11].

6   Conclusion

In this paper we presented a *persistent* information flow security property for stochastic processes specified as terms of a quantitative process algebra, namely Performance Evaluation Process Algebra (PEPA). Our property, named *Persistent Stochastic Non-Interference* (*PSNI*) is based on a bisimulation based observation equivalence for the PEPA terms which induces a lumping on the underlying Markov chain. The aim of our definition is that of protecting systems from maliciuos attachers which are able to measure also the timing properties of the system, e.g., the response time or the throughput.

In this paper we also deal with compositionality issues and prove that *PSNI* is compositional with respect to low prefix, cooperation on low actions and hiding.

As a future work we plan to relax the definition of Non-Interference by introducing metrics that allow us to measure the security degree of a system in terms of probabilities.

Acknowledgments. The work described in this paper has been partially supported by the Università Ca' Foscari Venezia - DAIS within the IRIDE program, by the Università di Udine PRID ENCASE project, and by GNCS-INdAM project Metodi Formali per la Verifica e la Sintesi di Sistemi Discreti e Ibridi.

References

1. Alzetta, G., Marin, A., Piazza, C., Rossi, S.: Lumping-based equivalences in markovian automata: algorithms and applications to product-form analyses. Inf. Comput. **260**, 99–125 (2018)
2. Bortz, A., Boneh, D.: Exposing private information by timing web applications. In: Proceedings of the 16th International Conference on World Wide Web (WWW), pp. 621–628. ACM (2007)
3. Brumley, D., Boneh, D.: Remote timing attacks are practical. Comput. Netw. **48**(5), 701–716 (2005)
4. Crafa, S., Rossi, S.: Controlling information release in the pi-calculus. Inf. Comput. **205**(8), 1235–1273 (2007)
5. Felten, E.W., Schneider, M.A.: Timing attacks on web privacy. In: Proceedings of the 7th ACM Conference on Computer and Communications Security (CCS), pp. 25–32. ACM (2000)
6. Focardi, R., Gorrieri, R.: Classification of security properties. In: Focardi, R., Gorrieri, R. (eds.) FOSAD 2000. LNCS, vol. 2171, pp. 331–396. Springer, Heidelberg (2001). https://doi.org/10.1007/3-540-45608-2_6
7. Gao, H., Bodei, C., Degano, P., Riis Nielson, H.: A formal analysis for capturing replay attacks in cryptographic protocols. In: Cervesato, I. (ed.) ASIAN 2007. LNCS, vol. 4846, pp. 150–165. Springer, Heidelberg (2007). https://doi.org/10.1007/978-3-540-76929-3_15
8. Goguen, J.A. Meseguer, J.: Security policy and security models. In: Proceedings of the 1982 Symposium on Security and Privacy, pp. 11–20. IEEE Computer Society Press (1982)
9. Hillston, J.: A Compositional Approach to Performance Modelling. Cambridge Press, Cambridge (1996)

10. Hillston, J., Marin, A., Piazza, C., Rossi, S.: Contextual lumpability. In: Proceedings of Valuetools 2013 Conference, pp. 194–203. ACM Press (2013)
11. Kemeny, J.G., Snell, J.L.: Finite Markov Chains. D, Van Nostrand Company Inc., New York (1960)
12. Marin, A., Rossi, S.: On the relations between Markov chain lumpability and reversibility. Acta Inf. **54**(5), 447–485 (2017)
13. Marin, A., Rossi, S.: On the relations between lumpability and reversibility. In: Proceedings of MASCOTS 2014, pp. 427–432 (2014)
14. McLean, J.: A general theory of composition for trace sets closed under selective interleaving functions. In: Proceedings of the IEEE Symposium on Security and Privacy (SSP 1994), pp. 79–93. IEEE Computer Society Press (1994)
15. Ryan, P.Y.A., Schneider, S.: Process algebra and non-interference. J. Comput. Secur. **9**(1/2), 75–103 (2001)
16. Sabelfeld, A., Myers, A.C.: Language-based information-flow security. IEEE J. Sel. Areas Commun. **21**(1), 5–19 (2003)
17. Smith, G., Volpano, D.M.: Secure information flow in a multi-threaded imperative language. In: Proceedings of ACM SIGPLAN-SIGACT Symposium on Principles of Programming Languages (POPL 1998), pp. 355–364. ACM Press (1998)
18. Sutherland, D.: A model of information. In: Proceedings of the 9th National Computer Security Conference, pp. 175–183 (1986)
19. Valmari, A., Franceschinis, G.: Simple $O(m \log n)$ time Markov chain lumping. In: Esparza, J., Majumdar, R. (eds.) TACAS 2010. LNCS, vol. 6015, pp. 38–52. Springer, Heidelberg (2010). https://doi.org/10.1007/978-3-642-12002-2_4

Towards Probabilistic Modeling
and Analysis of Real-Time Systems

Laura Carnevali[1]([⊠]), Luca Santinelli[2], and Giuseppe Lipari[3]

[1] DINFO, University of Florence, Florence, Italy
laura.carnevali@unifi.it
[2] ONERA, Toulouse, France
luca.santinelli@onera.fr
[3] LIFL, University of Lille, Lille, France
giuseppe.lipari@univ-lille1.fr

Abstract. Schedulability analysis of software-intensive systems requires solution techniques that go beyond worst-case assumptions, fostering a cross-fertilization between the areas of real-time systems and performance engineering. We address probabilistic schedulability analysis of tasks in single-processor non-preemptive real-time systems. To this end, we consider periodic tasks with offsets, scheduled by Fixed Priority (FP) or Earliest Deadline First (EDF), and managed by the discarding policy or the rejection policy to control deadline misses. Each task has a Worst Case Execution Time (WCET) which can be a deterministic value or a random variable, notably characterized by a non-Markovian distribution possibly with bounded support. A continuous-time stochastic model of task-set is specified through Stochastic Time Petri Nets (STPNs) and solved by regenerative transient analysis based on stochastic state classes. The evaluation of performance measures on resource allocation and missed deadlines enables the analysis of design choices and the estimation of over-provisioned resources that are likely to be unused at runtime. Feasibility and effectiveness of the approach are validated on randomly generated task-sets for different processor utilizations.

Keywords: Real-time systems
Probabilistic Worst Case Execution Time
Probabilistic schedulability analysis
Continuous-time stochastic models

1 Introduction

In real-time systems, the increasing complexity of safety-critical requirements and computing platforms cannot be handled through deterministic frameworks, which cannot capture uncertainties resulting from varying execution conditions and inherent system randomness. Indeed, probabilistic approaches are advocated to go beyond worst-case assumptions and provide guaranteed probabilities for

© Springer Nature Switzerland AG 2018
R. Bakhshi et al. (Eds.): EPEW 2018, LNCS 11178, pp. 157–172, 2018.
https://doi.org/10.1007/978-3-030-02227-3_11

timing properties. To this end, different research directions have been pursued in order to achieve probabilistic predictability of real-time components.

The real-time community has recently approached modeling and schedulability analysis with probabilities. The modeling problem involves the definition of the Worst-Case Execution Time (WCET) with random variables [3,8,9]. Then, schedulability analyses make use of probabilistic models to develop probabilistic feasibility criteria and to guarantee system timing behaviors [2,11,22–24]. Schedulability analysis with probabilities extends the results with confidence levels (e.g., probabilities) as the degree of respecting the schedulability conditions. In both modeling and analysis with probabilities, key elements for evaluating the quality of the obtained results are the enhancements of the amount and quality of information (thus the flexibility achieved capturing the natural variability that real-time systems have), the degree of formalism (thus the guarantees provided), and the implicit complexity due to probability composition.

The formal modeling and analysis community has developed formalisms and tools enabling timing analysis of systems subject to safety-critical requirements. Notably, timeliness analysis of non-preemptive hard real-time systems is addressed in [26], providing a mixed static/dynamic strategy for task acceptance and guarantee; the theory of timed automata is used to support model checking and testing of non-preemptive real-time systems [1], robust specification of real-time components [17], and timing analysis of systems running under preemptive scheduling, introducing clocks that can be occasionally stopped and resumed [12]; preemptive timed models with comparable expressivity are also proposed in [13,19,25], addressing both FP and EDF scheduling. Few probabilistic model-based approaches effectively address real-time systems by encompassing timers with bounded and deterministic support. In particular, the solution technique of [20] supports the analysis of models with multiple concurrent exponential and deterministic timers; the method of stochastic state classes evaluates models with multiple concurrent clocks having a non-Markovian distribution, possibly over a bounded interval [14], supporting deadline miss analysis of real-time systems scheduled by the non-preemptive FP policy, under the assumption of a simplified task-set model [7]; the approach of [15] evaluates the expected performance of a given schedule, notably enabling the synthesis of an optimal scheduler by means of a dynamic programming algorithm [16].

In this paper, we extend preliminary results of [7] through a general periodic task model with offsets and with deadlines possibly lower than periods, considering the FP and the EDF policies to schedule jobs, and the discarding and the rejection policies to manage late jobs, also solving priority/deadline ties. Performance measures are defined to evaluate deadline misses and to identify the time intervals during which the processor is likely to be free at run-time. A task-set is specified by Stochastic Time Petri Nets (STPNs) and analyzed by regenerative transient analysis based on the method of stochastic state classes [14], supporting modeling and analysis of real-time systems with non-Markovian (possibly bounded) execution times. An experimental evaluation is provided on randomly generated task-sets for different processor utilizations. In light of the obtained results, the approach appears to be a promising step towards bridging the gap between real-time scheduling theories and probabilistic model-based approaches.

In the rest of the paper: we formulate the problem and we define performance measures of interest (Sect. 2); we present the models under the different combinations of policies, we recall the salient traits of the analysis, and we illustrate how the performance measures are computed (Sect. 3); we present experimental results (Sect. 4); and, we provide a final discussion (Sect. 5).

2   Problem Formulation

Task Model. We consider a set of periodic tasks $\Gamma = \{T_1, \ldots, T_N\}$ running concurrently on a single processor. A task T_i releases a job with period $\pi_i \in \mathbb{N}$ such that $\pi > 0$ and offset $\theta_i \in \mathbb{N}$, i.e., the n-th job J_i^n of T_i is released at time $\rho_i^n = \theta_i + (n-1)\pi_i$, with $n > 0$. (see Fig. 1). Every job of T_i has a WCET ϕ_i [10], which can either *deterministic* (i.e., a strict upper bound on the execution time, that is never exceeded at run-time) or *probabilistic* (i.e., an upper bound on the execution time, associated with a given probability to be exceeded):

- a deterministic WCET ϕ_i is defined by a Dirac Delta function f_{ϕ_i} centered at $\phi_i^{\min} = \phi_i^{\max}$, i.e., $f_{\phi_i}(x) = \delta(x - \phi_i^{\min})$;
- a probabilistic WCET ϕ_i is characterized by a non-Markovian PDF f_{ϕ_i}, possibly with bounded support, i.e., $f_{\phi_i}(x) : [\phi_i^{\min}, \phi_i^{\max}] \to [0, 1]$ with $\phi_i^{\min} \in \mathbb{Q}^+$, $\phi_i^{\max} \in \mathbb{Q}^+ \cup \{\infty\}$, and $\phi_i^{\min} \neq \phi_i^{\max}$, where $\int_{\phi_i^{\min}}^{y} f_{\phi_i}(x)\,dx$ comprises the probability that the WCET of the task does not exceed y.

Each job of T_i has an absolute deadline equal to the job release time plus a relative deadline $\omega_i \leq \pi_i$, i.e., the absolute deadline of J_i^n is $\Omega_i^n = \rho_i^n + \omega_i$ (see Fig. 1). If J_i^n has not completed its execution by Ω_i^n, it is termed *late job*. Jobs do not use mutex semaphores to synchronize and cannot self-suspend before completion, thus being considered functionally independent. Each task T_i has also a static priority $\psi_i \in \mathbb{N}$, with higher numbers corresponding to higher priorities. Overall, a task T_i can be represented as a tuple $\langle \pi_i, \theta_i, f_{\phi_i}, \omega_i, \psi_i \rangle$.

Scheduling Policies. We consider two *non-preemptive* scheduling policies (i.e., a task cannot be interrupted and later resumed): *Fixed-Priority* (FP) and *Earliest Deadline First* (EDF). The FP policy schedules for execution the task with the highest static priority among tasks that are ready to run. In the particular case of *Rate Monotonic* (RM), static priorities are assigned through a

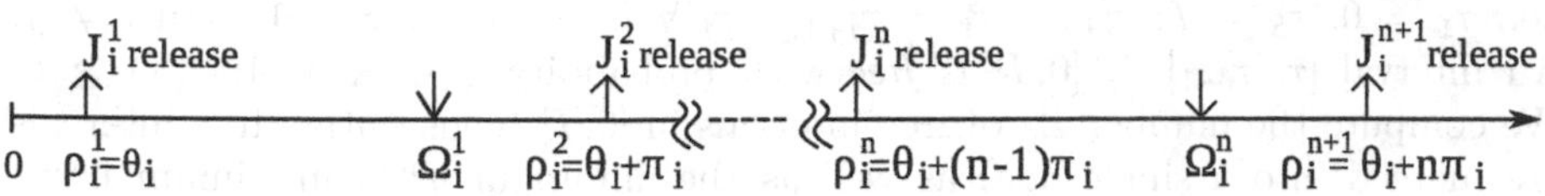

Fig. 1. Release times (↑) and absolute deadlines (↓) of jobs of a task T_i.

monotonically decreasing function of task periods, i.e., the shorter the period of a task is, the higher its static priority is. The EDF policy schedules to run the task whose job has the shortest absolute deadline among jobs of ready tasks.

Late Jobs Policies. As usual in real-time systems design, two policies are considered for late jobs, ensuring that no more than one job of each task is active in the system at any time: the *discarding* policy and the *rejection* policy [21].

- The discarding policy discards a job J_i^n of task T_i as soon as it misses its absolute deadline $\Omega_i^n = \theta_i + (n-1)\pi_i + \omega_i$. Hence, when the subsequent job J_i^{n+1} is released at time $\rho_i^{n+1} = \theta_i + n\pi_i$, job J_i^n is no more active ($\omega_i \leq \pi_i$ guarantees that $\Omega_i^n \leq \rho_i^{n+1}$). In so doing, late jobs are prevented from continuing execution, guaranteeing that the system gets back to the initial condition at times $\Theta + n \cdot \Pi$, where $n \in \mathbb{N}$, $\Theta = \max_{i|T_i \in \Gamma}\{\theta_i\}$ is the maximum offset, and $\Pi = \mathrm{lcm}_{i|T_i \in \Gamma}\{\pi_i\}$ is the least common multiple of task periods. According to this, based on the results of [18], it can be proved that the task-set Γ is schedulable if no deadline is missed by time $\Theta + (1 + \mathbb{1}_\Theta) \cdot \Pi$, where $\mathbb{1}_\Theta$ is equal to 0 if $\Theta = 0$ and equal to 1 otherwise.
- The rejection policy rejects a new job J_i^{n+1} of task T_i immediately upon release if the previous job J_i^n is still active (by construction, J_i^n has missed its absolute deadline when J_i^{n+1} has been released). While increasing the probability that a running job is eventually completed, this policy hinders schedulability verification, as it increases the length of paths where a job is being executed while multiple events occur (e.g., another job is released or misses its deadline). More specifically, if tasks have WCET with unbounded support, then no time bound exists by which the system can be analyzed and proved to be schedulable. Vice versa, based on the results of [18], it can be proved that, if WCETs have bounded support and the remaining execution time of each task is the same at time instants $\Theta + n \cdot \Pi$ and no deadline is missed by time $\Theta + (1 + \mathbb{1}_\Theta) \cdot \Pi$, then the task-set Γ is schedulable.

Performance Measures. We evaluate the following *transient rewards* on processor usage and deadline misses over the interval $[0, I]$ with $I := \Theta + (1 + \mathbb{1}_\Theta) \cdot \Pi$:

- $\alpha_i(t) := P\{\text{a job of task } T_i \text{ is running at time } t\}$;
- $\beta_i(t) := P\{\text{a job of task } T_i \text{ is running at time } t \text{ and its deadline has passed}\}$;
- $\gamma_i^k(t) := P\{\text{jobs of task } T_i \text{ have missed at least } k \in \mathbb{N} \text{ deadlines by time } t\}$;
- $A(t) := P\{\text{no job is running at time } t\} = 1 - \sum_{i \in \mathbb{N}|T_i \in \Gamma} \alpha_i(t)$.

where $\alpha_i(t)$, $\beta_i(t)$, and $A(t)$ are *instantaneous* rewards, while $\alpha_i^k(t)$ is *cumulative*. These measures are evaluated at S equispaced time instants $\tau_1, \ldots, \tau_S$ in $[0, I]$, i.e., $\tau_1 = 0$, $\tau_S = I$, $\tau_{i+1} - \tau_i = \tau_{j+1} - \tau_j \ \forall \ i, j = 1, \ldots, S - 1$ with $i \neq j$. An interval $[\tau_i, \tau_{i+1}] \subseteq [0, I]$ is *free* with probability $\zeta \in \mathbb{R}$ if $A(\tau_{i+1}) \geq \zeta$. We compute the number Z_ζ of free intervals in $[0, I]$ (consecutive free intervals are merged into a single one) as well as the minimum $\eta_\zeta^{\min}$, maximum $\eta_\zeta^{\max}$, average $\bar{\eta}_\zeta$, and standard deviation $\eta_\zeta^{\mathrm{std}}$ of the duration of free intervals.

3   Modeling and Analysis

3.1   Stochastic Time Petri Nets

Syntax. An STPN consists of a set P of places, a set T of transitions, and sets $A^- \subseteq P \times T$, $A^+ \subseteq T \times P$, and $A^{\cdot} \subseteq P \times T$ of precondition, postcondition, and inhibitor arcs, respectively. An initial marking $m_0 : P \to \mathbb{N}$ associates each place with a number of tokens. A transition t has an *earliest firing time* $EFT(t) \in \mathbb{Q}^+$, a *latest firing time* $LFT(t) \in \mathbb{Q}^+ \cup \{\infty\}$ such that $EFT(t) \leq LFT(t)$, and a static Cumulative Distribution Function (CDF) $F_t : [EFT(t), LFT(t)] \to [0, 1]$. A transition t has also a weight $\mathcal{C}(t) \in \mathbb{R}^+$, a priority $R(t) \in \mathbb{N}$, an enabling function $E(t) : \mathbb{N}^P \to \{true, false\}$ associating each marking with a boolean value (e.g., a transition may have an enabling function $\texttt{p1} + \texttt{p2} == 1$ which evaluates to true if the sum of tokens in places $\texttt{p1}$ and $\texttt{p2}$ is 1 and to false otherwise), and a *flush function* $L(t) \in \mathcal{P}(P)$ being a subset of P. A place p is an *input*, an *output*, or an *inhibitor* place for a transition t if $\langle p, t \rangle \in A^-$, $\langle t, p \rangle \in A^+$, or $\langle p, t \rangle \in A^{\cdot}$, respectively. A transition t is *immediate* (IMM) if $EFT(t) = LFT(t) = 0$ and *timed* otherwise; a timed transition t is *exponential* (EXP) if $F_t(x) = 1 - e^{-\lambda x}$ with $x \in [0, \infty]$ and $\lambda \in \mathbb{R}^+$, and *general* (GEN) otherwise; a GEN transition t is *deterministic* (DET) if $EFT(t) = LFT(t)$ and *distributed* otherwise; if t is distributed, we assume that F_t is absolutely continuous over its support and thus that there exists a PDF f_t such that $F_t(x) = \int_0^x f_t(y) dy$.

Semantics. The *state* of an STPN is a pair $\langle m, \tau \rangle$, where $m : P \to \mathbb{N}$ is a marking and $\tau : T \to \mathbb{R}^+$ associates each transition with a time-to-fire. A transition is *enabled* in a state if each of its input places contains at least one token, none of its inhibitor places contains any token, and its enabling function evaluates to true (typically, the enabling function of a transition does not constrain the marking of the input, output, and inhibitor places of such transition). An enabled transition t is *firable* if its time-to-fire is zero and, if t is IMM or DET, if its priority is not smaller than that of any other enabled IMM transition and of any other enabled DET transition with zero time-to-fire.

When multiple transitions are firable, one of them is selected to fire with probability $\text{P}\{t \text{ is selected}\} = \mathcal{C}(t) / \sum_{t_i \in T^f(s)} \mathcal{C}(t_i)$, where $T^f(s)$ is the set of firable transitions in state s. When t fires, $s = \langle m, \tau \rangle$ is replaced by a new state $s' = \langle m', \tau' \rangle$, where m' is derived from m by: *(i)* removing a token from each input place of t and assigning zero tokens to the places in $L(t) \subseteq P$, which yields an intermediate marking m_{tmp}, *(ii)* adding a token to each output place of t. Transitions enabled both by m_{tmp} and by m' are said *persistent*, while those enabled by m' but not by m_{tmp} or m are said *newly-enabled*; if t is still enabled after its own firing, it is regarded as newly enabled [4]. The time-to-fire of persistent transitions is reduced by the time elapsed in s, while that of newly-enabled transitions takes a random value sampled according to their CDF.

3.2   Model Under FP and RM Scheduling

The task-set model composes four submodels for each task, i.e., the *release sub-model*, the *job submodel*, the *deadline submodel*, and the *late jobs submodel*. Given a scheduling policy (i.e., FP or EDF), a late jobs policy (i.e., discarding or rejection), and a reward to compute on deadline misses (i.e., cumulative or instantaneous), the model of a task-set Γ is univocally derived from the specification of tasks, i.e., $T_i = \langle \pi_i, \theta_i, f_{\phi_i}, \omega_i, \psi_i \rangle \ \forall \ T_i \in \Gamma$. As a running example, Table 1 specifies three tasks T_1, T_2, and T_3 with period equal to 5 ms, 10 ms, and 10 ms, respectively, deadline equal to 5 ms, 8 ms, and 10 ms, respectively, and priority equal to 3, 1, and 2, respectively, clearly not assigned according to RM. T_3 has offset equal to 1 ms and a probabilistic WCET with expolynomial PDF $f_{\phi_3}(x) = 0.0150694 \cdot e^{-5x}$ supported over $[0.5, 1]$ ms, while T_1 and T_2 have null offset and deterministic WCET equal to 2 ms and 1 ms, respectively.

Table 1. A task-set Γ made of three tasks (times are expressed in ms).

Task	Period	Offset	WCET PDF	Deadline	Priority
T_3	$\pi_3 = 10$	$\theta_3 = 1$	$f_{\phi_3}(x) = 0.0150694 \cdot e^{-5x} \ \forall \ x \in [0.5, 1]$	$\omega_3 = 10$	$\psi_3 = 2$
T_2	$\pi_2 = 10$	$\theta_2 = 0$	$f_{\phi_2}(x) = \delta(2)$	$\omega_2 = 8$	$\psi_2 = 1$
T_1	$\pi_1 = 5$	$\theta_1 = 0$	$f_{\phi_1}(x) = \delta(1)$	$\omega_1 = 5$	$\psi_1 = 3$

The FP Model Under the Discarding Policy. Figure 2 shows the submodels of T_3 when task-set Γ runs under FP scheduling according to the discarding policy, and the cumulative reward $\gamma_i^k(t)$ is calculated $\forall \ T_i \in \Gamma$ for some $k \in \mathbb{N}$. The *release* submodel includes a DET transition representing the task offset (t_task3_offset, with value 1 equal to offset θ_3 in Table 1), a DET transition modeling job releases (t_task3_release, with value 10 equal to period π_3), and two IMM transitions accounting for task acceptance (t_task3_accept) and rejection (t_task3_reject), respectively. Under the discarding policy, a newly released job is always accepted, since any previous job either has finished or has been discarded due to a deadline miss. According to this, t_task3_accept has an enabling function that evaluates to true in any marking, while t_task3_reject has an enabling function that evaluates to false in any marking. The initial marking of the submodel puts a token either in p_task3_offset (if the task had a null offset, the initial marking would have assigned one token to place p_task3_ready and one to place p_task3_start).

   The *job* submodel has an IMM transition modeling processor acquisition (t_task3_wait), preconditioned by a place modeling processor availability (cpu), and a GEN transition accounting for job execution (t_task3_job), associated with the CDF of the task WCET ($F_{\text{t\_task3\_job}}(x) = \int_0^x f_{\phi_3}(y)dy$) and postconditioned by the place accounting for processor availability. As discussed later, the larger the priority of a task T_i is, the larger the priority of transition t_task$i$_wait is, guaranteeing that processor is acquired by the waiting job with the largest priority. Synchronization of jobs of different tasks on shared resources could be represented similarly, using a place to represent resource availability, and two IMM transition to model semaphore acquisition and release, respectively.

The *deadline* submodel includes a DET transition modeling the expiration of the deadline (t_task3_deadline, with value 10 equal to deadline ω_3), and two IMM transitions counting the number of deadlines missed by task T_3 (t_task3_deadlineMissCount) or ignoring it (t_task3_- deadlineMissIgnore), respectively. Given that the cumulative reward $\gamma_3^k(t) = \mathrm{P}\{$jobs of T_3 have missed at least k deadlines within time $t\}$ is computed, t_task3_deadlineMissCount has an enabling function evaluating to true if p_task3_deadlineMissCount $< k$ and false otherwise, t_task3_deadlineMissIgnore has an enabling function evaluating to true if p_task3_deadlineMissCount $== k$ and false otherwise, and t_task3_job has a flush function emptying place p_task3_deadline upon its firing. Conversely, the evaluation of the instantaneous reward $\beta_3(t) = \mathrm{P}\{$a job of task T_3 is running at time t and its deadline has passed$\}$ is not considered under the discarding policy, given that $\beta_3(t)$ would be equal to 0 for any time $t \in \mathbb{R}^+$.

The *late jobs* submodel implements the discarding policy by means of the IMM transitions t_task3_waitingJobDiscard and t_task3_running JobDiscard, preconditioned by p_task3_wait and p_task3_job, respectively, so as to discard a late job both when it is ready and when it is running, respectively.

Priorities are assigned to IMM and DET transitions so as to implement the FP scheduling policy and to avoid non-determinism. Let a task-set consist of N tasks having N different priority values, ordered by ascending priority, i.e., tasks $T_1, \ldots, T_N$ have priority $1, \ldots, N$, respectively. In the model of task T_i (where i is the task index in the above ordering), transitions have the following priorities: if t_task$i$_job is a DET transition (i.e., the WCET of T_i is deterministic), then it has priority $4N + i$; transitions in the *deadline* submodel and in the *late*

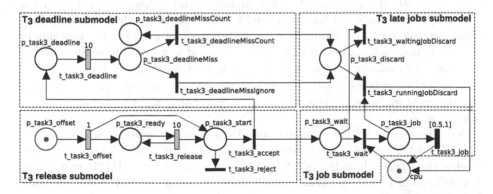

Fig. 2. A fragment of the STPN of the task-set of Table 1, when tasks run under FP scheduling and discarding policy, and the cumulative reward $\gamma_i^k(t)$ is computed for each task T_i for some $k \in \mathbb{N}$. IMM, DET, and GEN transitions are represented by thin black bars, thick gray bars, and thick black bars, respectively.

jobs submodel have priority $3N + i$; transitions in the *release* submodel have priority $2N + i$; t_task$i$_wait has priority i. For instance, in the model of Fig. 2: transitions in the *deadline* and *late jobs* submodels have priority 11; transitions in the *release* submodel have priority 8; and, t_task3_wait has priority 2. Note that t_task1_wait and t_task2_wait have priority 3 and 1, respectively, so that, in case jobs of different tasks are waiting to acquire processor at the same time, jobs of T_2 are never overtaken by any job, jobs of T_3 are overtaken by jobs of T_2, and jobs of T_1 are overtaken by jobs of both T_2 and T_3.

In the specific case of RM scheduling, tasks T_1, T_2, and T_3 would have priority 3, 2, and 1, respectively. According to this, in Fig. 2: transitions in the *deadline* and *late jobs* submodels would have priority 10; transitions in the *release* submodel would have priority 7; and, t_task3_wait would have priority 1.

The FP Model Under the Rejection Policy. If the rejection policy were assumed, the *late jobs* submodel of Fig. 2 would be empty. Additionally, in the *release* submodel, t_task3_accept and t_task3_reject would have an enabling function that evaluates to true if p_task3_wait + p_task3_job == 0 and if p_task3_wait + p_task3_job == 1, respectively, and to false otherwise. Moreover, if the instantaneous reward $\beta_3(t)$ were evaluated (instead of the cumulative reward $\gamma_3^k(t)$ considered in Fig. 2), t_task3_deadlineMissCount and t_task3_deadlineMissIgnore would have an enabling function that evaluates to false in any marking, and t_task3_job would have a flush function that empties places p_task3_deadline and p_task3_deadlineMiss.

Encompassing Tasks with Equal Priority. If H tasks belonging to a subset $\mathcal{H}$ of the task-set Γ had the same priority, then they would be assigned the processor in the order they become ready, and, in case they become ready at the same time, those with shorter period would run first. To this end, the *job* submodel of each task $T_i \in \mathcal{H}$ would be extended with a sequence of $H - 1$ IMM transitions chained through their input places, i.e., t_task$i$_queue$h$ $\forall h = 1, \ldots, H-1$. Transitions t_task$i$_queue$h$ would be assigned priority $N+i$, where N is the number of tasks in Γ and $i \in \mathbb{N}$ is the task index, assuming that tasks are ordered by ascending priority and, in case of priority ties, descending period. Transitions t_task$i$_queue$h$ $\forall h = 1, \ldots, H - 2$ would have an enabling function that evaluates to true if $\sum_{j \neq i | T_j \in \mathcal{H}}$ p_t_task$j$_queue$(h + 1)$ == 0, and false otherwise, while transition t_task$i$_queue$(H - 1)$ would have an enabling function that evaluates to true if $\sum_{j \neq i | T_j \in \mathcal{H}}$ p_t_task$j$_wait == 0, and to false otherwise.

For instance, if the task-set of Table 1 were added two tasks T_4 and T_5 with priority 2 and with period 20 ms and 30 ms, respectively, the *job* submodel of T_3 would be added two IMM transitions t_task3_queue1 and t_task3_queue2 with priority 9 and with enabling function evaluating to true if p_task4_queue2 + p_task5_queue2 == 0 and p_task4_wait + p_task5_wait == 0, respectively, and to false otherwise (see Fig. 3). Moreover, transitions in the *deadline* and *late jobs* submodels of T_3 would have priority 19; transitions in the *release* submodel would have priority 14; and, t_task3_wait would have priority 4.

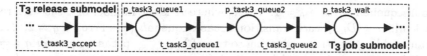

Fig. 3. A fragment of the STPN model of the task-set specified in Table 1 under the assumption that two tasks T_4 and T_5 with priority 2 are added to the task-set.

3.3 Model Under EDF Scheduling

The EDF Model Under the Discarding Policy. Let tasks in $T_1, \ldots, T_N$ be ordered by descending relative deadline and, in case of deadline ties, by descending period. Let $\mathcal{D} = \{D_1, \ldots, D_M\}$ be the set of relative deadlines of tasks in descending order, with $M \leq N$. The *deadline* submodel of task T_i (where i is the task index according to the above ordering) includes a sequence of $M - i + 1$ DET transitions, i.e., t_task$i$_deadline$d$ $\forall d = i, \ldots, M$, chained through their input places, with $f_{\text{t\_task}i\text{\_deadline}d}(x) = \delta(D_d - D_{d+1})$ and $D_{M+1} := 0$ ms. For instance, in the task-set of Table 1, tasks T_3, T_2, and T_1 have deadline $D_1 = 10$ ms, $D_2 = 8$ ms, and $D_3 = 5$ ms, respectively. As shown in Fig. 4, the *deadline* submodel of T_3 (which has index 1 according to the above ordering) includes 3 DET transitions t_task3_deadline1, t_task3_deadline2, and t_task3_deadline3, such that $f_{\text{t\_task3\_deadline1}} = \delta(2)$ (given that $D_1 - D_2 = 2$ ms), $f_{\text{t\_task3\_deadline2}} = \delta(3)$ $(D_2 - D_3 = 3$ ms), $f_{\text{t\_task3\_deadline3}} = \delta(5)$ $(D_3 - D_4 = 5$ ms). Hence, at run-time, during the interval of duration 2 ms going from the firing of t_task3_accept to that of t_task3_deadline1, the just released job of T_3 has the largest relative deadline, between 8 ms and 10 ms. Similarly, during the interval of duration 3 ms going from the firing of t_task3_deadline1 to that of t_task3_deadline2, the job of T_3 has relative deadline between 5 ms and 8 ms, which may be lower/larger than the relative deadline of a job of T_2. Finally, during the interval of duration 5 ms going from the firing of t_task3_deadline2 to that of t_task3_deadline3, the job of T_3 has relative deadline between 0 ms and 5 ms, which may be lower/larger than the relative deadline of a job of T_2 or T_1.

The *job* submodel is extended to guarantee that processor is acquired by the job with the largest relative deadline at run-time. To this end, the *job* submodel of T_i includes $M - i + 1$ subsubmodels $r_h \ \forall h = i, \ldots, M$, each related with transition t_task$i$_deadline$h$ in the *deadline* submodel and aimed at determining the position of T_i job in the queue of waiting jobs with relative deadline between D_h and D_{h+1}. Let H be the maximum queue length, i.e., the cardinality of the set $\mathcal{S}_h \subset \Gamma$ of tasks with relative deadline $\geq D_h$. The r_h subsubmodel consists of: H IMM transitions t_task$i$_queue$h$_q $\forall q = 1, \ldots, H$; $H - 1$ IMM transitions t_task$i$_queue$h$_$(q-1)$Toq $\forall q = 2, \ldots, H$; and, an IMM transition t_task$i$_wait$h$. Moreover, each transition t_task$i$_queue$h$_q has an enabling function that evaluates to true if p_task$i$_deadline$h$ == 1 && $\sum_{j|T_j \in \mathcal{S}_h, u=q+1, \ldots, H}$ p_task$j$_queue$h$_u == $H - q$ and false otherwise; each transition t_task$i$_queue$h$_q $\forall q = 2, \ldots, H$ has a flush function that empties

$\mathbf{p\_task}i\mathbf{\_queue}h - 1\_k \ \forall \ k = 1,\ldots,K$, where K is the number of tasks with relative deadline $\geq D_{h-1}$; each transition $\mathbf{t\_task}i\mathbf{\_queue}h\_(q-1)\mathbf{To}q \ \forall \ q = 2,\ldots,H$ has an enabling function evaluating to true if $\sum_{j|T_j \in \mathcal{S}_h} \mathbf{p\_task}j\mathbf{\_queue}h\_q == 0$; and, if $h < H$, $\mathbf{t\_task}i\mathbf{\_wait}h$ has a flush function emptying $\mathbf{p\_task}i\mathbf{\_queue}h + 1$.

For instance, the *release* submodel of T_3 shown in Fig. 4 includes three sub-submodels r_1, r_2, and r_3 ($M = 3$ is the number of distinct relative deadlines) representing the queue of waiting jobs with relative deadline between 8 ms and 10 ms, between 5 ms and 8 ms, and between 0 ms and 5 ms, respectively. The r_1 subsubmodel has a single IMM transition $\mathbf{t\_task3\_queue1\_1}$ given only T_3 job may have relative deadline larger than 8 ms. Conversely, the r_2 subsubmodel includes two IMM transitions $\mathbf{t\_task3\_queue2\_1}$ and $\mathbf{t\_task3\_queue2\_2}$, given that both T_2 and T_3 jobs may have relative deadline between 5 ms and 8 ms: the enabling function of $\mathbf{t\_task3\_queue2\_1}$ and $\mathbf{t\_task3\_queue2\_1To2}$ evaluates to true if $\mathbf{p\_task3\_deadline2} == 1 \ \&\& \ \mathbf{p\_task2\_queue2\_2} == 1$ and if $\mathbf{p\_task3\_deadline2} == 1 \ \&\& \ \mathbf{p\_task2\_queue2\_2} == 0$, respectively, and false otherwise. Hence, if T_2 job is already in the queue when T_3 job arrives, $\mathbf{t\_task3\_queue2\_1}$ is enabled and fires, queuing T_3 job; conversely, if the queue is empty, $\mathbf{t\_task3\_queue2\_2}$ is enabled and fires, enabling transition $\mathbf{t\_task3\_wait2}$ accounting for processor acquisition. In a similar manner, the r_3 subsubmodel includes three IMM transitions $\mathbf{t\_task3\_queue3\_}h \ \forall \ h = 1,2,3$.

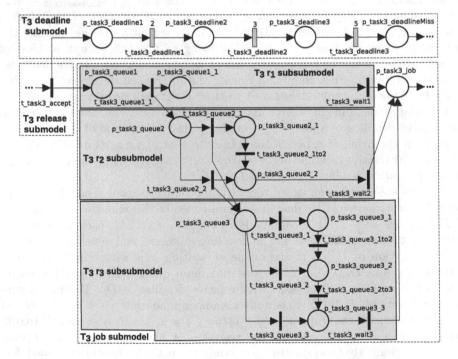

Fig. 4. A fragment of the STPN of the task-set of Table 1 scheduled by EDF.

Priorities are assigned to IMM and DET transitions so as to implement the EDF scheduling policy and to avoid non-determinism. In the model of task T_i (where i is the task index in the above stated ordering), transitions have the following priorities: if t_task$i$_job is a DET transition (i.e., the WCET of T_i is deterministic), then it has priority $5N + i$; transitions in the *deadline* submodel and in the *late jobs* submodel have priority $4N + i$; transitions in the *release* submodel have priority $3N + i$; transitions t_task$i$_queue$h$_q have priority $2N + i$ $\forall\, h = 1, \ldots, M, \forall\, q = 1, \ldots, H$; transitions t_task$i$_queue$h$_$(q - 1)Toq$ have priority $N + i$ $\forall\, h = 1, \ldots, M, \forall\, q = 2, \ldots, H$; and, t_task$i$_wait$h$ $\forall\, h = 1, \ldots, M$ has priority h. For instance, in Fig. 4, transitions in the *deadline* and *release* submodels have priority 13 and 10, respectively; t_task3_queue2_q has priority $7\ \forall\, q = 1, 2$; t_task3_queue2_1To2 has priority 4; t_task3_wait2 has priority 2.

As in the FP model, under the discarding policy, t_task$i$_accept has an enabling function that evaluates to true in any marking, while t_task$i$_reject has an enabling function that evaluates to false in any marking. Moreover, to evaluate the instantaneous reward $\beta_i(t)$, the flush function of t_task$i$_job empties any place in the *deadline* submodel.

The EDF Model Under the Rejection Policy. If the rejection policy were assumed, the enabling function of t_task$i$_accept would evaluate to true if every place in the *job* submodel is empty and false otherwise, while the enabling function of t_task$i$_reject would evaluate to true if some place in the *job* submodel contains a token and false otherwise. Moreover, if the cumulative reward $\gamma_i^k(t)$ were evaluated for some $k \in \mathbb{N}$, t_task$i$_job would have a flush function that empties any place in the *deadline* submodel, except for p_task3_deadlineMiss.

3.4   Analysis

The task-set model is analyzed by the regenerative transient analysis of [14] with time limit T, obtaining transient marking probabilities at any time $t \leq T$, i.e., $p_m(t) = P\{M(t) = m\}\ \forall\, t \leq T, \forall\, m \in \mathcal{M}$, where $\mathbb{M} = \{M(t),\ t \geq 0\}$ is the underlying marking process and $\mathcal{M}$ the set of reachable markings. Probabilities are aggregated to derive the performance measures of Sect. 2. Specifically, for each task $T_i \in \Gamma$: $\alpha_i(t) = \sum_{m \in \mathcal{M}_i^\alpha} p_m(t)$, $\beta_i(t) = \sum_{m \in \mathcal{M}_i^\beta} p_m(t)$, and $\gamma_i^k(t) = \sum_{m \in \mathcal{M}_i^{\gamma, k}} p_m(t)\ \forall\, k \in \mathbb{N}$, where $\mathcal{M}_i^\alpha$, $\mathcal{M}_i^\beta$, and $\mathcal{M}_i^{\gamma, k}$ are the sets of markings s.t. p_task$i$_job contains a token, p_task$i$_deadlineMiss contains a token, and p_task$i$_deadlineMissCount contains at least k tokens, respectively.

4   Experimentation

Experimental Setup. To explore multiple load conditions and different task-set implementations, we have developed a procedure for random generation of task-sets from a given utilization U, i.e., Algorithm 1, which includes a probabilistic extension of the UUnifast Algorithm presented in [6]. The utilization of the i-th generated task T_i is derived as $U_i = (U - \sum_{n=1}^{i-1} U_n) \cdot \mathcal{U}(0, 1)$ where $\mathcal{U}(0, 1)$

is the continuous uniform distribution over $[0,1]$ (Line 8 in Algorithm 1). A specification $T_i = \langle \pi_i, \theta_i, f_{\phi_i}, \omega_i, \psi_i \rangle$ is obtained as follows (Lines 9–12): a period π_i is extracted from a discrete uniform distribution $\mathcal{U}\{4,6,8,10,12,16,20\}$; a deterministic WCET ϕ_i is derived such that $f_{\phi_i} = \delta(\lfloor \pi_i \cdot U_i \rfloor)$; an offset θ_i is extracted from $\mathcal{U}\{0,1,\ldots,\pi_i - \lfloor \pi_i \cdot U_i \rfloor\}$; a deadline Ω_i is sampled from $\mathcal{U}\{\phi_i - \theta_i, \ldots, \pi_i\}$; a priority ψ_i is derived from $\mathcal{U}\{1,\ldots,N\}$, where N is the number of tasks. Then, according to a random choice, the deterministic WCET is maintained or used to derive a probabilistic WCET $f_{\phi_i}(x) : [\phi_i^{\min}, \phi_i^{\max}] \to [0,1]$ from an exponential distribution with rate λ sampled from $\mathcal{U}\{0.5, 0.55, \ldots, 1.5\}$ (Lines 2–3).

Algorithm 1. Random Generation

Input: $T_i = \langle \pi_i, \theta_i, f_{\phi_i}, \omega_i, \psi_i \rangle$ with deterministic WCET, i.e., $f_{\phi_i}(x) = \delta(\phi_i^{\min})$;
Output: $T_i = \langle \pi_i, \theta_i, f_{\phi_i}, \omega_i, \psi_i \rangle$ with probabilistic WCET, i.e., $f_{\phi_i}(x) : [\phi_i^{\min}, \phi_i^{\max}] \to [0,1]$;
1: **procedure** EXECUTION TIME PROBABILISTIC RANDOM GENERATION(T_i)
2:     $\lambda = \mathcal{U}\{0.5, 0.55, \ldots, 1.5\}$;
3:     $\phi_i^{\min} = \lfloor \pi_i \cdot U_i \rfloor$; $\Phi_i = \lfloor -\log(0.2)/\lambda \rfloor$; $\phi_i^{\max} = \phi_i^{\min} + \Phi_i$; $f_{\phi_i}(x) = \lambda e^{-\lambda x} / \int_{\phi_i^{\min}}^{\phi_i^{\max}} \lambda e^{-\lambda x}$;
4: **end procedure**
Input: Task-set utilization U, number of tasks N
Output: Task-set $\Gamma = \{\langle \pi_i, \theta_i, f_{\phi_i}, \omega_i, \psi_i \rangle \; \forall \; i = 1, \ldots, N\}$
5: **procedure** TASK SET RANDOM GENERATION(U,N)
6:     $sumU = 0$; $availableU = U$;
7:     **for** $i \in \{1, \ldots N\}$ **do**
8:         $U_i = availableU \cdot \mathcal{U}(0,1)$; $sumU = sumU + U_i$; $availableU = U - sumU$;
9:         $\pi_i = \mathcal{U}\{4,6,8,10,12,16,20\}$;
10:        $\phi_i^{\min} = \lfloor \pi_i \cdot U_i \rfloor$; $f_{\phi_i} = \delta(\phi_i^{\min})$;
11:        $\theta_i = \mathcal{U}\{0,1,\ldots,\pi_i - \lfloor \pi_i \cdot U_i \rfloor\}$;
12:        $\Omega_i = \mathcal{U}\{\phi_i - \theta_i, \ldots, \pi_i\}$;
13:        **if** $\mathcal{U}(0,1) > 0.5$ **then**
14:            Execution Time Probabilistic Random Generation$(\langle \pi_i, \theta_i, f_{\phi_i}, \omega_i, \psi_i \rangle)$
15:        **end if**
16:    **end for**
17: **end procedure**

Experimental Results. Ten task-sets made of five tasks have been generated for each utilization $U \in \{0.5, 0.6, 0.7, 0.8\}$ through Algorithm 1 implemented with the R tool. The corresponding STPN models have been automatically derived through an implementation developed on top of the ORIS API [5]. Each model has been analyzed for each scheduling policy (i.e., FP, RM, EDF), late jobs policy (i.e., discarding, rejection), and deadline miss reward (i.e., instantaneous, cumulative), computing the performance measures of Sect. 2 at 100 equidistant time points over the interval $[0, I]$. The analysis has been performed on an Intel Xeon 2.67 GHz with 32 GB RAM, requiring at most 180 s (10 s on average).

For each combination of scheduling policy, late jobs policy, and utilization, Table 2 shows the maximum probability that a task has missed a deadline by the time limit I, computed over all task-sets $\Gamma_1, \ldots, \Gamma_{10}$, i.e., $\max_{i|T_i \in \{\Gamma_1,\ldots,\Gamma_{10}\}} \gamma_i^1(I)$. As expected, EDF outperforms RM which, in turn, outperforms FP. The maximum deadline miss probability increases with the utilization, except for the peak value obtained with utilization 0.7 under FP scheduling, which is due to the fact that the task with the smallest period is the one with the lowest priority, which never occurs in randomly generated task-sets with utilization 0.6 and 0.8. Results also show that $\gamma_i^1(I)$ is insensitive to the late jobs policy, which is mainly ascribed to the fact that the way a late job is managed does not affect the probability that such job is late. In principle, it may have an effect on the completion time of subsequent jobs, which is nevertheless smoothed by non-preemptive scheduling in these experiments. Fig. 5 shows the performance measures for the task attaining the maximum deadline miss probability, i.e., task T_5 of a task-set with utilization 0.7. The remaining tasks belonging to the task-set of T_5 have larger priority than T_5 and never miss a deadline. Note that ramps and flats in $\gamma_5^1(t)$ correspond to peaks and zero-valued intervals in $\beta_5(t)$, respectively.

Table 2. Maximum probability of deadline miss by the time limit I.

	Utilization			
	0.5	0.6	0.7	0.8
FP–discarding/FP–rejection	0.0/0.0	0.00054/0.00054	0.85/0.85	0.32/0.32
RM–discarding/RM–rejection	0.0/0.0	0.0/0.0	0.0/0.0	0.29/0.29
EDF–discarding/EDF–rejection	0.0/0.0	0.0/0.0	0.0/0.0	0.0/0.0

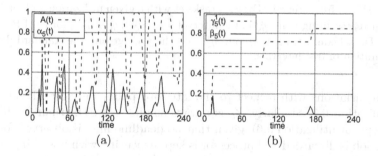

(a)   (b)

Fig. 5. For the task with maximum deadline miss probability in Table 2, i.e., task T_5 of a task-set with utilization 0.7: (a) the probability $\alpha_5(t)$ that a job of T_5 is running at t, and the probability $A(t)$ that no job in the task-set of T_5 is running at t; (b) the probability $\beta_5(t)$ that a job of T_5 is running at t and its deadline has passed, and the probability $\gamma_5^1(t)$ that a job of T_5 has missed a deadline by t.

Figures. 6(a)–(c) plot the number Z_ζ of intervals in $[0, I]$ that are free with probability not lower than $\zeta = 0.9$, their minimum duration $\eta_\zeta^{\min}$, and their maximum duration $\eta_\zeta^{\max}$, respectively, for all task-set with a given utilization. While $\eta_\zeta^{\min}$ is insensitive to the scheduling and the late jobs policy, with negligible variations with respect to the utilization, $\eta_\zeta^{\max}$ is larger for EDF than for RM and

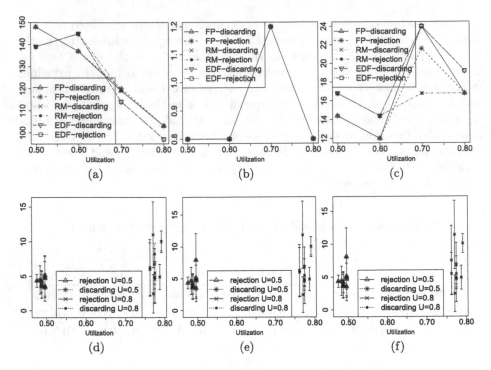

Fig. 6. For all task-sets with a given utilization and for $\zeta = 0.9$: (a) the number Z_ζ of free intervals in $[0, I]$; and, (b) the minimum duration $\eta_\zeta^{\min}$ and (c) the maximum duration $\eta_\zeta^{\max}$ of free intervals. For each task-set with a given utilization and for $\zeta = 0.9$: a segment representing point $\bar{\eta}_\zeta$ in the interval $[\bar{\eta}_\zeta - \eta_\zeta^{\mathrm{std}}; \bar{\eta}_\zeta + \eta_\zeta^{\mathrm{std}}]$ for (d) FP, (e) RM, and (f) EDF scheduling, where $\bar{\eta}_\zeta$ and $\eta_\zeta^{\mathrm{std}}$ are the average and the standard deviation of the duration of free intervals.

FP, with variations with respect to the late jobs policy only for FP scheduling with utilization 0.7. Similarly, Z_ζ is always smaller for EDF than for RM and FP (except for utilization 0.6), given that no deadline miss is observed for EDF, hence no job is discarded and processor is kept executing with less idling periods.

Figures 6(d)–(f) show the interval $[\bar{\eta}_\zeta - \eta_\zeta^{\mathrm{std}}; \bar{\eta}_\zeta + \eta_\zeta^{\mathrm{std}}]$ for each task-set with a given utilization and for $\zeta = 0.9$, where $\bar{\eta}_\zeta$ and $\eta_\zeta^{\mathrm{std}}$ are the average and the standard deviation of the duration of free intervals. Average values do not exhibit significant differences with respect to the scheduling and the late jobs policy, showing evident variability only for utilization, due to the different load.

5   Discussion

Experimental results show that the approach can be effectively applied to probabilistic analysis of real-time task-sets, suggesting further developments. The model expressivity could be improved encompassing task synchronization, which requires the investigation of suitable policies to avoid priority inversion (e.g., the priority ceiling protocol) and to prevent task discarding while being in the critical section. Both aspects could be accounted using modeling patterns similar to those discussed for priority ties and EDF scheduling. The model could be also extended to represent conditional execution of tasks, using random switches among IMM transitions to account for the probability of different paths.

The approach could be used also to predict time intervals during which the processor is likely to be unused due to tasks that may execute less than their WCET. While requiring an effort to reduce the computational burden of stochastic analysis, this could support online reclaiming of over-provisioned resources, finding its major application in resource allocation for mixed-criticality systems.

References

1. Hessel, A., Pettersson, P.: A global algorithm for model-based test suite generation. ENTCS **190**(2), 47–59 (2007)
2. Abeni, L., Manica, N., Palopoli, L.: Efficient and robust probabilistic guarantees for real-time tasks. J. Syst. Softw. **85**(5), 1147–1156 (2012)
3. Altmeyer, S., Cucu-Grosjean, L., Davis, R.I.: Static probabilistic timing analysis for real-time systems using random replacement caches. Real-Time Syst. **51**(1), 77–123 (2015)
4. Berthomieu, B., Diaz, M.: Modeling and verification of time dependent systems using time Petri nets. IEEE Trans. Softw. Eng. **17**(3), 259–273 (1991)
5. Biagi, M., Carnevali, L., Paolieri, M., Vicario, E.: An introdution to the ORIS tool. In: VALUETOOLS. ACM (2017)
6. Bini, E., Buttazzo, G.C.: Measuring the performance of schedulability tests. Real-Time Syst. **30**(1–2), 129–154 (2005)
7. Carnevali, L., Melani, A., Santinelli, L., Lipari, G.: Probabilistic deadline miss analysis of real-time systems using regenerative transient analysis. In: RTNS (2014)
8. Cazorla, F.J., Vardanega, T., Quinones, E., Abella, J.: Upper-bounding program execution time with extreme value theory. In: WCET (2013)
9. Cucu-Grosjean, L., et al.: Measurement-based probabilistic timing analysis for multi-path programs. In: ECRTS. IEEE (2012)
10. Cucu-Grosjean, L.: Independence-a misunderstood property of and for probabilistic real-time systems. In: Real-Time Systems: The Past, the Present and the Future, pp. 29–37 (2013)
11. Díaz, J.L., et al.: Stochastic analysis of periodic real-time systems. In: RTSS, pp. 289–300 (2002)
12. Cassez, F., Larsen, K.: The impressive power of stopwatches. In: Palamidessi, C. (ed.) CONCUR 2000. LNCS, vol. 1877, pp. 138–152. Springer, Heidelberg (2000). https://doi.org/10.1007/3-540-44618-4_12
13. Bucci, G., Fedeli, A., Sassoli, L., Vicario, E.: Timed state space analysis of real time preemptive systems. IEEE Trans. Softw. Eng. **30**(2), 97–111 (2004)
14. Horváth, A., Paolieri, M., Ridi, L., Vicario, E.: Transient analysis of non-Markovian models using stochastic state classes. Perf. Eval. **69**(7–8), 315–335 (2012)
15. Kempf, J.-F., Bozga, M., Maler, O.: Performance evaluation of schedulers in a probabilistic setting. In: FORMATS, pp. 1–17 (2011)
16. Kempf, J.-F., Bozga, M., Maler, O.: As soon as probable: optimal scheduling under stochastic uncertainty. In: TACAS, pp. 385–400 (2013)

17. Larsen, K.G., Legay, A., Traonouez, L.-M., Wasowski, A.: Robust specification of real time components. In: FORMATS, pp. 129–144 (2011)
18. Leung, J.Y.-T., Merrill, M.L.: A note on preemptive scheduling of periodic, real-time tasks. Inf. Process. Lett. **11**(3), 115–118 (1980)
19. Lime, D., Roux, O.H.: Formal verification of real-time systems with preemptive scheduling. Real-Time Syst. **41**(2), 118–151 (2009)
20. Lindemann, C., Thümmler, A.: Transient analysis of deterministic and stochastic Petri nets with concurrent deterministic transitions. Perform. Eval. **36–37**(1–4), 35–54 (1999)
21. Manolache, S., Eles, P., Peng, Z.: Schedulability analysis of applications with stochastic task execution times. ACM TECS **3**(4), 706–735 (2004)
22. Maxim, D., Cucu-Grosjean, L.: Response time analysis for fixed-priority tasks with multiple probabilistic parameters. In: RTSS, pp. 224–235 (2013)
23. Refaat, K.S., Hladik, P.-E.: Efficient stochastic analysis of real-time systems via random sampling. In: ECRTS, pp. 175–183 (2010)
24. Santinelli, L., Meumeu, P., Maxim, D., Cucu-Grosjean, L.: A component-based framework for modeling and analyzing probabilistic real-time systems. In: ETFA 2011 (2011)
25. Traonouez, L.-M., Lime, D., Roux, O.H.: Parametric model-checking of time Petri nets with stopwatches using the state-class graph. In: FORMATS (2008)
26. Vicario, E.: Static analysis and dynamic steering of time dependent systems using time Petri nets. IEEE Trans. Softw. Eng. **27**(1), 728–748 (2001)

An Ontology Framework for Generating Discrete-Event Stochastic Models

Ken Keefe[✉], Brett Feddersen, Michael Rausch, Ronald Wright,
and William H. Sanders

Information Trust Institute, University of Illinois at Urbana-Champaign,
Urbana, IL 61801, USA
{kjkeefe,bfeddrsn,mjrausc2,wright53,whs}@illinois.edu

Abstract. Discrete-event stochastic models are a widely used approach for studying the behavior of systems that have not been implemented or that it would be too costly to examine directly. Valuable analysis depends on carefully constructed, well-founded models, which are very difficult for humans to create. To address this problem, we propose a framework for generating detailed, low-level models from high-level, block-diagram-style graphical models. Our approach uses extensible, collaborative ontology libraries that contain information about the types of components in a system, the types of relationships that connect those components, and fragments of low-level models that can be constructed together based on the definition of a high-level system model. This framework has been implemented and used in several case studies. We describe the framework and how model generation works by examining its use to generate complex ADversary VIew Security Evaluation (ADVISE) models.

Keywords: Ontology · Model generation · Executable models
Discrete-event simulation

1 Introduction

Modeling is a critical element of system design and analysis. Through a formal, mathematical description of how the world works, a model provides a representation of a system that can be explored, evaluated, and tested in a scientific, repeatable way. Discrete-event stochastic models provide especially useful views of real-world system designs [1].

Creating accurate, complete stochastic models is very challenging. Typically, human modelers must make decisions about what details and behaviors are important to include in each system model they create. Tools that automatically explore an existing system to construct a complete model can help with the decision-making process, but function only on systems that have already been implemented [2,3].

This paper's contribution are (1) a formal description of an ontology framework that automatically generates detailed, discrete-event, stochastic models

© Springer Nature Switzerland AG 2018
R. Bakhshi et al. (Eds.): EPEW 2018, LNCS 11178, pp. 173–189, 2018.
https://doi.org/10.1007/978-3-030-02227-3_12

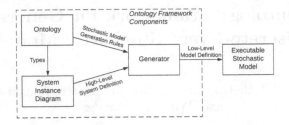

Fig. 1. An overview of the three parts of the ontology framework and how they work together to automatically generate executable, stochastic models.

from high-level system design primitives and (2) an implementation of the framework that generates ADVISE security models in the Möbius tool. Figure 1 shows how the pieces of our framework interact. Fine-grained models are generated from (1) an ontology of component and relationship types, as well as model fragment generation rules, and (2) a simple, formal description of a system that uses instances of the types from the ontology. We define the notion of a *system instance diagram (SID)* to be a graphical model of component instances and relationship instance arcs that connect component instances. From the ontology and SID, we use a custom semantic reasoner to automatically construct the low-level model.

We argue that our approach to model generation is inherently more useful, less prone to error, and more complete than conventional approaches. Once an ontology has been defined for certain classes of systems, it is relatively quick and easy to define a SID and generate rich and complex stochastic models. We can now create in hours a low-level model that previously would have taken weeks of painstaking effort. By separating the ontology and SID, ontologies can be refined over time by a community of experts and reused over many system studies. Instead of relying on a human modeler's diligence to be sure that all aspects of a system have been thoroughly and correctly modeled at a detailed level, one can count on the generation process to apply every stochastic model construction rule consistently and accurately. Further, making significant changes to a system design or comparing multiple designs is much faster at the SID level than it is at the traditional detailed stochastic model level.

Our ontology framework has been implemented and tested on a cybersecurity modeling formalism called ADversary VIew Security Evaluation (ADVISE) [4]. The generated ADVISE models are used by the Möbius tool [5] to evaluate custom quantitative metrics through discrete-event simulation [6].

This paper is organized as follows. Section 2 describes our ontology framework. Section 3 explains how the ontology framework is used to create ADVISE models. In Sect. 4, we provide an overview of two case studies that use our implementation of the ontology framework. In Sect. 5, we describe prior work that has similarities to our work. We conclude in Sect. 6.

2   Ontology Framework

An *ontology* is a formal specification of types, attributes of instances of those types, and relationships that can connect instances of those types [7]. The types, attributes, and relationships all have semantic interpretations that the ontology seeks to organize and formalize. A *knowledge base* is associated with an ontology and contains instances of the types from the ontology, values for the attributes associated with each instance's type, and relationships that connect two instances.

We define a *Möbius ontology* to contain a set of component, relationship, and model fragment classes. Each component class may have one or more attributes that can be any single basic data type. Relationship classes in a Möbius ontology define domain and range component class restrictions and provide a type for instances of semantic relationships that connect two component instances. Component and relationship classes have a disjoint inheritance structure that indicates that one type is a more specialized type of another. Model fragment classes are formal definitions of a piece of a detailed, low-level model. A model fragment is tied to a component class by the special *dependent* relationship.

The knowledge base in our framework is called a *system instance diagram (SID)*. When a component class is instantiated in the SID, each model fragment class that is a dependent of the instance's class is also instantiated. A model fragment class includes instructions for connecting the instances to other model fragment instances.

2.1   Formal Definition

Definitions 1 and 2 provide a formal definition of a Möbius ontology and a SID. A detailed discussion of these definitions is provided in subsequent sections.

Definition 1. *A* Möbius ontology *can be defined as the following tuple:*

$$<C, A, R, AF, SF, S, U, Type, Inherits, Attrib, Domain, Range, Dependents>,$$

where

- C *is the set of component classes.*
- A *is the set of attributes.*
- R *is the set of relationship classes.*
- AF *is the set of action model fragment classes.*
- SF *is the set of state variable model fragment classes.*
- $S \subseteq R$ *is the set of relationship classes that are symmetric.*
- $U \subseteq (AF \cup SF)$ *is the set that contains all universal fragment classes.*
- $Type: A \cup SF \rightarrow T$ *provides a type for every attribute or state variable model fragment. T is defined in Sect. 3.1.1 of [8].*
- $Inherits: C \cup R \rightarrow \mathcal{P}(C) \cup \mathcal{P}(R)$ *identifies the set of classes from which the given component class or relationship class inherits.*
- $Attrib: C \rightarrow \mathcal{P}(A)$ *identifies the set of attributes of a component class.*

- *Domain:* $R \rightarrow \mathcal{P}(C)$ *identifies the set of source types for the relationship.*
- *Range:* $R \rightarrow \mathcal{P}(C)$ *identifies the set of target types for the relationship.*
- *Dependents:* $C \rightarrow \mathcal{P}(AF \cup SF)$ *identifies the set of model fragments that are dependents of the given component type.*

Definition 2. *A* system instance diagram (SID) *can be defined as the following tuple:*

$$<o, CI, RI, AFI, SFI, Class, Value, Arc, Dependents>,$$

where

- *o is the SID's ontology.*
- *CI is the set of component instances.*
- *RI is the set of relationship instances.*
- *AFI is the set of action model fragment instances.*
- *SFI is the set of state variable model fragment instances.*
- *FI is the set of model fragment instances (AFI ∪ SFI).*
- *Class:* $CI \cup RI \cup AFI \cup SFI \rightarrow C \in o \cup R \in o \cup AF \in o \cup SF \in o$ *provides the class of the instance.*
- *Value:* $CI \times A \rightarrow V$ *provides the value of a component instance's attribute, and V is defined such that*

$$\forall ci \in CI, \forall a \in Attrib(Class(ci)), \forall v \in V,$$
$$Value(ci, a) = v \Rightarrow type(v) = Type(a)$$

where type *and* V *are defined in Sect. III.A.2 of* [8].
- *Arc:* $RI \rightarrow CI \times CI$ *provides the source and target component instances of a relationship instance.* $Arc_s(ri)$ *and* $Arc_t(ri)$ *denote the source and target component instance of the given relationship instance, respectively.*
- *DependentsI:* $CI \rightarrow \mathcal{P}(FI)$ *provides the set of model fragment instances that are dependents of the given component instance.*

2.2 Components, Attributes, and Relationships

Our ontology framework defines the notions of components, attributes, and relationships. *Components* are atomic pieces of a system, either physical or conceptual. For example, a component can be a network, a firewall, a human user, a password policy, or a collection of data in a database.

A *relationship* is a semantic connection between two component instances. Class constraints are applied to the *domain* and *range* of the relationship in order to limit instance types that are allowable as the source or target, respectively. For example, a *connectedTo* relationship could connect a firewall component to a network component and capture the information that the source component has an Ethernet connection to the target component. Ontology relationships are directed unless the relationship is in S, indicating that it is symmetric.

An *attribute* is a semantic reference between a component instance and a basic data type. Basic data types are like those described in Sect. III.A.1 of [8]. They are used to describe qualities of a component, such as the operational state of an IDS service on a network component, or whether malware has infected a network component.

2.3   Class Inheritance

In our ontology framework, classes may inherit features from other classes. Definition 3 defines class inheritance and its consequences. Inheritance plays a pivotal role in the definition of components, relationships, and attributes. Components and relationships have directed, acyclical hierarchies that define the inheritance structure among these classes. The inheritance structures for components and relationships are necessarily disjoint.

Definition 3. *A **child** class **inherits** from its **parent** class(es) and is a specialized subtype of its parent(s). The following properties hold.*

1. $\forall a, b \in C, b \in Inherits(a) \Rightarrow Attrib(b) \subseteq Attrib(a)$
2. $\forall a, b \in C, \forall r \in R, b \in Inherits(a) \wedge b \in Domain(r) \Rightarrow a \in Domain(r)$
3. $\forall a, b \in C, \forall r \in R, b \in Inherits(a) \wedge b \in Range(r) \Rightarrow a \in Range(r)$
4. $\forall q, r \in R, \forall a \in C, r \in Inherits(q) \wedge b \in Domain(r) \Rightarrow a \in Domain(q)$
5. $\forall q, r \in R, \forall a \in C, r \in Inherits(q) \wedge b \in Range(r) \Rightarrow a \in Range(q)$

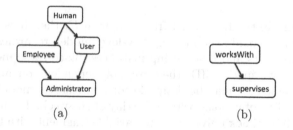

(a)   (b)

Fig. 2. Example component (a) and relationship (b) class inheritance hierarchies.

When a child component class inherits from a parent component class, every attribute ascribed to the parent will also be ascribed to the child (Definition 3.1). For example, in Fig. 2a, Human could have the attribute Name, and User could have the attribute Username. Given the rules of inheritance, an instance of type User would have two attributes, Name and Username.

A relationship that defines its range class constraints as the set {User} really has a range class constraints set of {User, Administrator} (Definition 3.2–3.3). Relationship classes can also have an inheritance structure. For example, in Fig. 2b, two relationship classes are defined in the example ontology; both have domain and range class constraints sets that are equal to {Employee}. worksWith means that two people work for the same employer, while **supervises** means that the source person oversees the work of the target person. It makes sense for inheritance to be defined between these two relationship classes, because if a person supervises another person at work, then both people work for the same employer (Definition 3.4–3.5).

2.4   Model Fragments

The primary objective of our framework is to automatically create detailed low-level models from high-level system instance diagrams (SIDs). Components, attributes, and relationships are the building blocks of the high-level model, and model fragments describe how the lower-level models will be constructed. The connection between the two levels is done through an explicit mapping that uses the *Dependents* (Definition 1) function.

Model fragments are classified into two types: state variable fragments and action fragments. *State variable fragments* describe variables that store a part of the low-level model's state, and *action fragments* describe low-level model actions that transition the model's state. Fragments in the ontology are not themselves state variables and actions, but rather are information about how to create sets of state variables and actions that will be included in the generated low-level model. More precisely, model fragments are classes in the ontology, and the state variables and actions that they create are instances in the knowledge base (SID). Unlike component and relationship instances, model fragment instances do not appear visually in a SID.

Universal Fragments. If a model fragment is in U, then it is considered to be an element that should exist in every low-level model, regardless of the composition of components and relationship instances. Since these model fragment instances are always in the SID, they are not dependent on any component instance. For example, it may be desirable for a stochastic model dealing with real-world scheduling of people to track the day of the week. To enable that, one could add a `DayOfTheWeek` universal state variable fragment with the type `char`. Regardless of how many users and which jobs are added to the SID, there will always be a single `DayOfTheWeek` state variable to track the day of the week in the generated stochastic model.

Variable Macros and Path Expressions. A variable macro describes an attachment between an action model fragment and a state variable model fragment. Our generator uses these definitions to connect together the generated model fragment instances. Depending on the semantics of the low-level model formalism, these variable macros can impact the model in a variety of ways. For example, in the ADVISE formalism, variable macros cause AEG arcs to be defined between state variable elements and attack steps. A variable macro includes a SID path expression tree to identify which state variables should be included in the variable macro's set.

Path expressions are used to explore the SID and collect a set of model fragment instances. Path expressions are a hierarchy of path constraints, which are often parameterized with a class constraint that is used to filter path steps according to the component's, relationship's, or model fragment's class. There are several kinds of individual path constraint nodes:

- $Dependent(t)$ explores the dependent model fragment instances with class t of the current component instance.
- $Component_{source}(t)$ explores the source component with the class t of the current relationship instance.
- $Component_{target}(t)$ explores the target component with the class t of the current relationship instance.
- $Relationship_{source}(t)$ explores the relationship instances with class t that have the current component instance as the source component.
- $Relationship_{target}(t)$ explores the relationship instances with class t that have the current component instance as the target component.
- And evaluates all child path constraints and returns the intersection.
- Or evaluates all child path constraints and returns the union.
- $Universal(t)$ returns the universal model fragments with class t.

Algorithm 1 defines how variable macro path expression trees are evaluated. The cases that explore $Component_{target}(t)$ and $Relationship_{target}(t)$ are omitted here to save space, but they are very similar to their *source* counterparts.

2.5   Model Generation Algorithm

The low-level stochastic model is generated in two phases. The first phase happens synchronously as components are added to or removed from the system instance diagram. Any state variable or action model fragments that are dependents of a component are created and added when a component is added to the SID. Likewise, the model fragment instances are removed from the SID when the component instance on which they depend is removed.

The second phase is performed once the SID has been defined. Algorithm 2 describes the execution of this phase. Every model fragment instance in the SID ($AFI \cup SFI$) is looped through. The component instance ci is stored for each model fragment instance fi. For each variable macro associated with the model fragment instance, the following two steps are performed: (1) find the set of variables by exploring the path expression defined in the variable macro by using the component instance as the starting point, (2) make formalism-specific changes to the model. Once Algorithm 2 has been executed, a well-formed low-level model has been generated.

Complexity. The factors that impact the time and space complexity of the first phase of the model generation algorithm include the number of model fragments that are dependents of each component class (d_c) in the ontology and the number of component instances of each component class (i_c) in the SID, giving a time

---

Algorithm 1. Path Expression Evaluation

1: Given path expression tree pet, and component or relationship instance cur
2: **function** FSV(pet, cur)
3:     $ret \leftarrow \emptyset$
4:     $pc \leftarrow rootOf(pet)$
5:     **switch** pc **do**
6:         **case** $Dependent(t)$
7:             **for all** $d \in Dependents(cur)$ **do**
8:                 **if** $Class(d) = t$ **then**
9:                     $ret \leftarrow ret \cup \{d\}$
10:        **case** $Component_{source}(t)$
11:            **if** $Class(Arc_s(cur)) = t$ **then**
12:                $ret \leftarrow ret \cup$ FSV($childOf(pc, 0), Arc_s(cur)$)
13:        **case** $Relationship_{source}(t)$
14:            **for all** $r \in RI$ **do**
15:                **if** $Arc_s(r) = cur$ & $Class(r) = t$ **then**
16:                    $ret \leftarrow ret \cup$ FSV($childOf(pc, 0), r$)
17:        **case** And
18:            $ret \leftarrow \mathbb{U}$
19:            **for** $i \leftarrow 0 \ldots n$ **do**
20:                $ret \leftarrow ret \cap$ FSV($childOf(pc, i), cur$)
21:        **case** Or
22:            **for** $i \leftarrow 0 \ldots n$ **do**
23:                $ret \leftarrow ret \cup$ FSV($childOf(pc, i), cur$)
24:        **case** $Universal(t)$
25:            **for all** $u \in U$ **do**
26:                **if** Class(u) = t **then**
27:                    $ret \leftarrow ret \cup \{u\}$
28:    **return** ret

Algorithm 2. Model Generation Algorithm

1: **for all** $fi \in AFI \cup SFI$ **do**
2:     $ci \leftarrow c \in CI \mid fi \in Dependents(c)$
3:     **for all** $vm \in VariableMacros(fi)$ **do**
4:         $vs \leftarrow FSV(PathExp(vm), ci)$
5:         $MakeFormalismSpecificChanges(vm, vs, fi)$

---

and space complexity of $\mathcal{O}(d_c i_c)$. However, phase 1 can be done synchronously during the creation of a SID, so, in practice, it is $\mathcal{O}(1)$.

For the second phase of the generation algorithm, the time complexity is $\mathcal{O}(vp)$, where v is the number of variable macros that must be evaluated across the entire SID and p is the maximum number of nodes in the variable macros' path expressions. The space complexity is entirely dependent on the formalism-specific $MakeFormalismSpecificChanges()$ function. It is typical to expect a formalism to add a single arc for each variable macro replacement, so the complexity would be $\mathcal{O}(v)$.

Scalability. To describe the scalability of our approach in more concrete terms, we will mention an example ontology and system that are pending publication and are the largest (that we know of) to date. The system domain is power distribution systems. The ontology contains about 100 component types, 20 relationship types, and approximately 200 model fragment classes. The system instance diagram contains about 50 component instances and 500 relationship instances. On a modern laptop, this system takes approximately 15 min to generate the 500 state variables, 200 actions (with 2,000 variable macro resolutions), and 1,400 arcs.

3   Generating ADVISE Security Models

To test the concepts described in Sect. 2, we have implemented our ontology framework and are able to generate Möbius ADVISE atomic models from SIDs. Möbius provides an interface through which multiple modeling formalisms can be used to define executable, discrete-event systems that can be combined together and evaluated by an array of solution methods implemented in the Möbius tool.

In the remainder of Sect. 3, we will give a brief overview of the ADVISE formalism, discuss the extensions to the generator that were implemented to accommodate ADVISE model generation, and go through a detailed example that should illuminate the formal definitions given in Sect. 2.

3.1   The ADVISE Atomic Model Formalism

ADversary VIew Security Evaluation (ADVISE) [4,9–11] is a security modeling formalism that models a system from the perspective of an adversary attempting to compromise the system and achieve custom-defined goals. An ADVISE model consists of an executable version of an attack tree called the *attack execution graph (AEG)* and an adversary profile that describes the initial assets of the adversary.

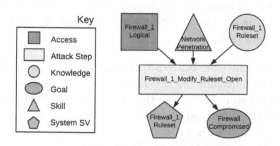

Fig. 3. An example AEG fragment.

Figure 3 shows a small example fragment of an attack execution graph. The yellow rectangles are the attack steps that change the model state, and every other shape is a state variable of some kind. Arcs connecting state variables to or from attack steps indicate that the state variable is used in the execution of the attack step.

Several case studies have used ADVISE to model potential attack scenarios against critical infrastructure systems [11–13]. However, these models were created through extensive manual effort of human modelers.

3.2   Implementing the ADVISE Generator Extensions

Access, goals, knowledge, skills, and system state variables (SSV) are all state variable elements of an ADVISE model. We defined five model fragment classes to serve as base classes for any ADVISE state variable model fragments defined in the ontology.

When formalism-specific extensions are added to the Möbius ontology framework, model fragments that store the component instance attribute values must be defined. In the ADVISE extension, component instance attributes are generated as system state variables, and the type of the attribute matches the type of the generated system state variable.

ADVISE models have only one kind of Möbius action, the attack step-outcome pair. These pairs are grouped together by the attack step to form Möbius groups (see [14]). The action fragments in the ontology framework work in a similar way, so that many actions can be joined together in a group. When a human ontology developer defines an attack step and its outcomes, he or she does so by creating child classes of the base attack step-outcome class. The same code expressions necessary to define attack steps and outcomes in ADVISE atomic models are also required in the definition of the attack step-outcome model fragment classes.

3.3   The Two Nets Example

We now present an example ontology, system instance diagram, and generated ADVISE model to illuminate the discussion presented so far. Consider a very simple ontology that is used to describe networks and the firewalls that bridge them. C, A, and R are defined:

- **Firewall:** Component that bridges traffic between connected networks.
- **Network:** Component that has a collection of hosts connected to it.
  - **isIDSOperational:** Attribute that stores the operational state of a network's intrusion detection service.
- **connectedTo:** Indicates that a firewall is connected to a network.
  - **Domain: {Firewall}. Range: {Network}.**

This ontology can define any organization of networks and firewalls. Figure 4 shows the Two Nets example's SID. It has two instances of Network (*Corporate LAN* and *SCADA LAN*) and one instance of Firewall (*Corp SCADA FW*).

Fig. 4. The system instance diagram for the Two Nets example.

In order to generate an ADVISE model, ADVISE model fragment classes must be defined in the ontology. The model fragment classes used in the Two Nets example are outlined below. Fragments below a component class are dependents of the component class.

- **Firewall**
  - **Defeat Firewall Attack Step:** This attack step defeats a firewall by using a brute-force approach. Upon successful completion, access is gained to any network connected to the firewall.
- **Network**
  - **IDS Operational SSV:** This SSV stores whether the network's IDS is currently operational. This model fragment's value is inferred from the *isIDSOperational* component attribute value.
  - **Install Malware on Network Attack Step:** This attack step installs malware on the network (on one of the network's hosts).
  - **Malware Installed SSV:** This SSV stores whether malware is installed.
  - **Network Access:** This access stores whether the adversary has some kind of access to the network.
- *Universal*
  - **Brute Force Skill:** This skill represents the ability of an adversary to effectively perform brute-force attacks.

In Fig. 5, the system instance diagram is presented in the left column. The center column shows the state variable model fragment instances that are generated for each of the associated component instances. The center column also shows the universal state variable model fragment instance that is generated for all ADVISE models that use this ontology. The right column shows the action model fragment instances that are generated for each component instance. The center and right columns combined show what the attack execution graph generation looks like after phase one of the generation process. In phase two, variable macro path expressions are evaluated, and AEG arcs are created. Precondition elements will create AEG arcs that target attack steps. Affected elements will create AEG arcs that are sourced from attack steps.

The outline below shows the structure of the variable macro path expression for the *Defeat Firewall Attack Step*. The *Install Malware on Network Attack Step* is omitted here because of space limitations. However, the *Defeat Firewall Attack Step* definition is complex enough to demonstrate the relevant concepts.

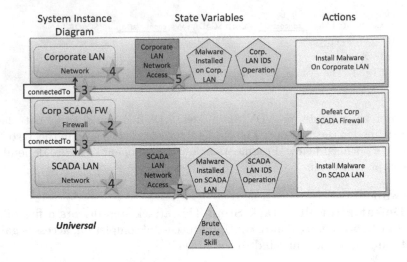

Fig. 5. The generated state variable and action model fragment instances.

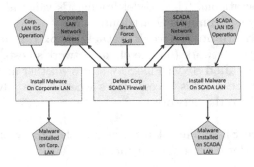

Fig. 6. The generated ADVISE attack execution graph for the Two Nets example.

- **Defeat Firewall Attack Step**
  - **bfs:** Precondition element.
    - $Universal$(BruteForceSkill)
  - **netAccesses:** Precondition (and affected) element.
    - $Relationship_{source}$(connectedTo)
      - $Component$(Network)
        - $Dependent$(Network Access)

The path for finding the universal brute-force skill is trivial, but the path of **netAccesses**, which finds all Network Access state variables of components connected to the firewall, requires some explanation. Using the orange stars in Fig. 5, we will step through the macro path exploration for the *netAccesses* variable macros. The origin of every path is always the component instance of which the macro's parent is a dependent. In this case, the macro's parent is the *Defeat Corp SCADA Firewall* attack step instance (star marked "1"). The component instance on which the attack step is dependent is shown as a star marked "2" and is the origin of the path constraints. The first step in the path expression is to find outgoing relationship instances of the `connectedTo` type, which are shown with stars marked "3." The next step in the path expression looks for components targeted by the discovered arcs with a type of `Network`. Those components are shown as stars marked "4." The final step in the path expression will look at the dependents of the "4" star components that have a class of `Network Access`. These network access instances are shown as stars marked "5." The end result is that AEG arcs will be drawn to and from the *Defeat Corp SCADA Firewall* attack step and will connect every `Network Access` element of a network component that is attached to the firewall component that this attack step is attacking.

Figure 6 shows the final generated attack execution graph that is created by the example ontology and the system instance diagram shown in Fig. 4. The central attack step and the arcs that connect it to the graph were created by the variable macros described earlier.

4 Case Studies

The Möbius ontology framework and its implementation have been used by dozens of test users in order to evaluate and refine the overall approach. Two in-depth case studies have been presented at peer-reviewed conferences.

In [15], the authors studied several designs of intrusion detection system deployments on a multi-tiered advanced metering infrastructure in power distribution systems. They calculated metrics that provided the expected cost to the system owner and the probability that the adversary would be detected. In [16], the authors used the Möbius ontology framework and ADVISE to construct a set of physical attack models for a railway station. From these models, the authors determined the likely sequence of attack steps for each class of attacker and identified which kinds of devices should receive additional monitoring resources to maximize the mitigation of attacks.

5 Related Work

We have not found work that attempts to automatically generate detailed, discrete-event stochastic models from an ontological definition of system components and a high-level specification of a general system based on those components. However, we have found many efforts that relate to our approach.

In [17], the authors automatically translate feature-based system models to PRISM models for the purpose of probabilistic model checking. In [18], software code models are translated to Petri-net-based performance models. If one considers the detailed model generation of our approach as a translation from a source model to a target discrete-event model, our source model is comprised of a high-level system description and a reusable, auditable, and extensible ontology of translation rules. We believe that this design difference is critical.

[19] generates attack trees from a π-calculus process language by using static analysis. [20] generates attack trees from a general system model by using a rigid set of rules that expand attack tree nodes based on locations, assets, actors, and processes. These approaches have some similarities in their generation parts, but their generated products are significantly different. They generate attack trees for static analysis, whereas we are generating executable, discrete-event, state-based models that can be evaluated through simulation or analytical solution. Furthermore, their input rules are not extensible.

In [21], the authors discuss an approach for generating code from high-level Petri nets and how it can be extended to generate code from general UML models with additional semantic information. That second part has a clear connection to our approach of coupling a high-level UML-like model with formal semantic definitions in the ontology to construct executable code. However, we generate executable graphical models as an end result, and we take a more formal approach in defining the ontology and system model, thereby enabling a much larger class of potential input models than the one on which [21] focuses.

[22] generates an executable, generalized stochastic Petri net model from a specialized class of UML models, sequence diagrams, and statecharts. [23] generates an OSAN from another restricted class of UML models with Petri net annotations. We believe that an ontology in the Möbius ontology framework can be defined that would generate executable stochastic models equivalent to those described by those authors; it might be an interesting topic for future work.

[24] and [25] construct ontologies that describe discrete-event simulation and use them to generate executable code to evaluate discrete-event models encoded in a knowledge base of the ontology. This approach has several connections to our work, but does not abstract the complexity of discrete-event models of real systems by allowing the user to think about and define the system at the level of custom component building blocks. In essence, the authors of [24] and [25] replicate the existing Möbius framework, but using an ontology to describe the atomic models instead of the variety of formalisms that Möbius provides.

There is a large body of work in the area of model-driven software engineering [26], including many well-known frameworks, such as the Eclipse Modeling Framework (EMF) [27]. These efforts often use formal meta-models to describe the architecture of a software application, and then use the meta-models to automatically generate significant portions of the source code necessary to define the application. The software meta-models can be thought of as a kind of knowledge base on a source code ontology. While it is clear that the Möbius ontology framework addresses a very different kind of problem, we pulled many lessons from the model-driven software engineering work as we developed our framework.

6 Conclusion

Building formal, mathematical models of real-world systems is a challenging endeavor for any human modeler. A vast array of design details must be encoded in complex modeling formalism primitives, often with many parameters on each primitive. Once complete, these low-level models are difficult for others to interpret and difficult for the human modeler to alter or vary to allow for experimental analysis of multiple designs. The development process of low-level models is a subjective effort, and different human modelers will produce different models.

To address those issues, we have developed an ontology framework that enables the formalization of the model development process in the form of an ontology. The low-level model generator uses an ontology and a SID to automatically construct the low-level model. Instead of working with low-level, complex, discrete-event modeling primitives, users create high-level, intuitive block diagram primitives by using familiar component and relationship notions. The ontologies developed in our framework can be shared, audited, improved over time, and reused. The task of constructing an effective ontology is still as challenging as that of creating low-level models in the original approach. However, the process can be collaborative, and once it is done, the ontology can be used for many system models and by many different people. Ontologies can be connected together through the use of the inheritance relationship among types in order to reuse previous ontology developments and to add greater detail.

We have implemented our framework in the Möbius tool and extended the framework's generator to construct Möbius ADVISE models in order to evaluate the efficacy of our approach. From simple system instance diagrams, rich and thorough attack execution graphs are generated. The implementation and underlying concepts of the Möbius ontology framework have been evaluated in two peer-reviewed case studies [15, 16] and shown to be useful and effective for defining complex models and easily evaluating multiple design alternatives.

References

1. Nicol, D.M., Sanders, W.H., Trivedi, K.S.: Model-based evaluation: from dependability to security. IEEE Trans. Dependable Secure Comput. **1**(1), 48–65 (2004)
2. Jajodia, S., Noel, S., O'Berry, B.: Topological analysis of network attack vulnerability. In: Kumar, V., Srivastava, J., Lazarevic, A. (eds.) Managing Cyber Threats: Issues, Approaches, and Challenges, pp. 247–266. Springer, Boston (2005). https://doi.org/10.1007/0-387-24230-9_9
3. Ortalo, R., Deswarte, Y., Kaâniche, M.: Experimenting with quantitative evaluation tools for monitoring operational security. IEEE Trans. Softw. Eng. **25**(5), 633–650 (1999)
4. LeMay, E.: Adversary-driven state-based system security evaluation. Ph.D. dissertation, University of Illinois at Urbana-Champaign, Urbana, Illinois (2011)
5. Clark, G., T. et al.: The Möbius modeling tool. In: Proceedings of the 9th International Workshop on Petri Nets and Performance Models, pp. 241–250, September 2001
6. Williamson, A.L.: Discrete event simulation in the Möbius modeling framework. Master's thesis, University of Illinois at Urbana-Champaign, Urbana, Illinois (1998)
7. Gruber, T.R.: A translation approach to portable ontology specifications. Knowl. Acquis. **5**(2), 199–220 (1993)
8. Deavours, D.D., et al.: The Möbius framework and its implementation. IEEE Trans. Softw. Eng. **28**(10), 956–969 (2002)

9. LeMay, E., Unkenholz, W., Parks, D., Muehrcke, C., Keefe, K., Sanders, W.H.: Adversary-driven state-based system security evaluation. In: Proceedings of the 6th International Workshop on Security Measurements and Metrics (MetriSec 2010), Bolzano-Bozen, Italy, 15 September 2010

10. Ford, M.D., Keefe, K., LeMay, E., Sanders, W.H., Muehrcke, C.: Implementing the ADVISE secrity modeling formalism in Möbius. In: Proceedigns of the 43rd Annual IEEE/IFIP International Conference on Dependable Systems and Networks (DSN 2013), pp. 1–8, June 2013

11. LeMay, E., Ford, M.D., Keefe, K., Sanders, W.H., Muehrcke, C.: Model-based security metrics using ADversary VIew Security Evaluation (ADVISE). In: Proceedings of the 8th Interantional Confernece on Quantitative Evaluation of SysTems (QEST 2011), Aachen, Germany, pp. 191–200, 5–8 September 2011

12. Rausch, M., Feddersen, B., Keefe, K., Sanders, W.H.: A comparison of different intrusion detection approaches in an advanced metering infrastructure network using ADVISE. In: Agha, G., Van Houdt, B. (eds.) QEST 2016. LNCS, vol. 9826, pp. 279–294. Springer, Cham (2016). https://doi.org/10.1007/978-3-319-43425-4_19

13. Wright, R., Keefe, K., Feddersen, B., Sanders, W.H.: A case study assessing the effects of cyber attacks on a river zonal dispatcher. In: Proceedings of the 11th International Conference on Critical Information Infrastructures Security (CRITIS), Paris, France, pp. 252–264, 10–12 October 2016

14. Deavours, D., Sanders, W.H.: Möbius: framework and atomic models. In: Proceedingso of the 10th International Workshop on Petri Nets and Performance Models, pp. 251–260, September 2001

15. Rausch, M., Keefe, K., Feddersen, B., Sanders, W.H.: Automatically generating security models from system models to aid in the evaluation of AMI deployment options. In: Proceedings of the 12th International Conferece on Critical Information Infrastructures Security (CRITIS), Lucca, Italy, 8–13 October 2017

16. Cheh, C., Keefe, K., Feddersen, B., Chen, B., Temple, W.G., Sanders, W.: Developing models for physical attacks in cyber-physical systems. In: Proceedings of the Cyber-Physical Systems Security and PrivaCy (CPS-SPC) Workshop, Dallas, Texas, USA, pp. 49–55, 3 November 2017

17. Chrszon, P., Dubslaff, C., Klüppelholz, S., Baier, C.: Family-based modeling and analysis for probabilistic systems – featuring PROFEAT. In: Stevens, P., Wąsowski, A. (eds.) FASE 2016. LNCS, vol. 9633, pp. 287–304. Springer, Heidelberg (2016). https://doi.org/10.1007/978-3-662-49665-7_17

18. Woodside, M., Petriu, D.C., Merseguer, J., Petriu, D.B., Alhaj, M.: Transformation challenges: from software models to performance models. Softw. Syst. Model. 13(4), 1529–1552 (2014)

19. Vigo, R., Nielson, F., Nielson, H.R.: Automated generation of attack trees. In: Proceedings of the IEEE 27th Computer Security Foundations Symposium, pp. 337–350, July 2014

20. Ivanova, M.G., Probst, C.W., Hansen, R.R., Kammüller, F.: Transforming graphical system models to graphical attack models. In: Mauw, S., Kordy, B., Jajodia, S. (eds.) GraMSec 2015. LNCS, vol. 9390, pp. 82–96. Springer, Cham (2016). https://doi.org/10.1007/978-3-319-29968-6_6

21. Philippi, S.: Automatic code generation from high-level Petri-nets for model driven systems engineering. J. Syst. Softw. 79(10), 1444–1455 (2006)

22. Bernardi, S., Donatelli, S., Merseguer, J.: From UML sequence diagrams and statecharts to analysable Petri net models. In: Proceedings of the 3rd International Workshop on Software and Performance, pp. 35–45. ACM (2002)

23. Kamandi, A., Azgomi, M.A., Movaghar, A.: Transformation of UML models into analyzable OSAN models. Electron. Notes Theor. Comput. Sci. **159**, 3–22 (2006)
24. Gheraibia, Y., Bourouis, A.: Ontology and automatic code generation on modeling and simulation. In: 6th Internatioal Conference on Sciences of Electronics, Technologies of Information and Telecommunications (SETIT), pp. 69–73. IEEE (2012)
25. Lacy, L.: Interchanging discrete event simulation process interaction models using PIMODES and SRML. In: Proceedings of the Fall 2006 Simulation Interoperability Workshop (2006)
26. Brambilla, M., Cabot, J., Wimmer, M.: Model-Driven Software Engineering in Practice. Morgan & Claypool Publishers, San Rafael (2012)
27. Steinberg, D., Budinsky, F., Merks, E., Paternostro, M.: EMF: Eclipse Modeling Framework. Pearson Education, New York (2008)

A Mixed Strategy for a Competitive Game in Delay Tolerant Networks

Thi Thu Hang Nguyen[1,2(✉)], Olivier Brun[1], and Balakrishna Prabhu[1]

[1] LAAS-CNRS, Université de Toulouse, CNRS, Toulouse, France
{tthnguye,brun,bala}@laas.fr
[2] Université de Toulouse, INSA, Toulouse, France

Abstract. We consider a non-cooperative game between N relays in Delay Tolerant Networks with one fixed source and one fixed destination. The source has no contact with the destination, so it has to rely on the relays when it has a message to send. We assume that the source has a sequence of messages and it proposes them to relays one by one with a fixed reward for the first transmission for each message. We analyse a symmetric mixed strategy for this game. A mixed strategy means a relay decides to accept relaying the kth message with probability q_k when it meets the source. We establish the conditions under which $q_k = 1; q_k = 0$ or $q_k \in (0, 1)$, and prove the existence and the uniqueness of the symmetric Nash equilibrium. We also give the formula to compute this mixed strategy as well as the probability of success and the delay of a given message. When k is large, we give the limiting value of the mixed strategy q and the probability of success for the messages.

Keywords: Delay Tolerant Networks · Incentive mechanism
Stochastic game

1 Introduction

In Delay Tolerant Networks (DTN) [3,9–11], the approach used by mobile nodes to communicate in the absence of a communication infrastructure is based on the so-called store-carry-forward paradigm: a source node gives a copy of its message to all mobile nodes that it meets, asking them to keep it until they can forward it to the destination. Although other routing schemes have been proposed [13,15], in this work we shall specifically consider two-hop routing DTNs [2,21], in which once a relay has the message, it can only transmit it to the destination.

The above approach implicitly assumes that mobile nodes accept to use their scarce energy resources for relaying messages of others out of altruism. In practice, it can be expected that some nodes will act as free-riders, that is, that they will use the network to send their own messages without offering their resources in exchange for relaying the messages of others. Clearly, if there are too many selfish nodes in a DTN, the network collapses and mobile nodes can no longer communicate with one another. A central issue in DTNs is therefore

© Springer Nature Switzerland AG 2018
R. Bakhshi et al. (Eds.): EPEW 2018, LNCS 11178, pp. 190–204, 2018.
https://doi.org/10.1007/978-3-030-02227-3_13

to convince mobile nodes to relay messages. Many incentive mechanisms have been proposed to avoid the free-rider problem in DTNs, including reputation-based schemes [12,16,22–24], barter-based schemes [4,5,20] and credit-based schemes [7,8,14,19,25,26]. In contrast to most of the incentive mechanisms proposed in the literature, explicit guarantees on the probability of message delivery and on the mean time to deliver a message have been obtained for the credit-based scheme considered in [17,18] (see also [19] for a closely-related mechanism).

The authors of [17,18] consider a source which promises a fixed reward to the relay who first delivers a message to the destination. The source is backlogged and only one message at a time is proposed by the source. Inter-contact times of relays with the source and the destination are exponentially distributed. When it meets the source, a relay has the choice to either accept the message or not, and if it accepts, it can decide to drop the message at any time in the future at no additional cost. The competition between relays is modelled as a stochastic game in which each relay seeks to minimize its expected net cost, that is, the sum of its expected energy and storage costs minus its expected reward. It is proven that the optimal policy of a relay is of threshold type: it accepts a message until a first threshold θ and then keeps it until it either meets the destination or reaches a second threshold γ (which can be infinite). Explicit formulas for computing the thresholds as well as the probability of message delivery are derived for the unique symmetric Nash equilibrium, in which all relays use the same thresholds and no player can benefit by unilaterally changing its policy.

The analysis in [17,18] implicitly assumes that the source tells the relays when a message was proposed for the first time, or, in other words, when this message was generated. Our objective in the present paper is to understand whether it is profitable for the source to give this information to the relays. We thus consider the same incentive mechanism, but assuming that when it meets the source, a relay has to make its decision without knowing for how long the message is in circulation. The only information available to the relay is the value R of the reward and the period of time T during which the message is proposed by the source.

Since it does not know for how long a message is available, we assume that a relay decides to accept a message according to a randomized policy, that is, when relay i meets the source, it accepts the kth message with probability q_k^i, and rejects it with probability $1 - q_k^i$. If it accepts the message, the relay keeps it until it reaches the destination. The value of q_k^i is computed by relay i so as to minimize its expected net cost, and it of course depends on R and T, but also on the number of relays competing for the delivery of the kth message (some relays may be busy delivering previous messages). We note that a similar setting was considered in [1], but with a different cost structure and assuming that the source has only one message to transmit.

We establish under which condition $q_k^i > 0$ for all i, and show that, under this condition, there exists a unique value $q_k > 0$ such that if all relays accept the kth message with probability q_k, no relay has anything to gain by unilaterally changing its acceptance probability. In other words, the situation in which all relays accept the kth message with probability q_k corresponds to a symmetric Nash equilibrium, and this equilibrium is unique. Explicit expressions for the probability of message delivery and the mean time to deliver a message at the symmetric Nash equilibrium are then derived. Assuming that q_k converges as $k \to \infty$, we also obtain an explicit characterization of the asymptotic value of the acceptance probability q_∞. Finally, we compare the performance obtained with the threshold-type strategy in the full information setting and with the randomized policy in the no information setting.

The rest of this paper is organized as follows. Section 2 is devoted to model description. In Sect. 3, we establish the conditions for the existence and uniqueness of symmetric Nash equilibria and present a method for recursively computing the acceptance probabilities q_k. The asymptotic value of the acceptance probability is also derived in Sect. 3. Explicit expressions for the main performance metrics at the symmetric Nash equilibrium are then derived in Sect. 4. Finally, numerical results pertaining to the comparison of the full information setting and the no information setting are given in Sect. 5.

2   Assumption and Model Description

We consider a two-hop network of N mobile nodes with one fixed source and one fixed destination. The source is backlogged, that is, it has an unlimited number of messages to send to the destination. Since the source and the destination are not in radio range of each other, the source cannot transmit its messages directly to the destination. Instead, it proposes a new message to the relays every T units of time, promising a fixed reward R to the first one to deliver the current message to the destination. We assume that the relays are moving randomly and that the inter-contact times of a given relay with the source (resp. destination) are i.i.d. and follow an exponential distribution with rate λ (resp. μ). This assumption holds (at least approximately) under the Random Waypoint Mobility model [6].

When it accepts a message, a relay incurs a one-time reception cost C_r for receiving it from the source. There is then a cost C_s per unit of time for keeping the message in its buffer. Finally, the relay incurs a transmission cost C_d for sending the message to the destination. We however assume that the latter cost is incurred by the relay if and only if the message has not been already delivered to the destination by another relay. If on the contrary the relay is the first one to deliver the message to the destination, it incurs the cost C_d but gets the reward R. In the following, we define $\bar{R} = R - C_d$.

When it proposes the current message (say message k) to relay i, the source informs it of the values of R and T, but does not tell it for how long the current message is available. The relay accepts message k with probability q_k^i, and rejects it with probability $1 - q_k^i$. If the kth message was rejected by relay i, then this relay cannot accept it later on when it meets again the source. We also assume that if the relay accepts the message, it has to keep it until it meets the destination. Finally, we assume that a relay can store only one message at a time and cannot drop a message to accept a new one.

Relay i computes its acceptance probability q_k^i so as to minimize its expected net cost, which depends on its probability to be the first one to deliver message k. Obviously, the latter probability in turn depends on the acceptance probabilities of the other relays. We say that a vector $(q_k^1, q_k^2, \ldots, q_k^N)$ is a Nash equilibrium if no relay i can decrease its expected net cost by unilaterally changing its acceptance probability q_k^i. A symmetric Nash equilibrium is a Nash equilibrium for which $q_k^i = q_k$ for all i, for some value q_k. In the following, we shall specifically focus on symmetric Nash equilibria.

3 Acceptance Probabilities Under the Symmetric Nash Equilibrium

3.1 Acceptance Probabilities

Consider a tagged relay and let us analyse the competition for the delivery of the kth message. Assume that all other relays accept the kth message with probability q_k. If the tagged relay accepts the message with probability q_k', its net expected cost is

$$q_k' \left(C_r + \frac{C_s}{\mu} - \bar{R}P_s(q_k) \right), \tag{1}$$

where $P_s(q_k)$ is the probability that the tagged relay be the first one to transmit message k to the destination, given the acceptance probability q_k of the others. In (1), C_r is the cost of accepting the message from the source and C_s/μ is the cost of storing the message until the relay meets the destination (recall that the inter-meeting times with the destination are exponentially distributed with mean $1/\mu$). The term $\bar{R}P_s(q_k)$ is the expected reward the relay gets the message. Thus, (1) gives the net expected cost for accepting the message.

For the tagged relay, the optimal value of q_k' is the one which minimizes (1). It follows that $q_k' = 0$ if $C_r + \frac{C_s}{\mu} - \bar{R}P_s(q_k) > 0$. Hence, we conclude that if $\bar{R} \le \bar{R}_{min} = C_r + \frac{C_s}{\mu}$, no relay will accept the kth message. In other words, the condition $\bar{R} > \bar{R}_{min}$ is a necessary condition for the relays to have an incentive to participate in message delivery. Assuming that this condition is met, we see that $q_k' = 1$ is the best response of the tagged relay if $\bar{R}_{min}/P_s(q_k) < \bar{R}$, while $q_k' = q_k$ is one of the possible best responses if $\bar{R}_{min}/P_s(q_k) = \bar{R}$. We thus need to analyse how $P_s(q_k)$ depends on q_k.

To this end, let p_k be the probability, as computed by the tagged relay, that an arbitrary other relay meets the source while it is proposing the kth message and that this relay is not already busy with a previous message. Obviously, for the first message we have $p_1 = 1 - e^{-\lambda T}$. The derivation of p_k for $k > 1$ is slightly more complex and we shall shortly explain how it can be computed by the tagged relay. From the definition of p_k, we obtain that $p_k q_k$ is the probability that an arbitrary other relay attempts the delivery of the kth message. Therefore, the number A_k of other relays that are in competition with the tagged relay for the delivery of the kth message follows a binomial distribution with parameter $p_k \, q_k$, which yields

$$P_s(q_k) = \mathbb{E}\left(\frac{1}{A_k+1}\right) = \frac{1 - (1 - p_k \, q_k)^N}{N \, p_k \, q_k}. \tag{2}$$

From (2), we can conclude that, if $\bar{R} > \bar{R}_{min}$, there exists a unique symmetric equilibrium with $q_k > 0$, as formally stated in Theorem 1 below.

Theorem 1. *If $\bar{R} > \bar{R}_{min}$, there exists a unique symmetric Nash equilibrium for the kth message with $q_k > 0$. Moreover, we have $q_k = 1$ if*

$$\bar{R} > \frac{Np_k}{1 - (1 - p_k)^N} \, \bar{R}_{min}, \tag{3}$$

while otherwise q_k is the unique solution in $(0,1)$ of

$$\bar{R} = \frac{Np_k \, q_k}{1 - (1 - p_k \, q_k)^N} \, \bar{R}_{min}. \tag{4}$$

Proof. See Appendix A.

The structure of the Nash equilibrium is illustrated in Fig. 1 for the first message. If $\bar{R} \leq \bar{R}_{min}$, no relay accepts the message. If $\bar{R} > \frac{N(1-e^{-\lambda T})}{1-e^{-\lambda NT}} \, \bar{R}_{min}$, at the unique Nash equilibrium all relays accept the message with probability 1. Otherwise, the relays use a randomized strategy with $0 < q_1 < 1$.

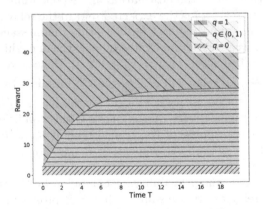

Fig. 1. Equilibrium acceptance probability q_1 as a function of R and T, when the values of the parameters are as follows: $\mu = 0.5, \lambda = 0.3, C_r = C_d = 2$ and $C_s = 0.4$.

3.2 Computation of the Probability p_k

For the first message, we already know the value of p_1. We now explain how the value of p_k can be computed by the tagged relay for subsequent messages $k > 1$. We need to consider the belief of the tagged relay regarding the number of other relays that are in competition with it for the delivery of the kth message. We assume that all relays play their equilibrium strategies q_i, $i = 1, \ldots, k-1$ for all previous messages. Define $\Phi_k(t)$ as the probability that an arbitrary relay enters into competition for message k on or before time t. By enter into competition on or before time t, we mean that there exists a time instant $t' < t$ such that the considered relay does not have any message with index smaller than k in the interval $[t', t]$. We shall denote by $\phi_k(t)$ the probability density function (pdf) corresponding to $\Phi_k(t)$. If this pdf is known by the tagged relay, then it can estimate the probability p_k as follows.

$$p_k = \int_{T(k-1)}^{Tk} \phi_k(x) \left(1 - e^{-\lambda(kT-x)}\right) dx.$$

Denote by $\delta_x(t)$ the Dirac delta function at point x. Following the same approach as in [18], we can the following result.

Lemma 1. *The density $\phi_k(t)$ obeys the recursion*

$$\phi_{k+1}(t) = h_1(k)\delta_{kT}(t) + \phi_k(t) + h_2(k)\mu e^{-\mu t}. \tag{5}$$

Here $h_1(k)$ represents the probability that a relay is free for the $(k+1)^{th}$ message at time kT, and is given by

$$h_1(k) = \int_{(k-1)T}^{kT} \phi_k(x)(1 - q_k I_k(x, kT)) dx, \tag{6}$$

and $h_2(k)e^{-\mu kT}$ is the probability that a relay be busy with the kth message at time kT, and is given by

$$h_2(k) = e^{\mu kT} \int_{(k-1)T}^{kT} q_k \phi_k(x) I_k(x, kT) dx. \tag{7}$$

In (6) and (7),

$$I_k(x, t) = \frac{\lambda}{\mu - \lambda} e^{-\mu t} e^{\lambda x} \left(e^{(\mu-\lambda)\min(t, kT)} - e^{(\mu-\lambda)x}\right),$$

represents the probability that a relay that comes into play at time $x < kT$ will meet the source and will not meet the destination by time t.

Since $h_2(i)e^{-\mu iT}$ is the probability that a relay has message i at iT, it can be seen that $h_2(i)e^{-\mu(k-1)T}$ is the probability that a relay has message i at time $(k-1)T$. Also, $h_1(k-1)$ is the probability that the relay does not have a message time $(k-1)T$. Since a relay either has a message or does not have one, we get the following relation:

$$h_1(k-1) + e^{-\mu(k-1)T} \sum_{i=1}^{k-1} h_2(i) = 1,$$

which yields

$$\sum_{i=1}^{k-1} h_2(i) = \frac{1 - h_1(k-1)}{e^{-\mu(k-1)T}}. \tag{8}$$

Using (5)–(8) and induction, we can prove that $h_1(k)$ obeys the recursions given below. We omit the proof due to lack of space.

Proposition 1. *The terms $h_1(k)$ can be computed with the recursion:*

$$h_1(k) = h_1(k-1)\left(1 - q_k I_k\left((k-1)T, kT\right)\right) + \left(1 - h_1(k-1)\right)\left(1 - e^{-\mu T}\right)$$
$$-\left(1 - h_1(k-1)\right)\frac{q_i \lambda \mu e^{-\mu T}}{\mu - \lambda}\left(\frac{e^{(\mu-\lambda)T} - 1}{\mu - \lambda} - T\right),$$

with the initial value: $h_1(1) = 1 - q_1 I(0, T)$. This leads to the following formulas for $h_2(k)$ and p_k:

$$h_2(k)e^{-\mu kT} = 1 - h_1(k) - (1 - h_1(k-1))e^{-\mu T}$$
$$p_k = h_1(k-1)\left(1 - e^{-\lambda T}\right)$$
$$+ (1 - h_1(k-1))\left(1 - e^{-\mu T} - \frac{\mu}{\mu - \lambda}\left(e^{-\lambda T} - e^{-\mu T}\right)\right). \tag{9}$$

Equation (9) has the following probabilistic interpretation. The probability that a relay can meet the source for message k can be conditioned on two events at time $(k-1)T$ (i.e., at the release time of message k): either the relay did not have a message or had one of the previous $k-1$ messages. The two terms in (9) correspond to each of the two events. In the case of the first event, the probability of picking up message k is just the probability of meeting the source in the interval $((k-1)T, KT]$. Since $h_1(k-1)$ is the probability of not having a message at time $(k-1)T$, the term $h_1(k-1)(1 - e^{-\lambda T})$ is the probability related to the first event. Next, we look at the second event. Suppose the relay has a message at time $(k-1)T$. It can take message k only if it meets the destination and then the source in an interval of length T starting from $(k-1)T$. This probability is the one inside the parenthesis of the second term in (9). Since $(1 - h_1(k-1))$, is the probability that the relay has a message at $(k-1)T$, the second term in (9) corresponds to the second event.

3.3   Asymptotic Analysis When $k \to \infty$

In this section, we shall do the analysis when k is large, that is, when the system is in steady-state or stationary regime. In this regime, the function ϕ_k will reach its limiting value so that each message will have statistically the same performance measures. This regime reflects the long-run characteristics which are obtained after a large number of messages have been transmitted. From numerical experiments, it will be seen that, for our model, after as few as 10 to 15 messages, the system reaches the steady-state.

Let $h_2'(k) = h_2(k)e^{-\mu kT}$. From Proposition 1 we get the following expressions for the limiting values of p_k, h_1, and h_2'. The proof is omitted.

Proposition 2. *When k is large, we have*

$$h_1(\infty) := h_1 = \frac{C(T)}{q_\infty I_\infty + C(T)}, \tag{10}$$

$$h_2'(\infty) := h_2' = (1 - h_1)(1 - e^{-\mu T}), \tag{11}$$

$$p_\infty = h_1(1 - e^{-\lambda T}) + (1 - h_1)D(T), \tag{12}$$

where

$$C(T) = 1 - e^{-\mu T} - \frac{q_\infty \mu \lambda}{\mu - \lambda}\left(\frac{e^{-\lambda T} - e^{-\mu T}}{\mu - \lambda} - Te^{-\mu T}\right),$$

$$D(T) = 1 - e^{-\mu T} - \frac{\mu}{\mu - \lambda}(e^{-\lambda T} - e^{-\mu T}), \tag{13}$$

$$I_\infty = \frac{\lambda}{\mu - \lambda}(e^{-\lambda T} - e^{-\mu T}). \tag{14}$$

From Proposition 2, we can write the relation between q_∞ and p_∞ as

$$p_\infty(q_\infty) = \frac{C(T)(1 - e^{-\lambda T})}{q_\infty I_\infty + C(T)} + \frac{q_\infty I_\infty D(T)}{q_\infty I_\infty + C(T)} \tag{15}$$

Now, we can establish the conditions when $q_\infty = 1$ and when $q_\infty < 1$.

Lemma 2. *If the following condition is satisfied, then $q_\infty = 1, p_\infty = p_\infty(1)$:*

$$\bar{R} - \frac{Np_\infty(1)(C_r + C_s/\mu)}{1 - (1 - p_\infty(1))^N} > 0 \tag{16}$$

Otherwise, p_∞ and q_∞ are the unique solution of the following system of equations:

$$\bar{R} - \frac{Np_\infty q_\infty(C_r + C_s/\mu)}{1 - (1 - p_\infty q_\infty)^N} = 0 \tag{17}$$

$$\frac{C(T)(1 - e^{-\lambda T})}{q_\infty I_\infty + C(T)} + \frac{q_\infty I_\infty D(T)}{q_\infty I_\infty + C(T)} = p_\infty \tag{18}$$

The proof follows directly from Theorem 1. Notice that in case of $q_\infty < 1$, there is unique solution since the left hand side of (17) is decreasing in q_∞.

Figure 2 presents the probability p_k that an individual relay, which is not busy with any previous message, meets the source while it is proposing the

k^{th} message. This probability is computed from analytical expressions as well as from simulations for different values of R, $T = 1.00357$ and $N = 10$ (the other parameters have the same value as in Fig. 1). In fact, the value of T is the value of $\hat{\theta}_\infty = \lim_{k\to\infty} \theta_{k+1} - \theta_k$ and the value of R is expressed as a multiple of $R_{min} = \bar{R}_{min} + C_d = C_r + \frac{C_s}{\mu} + C_d$. The simulations consist of generating meeting times of relays with the source and the destination, then each relay deciding whether to accept or not the message when it meets the source, and then determining which relay wins the reward. The value of p_k was then averaged over $2,000$ sample paths. For the same parameter values, Fig. 3 presents the acceptance probabilities q_k as well as their limiting value q_∞. From these figures, it can be seen that the steady-state is reached quite quickly (after 10 messages).

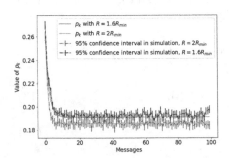

Fig. 2. Value of p_k.   **Fig. 3.** Value of q_k and its limiting value

4   Performance Metrics

In this section, we use the results obtained in Sect. 3 to establish explicit expressions for the probability of message delivery and the mean time to deliver a message at the symmetric Nash equilibrium. Together with Theorems 1 and (9), our first result, formally stated in Proposition 3, allows to compute the probability of message delivery of each message.

Proposition 3. *The probability of successful delivery of the kth message is* $\xi_k = 1 - (1 - q_k\, p_k)^N$.

Proof. Each individual relay participates to the delivery of the kth message with probability $q_k p_k$, from which the result follows.

Figure 4 shows the probability of message delivery for different values of R, and the following parameter values: $T = 1.00357$ and $N = 10$. The other parameters are the same as in Fig. 1. The probabilities obtained with event-driven simulations are also shown in Fig. 4. In the simulation, we generate the inter-contact times between the source, the destination and relays. We then let the

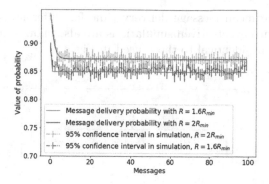

Fig. 4. Analytical probability of message delivery and simulated probability for different values of $\bar{R}$.

relays follow the mixed strategy with q_k computed from previous sections. We run the simulation 5000 times and take the average.

Proposition 4. *Let D_k denote the delay of the kth message. It holds that*

$$\mathbb{E}(D_k|D_k < \infty) = \frac{1}{\xi_k} \int_{(k-1)T}^{\infty} (1 - Q(t))^N - (1 - q_k p_k)^N dt$$

where, with the notation $m = \min(t, kT)$, $Q(t)$ is defined as

$$Q(t) = q_k \int_{(k-1)T}^{m} \phi_k(x) \left[1 - e^{-\lambda(m-x)} - I_k(x, t) \right] dx, \tag{19}$$

and represents the probability that an individual relay will deliver the kth message by time t.

Proof. The probability that an individual relay that comes into play at time x will meet the source by time $m \geq x$ and the destination by time $t \geq m$ is

$$\int_{x}^{m} \lambda e^{-\lambda(s-x)} \left(1 - e^{-\mu(t-s)} \right) ds = 1 - e^{-\lambda(m-x)} - I_k(x, t).$$

With $m = \min(t, kT)$, it follows that the probability that an individual relay will deliver the kth message by time t is

$$Q(t) = q_k \int_{(k-1)T}^{m} \phi_k(x) \left[1 - e^{-\lambda(m-x)} - I_k(x, t) \right] dx,$$

and hence the probability that the message is not delivered by time t is $\mathbb{P}(D_k > t) = (1 - Q(t))^N$. The proof now follows from

$$\mathbb{E}(D_k|D_k < \infty) = \int_{0}^{\infty} \mathbb{P}(D_k > t \mid D_k < \infty) dt,$$

$$= \frac{1}{\xi_k} \int_{0}^{\infty} \mathbb{P}(D_k < \infty) - \mathbb{P}(D_k \leq t) dt,$$

$$= \frac{1}{\xi_k} \int_{0}^{\infty} \mathbb{P}(D_k > t) - (1 - q_k p_k)^N dt.$$

Figure 5 shows the mean message delivery time for different values of R. The delays obtained with event-driven simulations are also shown on the figure. The parameter values are identical to those used in Fig. 4.

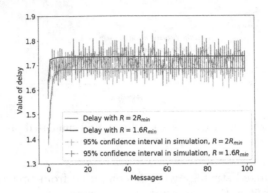

Fig. 5. Analytical delay and simulated delay.

5   Comparison Between the Threshold-Type Strategy and the Randomized Policy

In this section, we compare the performance obtained with the threshold-type strategy in the full information setting and with the randomized policy in the no information setting. We first consider the case where the source proposes each message for the same amount of time in both settings, that is, $T = \theta_k$ for the kth message (θ_k and γ_k are the first and second thresholds, respectively, for the kth message). Figure 6 shows the structure of the Nash equilibrium strategies for the first message in both settings. It turns out that the randomized policy is either to reject the message ($q = 0$) or to accept it ($q = 1$) depending on the value of R, but independently of the value of λ. In contrast, the value of γ in the threshold-type policy depends on the value of λ. We emphasize that when $q = 1$ and $\gamma = \infty$, the two policies coincide: all relays accept the message as long as it is proposed by the source and keep it until they meet the destination (this is not the case when $\gamma < \infty$ since relays can drop the message before meeting the destination). Therefore, in this situation, the source does not need to provide the birth-time of its messages. Moreover, the relays do not need to take care of time, they just decide to accept a message or not, and then keep the message until meeting the destination. Figure 7 compares the message delivery probabilities in both settings as T varies. In this case, we consider the steady-state message delivery probabilities, which are obtained as $k \to \infty$, for two different values of R. The figure also shows the asymptotic value of the acceptance probability q_∞ in the no information setting. For $R = 2R_{min} = 10$, we have $\theta = 0.65$ and $\gamma = \infty$ for the threshold policy. We observe that the message delivery probability in the no information setting increases as T grows: for $T \leq \theta$, the acceptance probability $q_\infty = 1$ and the message delivery probability is lower than in the full information setting. Both settings coincide when $T = \theta$, as expected. For $T > \theta$, the acceptance probability $q_\infty < 1$, but the message delivery probability keeps increasing until it reaches its limiting value, which is higher than in the full information setting. For $R = 3.5R_{min} = 17.5$, we have $\theta = 0.91$ and $\gamma = 3.07$. We observe a similar behavior of the message delivery probability in the no information setting, despite the fact that in this case $\gamma < \infty$. These results suggest that by using a value of T slightly larger than θ, and for the same reward value R, the source can increase its message delivery probability if it does not tell the relays when a message was generated.

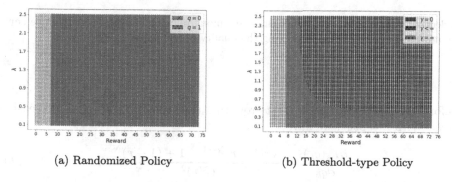

(a) Randomized Policy   (b) Threshold-type Policy

Fig. 6. Randomized and threshold-type policies as functions of R and λ for the first message when $T = \theta_1$. The values of the parameters are $\mu = 0.4, C_d = 2, C_r = 4, C_s = 0.5$ and $N = 3$.

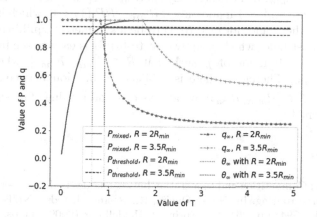

Fig. 7. The message delivery probability in mixed strategy and threshold strategy, with $\mu = 0.4, C_d = C_r = 2, C_s = 0.4, N = 10$ and $\lambda = 1.5$.

6   Conclusions

We analyzed a competitive DTN game between N relays in which the source does not give information on the message generation times to the relays. The equilibrium obtained is a mixed one in which a relay accepts a message with a certain probability. This contrasts with the threshold-based equilibrium in [18] in which the source gave message generation information to the relays. Simulations suggest giving no information on the message generation times can be advantageous to the source compared to giving information. By taking the duration for which a message is proposed to be slightly longer than the equilibrium threshold in [18], the source can improve the limiting value of its message delivery probability.

Acknowledgements. We thank the anonymous referees for their constructive comments that have helpful in improving the quality of the paper.

A   Proof of Theorem 1

Before proving the lemma, we first prove that the probability $P_s(q_k)$ is decreasing in q_k. With $r = p_k q_k$, we have

$$\frac{\partial P_s(q_k)}{\partial q_k} = \frac{Nr(1-r)^{N-1} - 1 + (1-r)^N}{(Nr)^2} \tag{20}$$

The numerator is negative since it has value 0 when $r = 0$ and it is decreasing in r (the derivative w.r.t r is negative), and thus in q_k. It follows that the expected net cost $\bar{R}_{min} - \bar{R} P_s(q_k)$ is increasing in q_k and reaches its maximum value for $q_k = 1$.

Assume $\bar{R} > \bar{R}_{min}$. If the other relays play $q_k = 1$, the best-response strategy of the tagged relay is $q'_k = 1$ if and only if $\bar{R}_{min} - \bar{R}P_s(1) < 0$, which is equivalent to (3). On the other hand, for $q_k \in (0,1)$ to be a symmetric equilibrium, $\bar{R}_{min} - \bar{R}P_s(q_k) = 0$ must hold, which is equivalent to (4). It is easy to see from (4) that $\bar{R}$ is an increasing function of q_k such that $\bar{R} \in [\bar{R}_{min}, \bar{R}_{max}]$, where $\bar{R}_{max} = \frac{Nq_k p_k}{1-(1-q_k p_k)^N} \bar{R}_{min}$. Therefore, there is a bijective function between $\bar{R}$ and q_k. Hence, for any $\bar{R} \in [\bar{R}_{min}, \bar{R}_{max}]$, we always can find a value of q_k such that the Eq. (4) is satisfied.

References

1. Altman, E.: Competition and cooperation between nodes in delay tolerant networks with two hop routing. In: Núñez-Queija, R., Resing, J. (eds.) NET-COOP 2009. LNCS, vol. 5894, pp. 264–278. Springer, Heidelberg (2009). https://doi.org/10.1007/978-3-642-10406-0_18

2. Basilico, N., Cesana, M., Gatti, N.: Algorithms to find two-hop routing policies in multiclass delay tolerant networks. IEEE Trans. Wirel. Commun. **15**(6), 4017–4031 (2016). https://doi.org/10.1109/TWC.2016.2532859

3. Benhamida, F.Z., Bouabdellah, A., Challal, Y.: Using delay tolerant network for the Internet of Things: opportunities and challenges. In: 2017 8th International Conference on Information and Communication Systems (ICICS), pp. 252–257, April 2017. https://doi.org/10.1109/IACS.2017.7921980
4. Buttyan, L., Dora, L., Felegyhazi, M., Vajda, I.: Barter-based cooperation in delay-tolerant personal wireless networks. In: IEEE International Symposium on a World of Wireless, Mobile and Multimedia Networks (2007)
5. Buttyan, L., Dora, L., Felegyhazi, M., Vajda, I.: Barter trade improves message delivery in opportunistic networks. Ad Hoc Netw. 8(1), 1–14 (2010)
6. Cai, H., Eun, D.: Crossing over the bounded domain: from exponential to power-law inter-meeting time in MANET. In: Proceedings of ACM/IEEE MOBICOM (2007)
7. Chahin, W., Sidi, H.B., El-Azouzi, R., Pellegrini, F.D., Walrand, J.: Incentive mechanisms based on minority games in heterogeneous DTNs. In: Proceedings of 25th ITC Conference, Sanghai, China, 10–12 September 2013
8. Chen, B.B., Chan, M.C.: MobiCent: a credit-based incentive system for disruption tolerant network. In: 2010 Proceedings IEEE INFOCOM, pp. 1–9, March 2010. https://doi.org/10.1109/INFCOM.2010.5462136
9. Fall, K.: A delay-tolerant network architecture for challenged internets. In: Proceedings of ACM SIGCOMM, Karlsruhe, Germany, pp. 27–34 (2003). https://doi.org/10.1145/863955.863960
10. Giannini, C., Calegari, P., Buratti, C., Verdone, R.: Delay tolerant network for smart city: exploiting bus mobility. In: 2016 AEIT International Annual Conference (AEIT), pp. 1–6, October 2016. https://doi.org/10.23919/AEIT.2016.7892779
11. Giannini, C., Shaaban, A.A., Buratti, C., Verdone, R.: Delay tolerant networking for smart city through drones. In: 2016 International Symposium on Wireless Communication Systems (ISWCS), pp. 603–607, September 2016. https://doi.org/10.1109/ISWCS.2016.7600975
12. He, Q., Wu, D., Khosla, P.: SORI: a secure and objective reputation-based incentive scheme for ad hoc networks. In: Proceedings of IEEE WCNC (2004)
13. Ito, M., Nishiyama, H., Kato, N.: A novel routing method for improving message delivery delay in hybrid DTN-MANET networks. In: 2013 IEEE Global Communications Conference (GLOBECOM), pp. 72–77, December 2013. https://doi.org/10.1109/GLOCOM.2013.6831050
14. Mahmoud, M.E., Shen, X.: PIS: a practical incentive system for multi-hop wireless networks. IEEE Trans. Veh. Technol. 59, 4012–4025 (2010)
15. Malathi, M., Jayashri, S.: Design and performance of dynamic trust management for secure routing protocol. In: 2016 IEEE International Conference on Advances in Computer Applications (ICACA), pp. 121–124, October 2016. https://doi.org/10.1109/ICACA.2016.7887935
16. Marti, S., Giuli, T.J., Lai, K., Baker, M.: Mitigating routing misbehavior in mobile ad hoc networks. In: Proceedings of MobiCom, pp. 255–265 (2000)
17. Nguyen, T.T.H., Brun, O., Prabhu, B.J.: Mean-field limit of the fixed-reward incentive mechanism in delay tolerant networks. In: 2018 16th International Symposium on Modeling and Optimization in Mobile, Ad Hoc, and Wireless Networks (WiOpt), pp. 1–8, May 2018. https://doi.org/10.23919/WIOPT.2018.8362810
18. Nguyen, T.T.H., Brun, O., Prabhu, B.: Performance of a fixed reward incentive scheme for two-hop DTNs with competing relays (long version), August 2017. https://hal.laas.fr/hal-01575320, this is the long version of the NetEcon paper, http://netecon.eurecom.fr/NetEcon2016/papers/Nguyen.pdf which is also in HAL, https://hal.archives-ouvertes.fr/hal-01365939

19. Seregina, T., Brun, O., Elazouzi, R., Prabhu, B.: On the design of a reward-based incentive mechanism for delay tolerant networks. IEEE Trans. Mob. Comput. **16**(2), 453–465 (2017)
20. Shevade, U., Song, H., Qiu, L., Zhang, Y.: Incentive-aware routing in DTNs. In: IEEE International Conference on Network Protocols (ICNP), pp. 238–247 (2008)
21. Torabkhani, N., Fekri, F.: Delay analysis of bursty traffic in finite-buffer disruption-tolerant networks with two-hop routing. In: 2013 IEEE International Conference on Sensing, Communications and Networking (SECON), pp. 541–549, June 2013. https://doi.org/10.1109/SAHCN.2013.6645026
22. Uddinand, M.Y.S., Godfrey, B., Abdelzaher, T.: RELICS: in-network realization of incentives to combat selfishness in DTNs. In: Proceedings of IEEE International Conference on Network Protocols (ICNP), pp. 203–212 (2010)
23. Wei, L., Cao, Z., Zhu, H.: MobiGame: a user-centric reputation based incentive protocol for delay/disruption tolerant networks. In: Proceedings of IEEE Global Telecommunications Conference (GLOBECOM), pp. 1–5 (2011)
24. Zhang, X., X.Wang, Liu, A., Zhang, Q., Tang, C.: Reputation-based schemes for delay tolerant networks. In: Proceedings of 2011 International Conference on Computer Science and Network Technology (2011)
25. Zhong, S., Chen, J., Yang, Y.R.: Sprite, a simple, cheat-proof, credit-based system for mobile ad-hoc networks. In: Proceedings of INFOCOM 2003, San Francisco, CA, USA, pp. 1987–1997, April 2003
26. Zhu, H., Lin, X., Lu, R., Fan, Y., Shen, X.: SMART: a secure multilayer credit-based incentive scheme for delay-tolerant networks. IEEE Trans. Veh. Technol. **58**(8), 4628–4639 (2009)

Second Order Fluid Performance Evaluation Models for Interactive 3D Multimedia Streaming

Enrico Barbierato[1], Marco Gribaudo[1], Mauro Iacono[2(✉)], and Pietro Piazzolla[1]

[1] Dip. di Elettronica, Informazione e Bioingegneria, Politecnico di Milano,
via Ponzio 34/5, 20133 Milano, Italy
{enrico.barbierato,marco.gribaudo,pietro.piazzolla}@polimi.it

[2] Dip. di Matematica e Fisica, Università degli Studi della Campania "L. Vanvitelli",
viale Lincoln 5, 81100 Caserta, Italy
mauro.iacono@unicampania.it

Abstract. Streaming of 3D content has become accessible and widespread thanks to inexpensive devices such as Google cardboard and Samsung Gear VR. In most of the applications the user is located at the center of a sphere where the interactive movie is projected, and she can look in different directions of the immersive world by tilting her head. The same technology can be used also to create different types of immersive content aimed at different goals.

This paper proposes a study for a system delivering object-centric as opposed to user-centric contents, where the subject of the action is in the center and the viewer can look at it from different directions. This type of multimedia content has many potential applications, ranging from product advertising to educational purposes. It also requires much more complex systems, which must be properly studied and sized to deliver the optimal performance required to support a good user experience. As the quality of the system depends heavily on the ability of its computing subsystem for computing image frames timely, and data streams to be processed depend on the geometry and setting of the acquisition subsystem, a preliminary performance analysis is needed to derive the specifications of the computing subsystem. This work exploits a Second Order Fluid Model to analyze and study the performances of the proposed system and defines a set of guidelines to properly develop a correct hardware and software solution.

1 Introduction

The cinema industry has presented since the last twenty years notable special effects oriented to tri-dimensional reconstruction of scenes.

Modeling of artificial or real scenes can be performed by using two approaches. The first technique uses a set of separate cameras deployed side by side in order to create a stereoscopic representation (based on the fact that the brain is "forced" to see a depth in the scene based on the inter-ocular distance),

© Springer Nature Switzerland AG 2018
R. Bakhshi et al. (Eds.): EPEW 2018, LNCS 11178, pp. 205–218, 2018.
https://doi.org/10.1007/978-3-030-02227-3_14

while the second converts a bi-dimensional representation into a tri-dimensional film, inevitably leading to a degradation of the original subject. More sophisticated approaches use stereo images called *anaglyphs* that exploit a red and a cyan colored filter, one per each eye, to visualize the image (for example, see [4]). The quality of the final result depends on many factors, such as the fidelity and coherence of the two cameras and the choice of good 3D glasses among the others.

More advanced methods integrate conventional image acquisition techniques and devices in complex computer based systems that offer a user with a real time, realistic, immersive view of the object, provided that performance parameters are properly tuned to achieve the quality of experience needed to satisfy the user. Designing performance parameters is crucial to both support the design and implementation of such systems and account for a proper compensation of the various variability factors that affect data acquisition, transfer, computing and rendering, keeping the experience realistic.

In this paper we present a preliminary performance evaluation based approach to design an advanced dedicated 3D visualization system and support early decision on design parameters. This approach is founded onto the exploration of system characteristics before the prototyping phase, to optimize costs and leverage guidance obtained by means of performance analysis for the acquisition and the specification of the components. As a result, the subsequent development phases is leaner and quicker. To provide more accurate prediction of the behavior of the to-be system, the approach is based on exploiting a Second Order Fluid Performance Model evaluation framework, which evolves an earlier work to include the presence of jitter in data transfer and acquisition. The idea is to provide the best possible tuning and account for real operating conditions. This choice is based on a previous work on fluid models within the SIMTHESys multisolution modeling framework [1,2] and extended here by implementing an experimental, dedicated second order evaluation engine based on previous work described in [9]. The approach to fluid modeling is founded onto [5].

The original contribution of this paper is twofold. As first - in a very preliminary design stage - a novel acquisition system based on Multi-View-plus-Depth (MVD) cameras, such as those exploiting Intel Real Sense Technology[1] able to combine image acquisition and depth acquisition is proposed. As second, a fluid performance modeling approach (applicable to all MVD different applications and accounting for practical issues, such as jitters) is proposed.

This paper is organized as follows: after this Introduction, next Section describes the visualization system on which we focus our attention, and its performance problems; Sect. 3 introduces the performance evaluation framework; Sect. 4 presents some significant experiments that demonstrate the approach; Sect. 5 reviews a short description of literature; finally, Sect. 6 draws conclusions.

---

[1] https://www.intel.com/content/www/us/en/architecture-and-technology/realsense-overview.html (Visited on: 5/2/2018).

2   The Target System

The target of our design is a system capable of allowing the 3D visualization of a subject or object (here called 'target') framed by a number of cameras, properly placed around it at the same distance so to cover 360°. It is assumed that each camera collects information about a part of the target colors and shape. The colors are taken by the standard camera sensor, while data about target shape are stored as a grayscale map of the depth sensor (part of said camera features). Both sets of data are stored as image files and provided to an application, able to produce a cloud of vertexes approximating the surface of the target and to color the resulting triangles accordingly. The perspective model and position matrix of each camera are also used to visualize the generated 3D mesh as its source target.

This application also allows a given user to visualize the target, freely rotating the view around it. An important goal of the target system is that it must be capable of real time streaming of information from the camera to the application, which must elaborate the 3D mesh from the data fed by each camera efficiently and fast enough to maintain a satisfying frame rate to ensure a quality experience for the final user.

We assume that by increasing the number of cameras used for data collection a more closely target resembling 3D mesh can be computed. This assumption, however, introduces a trade-off between visual quality and performances: increasing the number of image files to be transmitted to the application will also raise network load and computing costs for it, with a potential ruinous effect on the experienced frame rate. Another parameter to account for is the size of the images used for storing information as well as their bit-depth. Bandwidth can also easily became a bottleneck in case of very large image files from many camera sources. Lastly, computing power, provided by both CPU and graphics adapter, of the machine on which the application is run will play a major role in the overall system performances. All these factors heavily impact on the choice of the component of the system to-be. While the choice about suitable, state of the art cameras that fit our needs is relatively easy, the choice for all the other components benefits of a quite wide market. Specifically, the selection has to be driven by a model based analysis matching the needs that stem by the requirements and characteristics of available cameras. The general choices about camera features and their general setup in the system depend on technical considerations founded onto the background of perception physiology and psychology, cinema and direction and their professional practice, and will consequently not be analyzed in this paper. The analysis will be focused on the dimensioning of the computational characteristics of the architecture, limiting the parameters related to cameras to the essential ones.

In Fig. 1 we show an example setup of the target system with a focus on camera placement around the object to be filmed. The system is characterized by the following elements: a subject *Target* in a scene and two or more cameras $(C_1 \ldots C_N, N > 1)$ framing it at the same distance (d) but from different angles.

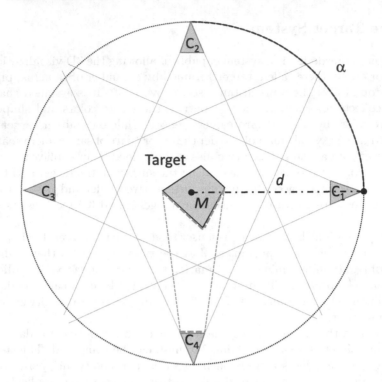

Fig. 1. A set of 4 cameras ($C_1 \ldots C_4$) all aiming at the same subject (*Target*) with partially overlapping fields-of-view. (Color figure online)

In order to give an even share of the target surface to all cameras, each camera C_n is placed with a look-at angle $\alpha = (n-1) \cdot 2\pi/N$ degrees. Thanks to the different angles of framing, each camera contributes to collect a portion of the surface data in terms of both colors and distance from the camera sensor, as shown for camera C_4 in Fig. 1.

All the cameras will rest on the same plane, at the same distance from the subject center of mass (M) and share the same field-of-view. The subject is considered framed in its entirety. In this preliminary stage of the study, we are considering only one plane for all the cameras to rest on, which is the one that allows them to maximize relevant surface data collection.

Figure 2 summarizes the workflow of the above presented system. In this specific experimental setup 8 cameras $C_1 \ldots C_8$ frame an actress in a scene from a musical, dancing at the center of the scene and captured from 8 different angles. The surface data collected by the cameras are streamed to an application for processing. This application is able to generate a cloud of vertexes approximating the actress' figure surface. This generation is required to be fast enough to support a frame per second rate able to allow target's animation to be experienced. To reduce the number of vertexes involved in the computation, clustering techniques are applied. Vertexes are then transformed in triangles to compose

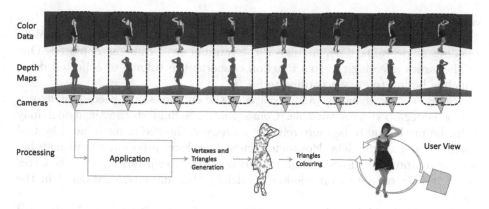

Fig. 2. A system setup composed of 8 cameras, all framing the same performing actress. (Color figure online)

the final mesh and then colored. The resulting 3D mesh is presented through an output window that allows the final user to navigate around it.

Summarizing, the main performance influencing parameters for the system are (i) network bandwidth, (ii) computing workloads for the acquisition and visualization subsystems, (iii) rate and resolution of images or camera aperture, (iv) number of cameras used for the acquisition.

3 Modeling Approach

System parameters depend on the characteristics of data streams fed by cameras to the computing subsystem. Each input data stream is composed of a compressed signal that includes in turn information about the video and the depth for the image. The number of data streams corresponds to the number of used cameras N. Each camera produces an amount of data that is proportional to its resolution. We consider (i) the number of pixels on the vertical axis as a fixed constant of the system (e.g. 720 or 1080), and (ii) the number of pixels on the horizontal axis dependent on aspect ratio a, which in turn is determined by the field view of the cameras. θ_h and θ_v denote respectively the horizontal and vertical field of view, it follows that:

$$a = \frac{\tan(\theta_h/2)}{\tan(\theta_v/2)} \qquad (1)$$

A larger aspect ratio increases the resolution of the captured object, and allows to use a smaller number of cameras. However, the total amount of data generated by the system is proportional to both the number of cameras N and their aspect ratio a. The data cardinality (expressed by the number of data collected per second) can be estimated by using *Blender* (www.blender.org), an open source 3d creation suite capable to integrate the full life-cycle rendering process. *Blender* is currently used in many heterogeneous fields such as modeling radio-wave propagation and character animation (see [10]). The opening angle of cameras is also a critical attribute, since a wrong value might cause the picture to overlap (see Fig. 1). The simulation must consequently be able to determine the minimum opening angle value v depending on the number n of cameras deployed. One of the issues affecting the goal function concerns the volume of collected data, which is bound to grow according to (N, v).

Being a scene dynamic (and because of the compression), each data stream entity is regarded as a variable. Consequently, a fluid stochastic model may help the prediction to be more reliable; moreover, the effects introduced by real components and the data dependency impact on local processing implementing stream compression, decoding and rendering, introduces jitters effects. The latter could impact on data transmissions as delays that must be considered in the model.

As for the workflow, the system acquires and transmits data to be decoded and then rendered by the computational subsystem. The capture process depends on the configuration of the acquisition section of the system, thus the number, aspect ratio and angle impact on the acquisition time. Its variability depends on complex interactions between data, scene variability and data compression, thus has to be described with a general stochastic characterization. The amount of data produced per capture operation depends on the duration, and affects both decoding and rendering length. Since the scenario deals with data streams, the modeling must consider that these processes are continuous. Visualization occurs by producing frames from rendered data, which must be available at fixed intervals depending on the number of frames per second required by the quality requirements of the system. As display happens in real time, if the system is not able to render a frame on time, related data have to be discarded and the incomplete frame has to be skipped, with a consequent loss of quality.

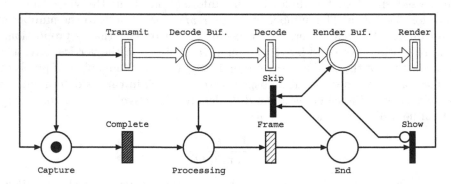

Fig. 3. A 2nd order FSPN model of the considered system.

Figure 3 shows a visual representation of the model of the proposed system by means of Second Order Fluid Stochastic Petri Nets [9]. This choice allows to take into account all the described features that the behavior of the system exhibits. Frame generation process is governed by transition `Complete`, which is characterized by a k_C stages Erlang distributed duration, whose average duration $\mu_C = a \cdot N \cdot \alpha$ is proportional both to the number of cameras and their aspect ratio. In this way, the model is kept as much general as possible, and additional tuning after the preliminary performance evaluation phase is provided. The quantity of data generated by the frame acquisition process is governed by fluid transition Transmit, characterized by average μ_T and variance σ_T^2. Fluid place Decode Buf. holds received data, and fluid transition Decode models the decompression of the color and depth streams for each camera. This process is characterized by an average speed μ_D and a variance σ_D^2. The last part of the process, which consists in the reconstruction of the selected view of captured scene, is modeled by fluid place Render Buf. and fluid transition Render (characterized by μ_R and σ_R^2). Firing of transition Complete moves a token from discrete place Capture to Processing to denote that now the frame can be generated. The system works with a double buffer strategy. To avoid synchronization issues, two image buffers are used: one for the frame being displayed, and another for the one being generated. To maintain a constant frame rate visualization, if an image is not completed in time, the next frame will be skipped. Deterministic transition Frame, of duration $\mu_F = \frac{1}{f_r}$ (where f_r is the reproduction frame rate) models synchronization with the display, moving the token to discrete place End. If the frame has been successfully created, it is displayed immediately by the firing of transition Show, which is enabled only if all the continuous places are empty[2]. If the generation process has taken more time than the available slot, transition Skip fires, and the test will be repeated when the next frame will be ready to be displayed.

3.1 Analysis

As a general overview, the model is analyzed using a specific discrete event simulation algorithm, based on the properties of the second order fluid model underlying the FSPN shown in Fig. 3.

Specifically, the simulation presented in this work implements a modeling language based on a subset of the Piecewise Deterministic Markov Processes introduced in [5] and described in [1,2] with the term Hybrid System Modeling Language (HSML).

The following sub-sections introduce some key notions that are exploited in Sect. 4.

Hybrid System. A *Hybrid System* is composed of a discrete and finite set of modes $\mathcal{M} = \{m_1, \ldots, m_M\}$. Specifically, a mode m_i is denoted by a finite number d_i of continuous *variables* $x_{i,j}$ (with $1 \leq j \leq d_i$), defined in turn on a compact subset of $\mathbb{R}$. The latter is included between a lower $l_{i,j}$ and an upper boundary $u_{i,j}$. Furthermore, a mode m_i is denoted by a *continuous domain* $D_i = \times_{j=1}^{d_i} [l_{i,j}, u_{i,j}]$, where $\times$ indicates the cartesian product of the corresponding sets.

---

[2] For sake of simplicity, in Fig. 3 only one inhibitor arc connecting fluid place Render Buf. to transition Show has been represented.

State. The tuple $\sigma = (m_i, \mathbf{x}_i)$ identify a *state*. Specifically, $\mathbf{x}_i = (x_{i,1}, \ldots, x_{i,d_i})$ indicates the values taken by the set of the continuous variables of the corresponding mode.

HSML Model Evolution. The *model dynamics* is defined by a state space $\mathcal{S} = \bigcup_{i=1}^{M} (\{m_i\} \times D_i)$ with $\sigma \in \mathcal{S}$. The HSML model evolves on the state space $\mathcal{S}$ according to the tuple $(\mathcal{S}, \Phi, E, \Lambda, \Psi, \sigma_0)$. The function $\Phi = \{\phi_1, \ldots, \phi_M\}$ defines the evolution of the states continuous components. For each mode $m_i \in \mathcal{M}$, the corresponding function $\phi_i : D_i \times \mathbb{R} \to D_i$ must be described. The advantage in using function ϕ_i consists of the ability to define the temporal evolution of the continuous variables, assuming that system remains in the same mode m_i a time interval $[t_a, t_b]$. In this case, $\sigma(t) = (m_i, \mathbf{x}_i(t))$ denotes the state at time t, with $t_a \le t \le t_b$. In case that the system endures in mode m_i in the considered time interval, as a result only the continuous element of the state is affected by t. Then, $\sigma(t_c) = (m_i, \mathbf{x}_i(t_c)) \implies \sigma(t_d) = (m_i, \phi_i(\mathbf{x}_i(t_c), t_d - t_c))$, $\forall t_a \le t_c \le t_d \le t_b$. Following the definition, it is possible to derive that $\phi_i(\mathbf{x}_i(t), 0) = \mathbf{x}_i(t)$. Each time one of N possible *events* $E = \{e_1, \ldots, e_N\}$ occurs, state $\sigma(t)$ changes. Events occur according to a state dependent rate denoted by function $\Lambda : S \times E \to \mathbb{R}_0^+$ In particular, $Pr\{e_k$ occurs in state $\sigma(t)$ during $\Delta t\} = \Lambda(\sigma(t), e_k) \cdot \Delta t + o(\Delta t)$. A function $\Psi : S \times E \times S \to [0,1]$ characterizes the effect of the event. The probability that the state $\sigma(t^-)$ becomes $\sigma(t^+)$ due to the occurrence of event e_k is denoted by a function $\Psi(\sigma(t^+)|e_k, \sigma(t^-))$. Both the mode and the continuous variables are probabilistically altered by a change of state, which motivates the behavior of function Ψ is defined such that $\Psi(\sigma(t^+)|e_k, \sigma(t^-)) = Pr\{\sigma(t^+) = (m_j, \mathbf{x}')$ with $x'_{j,1} \le x_{j,1}, \ldots, x'_{j,d_j} \le x_{j,d_j}|e_k, \sigma(t^-)\}$. A probability distribution depending on the current state $\sigma(t)$ is short-handed as $\Psi(e_k, \sigma(t)) = DIST(\sigma(t))$, using $DIST(\sigma(t))$. In other words, $\Psi(e_k, \sigma(t) = (m_i, \mathbf{x}_i)) = DET(m_l, \mathbf{x}_i)$ shows the effect of an event e_k changing deterministically (DET) the mode from m_i to m_l while leaving the continuous variables unaffected. Finally, $\sigma_0 \in \mathcal{S}$ denotes the initial state of the model.

Model Simulation. To simulate the model, as first, the *Erlang* distributed transition firing time t_C `Complete` is generated. The considered fluid processes correspond to a Brownian motion with positive (or negative) drift and a reflecting barrier. It is known that the distribution of a Brownian motion with drift μ and variance σ^2, at a given time t has the following cumulative distribution [6]:

$$P(Z(\mu, \sigma^2, t) \le z) = \Phi\left(\frac{z - \mu t}{\sigma\sqrt{t}}\right) - e^{\frac{2\mu z}{\sigma^2}} \Phi\left(\frac{-z - \mu t}{\sigma\sqrt{t}}\right) \tag{2}$$

where $\Phi(x)$ is the cumulative distribution of a standard normal distribution. Due to the particular structure of the model, the time required to (i) fill fluid place `Decode Buf.`, (ii) transfer the content, and (iii) empty place `Render Buf.` are all distributed according to Eq. 2. The simulator thus generates the instances of the corresponding times t_T, t_D and t_R, using the distribution in Eq. 2 and the corresponding values of parameters μ and σ^2. The time required to handle a frame of the process is thus computed as:

$$t_F = \max(t_T, t_D, t_R) \tag{3}$$

If $t_F < \mu_F$, then the frame will be displayed on time. Otherwise, the number of frames that will be skipped in this process is evaluated as:

$$f_s = \left\lfloor \frac{t_F}{\mu_F} \right\rfloor \tag{4}$$

4   Experiments

In order to use the proposed model to study the target system, we set parameters as follows, according to a tentative set of values that showed to be interesting and realistic:

$$\alpha = 1.4, \quad k_C = 20, \quad f_r = 50$$
$$\mu_T = 2, \quad \sigma_T^2 = \mu_T/4,$$
$$\mu_D = 1.5, \quad \sigma_T^2 = \mu_T/10,$$
$$\mu_R = 2.5, \quad \sigma_R^2 = 1.5\mu_T$$

Recalling Sect. 3, in order to determine the average firing time of the Erlang distribution μ_C, the aspect ratio a is computed it, so that the horizontal aperture of the camera allows to completely capture, from the different views, objects at a distance $d_1 < d$. In particular, from geometrical considerations, it is possible to derive that:

$$\theta_h = 2\tan^{-1}\left(d_1 \frac{\tan(180°/N)}{d - d_1}\right) \tag{5}$$

Then, Eqs. 5 and 1 determine $a(N)$ as function of the number of cameras N, setting $d = 3, d_1 = 1.5$ and $\theta_v = 86°$.

Figure 4 shows the average duration of the transmission, decoding and rendering, as well as of the entire processing. Since the aperture $a(N)$ required to frame the scene at the selected distance d_1 decreases, it is interesting to note that the time required to process a frame decreases as well, even if the number of camera increases. The figure shows the 95% confidence intervals of the measures: results were computed using Matlab on a commodity laptop.

In the previous study, the bottleneck of the system was the rendering. Figure 5 considers cases where the bottleneck is moved to the transmission ($\mu_T = 2.5, \mu_D = 1.5, \mu_R = 2$) and to the decoding ($\mu_T = 2, \mu_D = 2.5, \mu_R = 1.5$). All cases are characterized by the same average time at the bottleneck, but differ for what concerns σ^2. As expected, when the bottleneck is on the component with the highest variance, the system has the worst performances.

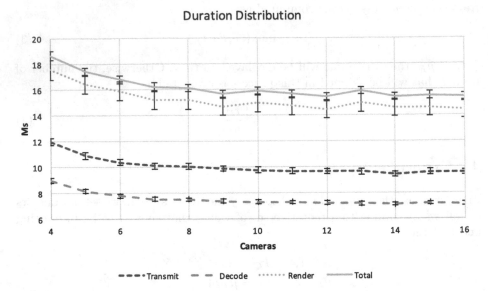

Fig. 4. Duration of the stages and of the frame generation with different number of cameras.

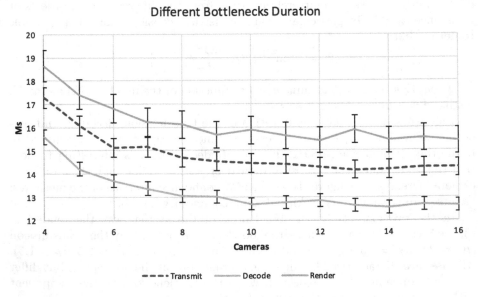

Fig. 5. Frame generation duration when changing the bottleneck of the system.

Frame Skip Distribution

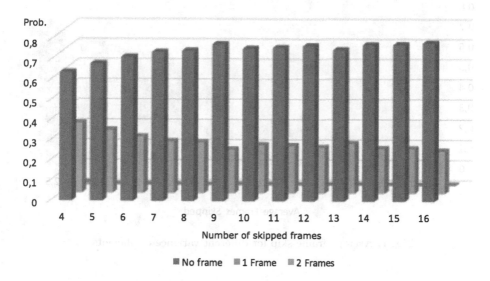

Fig. 6. Frame-skip distribution for different numbers of camera.

The proposed technique easily allows to study the distribution of the number of frames being skipped. This is an important quality measure, as it is shown in Fig. 6. Specifically, by considering the chosen planned configuration, the probability of skipping more than one frame is very limited, and in most of the cases the system is able to prepare the next image within the deadline. Since a relatively high rate to keep realistic movements (50 frame per second, as opposed to most of television programs that runs at 30 or 25) is considered, the proposed system is capable of producing a good quality of service.

Finally, we analyze the effects of changing the coefficient of variation of the processing time of a factor that ranges from 0.25 to 2.5 to explore the possibility of choosing computing hardware in different ranges of performances and account for variability effects. Figure 7 shows the average number of frame skipped, which seems to grow linearly with the variance of the system, confirming that it is generally well dimensioned with the reference configuration. To better investigate this effect, Fig. 8 shows the average duration of the transmission, decoding and rendering stages. As it can be seen, the effect on stages with a relatively low coefficient of variation (transmission and decoding) is almost negligible. However, the effect on the rendering stage, which is the one with the highest variability, is appreciable. This stage is the one that in the end drives the performances of the system and has to be considered in the definition of the specifications of the computing subsystem.

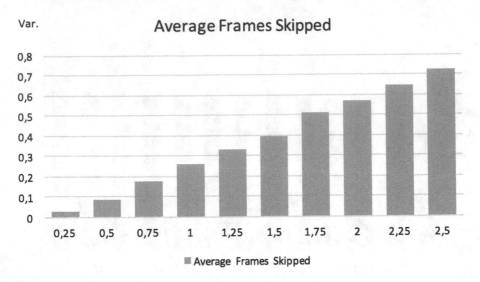

Fig. 7. Average frame-skip for different variance coefficients.

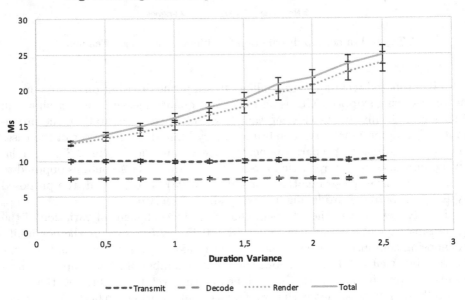

Fig. 8. Duration of the stages and of the frame generation with different variances of the considered stages.

5   Related Work

Many aspects characterize tri-dimensional image processing. Firstly, the compression of data, in guise of the MVD algorithm, present many interesting features besides being open to new developments. Secondly, the capability of creating a new view from a collection of generated views, is a technique articulated in different concepts such as (i) *view synthesis* [3], (ii) *view morphing* and (iii) *image metamorphosis* (see [12,14]). Other issues must be considered when the pixel virtualisation process generates uninitialized elements, whose size can vary according the distance from the reference system. The lack of precision linked to these pixels can be however recovered by applying different techniques (for example, see [7]).

The quality evaluation of the 3d image plays a crucial role in the tri-dimensional cinema and television industry. Existing literature covers two main fields regarding this subject, specifically stereoscopy, which aims at evaluating the quality data compression and Depth Image Based Rendering (DIBR). Regarding the former, two interesting views on the problem are presented in [8], which consider the ratio between weighted peak signal to noise ratio metric, and [13], where the authors propose an alternative complementary framework for quality assessment developing a structural similarity index. On the other hand, MIBR has been exploited to solve problems related to the depth compression and view prediction (see [11]).

6 Conclusions

This paper has presented a modeling approach to support the design of a novel 3D visualization system with an innovative MVD-based architecture.

The modeling approach aims to define a simulation technique that is founded onto a Second Order Fluid Stochastic Petri nets numerical evaluation framework, designed to be an extension of previous work of the authors. The proposed architecture has been analyzed with reference to different phenomena, showing significant results that provide a first guidance for the prototyping phase. Results seem to be promising both on the technical and the methodological point of view. From the methodological point of view, future work will include an enhancement of the modeling technique and its full integration into the SIMTHESys framework. From the application point of view, a prototype of the target system will be implemented, leveraging the results of the analysis, and including a refinement of our MVD approach to allow an easier application within different systems and scenarios.

References

1. Barbierato, E., Gribaudo, M., Iacono, M.: Modeling hybrid systems in SIMTHESys. Electron. Notes Theor. Comput. Sci. **327**, 5–25 (2016). https://doi.org/10.1016/j.entcs.2016.09.021. The 8th International Workshop on Practical Application of Stochastic Modeling, PASM 2016
2. Barbierato, E., Gribaudo, M., Iacono, M.: Simulating hybrid systems within SIMTHESys multi-formalism models. In: Fiems, D., Paolieri, M., Platis, A.N. (eds.) EPEW 2016. LNCS, vol. 9951, pp. 189–203. Springer, Cham (2016). https://doi.org/10.1007/978-3-319-46433-6_13

3. Chen, S.E., Williams, L.: View interpolation for image synthesis. In: Proceedings of the 20th Annual Conference on Computer Graphics and Interactive Techniques, SIGGRAPH 1993, pp. 279–288. ACM, New York (1993). https://doi.acm.org/10.1145/166117.166153

4. McAllister, D.F., Zhou, Y., Sullivan, S.: Methods for computing color anaglyphs (2010). https://doi.org/10.1117/12.837163

5. Davis, M.: Markov Models & Optimization. Monographs on Statistics & Applied Probability. Chapman & Hall/CRC, Taylor & Francis, Boca Roton (1993)

6. Dieker, A.: Reflected Brownian Motion. American Cancer Society (2011). https://doi.org/10.1002/9780470400531.eorms0711

7. Doan, H.N., Kim, B., Hong, M.-C.: Hole filling algorithm using spatial-temporal background depth map for view synthesis in free view point television. In: Ho, Y.-S., Sang, J., Ro, Y.M., Kim, J., Wu, F. (eds.) PCM 2015, Part II. LNCS, vol. 9315, pp. 598–607. Springer, Cham (2015). https://doi.org/10.1007/978-3-319-24078-7_61

8. Ekmekcioglu, E., Worrall, S., De Silva, D., Fernando, A., Kondoz, A.M.: Depth based perceptual quality assessment for synthesised camera viewpoints. In: Alvarez, F., Costa, C. (eds.) UCMEDIA 2010. LNICST, vol. 60, pp. 76–83. Springer, Heidelberg (2012). https://doi.org/10.1007/978-3-642-35145-7_10

9. Gribaudo, M., Manini, D., Sericola, B., Telek, M.: Second order fluid models with general boundary behaviour. Ann. Oper. Res. 160(1), 69–82 (2008). https://doi.org/10.1007/s10479-007-0297-7

10. Hornung, A., Dekkers, E., Kobbelt, L.: Character animation from 2D pictures and 3D motion data. ACM Trans. Graph. 26(1), 1 (2007). https://doi.org/10.1145/1189762.1189763

11. Martinian, E., Behrens, A., Xin, J., Vetro, A.: View synthesis for multiview video compression. In: Picture Coding Symposium (2006)

12. Seitz, S.M., Dyer, C.R.: View morphing, pp. 21–30

13. Wang, Z., Bovik, A.C., Sheikh, H.R., Simoncelli, E.P.: Image quality assessment: from error visibility to structural similarity. Trans. Image Process. 13(4), 600–612 (2004). https://doi.org/10.1109/TIP.2003.819861

14. Wolberg, G.: Digital Image Warping, 1st edn. IEEE Computer Society Press, Los Alamitos (1994)

Modeling the Effect of Parallel Execution on Multi-site Computation Offloading in Mobile Cloud Computing

Ismail Sheikh and Olivia Das[✉]

Electrical and Computer Engineering, Ryerson University, Toronto, Canada
misheikh@ryerson.ca, odas@ee.ryerson.ca

Abstract. As the smart mobile devices are becoming an inevitable part of our daily life, the demand for running complex applications on such devices is increasing. However, the limitations of resources (e.g. battery life, computation power, bandwidth) of these devices are restricting the type of applications that can run on them. The restrictions can be overcome by allowing such devices to offload computation and run parts of an application in the powerful cloud servers. The greatest benefit from computation offloading can be obtained by optimally allocating the parts of an application to different devices (i.e. the mobile device and the cloud servers) that minimizes the total cost—the cost can be the response time of the application or the mobile battery usage, or both. Normally, different devices can have different number of processing cores. *Unlike* prior work in the modeling of computation offloading, this work models the effect of parallel execution of different parts of an application—on different devices (external parallelism) as well as on different cores of a single device (internal parallelism)—on offloading allocation. This work considers each device as a multi-server queueing station. It *proposes* a novel algorithm to evaluate the response time and energy consumption of an allocation while considering both the application workflow as well as the parallel execution across the cores of different devices. For finding the near-optimal allocation(s), it uses an existing genetic algorithm that invokes our proposed algorithm to determine the fitness of an allocation. This work is more *advantageous* for cases where a workflow has multiple tasks that can execute in parallel. The results show that modeling the effect of parallel execution yields better near-optimal solution(s) for the allocation problem compared to not modeling parallel execution at all.

Keywords: Modeling · Multi-site computation offloading · Parallel execution

1 Introduction

In recent years, smart mobile devices are turning into an inevitable part of our daily life. Increasingly, more complicated applications are needed to run on these devices such as face recognition or interactive gaming. However, the resource limitations (e.g. in battery life, computation power and bandwidth) of these mobile devices are posing a challenge to execute complex applications on them [1, 2].

© Springer Nature Switzerland AG 2018
R. Bakhshi et al. (Eds.): EPEW 2018, LNCS 11178, pp. 219–234, 2018.
https://doi.org/10.1007/978-3-030-02227-3_15

One promising approach to deal with the resource limitations of mobile devices is to use computation offloading. Computation offloading is a solution to improve the capability of mobile applications by migrating heavy computation tasks of an application to powerful servers in clouds [1, 3, 4]. Computation offloading can save energy and prolong the battery life of mobile devices by running computation-intensive tasks in the cloud servers, which will drain a device's battery if executed locally [5–7]. Computation offloading can improve the response time of the mobile application by running some tasks on the cloud servers (assuming that the processing speed of the cloud servers is higher than the mobile device) [8]. However, there are certain factors that adversely affect the efficiency of offloading, for example, the amount of data that must be transferred among the mobile device and the cloud servers, and the communication bandwidth between them [9].

Thus, a mobile device should judiciously determine whether to offload computation, what tasks (i.e. parts) of an application should be offloaded, and to which servers in the cloud [10]. The offloading decisions must be taken for all the tasks of an application where one task may be dependent on other tasks for execution. The greatest benefit from computation offloading can be achieved by finding the optimal allocation for the tasks of an application to different devices (i.e. the mobile device and the cloud servers) that minimizes the total cost—the cost can be the response time of the application or the mobile battery usage, or both.

When the workflow—the execution sequence of tasks—of a mobile application is not linear, i.e. it contains tasks that can execute in parallel, offloading allocation can take advantage of this parallelism. It can reduce the response time of the application by allocating these tasks to different devices (in this work, termed as *external parallelism*) and to different processing cores of the devices (in this work, termed as *internal parallelism*) so that they can execute in parallel. As a result, the energy consumption in the mobile device will be affected as well.

The goal of this paper is to model the effect of *parallel execution* of different parts of an application on the offloading allocation problem. Although several works have addressed the offloading allocation problem [10–13], to the best of our knowledge this work is the first work that models the effect of parallel execution of different parts of an application—on different devices (external parallelism) as well as on different cores of the devices (internal parallelism)—on offloading allocation.

Our work assumes that different devices can have different number of processing cores. The cores inside a device are assumed to be homogenous (i.e. cores in a device have the same processing speed). The processing speed can vary across the devices though. Since finding the optimal multi-site offloading allocation is an NP-hard problem [10], our work applies an existing genetic optimization to evaluate multiple offloading allocations and subsequently arrive at the near-optimal allocation(s).

To evaluate an offloading allocation, we *propose* a new algorithm that computes the application's response time and the energy consumption on the mobile device. Our algorithm accounts for the execution dependencies of the tasks and the parallel execution of tasks across the cores of a device as well as across different devices.

In comparison to prior modeling approaches, our work is more advantageous for cases where the workflow of an application has multiple tasks that can execute in parallel. Our results show that considering the effect of parallel execution yields better near-optimal solution for the allocation problem compared to not accounting for parallelism at all.

The rest of the paper is organized as follows. Section 2 introduces the definitions for the key concepts related to computation offloading for mobile applications. Section 3 describes the optimal offloading allocation problem and our novel algorithm to compute the application's response time and the energy consumption on the mobile device for a given allocation. Section 4 illustrates the application of genetic algorithms in our work to find the near-optimal offloading allocation. Section 5 provides some evaluation and analysis of results. Section 6 reviews the related work. Finally, the paper is concluded in Sect. 7.

2 Definitions and Assumptions

This section provides the definitions for the key concepts related to computation offloading for mobile applications in this work.

Definition 1 (Mobile application). A mobile application is invoked by a mobile user through his/her mobile device for a particular purpose. A mobile application typically consists of several tasks.

Definition 2 (Mobile device). A mobile device is a cell-phone or any portable device that can connect to the internet and request execution of application tasks from computing clouds. The mobile device d_0 is a homogenous multi-core device which is modeled as a six tuple $<b_0, n_0, s_0, pc_0, pd_0, pi_0>$. Here b_0 is the current battery percentage of the mobile device, n_0 is the number of cores in the mobile device, and for each core—s_0 is the processing speed in million instructions per second (MIPS), pc_0 is the power consumption for computing in Watts (W), pd_0 is the power consumption for data transfer (uploading or downloading data), pi_0 is the power consumption while being idle.

Definition 3 (Remote Cloud Servers). In this work, a mobile device can offload its computation to more than one cloud servers. A cloud server is a homogenous multi-core device (e.g. a virtual machine) that can execute tasks of a mobile application. A cloud server d_c where $c = 1, 2, \ldots K$ is modeled as a two tuple $<n_c, s_c>$ where n_c is the number of cores in the cloud server and s_c is the speed of each core (in MIPS).

Definition 4 (Device-to-device bandwidth). The current data bandwidth between any two devices is known. This is necessary to estimate the communication time between the two devices for data transfer. Let $bandwidth(d_u, d_v)$ be the bandwidth between device d_u and device d_v, where $u, v = 0, 1, 2, \ldots K$ and u is not equal to v.

Definition 5 (Mobile Application Workflow). The workflow of a mobile application defines the execution sequence of the tasks. It is modeled as a workflow graph $G = (T, E)$ where the set of vertices $T = \{t_1, t_2, \ldots t_N\}$ represents the N tasks of the mobile application and the set of edges $E = \{e(t_i, t_j)$ such that $t_i, t_j \in T\}$ defines the interdependencies between the tasks.

A task of the mobile application receives some input data and produces some output data. All the tasks of a mobile application may not be suitable for offloading to remote cloud servers. A task may not be *offloadable* if it needs access to local components (such as camera or other sensors) or its execution on a remote cloud server might cause security problems.

In the workflow graph G, each task $t_i \in T$ is modeled as a two tuple $<o_i, \omega_i>$ where o_i is the type—true(T) for *offloadable* or false(F) for *non-offloadable*—of the task t_i and ω_i is the amount of CPU cycles (in million instructions (MI)) required for execution of task t_i. Each directed edge $e(t_i, t_j)$ such that $t_i, t_j \in T$ represents the dependency of t_j on t_i for execution. Each edge $e(t_i, t_j)$ is associated with a value $<\omega_{ij}>$ where ω_{ij} represents the amount of data that needs to be transferred between the devices executing the tasks t_i and t_j for communication. This data transfer does not happen if the tasks t_i and t_j are executed on the same device.

Let *source*(t_i) be the set of tasks on which the task t_i depends on for execution. Let *sink*(t_i) be the set of tasks which depends on task t_i for execution. We define the level of task t_i, *level*(t_i) be the maximum of the levels of the tasks on which t_i depends on for execution plus 1, i.e. $level(t_i) = \max \{level(source(t_i))\} + 1$.

Example-1. Figure 1(a) shows a workflow graph example consisting of seven tasks for a mobile application. Task t_1 must be executed first. When it is finished, the tasks t_2, t_3, t_4 and t_5 can execute in parallel. When task t_2 finishes, task t_6 can start its execution. When all the tasks t_3, t_4, t_5 and t_6 are finished, task t_7 can begin execution. Once task t_7 is finished, the execution of the mobile application is complete.

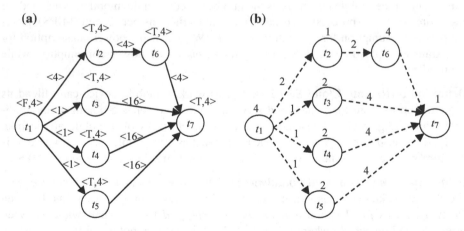

Fig. 1. (a). (Left) A simple workflow graph. (b). (Right) The time-weighted workflow graph corresponding to the offloading allocation $[d_0, d_2, d_1, d_1, d_1, d_0, d_2]$ for the graph in Fig. 1(a).

In Fig. 1(a), the task t_1 is *non-offloadable* task whereas tasks t_2, t_3, t_4, t_5, t_6 and t_7 are offloadable tasks. Each task in this example needs 4MI for execution. Each edge between t_i and t_j is labeled with the amount of data that needs to be transferred between the devices executing the tasks t_i and t_j for communication.

Definition 6 (Offloading Allocation). In a multi-server offloading scenario, each offloadable task of a mobile application can be allocated to run on either the mobile device or on one of the remote cloud servers. Each non-offloadable task must be allocated to run on the mobile device. An *offloading allocation* is defined as one such allocation of tasks to devices. An offloading allocation a is represented as $[f_1, f_2, \ldots f_N]$ where each $f_i = d_u$ where $u = 0, 1, 2, \ldots K$.

For a given offloading allocation $[f_1, f_2, \ldots f_N]$, we can construct a time-weighted workflow graph TWG = (T, E) from the workflow graph G as follows: Each vertex $t_i \in T$ is associated with a weight w_i that represents the time to execute the task t_i on device f_i. w_i can be computed by dividing the amount of CPU cycles required for execution of task t_i by the processing speed of a core for device d_u (where $f_i = d_u$), *i.e.* $w_i = \omega_i/s_u$. Each $e(t_i, t_j)$ such that $t_i, t_j \in T$ is associated with a weight w_{ij} that represents the communication time needed for transferring the data when task t_i will be executed on device d_u (i.e. $f_i = d_u$) and task t_j will be executed on device d_v (i.e. $f_j = d_v$). This communication time depends on the amount of the data that needs to be transferred and the bandwidth between the devices d_u and d_v. Thus, w_{ij} can be computed as: $w_{ij} = \omega_{ij}/bandwidth(d_u, d_v)$ where $d_u \neq d_v$ and $w_{ij} = 0$ otherwise.

Let us refer to the workflow graph of Example-1 (see Fig. 1(a)). We consider three devices here—the mobile device d_0 $<b_0, n_0, s_0, pc_0, pd_0, pi_0> = <95\%, 1, 1, 0.5, 0.25, 0.15>$, and two cloud servers d_1 $<n_1, s_1> = <1, 2>$ and d_2 $<n_2, s_2> = <1, 4>$. Let $bandwidth(d_0, d_1) = 1$ MB/sec, $bandwidth(d_0, d_2) = 2$ MB/sec, $bandwidth(d_1, d_2) = 4$ MB/sec. For the offloading allocation $[d_0, d_2, d_1, d_1, d_1, d_0, d_2]$, the time-weighted workflow graph corresponding to Fig. 1(a) is shown in Fig. 1(b). In this Figure, all the weights (on the vertices and the edges) are in seconds.

The computation of the response time RT_a and the energy consumption of the mobile device E_a for an offloading allocation a is given in the next section.

3 The Optimal Offloading Allocation Problem

Computation offloading can save battery *energy* for a mobile device by running computation-intensive tasks on the cloud servers which otherwise would have depleted battery of the mobile device if executed locally. Computation offloading can improve *response time* of the mobile application by running some tasks on the cloud servers (assuming that the processing speed of the cloud servers is higher than the mobile device). However, the amount of data that must be transferred among the devices and the communication bandwidth between them may adversely affect the application performance.

Depending on the current battery *energy* of the mobile device, the user may choose to minimize either response time or energy or both. The greatest benefit from computation offloading can be obtained by finding the optimal offloading allocation that minimizes the user-desired measures. The optimization problem can be a single-objective or a multi-objective optimization problem. For example, if the user chooses to minimize the response time and the mobile battery energy together, the multi-objective optimization problem can be stated as:

$Min \{RT_a\}$ and $Min \{E_a\}$ for $a \in A$ where A is the set of all possible allocations. (1)

Next, we show how to compute these two measures RT_a and E_a for an offloading allocation a. We show this for two different cases: The first case does not consider parallel execution of tasks. The second case considers parallel execution of tasks.

3.1 Not Considering Parallel Execution of Tasks

The previous works [e.g. 10, 11] on computation offloading expressed the response time of a mobile application as the sum of the task execution times and the communication times. These works assumed that the task executions are sequential although there may exist some tasks which—having been allocated on separate devices—can run simultaneously, depending on the workflow. The *external parallelism* among tasks was thus *ignored*. Additionally, the queueing within a device as well as the multiple cores in a device were not modeled. Thus, the *internal parallelism* among the tasks executing within a device was *also ignored* while making the computation offloading decision. Thus, the modeling of the effect of parallel execution, which may have resulted in a better allocation, was left out.

Following the philosophy of previous works [e.g. 10, 11], if we *ignore* both internal and external parallel execution of tasks, the response time RT_a for an offloading allocation $a = [f_1, f_2, \ldots f_N]$ can be computed from its time-weighted workflow graph as:

$$RT_a = \sum_{t_i \in T} w_i + \sum_{e(t_i, t_j) \in E} w_{ij} \qquad (2)$$

The previous work [e.g. 10] on multi-site computation offloading expressed the mobile battery energy consumption for executing a mobile application as the *sum of*—*execution energy* consumed for running the locally allocated tasks, *data transfer energy* consumed for communication of the mobile device with the other devices, and *idle energy* consumed when the mobile device is idle (the mobile device is considered idle in two cases—one, when tasks are executing in cloud servers (not in the mobile device), and second, when communication occurs between the cloud servers with no involvement of the mobile device). The computation assumed that the mobile device is a single core. This is because for a multi-core mobile device, it may be possible that one core is idling while others are either executing tasks or transferring data. Consequently, the energy consumption of the mobile device gets decided depending on which cores are idling, which cores are executing tasks, and which cores are transferring data. The aforementioned computation thus *did not* consider possible internal parallelism of the mobile device.

Following the philosophy of previous work [e.g. 10], if we *ignore* the internal parallel execution of tasks (i.e. internal to the mobile device) in the context of our work, the energy consumption E_a for an offloading allocation $a = [f_1, f_2, \ldots f_N]$ can be computed from its time-weighted workflow graph and the power consumption specification of the mobile device as:

$$E_a = \sum_{\substack{t_i \in T, \\ f_i = d_0}} w_i * pc_0 + \sum_{\substack{t_i \in T, \\ f_i \neq d_0}} w_i * pi_0 + \sum_{\substack{e(t_i, t_j) \in E, \\ f_i \neq f_j \text{ and} \\ \text{either } f_i = d_0 \\ \text{or } f_j = d_0}} w_{ij} * pd_0 + \sum_{\substack{e(t_i, t_j) \in E, \\ f_i \neq f_j \neq d_0}} w_{ij} * pi_0$$

$$(3)$$

Let us refer Fig. 1(b) of Example-1 that shows the time-weighted workflow graph for the offloading allocation $a = [d_0, d_2, d_1, d_1, d_1, d_0, d_2]$. Using (2), the response time for this allocation will be:

$RT_a = (4 + 1 + 2 + 2 + 2 + 4 + 1) + (2 + 1 + 1 + 1 + 2 + 4 + 4 + 4 + 2) = 37$ s

Using (3), the energy consumption on the mobile device for this allocation will be:

$E_a = 0.5 * (4+4) + 0.25 * (2+1+1+1+2+2) + 0.15 * [(4+4+4) + (1+2+2+2+1)] = 9.25$ J.

3.2 Considering Parallel Execution of Tasks

We now compute RT_a and E_a for an offloading allocation a considering both kinds of parallelism, internal and external.

To model the internal parallelism of a device d_u (where $u = 0, 1, 2, \dots K$) with r_u cores, we model d_u as a multi-server queueing station that consists of a job queue and r_u number of identical servers. To model the external parallelism, we assume that the parallelism can exist among the devices and each device maintains its own queue.

Let us assume that a *job* can be scheduled to execute on a device. There can be three kinds of jobs with respect to the execution of task t_i:

- *receiveJob(t_j, t_i)*: The execution of this job represents *receiving* of data—produced by task t_j—by the device hosting task t_i. This data will be needed for executing the task t_i. This job is relevant when tasks t_j and t_i are hosted in different devices.
- *executeJob(t_i)*: The execution of this job represents execution of the task t_i.
- *sendJob(t_i, t_j)*: The execution of this job represents *sending* of data—produced by task t_i—from the device hosting task t_i to the device hosting task t_j. This data will be needed for executing the task t_j. This job is relevant when tasks t_i and t_j are hosted in different devices.

Each job has *arrival time, start time, service time* and *end time*. The *arrival time* denotes the time when the job can be started to run if a server in the scheduled device is free. Otherwise, if all the servers are busy, then the job has to wait in the queue of the scheduled device. The *start time* denotes the time instant when one of the servers of the scheduled device actually starts processing the job. The *service time* denotes the time needed for processing the job. The *end time* denotes the time instant when the job processing is complete, i.e. *end time = start time + processing time*. Each job has a *depth*. The depth of a job captures its dependencies on other jobs. For example, a job with depth 2 will need information from one or more jobs at depth 1.

Each core in a device can be either in *busy* state or *idle* state. The core is in *busy* state means that it is busy processing a job. The core is in *idle* state means that the core is idle. Each core has *computation time* and *transmission time* associated with it. The *computation time* denotes the time the core spends in executing tasks. The *transmission time* denotes the time the core spends in sending or receiving data.

To compute RT_a and E_a for an offloading allocation $a = [f_1, f_2, \ldots f_N]$ from its time-weighted workflow graph, we *propose* the following new algorithm:

The Algorithm
Step-1: *In this step, we generate jobs and schedule them in relevant devices. We set the arrival times, service times and depth for the jobs.*
totalJobsList = {}
For each $t_i \in T$ processed in the order of increasing levels:
➤ receiveJobsList(t_i) = {}
➤ For each task $t_j \in source(t_i)$ where $f_j \neq f_i$:
  • Schedule a *receiveJob*(t_j, t_i) on the device f_i such that: (i) the *arrival time* of this job will be the *start time* of *sendJob*(t_j, t_i) (the job *sendJob*(t_j, t_i) should already be scheduled on device f_j), (ii) the *service time* of this job will be w_{ji}, (iii) the depth of this job will be the depth of *sendJob*(t_j, t_i) plus 1.
  • Add the job *receiveJob*(t_j, t_i) to the two lists *receiveJobsList*(t_i) and *totalJobsList*.
➤ *Schedule* a *executeJob*(t_i) on the device f_i such that: (i) the *arrival time* of this job will be the maximum of the *end times* of the jobs in the *receiveJobsList*(t_i), (ii) the *service time* of this job will be w_i (iii) the depth of this job will be $3*level(t_i)-2$.
➤ Add *the* job *executeJob*(t_i) to the list *totalJobsList*.
➤ For *each* task $t_k \in sink(t_i)$ where $f_k \neq f_i$:
  • Schedule a *sendJob*(t_i, t_k) on the device f_i such that: (i) the *arrival time* of this job will be the *end time* of the *executeJob*(t_i), (ii) the *service time* of this job will be w_{ik}, (iii) the depth of this job will be the depth of *executeJob*(t_i) plus 1.
  • Add the job *sendJob*(t_i, t_k) to the list *totalJobsList*.
Step-2: *In this step, we process all the jobs to set the start time and end time for each of them.*
Process each job in the *totalJobsList* in the order of increasing depths as follows:
➤ Obtain the time instant t when one of the cores of the job's scheduled device will be free. Let the core which will be free at time t be p.
  • If the *arrival time* of this job is greater or equal to t, then set the *start time* of this job = its *arrival time*. Otherwise, set the *start time* of this job = t.
  • Set the *end time* of this job = its *start time* + its *service time*. Let the time period, *end time* of this job minus *start time* of this job, be b.
  • Set the state of the core p to be *busy* for the time period b. If this job is an *executeJob*, add the time period b to the *computation time* of core p, otherwise add b to the *transmission time* of core p.
Step-3: *Compute the required measures as follows:*
(i) Compute RT_a = max of the *end times* of the jobs which are at the highest depth.
(ii) Compute $E_a = \sum_{p=1}^{n_0}$ (Energy consumption of each core p) where the energy consumption of each core p can be computed as: (*computation time* of p) $*$ pc_0 + (*transmission time* of p) $*$ pd_0 + (RT_a – *computation time* of p - *transmission time* of p) $*$ pi_0.

Now let us refer to Fig. 1(b) of Example-1 that shows the time-weighted workflow graph for the offloading allocation $a = [d_0, d_2, d_1, d_1, d_1, d_0, d_2]$. In this example, each of the three devices (the mobile device d_0 and the two cloud servers d_1 and d_2) has only one core. Hence, we do not have internal parallelism here. But we do have external parallelism since the three devices can execute in parallel.

The Step-1 and Step-2 of our algorithm generates the jobs, schedules them in different devices and sets their *depths*, *arrival times*, *service times*, *start times* and *end times*. We found that the mobile device spent 8 s for *computation*, and 9 s for data *transmission*. Also, the *end time* of job *execute*(t_7) was found to be 30 s. As per Step-3 of our algorithm, we compute:

RT_a = *end time* of job *execute*(t_7) since this job has the highest depth = 30 s
E_a = 0.5 * 8 + 0.25 * 9 + 0.15 * (30-17) = 8.2 J.

Thus, we find from Sects. 3.1 and 3.2 that for an allocation $a = [d_0, d_2, d_1, d_1, d_1, d_0, d_2]$ of Example-1, both the measures, RT_a and E_a are different when we consider external parallelism as opposed to not considering it.

4 Solution

To determine the optimal offloading allocation(s) of tasks to different devices that will minimize one or more performance measures, i.e., to solve the optimization problem given in (1), we have used genetic algorithm based solutions.

A genetic algorithm is a population based optimization method that evolves a population of candidate solutions (called individuals) toward better solutions. For single-objective optimization problems, it tries to find a globally optimized solution. For multi-objective optimization problems, it is used to approximate the Pareto optimal solutions in a single optimization run [14].

A genetic algorithm typically requires two things:

(i) a genetic representation of solutions. In our work, a *solution* represents a possible offloading allocation of tasks to different devices and it is encoded in an array of N integers $x_1, x_2, \ldots x_N$, ($0 \leq x_i \leq K$) where N is the total number of tasks in the mobile application. Each x_i represents a task and its integer value represents its allocation to a device. Here, the integer value 0 represents the mobile device d_0, integer value 1 represents the cloud server d_1, integer value K represents the cloud server d_K.

(ii) fitness function(s) to evaluate the solutions. In this work, we use the objective function RT_a or E_a or both to calculate the fitness of each individual.

A brief outline of a genetic algorithm that iteratively finds the near-optimal solution (s) is as follows. First, the initial search population is generated during the initialization process. The search population in each iteration is called a *generation*. Then, for each iteration, individuals are *selected*, recombined by *mutation* or *crossover* operations to generate offspring, and finally the search population is updated with these offsprings using a replacement strategy. This procedure is repeated until some termination condition is met, usually when the maximum number of evaluations of the solutions is reached.

In our work, we have implemented our proposed algorithm (that considers both internal and external parallelism) given in Sect. 3.2 to compute the measures RT_a and E_a. To compare the scenario of parallelism with that of non-parallelism, we have also implemented the computations of RT_a and E_a, given in Sect. 3.1, that ignores parallel execution of tasks. All our algorithms have been implemented in Java. We have combined our implementations in a genetic algorithm framework [15] so that it can invoke our algorithms for evaluating fitness of solutions.

5   Results and Discussions

In this section, we evaluate our offloading allocation algorithm to answer the following questions: (i) Does consideration of parallel execution of different tasks of an application while solving the offloading allocation problem influence the optimal solution? (ii) What is the effect of multi-core devices on the optimal solution of the offloading allocation problem?

5.1   Setup

To evaluate our offloading allocation algorithm, we adapt the call graph of a face recognition application from the work of Wu et al. [11]. We generate the workflow graph, as shown in Fig. 2, from that call graph. In their call graph, Wu et al. has specified the execution times in the mobile device, in milliseconds, for each task. For our workflow graph, we obtain the ω_i of task i as follows: we assume that the mobile device has one core with processing speed of 1000MIPS. Using this assumption, we convert the execution time of task i from milliseconds to million instructions. Similar to Wu et al., we assume that all the tasks are *offloadable* tasks except **main** and **checkAgainst** which are *non-offloadable*.

In our analysis, we consider offloading to a maximum of two cloud servers. Our assumptions of the specifications of mobile device, cloud servers, and device-to-device bandwidth is given in Table 1. We assume the values for pc_0, pd_0, pi_0 similar to Wu et al. In each of the following two sub-sections, we evaluate three cases: (i) *No-offloading* (**Case 1**)—In this case, all the tasks must execute locally in the mobile device d_0. (ii) *Single-site offloading* (**Case 2**)—In this case, we assume that there is one cloud server d_1 available for computation offloading. *Two-site offloading* (**Case 3**)—In this case, we assume that there are two cloud servers d_1 and d_2 available for computation offloading.

Our evaluations are run on a machine with Intel Core i7-6800 K CPU with 3.4 GHz with 16 GB of RAM. We have applied NSGA-II genetic algorithm [14, 15] with *binary tournament selection* with Pareto dominance and crowding distance, *subset crossover* and *uniform mutation* operators. We set the probability of applying the *subset crossover* operator to a decision variable to be 0.9. We further set the probability of applying the *uniform mutation* operator to a decision variable to be 1/(number of decision variables, i.e. number of tasks) = 1/15. We set the population size to 1000 and the maximum number of evaluations of solutions to 100000. Each run took a maximum of 21 s to obtain the near-optimal solution(s).

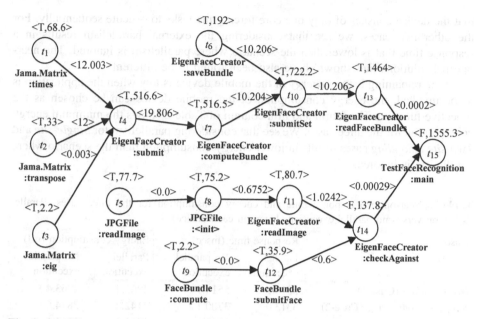

Fig. 2. Workflow graph of a face recognition application. It is generated from the call graph of [11]. A circle represents a task node. Below a task node, the top bold word is a class name, the bottom bold word after a colon is a method name of that class.

Table 1. Specifications of mobile device, cloud servers, device-to-device bandwidth

Parameter	Values
Mobile device, d_0 <b_0, n_0, s_0, pc_0, pd_0, pi_0>	<10%, 1 core, 1000MIPS, 0.9 W, 1.3 W, 0.3 W>
Cloud Server-1, d_1 <n_1, s_1>	<1 core, 2000MIPS>
Cloud Server-2, d_2 <n_2, s_2>	<1 core, 4000MIPS>
Bandwidth between any two devices	1 MB/s

5.2 Considering Versus not Considering Parallel Execution in Finding Optimal Offloading Allocation

This section tries to answer the question: Does consideration of parallel execution of different tasks of an application while solving the offloading allocation problem influences the optimal solution or not. We assume every device has one processing core. We therefore consider *only* external parallelism while comparing parallel versus non-parallel execution in this section.

Most often response time of an application is chosen to be the objective function. The second and third column of Table 2 shows the minimum response time for the three cases. Each case is evaluated while considering (Sect. 3.2) versus not considering (Sect. 3.1) the parallel execution of tasks. We observe that regardless of considering or not considering parallel execution, the minimum response time is the same for *No-offloading* case. This is because all the tasks must be allocated in the mobile device and that the device consists of only one core forcing the tasks to execute sequentially. For the other two cases, we see that considering the external parallelism results in a response time that is lower than the scenario where parallelism is ignored. The near-optimal solutions (not shown) have also been found to be different.

If the remaining battery *energy* of the mobile device is low when the application is to be invoked, the energy consumption of the mobile device can be chosen as the objective function. The fourth and fifth column of Table 2 shows the minimum energy consumption for the three cases. We see that considering parallelism for *Single-site* and *Two-site offloading* cases results in lower energy consumption than the scenario where parallelism is ignored.

Table 2. Near-optimal response time and energy consumption for the three cases. Parallel execution versus no parallel execution (1-core in each device)

Case	Response time (msec)		Energy consumption (mJ)	
	Parallel execution	No parallel execution	Parallel execution	No parallel execution
No-offloading (**Case-1**)	5514.9	5514.9	4963.4	4963.4
Single-site offloading (**Case-2**)	3313.0	3700.1	2142.2	3874.6
Two-site offloading (**Case-3**)	2434.2	2792.5	1861.4	2785.6

The results thus demonstrate that *modeling* the effect of external parallelism yields *better* near-optimal solution for the offloading allocation problem in comparison to *not modeling* parallelism at all.

5.3   Evaluating the Effect of Multi-core Devices on Optimal Offloading Allocation

This section tries to answer the question: What is the effect of multi-core devices on the optimal solution of the offloading allocation problem? We consider *both* internal and external parallelism here. We evaluate three cases—Case-1, Case-2 and Case-3 to show the effect of external parallelism. We vary the cores in each device—*1-core* versus *4-cores*—to show the effect of internal parallelism.

We consider minimizing both *response time* of the application and *energy consumption* of the mobile device together by solving the multi-objective optimization problem given in (1). We may not however end up with a single best solution that minimizes both objectives at the same time since a small improvement in one objective may deteriorate at least one other objective. Instead, we will have a Pareto-optimal set of solutions. Pareto optimality considers a solution to be *better* or *worse* in comparison to another solution only if it is *better* with respect to all objectives or *worse* with respect to all objectives. Any two solutions are non-dominated if neither dominates the other, i.e. neither one is *better* than the other. The set of all non-dominated solutions is captured by the Pareto-optimal set of solutions [15, 16].

For each case-core pair, Table 3 shows the values of the two objective functions for the Pareto-optimal set of solutions. A bold value in the table represents the minimum value of an objective function among the solutions in a Pareto-optimal set—for example, corresponding to the Pareto-optimal set for the case-core pair (*Case-2, 1-core*), the minimum response time is 3313.0 ms, and the minimum energy consumption is 2142.2 mJ.

For Case-1, we see that while the response time decreases, the energy consumption increases as we increase the number of cores in the mobile device from 1 to 4.

For the pair (*Case-2, 1-core*), there are four solutions in the Pareto-optimal set. If we have all the battery energy left in our mobile device, then the solution that yields the minimum response time of 3313.0 ms will be our choice. However, if we have less amount of energy left in the mobile device and as a result if saving energy becomes our prime concern, then the solution that yields minimum energy of 2142.2 mJ will be our choice. On the other hand, if both response time as well as energy consumption are our concern, then we have to make a selection from the last two solutions depending on our acceptable level of response time and energy consumption.

The solution for the pair (*Case-2, 4-core*) results in significant decrease in response time and energy consumption in comparison to the pair (*Case-1, 4-core*) by offloading some tasks to the cloud server d_1.

From Table 3, row 1 (i.e. Case-1), we see that when the number of cores increases from 1 to 4, the response time decreases from 5514.9 ms to 4843.1 ms and the energy consumption increases from 4963.4 mJ to 9120.7 mJ. We see similar effect for Case-2 and Case-3 as well, that is, as the number of cores in the mobile device increases, the response time decreases and the energy consumption of the mobile device increases.

Table 3. Effect of number of cores in each device

Case	1-core in each device		4-cores in each device	
	RT (ms)	Energy (mJ)	RT (ms)	Energy (mJ)
No-offloading **(Case-1)**	**5514.9**	**4963.4**	**4843.1**	**9120.7**
Single-site offloading **(Case-2)**	3370.5	2142.2	3170.3	4939.8
	3313.0	2193.9		
	3331.6	2177.2		
	3351.8	2159.0		
Two-site offloading **(Case-3)**	**2434.2**	**1861.4**	**2364.4**	**3968.4**

Let us consider Case-1 versus Case-2 versus Case-3 with 1-core in each device. We find that the near optimal solution for Case-3 yields a response time of 2434.2 ms and an energy of 1861.4 mJ which is lower than the response time of Case-1 (5514.9 ms) and Case-2 (3313.0 ms) as well as energy consumption of Case-1 (4963.4 mJ) and Case-2 (2142.2 mJ). We see this improvement in response time because two cloud servers d_1 and d_2 are utilized simultaneously in Case-3. Moreover, in Case-3 the mobile device is doing less computation—in comparison to Case-1 and Case-2—by offloading some tasks to the two cloud servers. Consequently less energy is consumed in the mobile device. Thus, two-site offloading is more beneficial than the other two cases.

In summary, depending on the mobile application workflow, increase in the internal parallelism results in the decrease in response time but increase in energy consumption of the mobile device. On the other hand, exploiting larger number of cloud servers (i.e. increasing the external parallelism) may be beneficial both in terms of response time and energy consumption.

6 Related Work

Computation offloading is a promising solution to deal with the resource limitations of mobile devices. Surveys on computation offloading techniques can be found in [1, 13]. Research themes in computation offloading are mostly related to drawing optimal offloading decisions and to develop offloading infrastructures [e.g. 17]. Since in this paper we focus on the offloading decision, we will review the related work and explain the differences with ours.

Most of the previous works have focused on single-site offloading, where an application is divided between the mobile device and a single remote cloud server [eg. 6, 11, 12, 18–22]. On the contrary, offloading to multiple remote cloud servers may result in more parallel computation and hence reduced response time as well as reduced energy consumption in the mobile device [4]. We are aware of only a few works that considered such multi-site offloading [10, 23–25]. Yet, in these works, the response time is formulated as a sum of the task execution times and the communication times. Thus, these works assume a sequential execution of the tasks in their decision model. Therefore, although tasks allocated on separate devices are able to run simultaneously, these works do not consider the effect of this external parallelism in the response time formulation.

Similarly, when the multi-site works formulate the energy consumption model for the mobile device, it is done as a sum of the execution energy, data transfer energy, and idle energy consumed by the device assuming that the device is a single-core mobile device. Since these works do not consider multiple cores (that can execute simultaneously), the effect of the internal parallelism is ignored in such energy consumption model.

Overall, unlike us, to the best of our knowledge, none of the modeling approaches on multi-site computation offloading consider the effect of parallelism—either internal or external—in their offloading decision model for response time and/or energy consumption objectives.

7 Conclusions

This paper models multi-site computation offloading for mobile applications. Our work goes beyond existing modeling approaches by considering parallel execution of tasks during offloading decision in contrast to other works that primarily focused on sequential executions. *Unlike* prior models in computation offloading, our work considers the effect of parallel execution of different parts of an application—on different devices (*external parallelism*) as well as on the different cores of the devices (*internal parallelism*)—on offloading allocation. For a given allocation, we *proposed* a novel algorithm to compute the response time and energy consumption taking into account the external and internal parallelism. To compute near-optimal solution(s), we used a genetic algorithm that invokes our proposed algorithm to evaluate the fitness of solutions. The results show that modeling the effect of parallel execution yields better near-optimal solution for the allocation problem compared to not modeling the parallel execution at all.

Our offloading technique can be used to dynamically partition a mobile application into local and remote cloud servers while minimizing the total cost where the cost can be energy consumption or response time of an application, or both. The dynamic nature is addressed by taking the user's context information such as bandwidth, user-preference on one or more objectives (that need to be minimized), etc. into account. To use our technique dynamically, one need to use static analysis to obtain the workflow graph of an application, and then use runtime profiling information to obtain the time-weighted workflow graph based on the user's context. Once such a graph is obtained, one can run our optimization algorithm to find the optimal offloading decision.

In future, we would like to consider the variation of the user's context—over a period of time—that may happen due to the movement of the mobile user across locations.

In this work, we assumed that a device is a homogenous multi-core device. We further plan to study the effect of parallelism for heterogeneous multi-core devices. Our future work rests on integrating our offloading decision-maker with software framework that will automatically distribute the tasks of a mobile application to cloud servers based on the near-optimal offloading allocation generated by our decision-maker.

Acknowledgment. We acknowledge support of NSERC through Discovery Grant of Olivia Das.

References

1. Kumar, K., Liu, J., Lu, Y.-H., Bhargava, B.: A survey of computation offloading for mobile systems. Mob. Netw. Appl. **18**(1), 129–140 (2013)
2. Liu, F., et al.: Gearing resource-poor mobile devices with powerful clouds: architectures, challenges, and applications. IEEE Wirel. Commun. **20**(3), 14–22 (2013)
3. Kumar, K., Lu, Y.-H.: Cloud computing for mobile users: can offloading computation save energy? Computer **43**(4), 51–56 (2010)
4. Zhang, W., Wen, Y., Wu, D.O.: Energy-efficient scheduling policy for collaborative execution in mobile cloud computing. In: IEEE INFOCOM, pp. 190–194 (2013)
5. Qian, H., Andresen, D.: Extending mobile device's battery life by offloading computation to cloud. In: 2nd ACM International Conference on Mobile Software Engineering and Systems, pp. 150–151 (2015)
6. Yang, K., Ou, S., Chen, H.-H.: On effective offloading services for resource-constrained mobile devices running heavier mobile Internet applications. IEEE Commun. Mag. **46**(1), 56–63 (2008)

7. Xian, C., Lu, Y.-H., Li, Z.: Adaptive computation offloading for energy conservation on battery-powered systems. In: International Conference on Parallel and Distributed Systems, pp. 1–8 (2007)
8. Wu, H., Wang, Q., Wolter, K.: Tradeoff between performance improvement and energy saving in mobile cloud offloading systems. In: IEEE International Conference on Communications Workshops, pp. 728–732 (2013)
9. Liu, Y., Lee, M.J., Zheng, Y.: Adaptive multi-resource allocation for cloudlet-based mobile cloud computing system. IEEE Trans. Mob. Comput. 15(10), 2398–2410 (2016)
10. Sinha, K., Kulkarni, M.: Techniques for fine-grained, multi-site computation offloading. In: 11th IEEE/ACM International Symposium on Cluster, Cloud and Grid Computing (CCGrid), pp. 184–194 (2011)
11. Wu, H., Knottenbelt, W., Wolter, K., Sun, Y.: An optimal offloading partitioning algorithm in mobile cloud computing. In: Agha, G., Van Houdt, B. (eds.) QEST 2016. LNCS, vol. 9826, pp. 311–328. Springer, Cham (2016). https://doi.org/10.1007/978-3-319-43425-4_21
12. Deng, S., Huang, L., Taheri, J., Zomaya, A.Y.: Computation offloading for service workflow in mobile cloud computing. IEEE Trans. Parallel Distrib. Syst. 26(12), 3317–3329 (2015)
13. Wu, H.: Multi-objective decision-making for mobile cloud offloading: a survey. IEEE Access 6, 3962–3976 (2018)
14. Deb, K., Pratap, A., Agarwal, S., Meyarivan, T.: A fast and elitist multiobjective genetic algorithm: NSGA-II. IEEE Trans. Evol. Comput. 6(2), 182–197 (2002)
15. Hadka, D.: MOEA Framework - A Free and Open Source Java Framework for Multiobjective Optimization. Version 2.12 (2015). http://www.moeaframework.org/
16. Zitzler, E., Deb, K., Thiele, L.: Comparison of multiobjective evolutionary algorithms: empirical results. Evol. Comput. 8(2), 173–195 (2000)
17. Kemp, R., Palmer, N., Kielmann, T., Bal, H.: Cuckoo: a computation offloading framework for smartphones. In: Gris, M., Yang, G. (eds.) MobiCASE 2010. LNICST, vol. 76, pp. 59–79. Springer, Heidelberg (2012). https://doi.org/10.1007/978-3-642-29336-8_4
18. Gu, X., Messer, A., Greenberg, I., Milojicic, D., Nahrstedt, K.: Adaptive offloading for pervasive computing. IEEE Pervasive Comput. 3(3), 66–73 (2004)
19. Cuervo, E., et al.: MAUI: making smartphones last longer with code offload. In: MobiSys, pp. 49–62 (2010)
20. Chun, B.-G., Ihm, S., Maniatis, P., Naik, M., Patti, A.: CloneCloud: elastic execution between mobile device and cloud. In: EuroSys, pp. 301–314 (2011)
21. Wu, H., Wolter, K.: Tradeoff analysis for mobile cloud offloading based on an additive energy-performance metric. In: 8th International Conference on Performance Evaluation Methodologies and Tools (VALUETOOLS), pp. 90–97 (2014)
22. Li, Z., Wang, C., Xu, R.: Computation offloading to save energy on handheld devices: a partition scheme. In: International Conference on Compilers, Architecture, and Synthesis for Embedded Systems (CASES), pp. 238–246 (2001)
23. Niu, R., Song, W., Liu, Y.: An energy-efficient multisite offloading algorithm for mobile devices. Int. J. Distrib. Sens. Netw. 9(3), 1–6 (2013)
24. Ou, S., Yang, K., Liotta, A.: An adaptive multi-constraint partitioning algorithm for offloading in pervasive systems. In: Fourth Annual IEEE International Conference on Pervasive Computing and Communications (PERCOM), pp. 116–125 (2006)
25. Terefe, M.B., Lee, H., Heo, N., Fox, G.C., Oh, S.: Energy-efficient multisite offloading policy using Markov decision process for mobile cloud computing. Pervasive Mob. Comput. 27, 75–89 (2016)

An OpenFlow Controller Performance Evaluation Tool

Zhihao Shang[✉], Han Wu, and Katinka Wolter

Free University of Berlin, Berlin, Germany
{zhihao.shang,han.wu,katinka.wolter}@fu-berlin.de

Abstract. SDN (Software Defined Networking) provides a way to flexible networks and makes the management easy. This is achieved by the programmable controllers. OpenFlow is a popular SDN protocol. In an OpenFlow network, the controller is the only part implemented logically, all the switches can only execute the instructions from the controller. Therefore, it is important to understand how a controller impacts an OpenFlow network for researchers and network managers. In this paper, we present a user-friendly OpenFlow controller performance evaluation tool that aims to help network researchers building performance models of OpenFlow controllers and network manager to understand the behavior of OpenFlow controllers. The tool uses a virtual OpenFlow switch sending OpenFlow messages to a controller and measures the response time. It fits the response time to a hyper-Erlang distribution. Through the fitted distribution, The tool can offer more clearly performance characteristic than the existing tools. The tool can export its result into JMT, it helps users to build and evaluate their performance models.

Keywords: Controller performance · Software defined networking
Distribution fitting

1 Introduction

SDN has emerged as an important way towards the future network. The key idea behind is a separation between the data plane and the control plane. The control plane is split from the network devices and implemented as a centralized controller. SDN introduces new possibilities for network management and operation by the programmable controllers, and it solves classical network management problems [11]. The SDN controllers manage all the data plane resources and provide interfaces to network applications.

OpenFlow [13] is a popular SDN protocol. It has matured strongly in the last decade. In OpenFlow networks, the switches send requests to the controllers when a new flow arrives. The controllers manage all the flows, build a global view of the network and offer interfaces to the network applications. A typical OpenFlow network is shown in Fig. 1. All the switches connect to a centralized controller. If a packet arrives at a switch and the switch find any matches for

© Springer Nature Switzerland AG 2018
R. Bakhshi et al. (Eds.): EPEW 2018, LNCS 11178, pp. 235–249, 2018.
https://doi.org/10.1007/978-3-030-02227-3_16

the packet, the packet will forwarded following the instructions. If there are no matches for the packet, the packet will be sent to the controller via a packet-in message, and the controller install a flow entry into the switch, then the other packets in the same flow will not trigger packet-in messages.

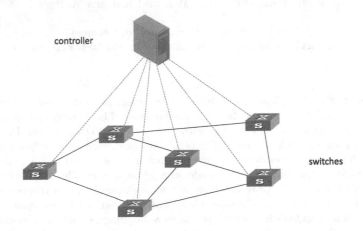

Fig. 1. A typical OpenFlow network

The performance of the controllers impact the performance of the networks significantly, especially in a large network [3]. Most studies on SDN focus on availability, scalability and functionality. Understanding the performance of OpenFlow controllers is an essential issue for wide deployment. The latency of flow entry installations and modifications must be considered during the design and deployment phase of OpenFlow networks. The controller plays an important role in an OpenFlow network. Since the OpenFlow specification does not dictate how a controller should be implemented, there are different controllers developed by different organizations in different programming languages. That makes each controller better suited for certain scenarios than others. The current OpenFlow ecosystem is fragmented due to the variety of controller platforms. We must understand the difference between the controllers to choose an implementation or to analyze the behavior of an OpenFlow network.

There are already benchmark tools to analyze the performance of OpenFlow controller, such as Cbench [17]. Cbench can provide users the minimum, maximum throughput as well as the mean and variance of throughput. This may be enough for some users. But researchers who want to build a performance model for OpenFlow controller or people who want to understand the reason of the behaviors may need more detail. The mean and variance of response time are the most commonly used metrics in application performance management. However, in reality, the response time often has a long tail, the mean and variance cannot provide a deep insight into of the performance. So it is better to provide a distribution of response time, in this paper, we introduce a user friendly tool to obtain the performance of OpenFlow controllers. Unlike other benchmark tools that focus on throughput, our tool helps users build models for OpenFlow networks and evaluate the performance of the controllers with the models. So we can understand the behavior of OpenFlow controllers and get a detailed analysis of the performance. Our tool aims to provide a simple way to analyze the performance of OpenFlow controllers. They can estimate the performance of their network design with the model. To achieve this, we develop a tool named OFCP to help researchers building models. There is a virtual switch in OFCP, which can send messages to and receive messages from an OpenFlow controller. Packet-in messages are the most frequent in an OpenFlow channel. So this tool focuses on the performance of the controller processing the packet-in messages. The tool sends a packet-in messages to an OpenFlow controller, receives a flow-modify message, records the round trip time, and fits the times into a hyper-Erlang distribution.

In this paper, we discuss our OpenFlow controller performance evaluation tool. It is a tool with a graphical user interface to help users build performance model of OpenFlow controllers. We provide a discussion of the implementation and the use of OFCP in common tasks. OFCP implements a virtual switch to measure the response time of OpenFlow controllers and a distribution fitting algorithm to fit the response time to a hyper-Erlang distribution. Our focus will be on the illustration of OFCP in typical scenarios. With the tool, users can gather the response time of OpenFlow controllers and fit the response time with a hyper-Erlang distribution. Furthermore, they can export the result into other modeling tools to build and evaluate their model.

The rest of this paper is structured as follows. In Sect. 2 we introduce the mathematical background about hyper-Erlang distribution. In Sect. 3 we present the implementation of OFCP. In Sect. 4 we present the fitting algorithm used in the tool. In Sect. 5 we discuss how to use the tool and present a performance evaluation result. We provide some related work in Sect. 6. Finally, we conclude this paper in Sect. 7.

2   An Overview of Hyper-Erlang Distribution

Hyper-Erlang distributions are a subclass of phase-type distribution. They are a very flexible class of distributions for performance modeling. As hyper-Erlang distributions have Markovian representation, they can easily be used in analytical and simulation approaches for performance evaluation. Hyper-Erlang distributions are typically applied to approximate empirical data sets.

A hyper-Erlang distribution is a mixture of Erlang distributions. An Erlang distribution is a special case of the Gamma distribution. It is the distribution of a sum of k independent exponential variables with mean $1/\lambda$. A hyper-Erlang distribution consists of M independent Erlang distributions weighted with initial probabilities $\alpha_1, \alpha_2, ..., \alpha_M$, where $0 < \alpha_m \leq 1$ and $\sum_{m=1}^{M} \alpha_m = 1$. A hyper-Erlang distribution corresponds to an absorbing continuous-time Markov chain. The absorbing state is shown as a dashed circle in Fig. 2.

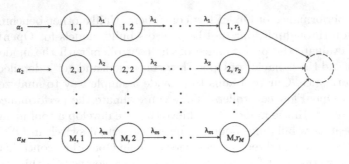

Fig. 2. State transition of a hyper-Erlang distribution

The number of phases in the mth Erlang distribution is denoted with r_m and the rate parameter of the mth Erlang distribution is denoted λ_m. The generator matrix of mth Erlang distribution is a $r_m \times r_m$ matrix $\mathbf{Q}_m$.

$$\mathbf{Q}_m = \begin{pmatrix} \lambda_m & 0 & & \\ 0 & \lambda_m & \ddots & \\ & \ddots & \ddots & 0 \\ & & 0 & \lambda_m \end{pmatrix} \tag{1}$$

The pdf of the mth Erlang distribution is

$$f(x) = \frac{\lambda_m^{r_m} x^{r_m-1} e^{-\lambda_m x}}{(r_m - 1)!} \tag{2}$$

and the cdf is

$$F(x) = 1 - \sum_{n=0}^{r_m-1} \frac{1}{n!} e^{-\lambda x} (\lambda x)^n \tag{3}$$

The hyper-Erlang distribution is commonly represented by a vector-matrix tuple $(\alpha, \mathbf{Q})$, where α is the vector of initial probabilities and $\mathbf{Q}$ is the generator matrix. They are presented in (4) and (5).

$$\alpha = (\alpha_1, \alpha_2, ..., \alpha_M) \tag{4}$$

$$\mathbf{Q} = \begin{pmatrix} \mathbf{Q}_1 & 0 & & \\ 0 & \mathbf{Q}_2 & \ddots & \\ & \ddots & \ddots & 0 \\ & & 0 & \mathbf{Q}_m \end{pmatrix} \tag{5}$$

Let $\mathbf{X}$ be a hyper-Erlang random variable. The probability density function for $\mathbf{X}$ is

$$f_X(x) = \sum_{m=1}^{M} \alpha_m \frac{(\lambda_m x)^{r_m-1}}{(r_m - 1)!} \lambda_m e^{-\lambda_m x} \tag{6}$$

and the cumulative distribution function is

$$F_X(x) = 1 - \sum_{m=1}^{M} \alpha_m \sum_{i=0}^{r_m-1} \frac{(\lambda_m x)^i}{i!} e^{-\lambda_m x} \tag{7}$$

The i-th moment is

$$E[X^i] = \sum_{m=1}^{M} \alpha_m \frac{(r_m + i - 1)!}{(r_m - 1)!} \frac{1}{\lambda_m^i} \tag{8}$$

3 The OFCP Tool

In this section we introduce OpenFlow briefly and present the implementation of our performance evaluation tool. First, we explain the design goal of the tool. Then we present the architecture of the tool and how we implemented it.

3.1 Design Goal

The OpenFlow protocol introduce new forwarding delay into the networks because of the communications between the switches and the controller. It may become a bottleneck in a large network. Many researchers have noticed this problem and built queueing model for OpenFlow networks to measure the impact of the communications. Many studies assume the message processing time of controllers following exponential distribution [9,19]. Based on our measurements, the exponential distribution cannot fit the message processing very well. At the same time, there are no tools that offer the response time for individual messages, so we develop this tool. We develop this tool not only to help users evaluating the performance of OpenFlow controllers also help researchers building performance models for OpenFlow controllers. Researchers can use this tool to analyze the response time of an OpenFlow controller and obtain the distribution of the response time. They can use the distribution in their model. One of our design objectives is to build a tool that is interactive and easy to use. The architecture of OFCP is guided by the following design goals.

- *Detailed analysis:* The main purpose of this tool is to help researchers building their models of OpenFlow controllers. To achieve this, the mean response time and the variance is not enough. Our performance evaluation tool should provide the response time and the fitted distribution of the response time. If the users are not satisfied with the fitted result, they can also use other fitting tools. It also provides the performance metrics such as the number of outstanding packets.
- *Interaction with modeling tools:* This tool is used for building performance models of OpenFlow controllers, but we only focus on the response time analysis. Users need modeling tools to build and evaluate their models. It would be helpful if this tool can interact with other modeling tools, e.g. JMT

[4]. Users obtain controller response time, analyze the response time in this tool and export the result to other modeling tools to build and evaluate their models.

– *Flexibility:* By default, the tool sends a message to the controller, waits for the response, and sends next message when a response message is received. This means that the tool can only analyze the response time of controller. Researchers may want to control the arrival process of the messages in the performance evaluation. This is a common operation in a queueing model. In addition, the researchers may have different demanding for different topics. The tool should be adaptable to new scenarios. We want to develop a flexible tool to make it easy to adapt to different arrival processes.

– *User-friendly:* There are other open source OpenFlow benchmark tools, such as Cbench [17], OFCBenchmark [8]. They are both command line tools and only work on Linux platform. One of our goals is to develop a user-friendly performance evaluation tool with a graphical user interface. Users can get the performance metrics with some simple clicks.

3.2　Architecture

There are four main components in OFCP: virtual switch, time measurement, arrival process configuration and distribution fitting. They are illustrated in Fig. 3.

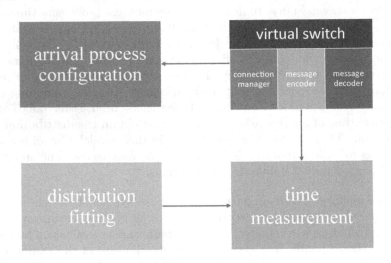

Fig. 3. The architecture of OFCP

The key component of the OFCP is the virtual switch and the distribution fitting. Figure 2 shows the structure of the virtual switch. It holds a connection to an OpenFlow controller, through which it sends OpenFlow messages to the controller and receives messages from the controller. The message encoder transfers OpenFlow messages into bytes and the message decoder does the reverse. The time measurement component stores the time when an OpenFlow message is sent or received. The time measurement is triggered by the message encoder and decoder. It records a time stamp when the message encoder or decoder transfers each message. After the time measurement, the distribution fitting component fits the response time of the OpenFlow controller into a hyper-Erlang distribution.

By default, the virtual switch sends the next OpenFlow messages after it receives the response for the previous one. That makes the controller only processes one request at any time. The users may want to change the arrival process to meet their demands. The arrival process configuration component is for this. The users can define the arrival process of the OpenFlow messages in this component.

3.3   Implementation

OFCP is written in Java using the OpenFlowJ library [15], which exposes the OpenFlow protocol through a Java API. Experiments can be configured directly via the graphical user interface. Configuration options include measurement time, arrival process, etc.

When a virtual switch is created, it reads the configuration, performs the OpenFlow handshake process and answers other controller requests. After the handshake is finished, an inside packet-generator creates packet-in messages and send them to the controller. The time between two message can be configured in the arrival process configuration component. Each packet-in message contains a packet header that the controller has not yet encountered. A packet-in message is identified by its buffer id. The controller responds to each packet-in message with a packet-out message or flow-modify message using the same buffer id to identify the corresponding packet-in message.

The time measurement component is informed that a request or response arrives by the encoder and decoder. Before a packet-in message can be sent, it should be encoded into bytes. The encoder informs time measurement component the buffer id, The time measurement component record the buffer id and the time stamp. After a packet-out or flow-modify message is received, the message decoder transfers the bytes into an OpenFlow message, it parses the buffer id and informs the time measurement component. The time measurement component gets another time stamp and calculates the response time for the request.

After the measurement is finished, the distribution fitting component gets the measured samples from the time measurement component and fits the response time to a hyper-Erlang distribution using the fitting algorithm described in Sect. 4.

The OFCP has a graphical user interface, the users can see the response time in real time. They can also see cdf and pdf of the distribution of the response time after the distribution fitting.

4 The Fitting Algorithm

In this section we discuss the theoretical aspects of the fitting algorithm. The fitting algorithm is used in our tool to fit a hyper-Erlang distribution to the response time of OpenFlow controllers. The fitting algorithm uses a cluster-based fitting approach. The main idea of the fitting algorithm is splitting the samples into clusters and fitting each cluster with an Erlang distribution. We get the hyper-Erlang distribution by combining all the Erlang distribution in a branch structure.

There are two steps in the clustering, initial clustering and refinement. In the initial clustering step, the samples are clustered using the k-means algorithm. Randomly choose M samples, $c_1, c_2, ..., c_m$, as initial cluster centers, each sample s_i is assigned to the closet cluster C_j.

$$\underset{j}{argmin}\{|c_j - s_i|, j = 1, 2, ..., M\} \Rightarrow s_i \in C_j \tag{9}$$

Then, each cluster center c_j is set to be the mean of the samples in the cluster C_j.

$$c_j = \frac{1}{|C_j|} \sum_{s_i \in C_j} s_i \tag{10}$$

Both these steps are repeated until the cluster centers converge.

After the initial clustering, we fit each cluster with an Erlang distribution and do the cluster refinement based on the pdf of clusters. There are two steps in each iteration, the fitting of Erlang distribution to the clusters and the refinement of the samples assignments to clusters. We first fit a hyper-Erlang distribution to each cluster C_j using the maximum expectation approach according to [14].

$$r_j = \frac{3 - s + \sqrt{(s - 3)^2 + 24s}}{12s} \tag{11}$$

where s is

$$s = ln(\frac{1}{|C_j|} \sum_{x_i \in C_j} x_i) - \frac{1}{|C_j|} \sum_{x_i \in C_j} ln(x_i) \tag{12}$$

r_j must be an integer in an Erlang distribution, but it is not for most cases if we compute it by this method. So we use $\lfloor r_j \rfloor$ or $\lceil r_j \rceil$ to be the phase of the cluster C_j based on maximum likelihood. We make $r_{j1} = \lfloor r_j \rfloor$ and $r_{j2} = \lceil r_j \rceil$ and the likelihoods for both r_{j1} and r_{j2} are

$$H_1 = \sum_{s_i \in C_j} f_{j1}(s_i) \tag{13}$$

$$H_2 = \sum_{s_i \in C_j} f_{j2}(s_i) \tag{14}$$

where f_{j1}, f_{j2} are the pdfs of the fitted Erlang distribution with parameter r_{j1} and r_{j2}.

Then we get r_j as follows:

$$r_j = \begin{cases} \lfloor r_j \rfloor & \text{if } H_1 \geq H_2 \\ \lceil r_j \rceil & \text{if } H_1 < H_2 \end{cases} \qquad (15)$$

λ_j can be computed as

$$\lambda_j = \frac{r_j}{E_j} \qquad (16)$$

where E_j is the mean of samples in cluster C_j.

We can get the generator matrix for the cluster C_j

$$\mathbf{Q}_j = \begin{pmatrix} \lambda_j & 0 & & \\ 0 & \lambda_j & \ddots & \\ & \ddots & \ddots & 0 \\ & & 0 & \lambda_j \end{pmatrix} \qquad (17)$$

$\mathbf{Q}_j$ is not the final result for the cluster C_j, it will be adjusted in each iteration of re-assignment. After the re-assignment is finished, we will get a final Erlang distribution for each cluster, and the generator matrix of the clusters are used to construct the generator matrix of the hyper-Erlang distribution.

We then re-assign samples to clusters using a probabilistic re-assignment strategy. For each sample s_i, we compute a pdf vector,

$$\pi = \frac{1}{\sum_{j=1}^{M} f_j(s_i)} (f_1(s_i), f_2(s_i), ..., f_M(s_i)) \qquad (18)$$

where f_j is the estimated pdf of the jth cluster. We use the pdf vector to estimate the probability that sample s_i is in cluster C_j. We draw a uniform random variable τ in $[0, 1]$, and assign the sample s_i to cluster C_j if

$$\sum_{i=1}^{j-1} \pi_i < \tau \leq \sum_{i=1}^{j} \pi_i \qquad (19)$$

After the probabilistic re-assignment, all the clusters are updated, we fit each cluster to an Erlang distribution again. The probabilistic re-assignment often does not converge, so we repeat the Erlang distribution fitting and the probabilistic re-assignment until a maximal number of iterations has been exceeded.

After the refinement process is done, we get M clusters, each cluster is associated with an Erlang distribution. The complete hyper-Erlang distribution can be obtained as a mixture of the Erlang distributions. The initial probabilities can be computed according to the relative cluster size:

$$\alpha = (\frac{|C_1|}{N}, \frac{|C_2|}{N}, ..., \frac{|C_M|}{N}) \qquad (20)$$

where N is the number of samples. The generator matrix of can be computed by combining the sub-generator matrix according to Eqs. 5 and 17.

5   Performance Evaluation Result

In this section we demonstrate the usage of our tool. We discuss its functionality and show an example of the performance evaluation of Ryu controller [16], which is a component-based OpenFlow framework written in python.

Table 1. The detailed configuration

Parameter	Default	Comment
IP address	127.0.0.1	IP address of the controller
Port	6633	TCP port of the controller
Mode	Latency	The measurement mode (latency or throughput)
Duration	30	How long the measurement lasts (in seconds)
Sample number	10000	How many samples to gather
Arrival mode	Once a time	The mode of packet-in arrival at the controller
Arrival rate	500	The arrival rate of Poisson process

The tool aims to help researchers to build performance model of OpenFlow controllers and the network managers to understand the behaviors of OpenFlow controllers. It measures the response time of the controller and fits the response time to a hyper-Erlang distribution. The users can use the distribution to build and validate their model. So the first step is to measure the performance of OpenFlow controllers. There are two modes, latency and throughput. In latency mode, the tool measure the response of the controller, it sends packet-in messages following the given arrival process and measures the response time. In throughput mode, the tool sends packet-in messages as many as possible, and measure how many response messages it receives. the default mode is to measure the response time because we think the response time is more relevant for building models. The users can also configure the duration of the measurement. There are two ways to configure it, measurement time and sample number. By configuring the measurement time, the measurement will last for the given time. If a sample number is given, the tool will gather samples until reaching the given number. The arrival process is essential in a queueing model. The users can give an arrival rate to the tool, by which the tool will send packet-in messages following the given arrival rate. For now, the tool only supports Poisson process. By default, after the response for the previous one is received. It makes the controller only process one message at any time. All the configurations can be set on the right panel of the tool. The detailed configuration are shown in Table 1.

We set up a Ryu controller and use the tool to measure the response time of Ryu. The Ryu controller runs on ubuntu 18.04 with 4G memory and 2.3 GHz CPU. There is a Ryu application for benchmark in the Ryu repository. We modify the benchmark application to make it send flow-modify message with a buffer id. Then we run the it and measure the response time. The measurement process is shown is Fig. 4, and the result is shown in Fig. 5.

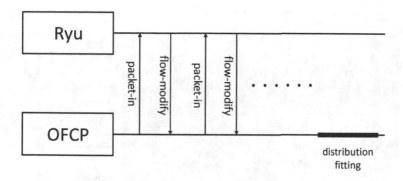

Fig. 4. The measurement process

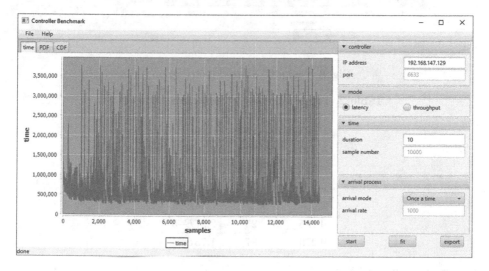

Fig. 5. The response time of Ryu controller

We can see the configuration on the right of Fig. 5. We use latency mode to measure the response time of the controller, and the measurement runs for 10 seconds. On the left of Fig. 5, the response time of Ryu controller is shown. The x-axis shows the number of the gathered samples, and the y-axis shows the response time in nanosecond. The line chart is updated in real time when the measurement is running.

After the measurement is done, we fit the distribution to the measuring response time. The pdf of the fitted distribution is shown in Fig. 6. The tool uses the fitting algorithm described in Sect. 4. It fits a hyper-Erlang distribution to the samples. We can see in the figure that there is a long tail in the distribution, which happens often in the real world. As illustrated in the figure, the result is well fitted. It even captures the little peak in the long tail. The fitted distribution is a hyper-Erlang distribution with 6 Erlang branches. The parameters of the Erlang branches are shown in Table 2.

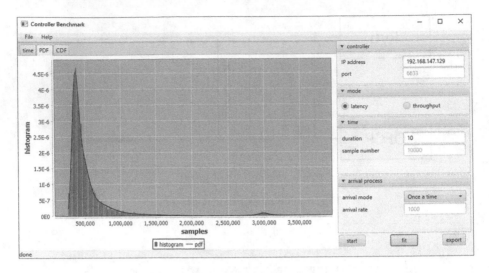

Fig. 6. The pdf of fitted distribution

Table 2. The parameters of the Erlang branches

Probability	Phase	Rate
0.349	134	$3.16E{-}4$
0.01	590	$2.01E{-}4$
0.203	48	$7.99E{-}5$
0.051	11	$7.54E{-}6$
0.105	25	$2.97E{-}5$
0.279	87	$1.73E{-}4$

6   Related Work

SDN is a new network architecture that promises to reduce the limitations of current networks by splitting the control plane from the hardwares, providing a centralized management, and introducing the programmability to networks [5,12]. By this way, SDN uses a centralized software to control a network. The centralized controller offers flexible, and programmable functionality to networks, and many other advantages such as reduced complexity, easier management [7]. However, these advantages come with a performance penalty because the split software controller decreases the packet processing speed and throughput [6]. The involvement of a remote controller in all forwarding devices comes at a the extra expense in the networks.

A controller manages all network devices in an SDN network and provides a programmatic interface to network applications. It plays a critical role in the SDN architecture, its performance impacts the networks significantly [1]. Therefore, it is necessary to understand the performance of the controllers in SDN. There are many researchers trying to study the performance of the controller in different ways. In [17], Sherwood et al. developed Cbench to benchmark different controller implementations. Cbench creates a set of virtual switches sending requests to OpenFlow controllers. By hence, Cbench can be used to measure the controller performance, However, it can only get the coarse-grained performance metrics. The performance metrics is not enough to build a model, and it is hard to derive the controller behaviors from the benchmark result. Tootoonchian [18] used the Cbench to measure several performance aspects of different OpenFlow controllers. The authors measured the minimum and maximum controller response time, maximum throughput, and the throughput and latency of the controller with a bounded number of packets. Their experimental results showed that a single controller is not enough to manage a sizeable network. In [8], Jarschel further developed OFCBenchmark, a more flexible benchmark tool based on Cbench. Unlike Cbench creates independent switches, OFCBenchmark creates a set of virtual switches that generate and send LLDP packets to each other. So the switches act more like a network. OFCBenchmark can get performance statistics for each virtual switch.

Besides the measurement, there are also researchers studying the performance of controller based on models. Azodolmolky et al. presented a model based on network calculus to report the performance of SDN. They defined a closed form of packet delay and buffer length inside OpenFlow switches for given cumulative arrival process and the service rate of the SDN controller [2]. Jarschel et al. used an on $M/M/1$ queueing model to estimate the packet sojourn time and blocking probability of an OpenFlow network [9]. They validated it in OMNeT++, their result showed that the packet sojourn time mainly depends on the controller performance for installing new flows.

Xiong et al. modeled the packet-in message processing of OpenFlow controller respectively using $M^x/M/1$ and $M/G/1$ queueing model [19]. Subsequently, they built a queueing model of OpenFlow networks, and derived a closed-form expression of average packet sojourn time in OpenFlow switches and the corresponding probability density function. They used Cbench to gather the response time of OpenFlow controller and validated their model in Mininet environment. In [10], the authors presented a $M/G/1$ queueing model using a log-normal mixture model as the service time. Their result showed that the $M/G/1$ model is more accurate than the $M/M/1$ model. They validated the proposed model with experimental data and demonstrated it to be a good fit to empirical measurements.

7 Conclusion and Future Work

OpenFlow controller is an essential component in OpenFlow networks. It is key to understand the performance for researchers and managers of productive networks. In this paper, we introduce our tool to evaluate the performance of OpenFlow controllers. It helps users not only get the performance metrics also fits the distribution of the response time of the OpenFlow controller. Through the distribution of response time, users can understand the underlying reason for the controllers' behaviors. We also present a cluster-based fitting algorithm that fits the samples into hyper-Erlang distribution. The fitting result shows that the algorithm can fit the response time of OpenFlow well. Since hyper-Erlang distributions have Markovian representation, the fitted result can be easily used in analytical and simulation approaches to performance evaluation. In our future work, we will continue to develop our performance evaluation tool. We aim to further investigate the performance of OpenFlow controller. The tool should support a more complex arrival process and generate queueing model metrics of given arrival process.

References

1. Alencar, F., Santos, M., Santana, M., Fernandes, S.: How software aging affects SDN: a view on the controllers. In: Global Information Infrastructure and Networking Symposium, GIIS 2014, pp. 1–6. IEEE (2014)
2. Azodolmolky, S., Nejabati, R., Pazouki, M., Wieder, P., Yahyapour, R., Simeonidou, D.: An analytical model for software defined networking: a network calculus-based approach. In: 2013 IEEE Global Communications Conference (GLOBECOM), pp. 1397–1402, December 2013. https://doi.org/10.1109/GLOCOM.2013.6831269
3. Benamrane, F., Mamoun, M.B., Benaini, R.: Short: a case study of the performance of an openFlow controller. In: Noubir, G., Raynal, M. (eds.) NETYS 2014. LNCS, vol. 8593, pp. 330–334. Springer, Cham (2014). https://doi.org/10.1007/978-3-319-09581-3_25
4. Bertoli, M., Casale, G., Serazzi, G.: JMT: performance engineering tools for system modeling. ACM SIGMETRICS Perform. Eval. Rev. **36**, 10–15 (2009)
5. Farhady, H., Lee, H., Nakao, A.: Software-defined networking: a survey. Comput. Netw. **81**, 79–95 (2015)
6. Gelberger, A., Yemini, N., Giladi, R.: Performance analysis of software-defined networking (SDN). In: 2013 IEEE 21st International Symposium on Modeling, Analysis & Simulation of Computer and Telecommunication Systems (MASCOTS), pp. 389–393. IEEE (2013)
7. Hu, F., Hao, Q., Bao, K.: A survey on software-defined network and OpenFlow: from concept to implementation. IEEE Commun. Surv. Tutor. **16**(4), 2181–2206 (2014)
8. Jarschel, M., Lehrieder, F., Magyari, Z., Pries, R.: A flexible OpenFlow-controller benchmark. In: 2012 European Workshop on Software Defined Networking (EWSDN), pp. 48–53. IEEE (2012)
9. Jarschel, M., Oechsner, S., Schlosser, D., Pries, R., Goll, S., Tran-Gia, P.: Modeling and performance evaluation of an OpenFlow architecture. In: Proceedings of the 23rd International Teletraffic Congress, pp. 1–7. International Teletraffic Congress (2011)
10. Javed, U., Iqbal, A., Saleh, S., Haider, S.A., Ilyas, M.U.: A stochastic model for transit latency in OpenFlow SDNs. Comput. Netw. **113**, 218–229 (2017). 10.1016/j.comnet.2016.12.015, https://doi.org/10.1016/j.comnet.2016.12.015
11. Kim, H., Feamster, N.: Improving network management with software defined networking. IEEE Commun. Mag. **51**(2), 114–119 (2013)
12. Kreutz, D., Ramos, F.M., Verissimo, P.E., Rothenberg, C.E., Azodolmolky, S., Uhlig, S.: Software-defined networking: a comprehensive survey. Proc. IEEE **103**(1), 14–76 (2015)

13. McKeown, N.: OpenFlow: enabling innovation in campus networks. ACM SIG-COMM Comput. Commun. Rev. **38**(2), 69–74 (2008)
14. Minka, T.P.: Estimating a gamma distribution. Technical report, Microsoft Research, Cambridge, UK (2002)
15. Networks, B.S.: OpenFlowJ. https://github.com/floodlight/loxigen/wiki/OpenFlowJ-Loxi
16. NTT: Ryu. https://osrg.github.io/ryu/
17. Sherwood, R., Yap, K.: Cbench controller benchmarker. Accessed Nov 2011
18. Tootoonchian, A., Gorbunov, S., Ganjali, Y., Casado, M., Sherwood, R.: On controller performance in software-defined networks. Hot-ICE **12**, 1–6 (2012)
19. Xiong, B., Yang, K., Zhao, J., Li, W., Li, K.: Performance evaluation of OpenFlow-based software-defined networks based on queueing model. Comput. Netw. **102**, 172–185 (2016). https://doi.org/10.1016/j.comnet.2016.03.005

Product-Form Queueing Networks with Batches

P. G. Harrison$^{(\boxtimes)}$

Department of Computing, Imperial College London, London, UK
pgh@ic.ac.uk

Abstract. A Markovian queue, with both batch arrivals and batch departures, is first shown to have a geometric queue length probability distribution at equilibrium under certain conditions. From this a product-form solution follows directly for networks of such queues at equilibrium, by application of the reversed compound agent theorem (RCAT). The method is illustrated using small batches of sizes 1 and 2, as well as geometric sizes.

1 Introduction

Queueing networks with batch movements, including so-called bulk arrivals, are appropriate for modelling burstiness that has been observed in internet traffic for some years, which has a degrading effect on network performance. Such systems may also be used to provide quantitative analysis of algorithms and schedules that reduce energy consumption, where large numbers of devices of various sorts are switched off when not in use and switched on again when they are next required. This switching inherently increases burstiness, not only in power consumption but also in the performance delivered – typically measured by device utilisation, throughput and response time.

In the next section, we define the batch-queues for which we obtain conditions for a geometric queue length probability distribution at equilibrium. These have regular batch arrivals and batch departures, as well as a special batch arrival stream that is activated only when the queue is empty, and a special batch departure stream that clears the queue. The special streams could represent the switching off of a device and the backlog of work when it is restarted in a power-control system. The geometric distribution, when it exists, allows a product-form to be derived for networks of such queues, called batch-networks; this is simply proved using the reversed compound agent theorem (RCAT) of [8] in Sect. 3. The method is illustrated using small batches of sizes 1 and 2, as well as geometric sizes. The basic results of Sect. 2 were summarised as preliminaries to the work on asymptotics in [7], but important new properties are also obtained here. The paper concludes in Sect. 4, with applications and future potential of the method.

© Springer Nature Switzerland AG 2018
R. Bakhshi et al. (Eds.): EPEW 2018, LNCS 11178, pp. 250–264, 2018.
https://doi.org/10.1007/978-3-030-02227-3_17

2 Geometric Batch-Queues

As noted in the introduction, batches occur in networks of queues in both the departure and arrival processes of the constituent nodes. Typically, but not necessarily, a batch of a given size departing from one node arrives as a batch of the same size at another node. However, a departing batch may be re-batched, e.g. divided into sub-batches, before being forwarded to another node, or perhaps to several other nodes probabilistically. To obtain a product-form in such a Markovian queueing network, we appeal to RCAT [8]. The primary requirement of this theorem is that the reversed rates of all the instances of each active, synchronising action (the output actions in one node that are awaited by another node) must be the same. In particular, every departure transition for a batch of a given size k at a given node must have the same reversed rate, which can be calculated directly from the node's equilibrium probabilities by a standard result; see, for example, [8,13]. If the forward rate μ_k is independent of the local state of the node it is departing from, the reversed rate of a batch-transition from state $i + k$ to state i is $\pi_{i+k}\mu_k/\pi_i$ for all $i \geq 0$, where $\boldsymbol{\pi}$ is the equilibrium probability vector. The reversed rate is therefore the same for all destination states i whenever the equilibrium state probability $\pi_i = (1 - \omega)\omega^i$ for some ω. We therefore seek conditions on the batch size probability distributions and the corresponding instantaneous transition rates that render the equilibrium state probabilities geometric. Product-forms in networks of such queues are then easy to identify and write down, using RCAT. It is well known that no such product-form exists for queues with only the arrival and departure batches described above – unless these are unit-sized with probability one. We therefore introduce additional, "special" batches that can arrive only when the queue is empty and can only depart so as to leave the queue empty. This idea itself is not new and product-forms have been obtained for special cases in [4,9].

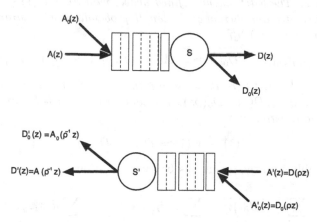

Fig. 1. Batch queue and its reversed process

Our model of batch movements in a single server queue is illustrated in Fig. 1 and defined as follows, where we assume that the rates are bounded so that the infinite sums exist:

- The state space S of the queue is the set of non-negative integers;
- *Normal* batch arrivals of size $k \geq 1$ are represented by transitions with constant instantaneous rate $a_k : i \to i + k$ $(i \geq 0)$, i.e. from states i to $i + k$;
- Additional *special* batch arrivals of size $k \geq 1$ to an empty queue are represented by transitions with constant instantaneous rate $a_{0k} : 0 \to k$;
- Normal batch departures of size k are represented by transitions with constant instantaneous rate $d_k : i + k \to i$ $(i \geq 0)$;
- Special batch departures of size k, leading to an empty queue, are represented by transitions with constant instantaneous rate $d_{k0} : k \to 0$;
- The ordering of individual tasks in the queue is strictly first come first served (FCFS).

We call this a *batch-queue*. Rate generating functions are defined for each batch movement as follows:

$$A(z) = \sum_{k=1}^{\infty} a_k z^k; \quad A_0(z) = \sum_{k=1}^{\infty} a_{0k} z^k; \quad D(z) = \sum_{k=1}^{\infty} d_k z^k; \quad D_0(z) = \sum_{k=1}^{\infty} d_{k0} z^k.$$

We assume that $A(1), A_0(1) < \infty$, to avoid null mean state holding times (i.e. infinite total instantaneous transition rate out of a state), and $D(1) < \infty$ similarly, to avoid unbounded total transition rates. The functions $A(z), A_0(z), D(z)$ are therefore absolutely convergent and analytic inside the unit disk, which lies inside their circles of convergence. The following proposition gives conditions for the length of the batch-queue to have a geometric equilibrium probability distribution, so that product-forms become facilitated in networks by application of RCAT.

Proposition 1. *The batch-queue defined above, with $A(1), D(1) < \infty$, has geometrically distributed equilibrium queue length probabilities with parameter $\rho < 1$, $\pi_n = (1 - \rho)\rho^n$ for $n \geq 0$, iff*

$$(1 - \rho z)[A_0(z) - D_0(\rho z)] = [A(1) - D(\rho)]\rho z - A(z) + D(\rho z) \quad (1)$$

for $|z| < \min(\rho^{-1}, R)$, where R is the minimum of the radii of convergence of the series $A(z), A_0(z), D(\rho z), D_0(\rho z)$. The total rates of the batch arrival streams then satisfy the constraint:

$$A(1) + A_0(1) = D(\rho) + D_0(\rho) \quad (2)$$

Proof. At equilibrium, the queue has balance equations

$$\left(A(1) + \sum_{j=1}^{i} d_j + d_{i0}\right)\pi_i = \sum_{j=1}^{i} a_j \pi_{i-j} + \pi_0 a_{0i} + \sum_{j=1}^{\infty} d_j \pi_{i+j} \quad (i \geq 1) \quad (3)$$

$$(A(1) + A_0(1))\pi_0 = \sum_{j=1}^{\infty}(d_j + d_{j0})\pi_j \quad (4)$$

Taking $\pi_i = (1-\rho)\rho^i$ as a trial solution, multiplying Eq. 3 by z^i and summing from $i = 1$ to ∞ leads to the following equation, where $\Pi(z) = \sum_{i=0}^{\infty}(1-\rho)\rho^i z^i = (1 - \rho)/(1 - \rho z)$ for $|z| < \rho^{-1}$:

$$A(1)(\Pi(z) - \pi_0) + \sum_{i=1}^{\infty}\sum_{j=1}^{i} d_j\pi_i z^i + \sum_{i=1}^{\infty} d_{i0}\pi_i z^i = A(z)\Pi(z) + \pi_0 A_0(z) + \sum_{i=1}^{\infty}\sum_{j=1}^{\infty} d_j\pi_{i+j}z^i$$

Dividing by $1 - \rho$, this becomes

$$\frac{A(1)\rho z}{1 - \rho z} + \sum_{j=1}^{\infty}\sum_{i=j}^{\infty} d_j\rho^i z^i + \sum_{i=1}^{\infty} d_{i0}\rho^i z^i = \frac{A(z)}{1 - \rho z} + A_0(z) + \sum_{i=1}^{\infty}\sum_{j=1}^{\infty} d_j\rho^{i+j}z^i$$

so that, multiplying by $1 - \rho z$ and summing all but one of the remaining series,

$$A(1)\rho z + \sum_{j=1}^{\infty} d_j(\rho z)^j + (1 - \rho z)D_0(\rho z) = A(z) + (1 - \rho z)A_0(z) + D(\rho)\rho z$$

Equation 1 now follows. The converse is proved by dividing Eq. 1 by $1 - \rho z$, expanding in powers of z and comparing coefficients.

At $z = 1$, Eq. 1 becomes

$$[A(1) - D(\rho) + A_0(1) - D_0(\rho)]\rho = A(1) - D(\rho) + A_0(1) - D_0(\rho)$$

so that for $\rho < 1$,

$$A(1) - D(\rho) + A_0(1) - D_0(\rho) = 0$$

as required. In fact, this also follows from the redundant Eq. 4. The trial solution is therefore valid and the proposition follows by uniqueness of the equilibrium probabilities of an irreducible Markov process. $\square$

This proposition states that, given the generating functions $A(z), D(z)$ for the normal batches, there is *always* a geometric, equilibrium queue length probability distribution with *any* parameter value $\rho \in (0,1)$, provided the special batch generating functions satisfy the equation

$$A_0(z) - D_0(\rho z) = \frac{[A(1) - D(\rho)]\rho z - A(z) + D(\rho z)}{1 - \rho z} \tag{5}$$

Notice that this equation does not uniquely define the individual generating functions $A_0(z), D_0(z)$. However, it is usually required to minimise the effect caused by the additional transitions introduced to secure the geometric probabilities; and hence product-form in a network. This is aided by the following corollary.

Corollary 1. *Suppose that $A(z), D(z)$ are given and that $A_0(z), D_0(z)$ are chosen to give geometric, equilibrium queue length probabilities with parameter ρ according to Proposition 1. Then the following properties hold:*

1. $A_0(z) - D_0(\rho z)$ has radius of convergence less than $1/\rho$ unless

$$A(\rho^{-1}) + D(\rho) = A(1) + D(1) \tag{6}$$

   In particular, ρ must satisfy this equation for $A_0(z) - D_0(\rho z)$ to have infinite radius of convergence, e.g. finitely many terms.

2. If there exists a real number $r \in (0,1)$, such that r^{-1} is less than the radius of convergence of $A(z)$ and $A(r^{-1}) > A(1) + D(1) - D(r)$, e.g. if $A(z)$ has infinite radius of convergence and so is unbounded, the equation $A(x^{-1}) + D(x) = A(1) + D(1)$ has a unique root $x_0 \in (0,1)$ if and only if $\dot{D}(1) > \dot{A}(1)$, where "dot" denotes differentiation with respect to z, the derivatives being well defined by analyticity of $A(z)$ and $D(z)$. The equilibrium queue length is then geometric, with parameter x_0.

3. Conversely, the existence of a geometric, equilibrium probability distribution, with parameter ρ, implies that $A(\rho^{-1}) + D(\rho) = A(1) + D(1)$, provided that $A(\rho^{-1}) < \infty$.

Proof. By Eq. 5, $A_0(z) - D_0(\rho z)$ is a power series, which is singular at the point $z = \rho^{-1}$ unless the numerator $[A(1) - D(\rho)]\rho z - A(z) + D(\rho z)$ vanishes when $z = \rho^{-1}$, i.e. unless Eq. 6 is satisfied. The point $z = \rho^{-1}$ must therefore lie outside the circle of convergence.

For the second part, let $f(x) = A(x^{-1}) + D(x) - A(1) - D(1)$. Then $f(r) > 0$ and $f(1) = 0$. There is therefore at least one solution to the equation $f(x) = 0$ in the open interval $(r,1)$ if and only if $\dot{f}(1) > 0$ (whereupon $f(1^-) < 0$), i.e. $\dot{D}(1) - \dot{A}(1) > 0$, since $D(z)$ and $A(z^{-1})$ are analytic in the unit disk and the annulus with inner radius r and outer radius 1 respectively, and so are continuous, in $(r,1)$. Substituting into Eq. 1, the batch queue has geometric equilibrium queue length probability distribution with parameter x_0, which is unique; hence x_0 is unique.

For the last part, setting $z = \rho^{-1}$ in Eq. 1 yields $A(1) - D(\rho) = A(\rho^{-1}) - D(1)$ giving Eq. 6. $\qquad\square$

Notice that the derivatives at $z = 0$, $\dot{A}(1)$ and $\dot{D}(1)$ are the task-arrival and task-departure rates respectively, so that $\dot{D}(1) > \dot{A}(1)$ is the expected stability condition for the batch-queue.

We call a queue satisfying the conditions of Proposition 1 a *geometric batch-queue with parameter* ρ. Notice that whenever the corollary holds, the parameter ρ is determined independently of the generating functions $A_0(z)$ and $D_0(z)$, which thereby become constrained by Eq. 1 of the main proposition.

Proposition 1 is a generalisation of a result in [9] where the extra departures to state 0 were restricted to being due to (normal) departure batches that were larger than the current queue length. Then *any* departure batch size k could occur at any queue length n: if $k \le n$, the state becomes $n-k$ after the departure; if $k > n$ (an excess batch of size k), the state becomes 0. In the present model, this is represented by $d_{k0} = \sum_{j=k+1}^{\infty} d_j$, but of course this is a special case. We use this case below and now calculate its rate generating function:

$$D_0(z) = \sum_{k=1}^{\infty} \sum_{j=k+1}^{\infty} d_j z^k = \sum_{j=2}^{\infty} \sum_{k=1}^{j-1} d_j z^k = \sum_{j=2}^{\infty} d_j \frac{z - z^j}{1 - z} = \frac{zD(1) - D(z)}{1 - z} \tag{7}$$

Plugging this expression for $D_0(z)$ into Eq. 5 now determines $A_0(z)$ as

$$A_0(z) = \frac{[A(1) + D(1) - D(\rho)]\rho z - A(z)}{1 - \rho z} \tag{8}$$

Notice, therefore, that such queues are entirely determined by just the two normal generating functions $A(z)$ and $D(z)$, which can be arbitrary, up to the existence of equilibrium of the queue.

If, in addition, Eq. 6 is satisfied, the expression simplifies to

$$A_0(z) = \frac{\rho z A(\rho^{-1}) - A(z)}{1 - \rho z} \tag{9}$$

Such queues are used in an "assembly-transfer network" in Chap. 8 of [4], which is appropriate for models of certain manufacturing systems. The interpretation is that batches of size less than or equal to the queue length are "full batches" and the others are "partial batches" (referring to a size equal to the queue length n which is less than the intended batch size k), which are discarded in the assembly line. We therefore call this the "discard" model, or a *discard batch-queue*; a *minimal discard batch-queue* when the parameter ρ is determined by Eq. 6.

Proposition 2. *In a minimal discard batch-queue defined by the generating functions $A(z), D(z)$,*

1. *$A_0(z)$ has finitely many terms if and only if $A(z)$ has finitely many terms.*
2. *If $A(z) = \sum_{i=1}^{n} a_i z^i$ for $1 \leq n \leq \infty$, $A_0(z) = \sum_{j=1}^{n-1} (\rho z)^j \sum_{i=j+1}^{n} a_i \rho^{-i}$.*
3. *If $A(z)$ is geometric with parameter α, i.e. $A(z) = A(1)(1 - \alpha)z/(1 - \alpha z)$, $A_0(z) = \frac{\alpha}{\rho - \alpha} A(z)$.*

Proof. 1. First, as in part 1 of Corollary 1 and using Eq. 8, the point $z = \rho^{-1}$ is a singularity of $A_0(z)$ unless Eq. 6 is satisfied, i.e. unless the discard batch-queue is minimal. Hence, $A_0(z)$ can only have finitely many terms in a minimal discard batch-queue. Since the numerator of Eq. 8 vanishes at $z = \rho^{-1}$, the denominator is a factor. Thus, if $A(z)$ has finitely many terms – and is of degree n, say – then $A_0(z)$ also has finitely many terms and has degree $n - 1$. Conversely, $A(z) = \rho z A(\rho^{-1}) - (1 - \rho z)A_0(z)$ and so has finitely many terms if $A_0(z)$ does.
2. Substitution into Eq. 9 and rearranging gives

$$A_0(z) = \frac{z \sum_{i=2}^{n} a_i \rho^{-(i-1)}(1 - (\rho z)^{i-1})}{1 - \rho z}$$

But $1 - (\rho z)^{i-1} = (1 - \rho z) \sum_{j=0}^{i-2} (\rho z)^j$ and so

$$A_0(z) = z \sum_{i=2}^{n} \sum_{j=0}^{i-2} a_i \rho^{-(i-1)} (\rho z)^j = \sum_{j=0}^{n-2} \sum_{i=j+2}^{n} a_i \rho^{-i} (\rho z)^{j+1}$$

3. The result follows by substituting into Eq. 9.

$\square$

2.1 Example

Suppose all batches have size either 1 or 2 in a minimal discard batch-queue and define $A(z) = \lambda_1 z + \lambda_2 z^2$, $D(z) = \mu_1 z + \mu_2 z^2$ so that $D_0(z) = \mu_2 z$. Equation 6 then yields $\mu_2 \rho^4 + \mu_1 \rho^3 - (\lambda_1 + \lambda_2 + \mu_1 + \mu_2)\rho^2 + \lambda_1 \rho + \lambda_2 = 0$ which factorises into $(\rho - 1)P(\rho) = 0$, where $P(x) = \mu_2 x^3 + (\mu_1 + \mu_2)x^2 - (\lambda_1 + \lambda_2)x - \lambda_2$. We therefore seek a root of the cubic equation $P(x) = 0$, i.e. of

$$\mu_2 x^3 + (\mu_1 + \mu_2)x^2 - (\lambda_1 + \lambda_2)x - \lambda_2 = 0 \tag{10}$$

Now, $P(0) < 0$ and $P(1) = 2\mu_2 + \mu_1 - (2\lambda_2 + \lambda_1) > 0$ under the stabilility condition, so that there is a geometric equilibrium probability distribution for the queue length.

Equation 9 (or part 2 of Proposition 2 directly) gives the arrivals-in-state-0 rate generating function $A_0(z) = \frac{(\rho z(\lambda_1/\rho + \lambda_2/\rho^2) - \lambda_1 z - \lambda_2 z^2}{1 - \rho z} = \lambda_2 z/\rho$. Thus, only unit-batch special arrivals are required for a geometric solution to exist. In the special case that arrivals are always single, $\lambda_2 = 0$ and we find $A_0(z) = 0$. Indeed, provided that arrivals are single, part 2 of Proposition 2 ensures that if departure batches with *any* choice of rates are introduced into an M/M/1 queue, a geometric equilibrium queue length probability distribution is preserved (assuming equilibrium exists) without introducing any special arrivals in the empty queue state.

2.2 The Reversed Batch-Queue

Although to apply RCAT requires the reversed rates of only the active actions – in our case the normal departures – we will need the whole reversed process later when we consider sojourn times in a network of batch-queues. Notice that the structure of a batch-queue is symmetric: normal batch arrivals and departures together with special batch arrivals and departures, out of and into state 0 only, respectively. Any such queue is specified entirely by its four corresponding rate generating functions A, A_0, D, D_0. Because of the symmetry, the reversed process is also a batch-queue with rate generating functions A', A_0', D', D_0', say. We now calculate these and confirm, using Proposition 1, that the reversed queue has the same geometric queue length probability distribution at equilibrium (assumed to exist, with $\rho < 1$) as the original (forward) queue.

Proposition 3. *The reversed process of a geometric batch-queue with parameter ρ and rate generating functions $A(z), A_0(z), D(z), D_0(z)$ is also a geometric batch-queue with parameter ρ and rate generating functions:*

$$A'(z) = D(\rho z); \quad A_0'(z) = D_0(\rho z); \quad D'(z) = A(\rho^{-1}z); \quad D_0'(z) = A_0(\rho^{-1}z).$$

Proof. We calculate the rates of the individual transitions in the reversed process, denoted by primes, by multiplying the corresponding forward rates by the appropriate ratio of equilibrium probabilities (for the source and destination states of the transition). In the reversed process, the reversed arrival transitions cause decreases in the queue length and so become departures, and similarly, the reversed departure transitions become arrivals. Moreover, by the symmetry of the model, the special transitions out of/into state 0 map into special transitions in the reversed process into/out of state 0, respectively. We now easily obtain, using the hypothesis that the equilibrium queue length probabilities are geometric:

$$a'_k = \rho^k d_k; \quad a'_{0k} = \rho^k d_{k0}; \quad d'_k = \rho^{-k} a_k; \quad d'_{k0} = \rho^{-k} a_{0k}.$$

The rate generating functions of the reversed process then follow as stated.

Finally, since $A'(1) = D(\rho) < \infty, D'(\rho) = A(1) < \infty, A'(1) - D'(\rho) = -(A(1) - D(\rho)), A'(z) - D'(\rho z) = -(A(z) - D(\rho z))$ and $A'_0(z) - D'_0(\rho z) = -(A_0(z) - D_0(\rho z))$, the reversed process satisfies the conditions of Proposition 1 and has equilibrium queue length probability distribution with the same parameter ρ. □

3   Product-Form Batch-Networks

By construction, networks of geometric batch-queues – call them batch-networks – may have product-forms when their nodes are interconnected such that normal batch-departures become the normal batch-arrivals at another node. The special departures must leave the network and the special arrivals must also be external[1]; their parameters are determined by the rate equations of RCAT combined with Eq. 9 or Proposition 2. Normal internal departure streams may be split probabilistically to several other nodes by using parallel active departure transitions, just as in conventional queueing networks [6,11,12]. Thus, the enabling constraints of RCAT are satisfied in that the passive transitions are normal arrivals that are enabled in every state and, similarly, the active transitions come into every state, these being normal departures. It remains to solve the rate equations which equate the reversed rates of the active transition types, a say, to an associated variable x_a – see [10] for a practical description. Notice that the reversed rates will in general depend on the set of x_a and can be found from Proposition 3. This leads to the product-form given below in Theorem 1.

---

[1] This is because the special departures are active transitions, with the empty queue as their only possible destination-state, whereas RCAT requires all states to be possible destinations [8]. Similarly, the special arrivals are passive but enabled only in the empty queue, i.e. not in every state, as required by RCAT. One could consider the special departures as passive and the special arrivals as active, provided they could occur in, or lead to, every state, respectively. However, a special arrival transition from the empty state to itself would then be required – i.e. an active "invisible transition". This would lead to an increased rate of special departures in the synchronising queue, changing the model's specification. Worse still, the special arrival rates would have to be carefully chosen (geometrically) so as to ensure constant reversed rates. Similarly, an invisible, passive, special departure transition would also be needed on the empty state, allowing spontaneous special arrivals at the synchronising queue, which again would probably not be wanted.

3.1   Product-Form Theorem

In a Markovian network of M batch-queues (or nodes), in which the mean service times of node i are respectively $\mu_{ik}^{-1}, \mu_{0ik}^{-1}$ and the mean external arrival rates at node i are respectively $\lambda_{ik}, \lambda_{0ik}$ for normal, special batches of size $k \geq 0$, we define the rate generating functions:

$$A_i(z) = \sum_{k=1}^{\infty} \lambda_{ik} z^k; \; A_{0i}(z) = \sum_{k=1}^{\infty} \lambda_{0ik} z^k; \; D_i(z) = \sum_{k=1}^{\infty} \mu_{ik} z^k; \; D_{0i}(z) = \sum_{k=1}^{\infty} \mu_{0ik} z^k.$$

The "routing probability" p_{ikjl} $(1 \leq i \neq j \leq M; k, \ell \geq 1)$ is the probability that a normal batch of size k that completes service at node i immediately proceeds to node j as a batch of size ℓ^2. We define $B_{ij}(\rho, z)$ to be the generating function of the reversed rates (depending on the local geometric parameter ρ_i at node i) of the normal departure transitions at node i that go to node j as batches of size $\ell \geq 1$:

$$B_{ij}(\rho_i, z) = \sum_{\ell=1}^{\infty} \sum_{k=1}^{\infty} p_{ikjl} \mu_{ik} \rho_i^k z^\ell.$$

Note that typically $p_{ikjl} = p_{ikj} \delta_{kl}$ for certain quantities p_{ikj}, i.e. there is no change to the batch size in transit. With no re-batching, therefore, $B_{ij}(\rho_i, z) = \sum_{k=1}^{\infty} p_{ikj} \mu_{ik} (\rho_i z)^k$. Furthermore, if the routing probabilities are the same for all batch sizes, i.e. $p_{ikjl} = p_{ij} \delta_{kl}$, we have $B_{ij}(\rho_i, z) = p_{ij} D_i(\rho_i z)$.

Our main product-form result now follows by construction: the detailed proof is omitted, being the simple application of RCAT just described.

Theorem 1. *A network of M minimal discard batch-queues at equilibrium, specified according to the above notation, has equilibrium joint queue length probability distribution with the product-form $\mathbb{P}(\boldsymbol{N} = \boldsymbol{n}) = \prod_{j=1}^{M} (1 - \rho_j) \rho_j^{n_j}$, where N_j is the equilibrium queue length random variable at node j, if the numbers $\rho_1, \ldots, \rho_M$ are the solution of the system of non-linear equations, for $1 \leq j \leq M$:*

$$A_j(\rho_j^{-1}) + \sum_{1 \leq k \neq j \leq M} B_{kj}(\rho_k, \rho_j^{-1}) + D_j(\rho_j) = A_j(1) + \sum_{1 \leq k \neq j \leq M} B_{kj}(\rho_k, 1) + D_j(1).$$

(11)

Furthermore, the special arrival streams to empty queues (only) have rate generating functions:

$$A_{0j}(z) = \frac{\rho_j z \left[A_j(\rho_j^{-1}) + \sum_{1 \leq k \neq j \leq M} B_{kj}(\rho_k, \rho_j^{-1}) \right] - A_j(z) - \sum_{1 \leq k \neq j \leq M} B_{kj}(\rho_k, z)}{1 - \rho_j z}$$

at node j.

To clarify, we observe that Eq. 11 is simply Eq. 6 applied to node j, which has additional normal batch-arrivals with rates defined by the reversed rates of the

---

^{2} We exclude feedback from a node to itself, so that $j \neq i$ or, equivalently, we can define $p_{ikjl} = 0$ whenever $i = j$.

feeding normal departures at other nodes, given by the generating functions $B_{kj}(\rho_k, z)$. The special arrival streams necessary to ensure the product-form are given by the rate generating functions $A_{0j}(z)$, computed from Eq. 9 or explicitly from part 2 of Proposition 2, with parameter ρ equal to the jth component of the vector computed for the solution of the equations in the theorem.

Necessary and sufficient conditions for equilibrium to exist are difficult to obtain, as in even simple open queueing networks, but the following sufficient condition can turn out to be useful.

3.2   Sufficient Stability Condition

The necessary and sufficient condition for equilibrium to exist is that a vector ρ with $0 < \rho_i < 1$, for $1 \leq i \leq M$, can be found that satisfies Proposition 1 and, in the case of a minimal discard batch-queue, Eq. 6. It then follows that the net task-arrival rate at each node j is strictly less than the task-service rate, i.e. $\dot{A}_j(1) + \sum_{1 \leq k \neq j \leq M} \dot{B}_{kj}(\rho_k, 1) < \dot{D}_j(1)$. This is a rather useless a priori condition because the quantities ρ_k are unknown, but since each $\rho_k < 1$, a sufficient condition for equilibrium to exist is that

$$\dot{A}_j(1) + \sum_{1 \leq k \neq j \leq M} \dot{B}_{kj}(1,1) < \dot{D}_j(1) \text{ for } 1 \leq j \leq M \tag{12}$$

$\dot{B}_{kj}(\rho_k, z)$ being monotonically increasing in ρ_k, which is easy to check.

For the case of no re-batching and routing probabilities p_{ij} that do not depend on the batch size, this simplifies to $\dot{A}_j(1) + \sum_{1 \leq k \neq j \leq M} p_{kj} \dot{D}_k(1) < \dot{D}_j(1)$, a more conventional type of "traffic constraint".

3.3   Open and Pseudo-closed Networks

First, notice that all non-trivial (i.e. with at least one non-unit batch size) batch-networks are open in the sense that they have external (special) arrivals and departures from the network. Moreover, this means that all nodes have unbounded queue lengths, whatever the batch size probability distributions; even when special batches are a.s. finite, with positive probability some node in the network is empty and so the total network population can increase due to special arrivals at that node. Again, with positive probability, a node may subsequently become empty before any special departure occurs to reduce the total population. In this way it is possible for the network population to increase indefinitely (with probability one), so that it is unbounded; the same therefore applies to each queue length. Contrary to plain queueing networks, therefore, it must always be the case that $\rho_i < 1$ at each node i. Notwithstanding these remarks, we define an *open batch network* to be one in which there are external normal arrivals or departures at one or more nodes, and a *pseudo-closed batch network* (mixed open-closed) to be one with no external normal arrivals or departures (Figs. 2 and 3).

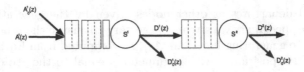

Fig. 2. Open batch-network

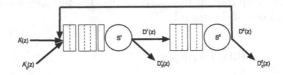

Fig. 3. Pseudo-closed batch-network: closed for normal tasks, open for special tasks

Consider, as a simple example, a cycle of two discard batch-queues of the type considered above and illustrated in Fig. 3, with batch sizes restricted to 1 or 2. Without loss of generality, we assume that departing batches of size 2 become arriving batches of size 2 at the other node; however we could just as easily choose to have departing batches change their size probabilistically (from 1 to 2 and/or 2 to 1 here) when they arrive at the other node. Denote the types of the transitions synchronising node 1 departures with node 2 arrivals by α_{21}, α_{22}, with rates $d_{11} = \mu_{11}, d_{12} = \mu_{12}$ (corresponding to batch sizes 1 and 2) respectively, and similarly for the corresponding transitions synchronising node 2 departures with node 1 arrivals. Further, let the external arrival rate of normal batches of size j at node i be λ_{ij}, so that the generating function of all the normal arrival rates at node i is $\sum_{j=1}^{2} a_{ij} z^j$, where $a_{ij} = x_{\alpha_{ij}} + \lambda_{ij}$ for $i = 1, 2; j = 1, 2$. The special batch external arrival rates and their generating functions $A_{i0}(z)$ are then determined by Eq. 8. To illustrate more clearly, proceeding from first principles, the rate equations are:

$$x_{\alpha_{21}} = \rho_1 \mu_{11}; \quad x_{\alpha_{22}} = \rho_1^2 \mu_{12}; \quad x_{\alpha_{11}} = \rho_2 \mu_{21}; \quad x_{\alpha_{12}} = \rho_2^2 \mu_{22}$$

where ρ_i is the solution of the equation

$$\mu_{i2} \rho_i^3 + (\mu_{i1} + \mu_{i2}) \rho_i^2 - (\lambda_{i1} + \lambda_{i2} + x_{\alpha_{i1}} + x_{\alpha_{i2}}) \rho_i - \lambda_{i2} - x_{\alpha_{i2}} = 0$$

for $i = 1, 2$, which arises immediately from Eq. 10. This pair of simultaneous cubic equations must be solved numerically.

Equivalently, just applying Theorem 1, we obtain – in the more general case where departing batches from node i may choose to leave the network with probability $1 - p_{ij}$ or to pass to the other node with probability p_{ij} ($i \neq j \in \{1, 2\}$):

$$A_1(\rho_1^{-1}) + p_{21} D_2(\rho_2/\rho_1) + D_1(\rho_1) = A_1(1) + p_{21} D_2(\rho_2) + D_1(1)$$
$$A_2(\rho_2^{-1}) + p_{12} D_1(\rho_1/\rho_2) + D_2(\rho_2) = A_2(1) + p_{12} D_1(\rho_1) + D_2(1)$$

However, these are simultaneous quartic equations, the invalid roots $\rho_1, \rho_2 = 1$ not being factored out as in Eq. 10.

The sufficient stability conditions for this network are

$$\dot{A}_1(1) + p_{21}\dot{D}_2(1) < \dot{D}_1(1) \text{ and } \dot{A}_2(1) + p_{12}\dot{D}_1(1) < \dot{D}_2(1),$$

which yield $\lambda_{11} + 2\lambda_{12} + p_{21}(\mu_{21} + 2\mu_{22}) < \mu_{11} + 2\mu_{12}$ and a similar inequality, interchanging the node-subscripts 1 and 2.

A numerical instance of this example has $\mu_{11} = 10; \mu_{12} = 2; \mu_{21} = 5; \mu_{22} = 3; \lambda_{11} = 4; \lambda_{12} = 0; \lambda_{21} = 3; \lambda_{22} = 0; p_{12} = 0.4; p_{21} = 0.6$. The sufficient stability conditions require, respectively, that $10.6 < 14$ and $8.6 < 11$, which are satisfied, and the solution for the product-form is $\rho_1 = 0.584, \rho_2 = 0.615$.

If we increase the external arrival rate at node 2 to $\lambda_{21} = 6$ the second sufficient stability conditions becomes $11.6 < 11$ so is not satisfied. However, in this case a solution $\rho_1 = 0.767, \rho_2 = 0.931$ exists and the network is stable; the second *exact* stability condition is $\lambda_{21} + 2\lambda_{22} + p_{12}\rho_1(\mu_{11} + 2\mu_{12}\rho_1) < \mu_{21} + 2\mu_{22}$, i.e. $10.01 < 11$.

3.4   Pseudo-closed Networks

It is well known that, in a closed Jackson network [12], the (traffic) rate equations have a unique solution only up to a multiplicative constant, these being the solution of a set of homogeneous linear equations. With batches in minimal discard queues, as we have already pointed out, the network's population is not bounded and certainly not constant because of the external special arrivals. Furthermore, the rate equations are non-linear. However, pseudo-closed networks, with no external normal arrivals, do have a different type of constraint, arising from Eq. 11 which, for a pseudo-closed network becomes:

$$\sum_{1 \leq k \neq j \leq M} B_{kj}(\rho_k, \rho_j^{-1}) + D_j(\rho_j) = \sum_{1 \leq k \neq j \leq M} B_{kj}(\rho_k, 1) + D_j(1) \qquad (13)$$

for $1 \leq j \leq M$. When batch sizes do not change in transit and the routing probabilities are the same for all batch sizes, the equation becomes

$$\sum_{1 \leq k \neq j \leq M} p_{kj} D_k(\rho_k/\rho_j) + D_j(\rho_j) = \sum_{1 \leq k \neq j \leq M} p_{kj} D_k(\rho_k) + D_j(1) \qquad (14)$$

Summing over j then gives, setting $p_{jj} = 0$ for $1 \leq j \leq M$,

$$\sum_{j=1}^{M} \sum_{k=1}^{M} p_{kj} D_k(\rho_k/\rho_j) + \sum_{j=1}^{M} D_j(\rho_j) = \sum_{j=1}^{M} \sum_{k=1}^{M} p_{kj} D_k(\rho_k) + \sum_{j=1}^{M} D_j(1)$$

Interchanging the order of summation on the right hand side and noting that for pseudo-closed networks $\sum_{j=1}^{M} p_{kj} = 1$ for all k, two of the sums cancel and we are left with

$$\sum_{j=1}^{M} \sum_{k=1}^{M} p_{kj} D_k(\rho_k/\rho_j) = \sum_{j=1}^{M} D_j(1)$$

This is a constraint on all the pairwise ratios of the nodes' utilisations – the parameters of the required geometric distributions at each node. Notice that this does not apply to open batch networks because the corresponding equation would include the term $\sum_{j=1}^{M} A_j(\rho_j^{-1})$, which is neither constant nor a function of the utilisation-ratios.

Clearly one solution to this equation has $\rho_1 = \rho_2 = \ldots = \rho_M$, whereupon we may write

$$(\mathbf{D}(\rho) - \mathbf{D}(1))(I - P) = \mathbf{0}$$

where $\rho = (\rho_1, \ldots, \rho_1)$, $\mathbf{D}(\mathbf{z})$ is the vector $(D_1(z_1), \ldots, D_M(z_M))$, $\mathbf{1}$ is the vector of ones $(1, \ldots, 1)$ of length M, the matrix $P = (p_{ij} \mid 1 \leq i, j \leq M)$ and I is the identity $M \times M$ matrix. Since P is singular for a pseudo-closed network, these equations have a unique solution up to an arbitrary multiplicative constant (the rank of P being $M - 1$ in a connected network). Hence we obtain

$$D_j(\rho_1) - D_j(1) = \kappa_j(D_1(\rho_1) - D_1(1))$$

for $2 \leq j \leq M$, where the vector $(1, \kappa_2, \ldots, \kappa_M)$ is a solution to the linear equations $\mathbf{x}.(I - P) = \mathbf{0}$, i.e. a left eigenvector of $I - P$ with eigenvalue 0. It therefore remains to solve each of the non-linear equations $D_j(y) - D_j(1) = \kappa_j(D_1(y) - D_1(1))$ for $j = 2, \ldots, M$, each of which must have the same solution $y = \rho_1$. In general, this will be highly constraining on the parameters of the network, but for a two-node network there is only one such equation to solve, namely (since $\kappa_2 = 1$) $D_2(\rho) - D_2(1) = D_1(\rho) - D_1(1)$, or, after factorisation,

$$(\rho - 1)[(\mu_{22} - \mu_{12})\rho - (\mu_{11} + \mu_{12} - \mu_{21} - \mu_{22})] = 0$$

The only valid solution (with $\rho_1 = \rho_2 = \rho$) is therefore $\rho = -1 - \delta_1/\delta_2$ where $\delta_i = \mu_{1i} - \mu_{2i}$ for $i = 1, 2$. For $0 < \rho < 1$ we therefore require that either $\delta_1 > 0, \delta_2 < 0, -\delta_2 < \delta_1 < -2\delta_2$ or $\delta_1 < 0, \delta_2 > 0, \delta_2 < -\delta_1 < 2\delta_2$.

Consider the following pseudo-closed 2-node example, for which we must have $p_{12} = p_{21} = 1$. Let $\mu_{11} = 2, \mu_{12} = 1; \mu_{21} = 2.6$ and μ_{22} be left unspecified. Then $\delta_1 = -0.6$ and $\delta_2 = 1 - \mu_{22}$, so we have the second case and require $0.4 < \mu_{22} < 0.7$. No solutions were found for μ_{22} outside this range and all solutions with μ_{22} in the range had $\rho_1 = \rho_2$. For example, when $\mu_{22} = 0.699$ we find $\rho_1 = \rho_2 = 0.9934$; when $\mu_{22} = 0.401$, $\rho_1 = \rho_2 = 0.0017$; and when $\mu_{22} = 0.5$, $\rho_1 = \rho_2 = 0.2$. In fact, it can be shown via tedious algebra that there are no other solutions to Eq. 14 when $M = 2$ other than $\rho_1 = \rho_2$. Whilst being a challenge to generalize this to arbitrary pseudo-closed networks, this is not the point of the present paper and the urgency of such a result is not clear.

4   Conclusion

As noted in the introduction, batch-networks of this type are well suited to modelling bursty traffic that occurs in networks of various types, for example router networks and file transfers in storage systems. Data centres, in particular, consume vast amounts of energy, often requiring their own power plants to be constructed, and demand for their services is set to continue growing rapidly. Thus both economics and social responsibility demand the minimisation of energy use and certainly that energy not be wasted. One way this is being done is to construct devices with several power levels of operation, at least including "on" and "off", and probably with "sleep" or "standby" intermediate levels as well. When a device is not in use, its power level decreases, e.g. it is switched off, and conversely when it is required again, it is switched on. If the offered workload is "smooth", i.e. devices do not have long idle periods, there is no benefit in shutting them down or reducing their power level; they will quickly have to be powered up again, with increased energy (and wear) overheads, resulting in a penalty, not a saving in energy [15]. Therefore in energy-efficient systems, workload has to be scheduled to introduce *bursts* into the workload, with longer idle periods, and these are well modelled by batch movements in a network. To minimise energy consumption subject to adequate quality of service (QoS), and *vice versa*, therefore requires models that account for burstiness.

In a batch-network, the scheduled regular traffic can be represented by normal batches. When a device is switched off, it may lose work that has either already arrived or is on the way, for example in a control unit buffer. Conversely, when the device starts up again, it may be that a backlog of work has built up and so there is a sudden burst of activity. Such events – switching off and on again – are well described by a batch-queue's special departure and arrival streams. Efficient, product-form, batch-networks therefore have the potential to provide a way to suggest alternative scheduling algorithms that can be assessed quickly, even in real time.

Of course there is the objection that, even if batch-networks provide a good representation, it is unlikely that the conditions will be met that lead to a product-form – and hence efficient solution. However, direct analytical solutions (solving the underlying Markov chain's global balance equations) are intractable numerically and simulation is expensive and time consuming. Therefore approximations are generally used. This gives at least three important roles for product-forms:

- To provide exact results when their conditions are met;
- To provide a benchmark against which to assess approximate methods and simulation: a parameterisation of a model would be chosen that does satisfy the conditions for product-form and the ensuing exact solution would be compared with the inexact model's output;
- Product-forms themselves are (usually) approximations and may lead to upper and/or lower bounds on the exact solution.

In fact the generality of the RCAT approach allows batch-queues to be incorporated into any other product-form networks, for example G-networks or BCMP networks, or even be mixed with product-form Petri nets [1–3,5,11]. Current work is investigating a pair of batch queues with finite batch sizes and *without* any special arrivals or departures. The essence of the approach is to observe that above a certain pair of queue lengths, the steady state balance equations are the same with or without the special batches. Below these thresholds, the method of spectral expansion is used to yield an "almost" product-form solution [14].

References

1. Marin, S.B.A., Harrison, P.G.: Analysis of stochastic petri nets with signals. Perform. Eval. **69**, 551–572 (2012)
2. Balsamo, S., Harrison, P.G., Marin, A.: Methodological construction of product-form stochastic petri nets for performance evaluation. J. Syst. Softw. **85**, 1520–1539 (2012)
3. Baskett, F., Chandy, K.M., Muntz, R.R., Palacios, F.G.: Open, closed and mixed networks of queues with different classes of customers. J. ACM **22**(2), 248–260 (1975)
4. Chao, X., Miyazawa, M., Pinedo, M.: Queueing Networks: Customers, Signals and Product Form Solutions. Wiley, New York (1999)
5. Gelenbe, E.: G-networks with triggered customer movement. J. Appl. Prob. **30**, 742–748 (1993)
6. Gross, D., Harris, C.M.: Fundamentals of Queueing Theory. Wiley, New York (1985)
7. Harrison, P.G., Hayden, R.A., Knottenbelt, W.J.: Product-forms in batch networks: approximation and asymptotics. Perform. Eval. **70**(10), 822–840 (2013)
8. Harrison, P.G.: Turning back time in Markovian process algebra. Theoret. Comput. Sci. **290**(3), 1947–1986 (2003)
9. Harrison, P.G.: Compositional reversed Markov processes, with applications to G-networks. Perform. Eval. **57**, 379–408 (2004)
10. Harrison, P.G.: Turning back time - what impact on performance? Comput. J. **53**(6), 860–868 (2010)
11. Harrison, P.G., Patel, N.M.: Performance Modelling of Communication Networks and Computer Architectures. Addison-Wesley, Boston (1992)
12. Jackson, J.R.: Jobshop-like queueing systems. Manag. Sci. **10**(1), 131–142 (1963)
13. Kelly, F.P.: Reversibility and Stochastic Networks. Wiley, New York (1979)
14. Mitrani, I., Chakka, R.: Spectral expansion solution for a class of Markov models: application and comparison with the matrix-geometric method. Perform. Eval. **23**, 241–260 (1995)
15. Papathanasiou, A.E., Scott, M.L.: Energy efficiency through burstiness. In: 5th IEEE Workshop on Mobile Computing Systems and Applications (2003)

Author Index

Printed in the United States
By Bookmasters